This book is about the radical transformation of British literary culture during the period 1880 to 1914 as seen through the early publishing careers of three highly influential writers, Joseph Conrad, Arnold Bennett, and Arthur Conan Doyle. Peter D. McDonald examines the cultural politics of the period by considering the social structure of the literary world in which these writers were read and understood. Through a wealth of historical detail, he links the publishing history of key texts with the wider commercial, ideological and literary themes in the period as a whole. By tracing the complex network of relationships among writers, publishers, printers, distributors, reviewers, and readers, McDonald demonstrates that the discursive qualities of these texts cannot be fully appreciated without understanding the material conditions of their production. In so doing, he makes social history a central part of literary studies, and shows the importance of the history of publishing in questions of critical interpretation.

BRITISH LITERARY CULTURE AND
PUBLISHING PRACTICE
1880–1914

CAMBRIDGE STUDIES IN
PUBLISHING AND PRINTING HISTORY

GENERAL EDITORS

David McKitterick

TITLES PUBLISHED

*The Provincial Book Trade in
Eighteenth-Century England*
by John Feather

Lewis Carroll and the House of Macmillan
edited by Morton N. Cohen and Anita Gandolfo

The Correspondence of Robert Dodsley 1733–1764
edited by James E. Tierney

Book Production and Publication in Britain 1375–1475
edited by Jeremy Griffiths and Derek Pearsall

*Before Copyright: The French Book-Privilege
System 1486–1526*
by Elizabeth Armstrong

The Making of Johnson's Dictionary, 1746–1773
by Allen Reddick

*Cheap Bibles: Nineteenth-century Publishing and
the British and Foreign Bible Society*
by Leslie Howsam

*Print Culture in Renaissance Italy
The Editor and the Vernacular Text, 1470–1600*
by Brian Richardson

*American Literary Publishing in the Mid-Nineteenth Century
The Business of Ticknor and Fields*
by Michael Winship

*Fiction and the American Literary Marketplace: The Role of
Newspaper Syndicates, 1860–1900*
Charles Johanningsmeier

BRITISH LITERARY CULTURE
AND PUBLISHING PRACTICE
1880–1914

PETER D. McDONALD

ST HUGH'S COLLEGE, OXFORD

Published by the Press Syndicate of the University of Cambridge
The Pitt Building, Trumpington Street, Cambridge CB2 1RP, United Kingdom

CAMBRIDGE UNIVERSITY PRESS
The Edinburgh Building, Cambridge CB2 2RU, United Kingdom
40 West 20th Street, New York, NY 10011-4211, USA
10 Stamford Road, Oakleigh, Melbourne 3166, Australia

First published 1997

Printed in the United Kingdom at the University Press, Cambridge

Typeset in Baskerville 10/12 pt

A catalogue record for this book is available from the British Library

Library of Congress cataloguing in publication data
McDonald, Peter D.
British literary culture and publishing practice, 1880–1914 / Peter D. McDonald.
p.   cm. – (Cambridge Studies in Publishing and Printing History)
Includes bibliographical references and index.
ISBN 0 521 57149 9 (hardback)
1. English fiction – 19th century – History and criticism.
2. Authors and publishers – Great Britain – History – 19th century.
3. Authors and publishers – Great Britain – History – 20th century.
4. Literature publishing – Great Britain – History – 19th century.
5. Literature publishing – Great Britain – History – 20th century.
6. English fiction – 20th century – History and criticism.
7. Conrad, Joseph, 1857–1924 – Publishers.
8. Bennett, Arnold, 1867–1931 – Publishers.
9. Doyle, Arthur Conan, Sir, 1859–1930 – Publishers.
1. Title.   11. Series.
PR878.P78M39   1997
823'.809 – dc21   96–39743   CIP

ISBN 0 521 57149 9 hardback

CE

For my father and
in memory of my mother

ACKNOWLEDGEMENTS

Many friends, colleagues, and institutions have helped me at various stages in the process of researching and writing this book, all of whom deserve my sincere thanks. For access to research materials both published and unpublished, I am indebted to the curators and librarians at the Bodleian and English Faculty Libraries, Oxford; the British Library; University College Library, London; Reading Library; the Berg Collection, New York Public Library; the Pierpont Morgan Library, New York; and the Metropolitan Toronto Library. For permission to reproduce previously unpublished material, I am grateful to the Arnold Bennett Estate; the W. E. Henley Estate; A. P. Watt, Ltd; the Berg Collection; the Pierpont Morgan Library; and the Royal Literary Society. I am also grateful to the editors of *The Conradian*, *The Papers of the Bibliographical Society of America*, and *The Victorian Periodicals Review*, who published various parts of this book in article form, for kindly allowing me to use some of that material here again. I should also like to offer my warm thanks to the Fellows of New College, Oxford, and the benefactor of the Weston Junior Research Fellowship, for giving me two wonderful, undistracted years in which to complete this study; and the Human Sciences Research Council, the Ernest Oppenheimer Memorial Trust, Rhodes University, and Wolfson College for providing financial assistance in the form of grants and scholarships. The opinions expressed in this book, like its errors, are my own, of course, and should not be attributed to any of these institutions.

My deepest gratitude, however, must go to those I have pestered to read parts of this book in manuscript form, especially Damien Atkinson, Freddie Baveystock, Bill Bell, Amit and Rinka Chaudhuri, Robert Darnton, Simon Eliot, John Gouws, Anne Goriely, Eddie Greenwood, Michael Hechter, Kinch Hoekstra, Tony Nuttall, Michael Suarez, Michael Turner and my anonymous reader at Cambridge University Press. They have all given me extremely helpful critical advice and encouragement which has made this a better book, but they should not be held responsible for a word of it. Finally, I should like, above all, to offer my warmest thanks to John Carey, who was the most generous of supervisors, and Don McKenzie, who transformed my understanding of texts by teaching me how to read a blank book.

ABBREVIATIONS

CL1–4	*The Collected Letters of Joseph Conrad,* vols. 1–4
LAB1–3	*The Letters of Arnold Bennett,* vols. 1–3
NO	*The National Observer*
NR	*The New Review*
SO	*The Scots Observer*
SM	*The Strand Magazine*
TB	*Tit-Bits*
TPW	*T. P.'s Weekly*
YB	*The Yellow Book*

INTRODUCTION · THE LITERARY FIELD IN THE 1890s

What is obvious and indisputable is this: that with the dissemination of ignorance through the length and breadth of our island, by means of the Board School, a mighty and terrible change has been wrought in the characters both of the majority of readers and of the majority of writers. The 'gentleman scholar' who still flourished when I was young, has sunken into unimportance both as reader and writer. The bagman and the stockbroker's clerk (and their lady wives and daughters) 'ave usurped his plyce and his influence as readers; and the pressman has picked up his fallen pen, – the pressman, sir, or the presswoman!

'The Yellow Dwarf', *Yellow Book*, October 1895[1]

IN APRIL 1891, EDMUND GOSSE (1849–1928) contributed an essay to the *Contemporary Review* entitled 'The Influence of Democracy on Literature'. It was a studiously even-handed piece intended to assuage his more 'gloomy' peers who thought that, in the new democratic climate of the 1890s, 'poetry is dead, the novel sunken into its dotage, all good writing obsolete, and the reign of darkness begun'. There were, he granted, grounds for 'grave apprehension'. The 'enlargement of the circle of readers' meant 'an increase of persons who, without ear, are admitted to the concert of literature'; and this wider audience, in turn, attracted publishers who 'seduced' authors 'capable of doing better things' into writing simply 'for the sake of money'. Yet, after reviewing the 'whole field', he also saw 'much that may cheer and encourage us'. He pointed out that the 'principal poetical writers of our time seem to be unaffected by the pressure of the masses' – he was less sanguine about the novelists – and, more positively, that the newspapers, the 'most democratic vehicles of thought', now treated 'literary subjects' as 'of immediate public interest'. 'When an eminent man of letters dies', he wrote, 'the comments which the London and country press make upon his career and the nature of his work are often quite astonishing'. Finally, there was the inspiring example of Tennyson whose popularity was 'one of the most singular, as it is one of the most encouraging features of our recent literary history'. While the laureate had 'never courted the public, nor striven to serve it', he had none the less come to occupy an 'extraordinary place in the affections of our people'. 'Let no man', Gosse concluded, 'needlessly dishearten his brethren in this world of disillusions, by losing faith in the ultimate survival and continuance of literature.'[2]

Eighteen months later, on witnessing the enormous crowd gathered outside

Westminster Abbey on the occasion of Tennyson's stately burial, Gosse panicked and completely changed his mind. As he observed, now in an intemperate diatribe published in the *New Review* for November 1892, the funeral on 12 October was not simply a momentous public event. It was an alarming 'parable' of contemporary literary culture, the meaning of which lay in the 'symbolic contrast' between the ambience inside and that outside the Abbey.

Inside, the grey and vitreous atmosphere, the reverberations of music moaning somewhere out of sight, the bones and monuments of the noble dead, reverence, antiquity, beauty, rest. Outside, in the raw air, a tribe of hawkers urging upon the edges of a dense and inquisitive crowd a large sheet of pictures of the pursuit of a flea by a 'lady,' and more insidious salesmen doing a brisk trade in what they falsely pretended to be 'Tennyson's last poem'.

Though he felt sure this 'half-terrifying' contrast 'must have occurred to others', the newspaper reports seemed to suggest otherwise. His version of their version of events was socially and politically revealing. The papers offered 'affecting accounts of the emotion displayed by the vast crowds outside the Abbey – horny hands dashing away the tear, seamstresses holding the "little green volumes" to their faces to hide their agitation'. For Gosse, this was all nonsense invented by those who could see things only 'with their fairy telescopes out of the garrets of Fleet Street'. Giving himself the authority of an eye-witness, while nimbly modulating into the first-person plural, he claimed that inside the Abbey 'we distinguished patience, good behaviour, cheerful and untiring inquisitiveness'; while, on leaving, not only 'poetry' but 'authority, the grace and dignity of life, seemed to have been left behind us for ever'. The 'impression was one almost sinister in its abrupt transition', and he was relieved to have been 'conducted by courteous policemen through the unparalleled masses of the curious'.[3]

Not surprisingly, the actual newspaper coverage of the event bore little resemblance to Gosse's peremptory synopsis. It was, in fact, more in keeping with the remarks he made a year and a half earlier. For one thing, most papers focused on the formalities inside the Abbey. Even the Radical *Reynolds's Newspaper,* one of the most popular working-class Sunday broadsheets, devoted the bulk of its report to the 'effective and imposing character' of the service, though it emphasized that 'only an insignificant fraction of people' were allowed into the Abbey itself.[4] Moreover, opinions about the character and significance of the ceremony varied. The conservative *Times* briefly mentioned the 'seething crowd of men and women without', but it dwelt on the service which occasioned, in its view, a solemn moment of unity among the nation's elite: 'Statesmen of either party stood in common sorrow at the grave-side; medicine, the law, art, the drama, poetry, literature, science, and even the crude socialism of the day were represented by leading men, who shared in one deep feeling of general loss.' It called the event 'a piece of English history'.[5] For the Liberal *Daily Telegraph*, it was a more democratic triumph, since one could 'discern that every rank and walk in daily English life had representatives there, drawn by the genius of the dead man to come together'. The 'dignity' of the service, it added, surpassed any 'Emperor's coronation or burial'.[6] Politically divergent though they were, these reports all at least saw the ceremony in a positive light. Yet, as Martin indicates in his biography of Tennyson, not everyone agreed. Many thought it 'disappointingly impersonal and conventional'. While Henry James reckoned it lacked 'real impressiveness', Edward Burne-Jones felt it 'flat and flattening' and hated it 'heartily'.[7] The fiercely Tory and Imperialist *National Observer* echoed these private misgivings, complaining that the service left 'small room for emotion'. It was 'redeemed of banality', the report said, only by the presence of such men as the Tory leader Lord Salisbury, the 'Statesman who guards the Empire' Tennyson 'loved', and by the fact that the laureate's 'coffin was covered by our flag'.[8]

In dismissing the papers for their allegedly universal democratic and working-class enthusiasms, Gosse was not, of course, pretending to make a judicious claim based on an impartial survey of opinion. He was using a convenient rhetorical ploy. Yet even the papers whose reports seemed to justify his cursory comments laid bare his prejudices. The Radical halfpenny *Star*, for instance, offered a discriminating, and mildly sardonic, account of the crowds outside the Abbey. It noted that the funeral coincided with the Westminster Palace Yard's seasonal handout of plants, and that, consequently, 'many people who bore bundles of green stuff had come with no express intention to honor [sic] the dead, but sought rather the possession of something to cheer themselves'. It did mention, however, that 'many of the crowd' were 'so full of emotion that they carried green-backed volumes of the dead poet's works as signs of their devotion'. To this its wry reporter, who liked colourful incongruities, added that 'American tourists improved the occasion by linking the poet's book in strange conjunction with the red Baedecker.'[9] Yet, for all its interest in the working classes, the *Star* wisely did not single out any coy seamstresses from this diverse crowd. No doubt some devotees brought along Macmillan's enormously successful one-volume *Complete Works*, bound in green sand-grain cloth boards, which had been selling between 15,000 and 19,000 copies a year since its first publication in 1884 (and, it should be noted, yielding Tennyson over £1,500 annually in royalties).[10] Retailing at 7s 6d this neat volume would have been an extraordinary extravagance for a seamstress on a weekly wage of 15s.[11]

This book is not about Gosse, nor is it about the death of Tennyson. It is, however, centrally occupied with the problem of how to interpret Gosse's 'depressed and terrified' reaction to the 'the ten thousand persons refused admittance to the Abbey'. Though it recognizes that this is partly a task for the literary critic or historian of ideas, it argues that it is *necessarily* also a question for the sociologist of culture. This is because it maintains there is a productive, albeit treacherous, mediation between the discursive and the non-discursive, the text and the world, literary criticism and social history. Reading Gosse's diatribe, or, indeed, any written text, entails on this analysis attending to the dialectic between its qualities as a particular form of written discourse – its rhetorical and intertextual character – and the multiple determinations of its non-discursive context. Having said this, however, Gosse's essay immediately raises a central methodological problem for this book and, I would argue, for literary and cultural studies. In its obvious disdain towards seamstresses, for example, it clearly exploits the language of class prejudice. But does this make it an expression of Gosse's *class* interests? Or, again, does its dependence on the rhetoric of political fear – he had long 'dreaded' the 'eruption of a sort of Commune in literature' – mean it should be read as a *political* tract?[12] Without denying the importance of these larger socio-political commitments and contexts, this book makes a case for the relevance of a more specific set of interests, peculiar to a more limited social context which I shall call, following the French sociologist Pierre Bourdieu, the 'literary field'. This does not mean that the broader dimensions of Gosse's hostile reaction cease to be significant. It simply means they have to be accorded their proper place in the hierarchy of determinations which constitutes the non-discursive context in which he wrote. The argument of this book, in short, requires that one read his diatribe, not only as a discourse on the literary field in the 1890s, but as a view from a particular non-discursive position within it. In the second part of this introduction, I shall give a more detailed account of Bourdieu's concept of the 'field' and examine some of its methodological implications for literary and cultural studies, but, at this point, I would like to look more closely at Gosse's essay itself in order to discuss some of the general issues at stake in the literary field at the end of the nineteenth century, and to elaborate on the relationship between his anxieties and his particular position in it.

Despite the tenor of some of his language, then, his reaction should not be read as another instance of an intellectual's *social* animus against the 'masses', nor as the expression of a *political* reactionary. His were, rather, the anxieties of an established man of letters and a minor avant-garde poet. By 1892, aged 43, he had a modest but respectable reputation as the author of four delicate volumes of verse – *Madrigals, Songs and Sonnets* (1870), *On Viol and Flute* (1873), *New Poems* (1879), and *Firdausi in Exile and Other Poems* (1885) – all of which bore traces of his early associations with the Pre-Raphaelites and Swinburne in particular; and, despite some notorious setbacks, he had established himself as an authority on English and Norwegian literature (among other things, he was Ibsen's first British advocate). For six years in the 1880s he was Clark Lecturer in English Literature at Trinity College, Cambridge, during which time he also went on a lecture tour of America. By the 1890s, he had overcome his early prejudices against fashionable society and begun to make a name for himself as the aristocratic lady's literary man of London.[13] The clearest index of his cultural status, however, was his renowned library which contained, besides a large collection of Restoration drama, an extensive selection of 'recent books'. Mostly first editions personally inscribed by their authors, these were, Gosse claimed, 'largely records of friendships'.[14] They included works by Arnold, Browning, Bridges, Dobson, Hardy, Henley, Ibsen, James, Meredith, Pater, the Rossettis, Stevenson, Swinburne, Tennyson, Whistler, Whitman, Wilde, and, among the emergent generation, Richard Le Gallienne, Lionel Johnson, Kipling, and Yeats. This private canon of predominantly male authors, materially embodied in his library, at once encompassed contemporary literate culture for Gosse and testified to his own central place in it. It was, moreover, the specific authority of this 'literary hierarchy' that the 'vast black crowd' outside the Abbey seemed to threaten. In his 'parable', the Abbey represented the great traditions of British literate culture, which he traced from Chaucer to Tennyson, while the crowd, and its attendant 'salesmen', signified the advent of a new subversive order in the 1890s. Developing this anxious line of thought, he refigured the Abbey as a 'beautiful pinnacled structure' made of 'carven ice' which was 'kept standing' by 'a succession of happy accidents' and by an 'effort of bluff on the part of a small influential class'. 'It needs nothing', he noted with dismay, 'but that the hot popular breath should be turned upon it to sink into so much water'.[15]

It is important to be clear about the source of Gosse's sudden anxiety attack. Despite his passing remark about the 'hawkers' selling their 'pictures of the pursuit of a flea by a "lady"', he was not really worried that the crowd might represent a dominant and wholly independent counter-culture, vulgar in its appeal and commercial in its aims. In this and other respects, it should be noted, his all-too-visible crowd differed significantly from the 'unknown public' Wilkie Collins claimed to have stumbled upon some twenty years earlier. In a now much cited essay of 1858 entitled 'The Unknown Public', Collins presented readers of *Household Words* with what he considered a 'new and surprising' discovery. He claimed to have found a hidden network of anonymous authors, obscure publishers, and unknown readers which extended from Whitechapel to 'a dreary little lost town at the north of Scotland'. This 'neglected' network seemed to exist beyond the 'pale of literary civilisation', and, indeed, beyond the reach of the book. It supplied some three million readers (domestic servants mainly, he thought) with 'unbound picture quarto[s]', priced at one penny, and distributed them through 'fruit-shops', 'oyster-shops', and 'lollipop-shops'. Collins knew his own audience, and so his article reads more like a short adventure tale than a dryly dispassionate sociological survey. He speaks of the 'mysterious', of a 'locust-flight of small publications', of a 'new species of literary production', and of the 'outlawed majority'. Yet, for all this moonstone rhetoric, he did not consider this cultural world apart a danger. He saw it as a humbling curiosity which revealed that the 'eminent publishing houses', the 'members of book-clubs and circulating libraries', and the 'purchasers and borrowers of newspapers and reviews' – in short, what he called 'the literary world' – constituted 'nothing more than a minority' in the actual scheme of things. This was no cause for alarm, however, as he felt sure the 'unknown public' would 'obey the universal law of progress'. 'Sooner or later' it would 'learn to discriminate', and when that happens 'the great writer will have such an audience as has never yet been known'.[16]

Gosse shared neither Collins's populist enthusiasm, nor his confidence. For him, the problem was precisely that the 'unknown public' had obeyed the 'law of progress', and emerged in 1892, not as an invitingly large 'audience', but as a vast and culturally ambitious 'crowd'. The focus of his anxieties was not, therefore, the hawkers and their vulgar pictures – the counter-culture – but the 'more insidious salesmen' with their specious 'last poem' and the seamstresses with their 'little green volumes'. He most feared the poachers within literate culture, not the philistines without. There were two reasons for this. First, he now maintained that cultural democratization *necessarily* entailed devaluation. This was especially true for poetry which was, in his view, 'not a democratic art'. Its 'essence' was 'aristocratic', that is to say, 'dependent on the suffrages of a few thousand persons who happen to possess, in greater or lesser degree, certain peculiar qualities of mind and ear'. Allied to this was his theory that any feeling's authenticity was inversely proportional to the number of people who shared in it, so 'the excitement about Tennyson's death has been far too universal to be sincere'.[17] Importantly, these assumptions also informed his long-held belief in the superiority of poetry to prose. The most damning thing he could say about the novel form, for instance, was that it 'appeals to all': 'It is so broad and flexible, includes so vast a variety of appeals to the emotions, makes so few painful demands upon the overstrained attention, that it obviously lays itself out to please the greatest number.' This was in an essay entitled 'The Tyranny of the Novel' of April 1892. The fact that women (particularly young married women, he thought) formed 'the main audience of the novelist' only made matters worse. These opinions admittedly put him in an awkward position as the friend and critical supporter of the likes of Hardy, Meredith, and James. He safeguarded them, however, by arguing that 'it is probably to the approval of male readers that most eminent novelists owe that prestige which ultimately makes them the favourites of the women'.[18] In private he put it more bluntly. When *Tess of the D'Urbervilles* (1891) was anonymously attacked in the *Saturday Review*, he told Hardy the review was probably the work of some 'ape-leading and shrivelled spinster' and reassured him that 'you have strengthened your position tremendously, among your own confrères and the serious male public'.[19] Far from being intrinsic, then, the value of literary forms was, for Gosse, dependent on the limited size and specific gender of their readership. Now the full metonymic horror of the seamstresses hiding their emotion with their volumes of poems becomes clear.

6

Yet the danger did not lie simply in democratization *per se*, since, for Gosse, the *process* of popular appropriation now also seemed to involve corruption. At this point the real issue at stake in his diatribe emerges. What worried him was how such a large crowd came to be mourning Tennyson's death in the first place. As his earlier essay suggests, such concerns formed part of the debate about what Henry Harland's 'Yellow Dwarf' called the 'mighty and terrible' changes in late-Victorian culture, the causes of which were a recurrent topic of discussion among contemporary commentators. The electoral reforms, which steadily created a universal male franchise, featured prominently, but the most popular explanation, as we shall see, was that the Education Acts passed between 1870 and 1891, which gradually led to free, universal, and compulsory elementary education, had created a new culturally aspiring 'mass' readership. In a characteristically disdainful article responding to Gosse's piece on Tennyson, the *National Observer* also pointed to the influence of the university extension scheme, the Oxbridge initiative of the 1860s.

It is not for nothing that a cheap pretence of education has been extended – in the name of the Universities – to the suburbs and remoter provinces. Now every housemaid can lisp the poet's name, and tell you accurately the place he occupies in her literary text-book.[20]

In fact, Read indicates that, while the system was immensely successful – 'in the peak year of 1891–2 Oxford and Cambridge together provided 722 extension classes attended by nearly 47,000 people' – only a 'minority of these came from the working classes'.[21] As Harland hinted, however, these political and educational initiatives coincided with wider changes in late-Victorian society, including the rise of the lower middle classes, the professional advancement of women, and the advent of the 'New Journalism', which combined to challenge the pre-eminence of the mid-Victorian 'gentleman scholar'. Speaking as a member of that endangered genteel tradition, and once again disclaiming his earlier remarks, Gosse now put the blame squarely on the new developments in popular journalism. Like Hall Caine, whose article in the *Times* for 17 October 1892 he cited, he felt the 'whole enormous popular manifestation', and the transformation of the literary field it implied, was the effect of excessive news coverage.[22] Caine, one of the best-sellers of the period, liked to think of himself as the champion of 'primitive simplicity' in a corrupt modern age. A devotee of Dante Gabriel Rossetti, he believed that such virtues were being eroded by the 'spread of education' and that his duty, as an historical novelist, was to show the new generation the 'tenderness of the higher life, the courtly golden life, so fast passing from our midst'.[23] In keeping with this general outlook, his *Times* article contrasted Wordsworth's 'unreported and half-known' funeral at Grasmere – 'noble and touching in its simplicity' – with the papers' unwelcome 'garrulity' at the death of his successor to the laureateship. There was, he added, 'something out of tune in the spectacle of Tennyson, who had hidden himself from the world throughout his life, exposed to its gaze in his coffin'.[24] Five years later, by the way, Caine was publicly rebuked for exploiting the press for his own worldly self-promotion.

Gosse readily concurred. Yet, for him, the problem lay not only with the quantity, but with the style, of modern reporting. With its instinct for 'mere commercial success', the new periodical press, in his view, emphasized the 'personal' at the expense of the 'purely literary' aspects of authorship, and so ran the risk of making 'the artist more interesting than his art'.

This was a peril unknown in ancient times. The plays of Shakespeare and his contemporaries were scarcely more closely identified with the man who wrote them than Gothic cathedrals were with their architects.

Now, however, an 'interesting or picturesque figure, if identified with poetry, may attract an amount of attention and admiration which is spurious as regards the poetry, and of no real significance'.[25] Having had his faith in the resilience of literature severely tested, Gosse now shared his friend Henry James's contempt for 'this age of advertisement and newspaperism, this age of interviewing'.[26] Indeed, James's short story, 'The Death of the Lion', which first appeared in the *Yellow Book* for April 1894, reiterated Gosse's earlier anxieties in fictional form. The satirical story, which describes the death of the author, Neil Paraday, who falls victim to a paper called the *Empire* and its interviewers, is filtered through the consciousness of a young penitent male journalist. As he makes clear, the guilt for Paraday's death does not fall only on the brazen papers. Women are as much to blame. At one point, he turns on one of Paraday's many new-style Thracian fans, a young American 'terrible and laughable in her bright directness':

'Ah that dreadful word "personal"!' I wailed; 'we're dying of it, for you women bring it out with murderous effect. When you meet with a genius as fine as this idol of ours let him off the dreary duty of being a personality as well. Know him only by what's best in him and spare him for the same sweet sake.'[27]

In reality, the 'New Journalists' of the 1890s were unrepentant. Though the 'personal' interview was imported from America by the enterprising editor of the *World*, Edmund Yates, in the late 1870s – his series 'Celebrities at Home' included Tennyson at Haslemere – the most famous exponent of the genre in the 1890s was Raymond Blathwayt.[28] He mounted a robust defence of his new style of reporting, claiming that

It is in America that interviewing first rose to the status of a trade. In England we hope to give it the dignity of a profession.

He identified the interviewer with the modern 'scientific spirit', called him the 'veritable photographer and preserver of the history of his own time', defended his role as a mediator between 'the public and the novelist', and dignified the much disparaged genre by tracing it back to Boswell and even to the Gospels.[29]

Blathwayt's celebrity interviews appeared in new popular papers like *Great*

Thoughts (1884), the *Review of Reviews* (1890), *Black and White* (1891), *Bookman* (1891), and the *Idler* (1892), but, for Gosse, the blame for the new trend in 'personal' journalism fell on 'the *Tit-Bits* and *Pearson's Weeklies* in the world'.[30] This was uncharitable. The new-style late-Victorian penny weeklies, pioneered by George Newnes's *Tit-Bits* (1881), did publish some interviews, but they were hardly responsible for the success of the genre. Their staple was the anecdote, typified by the following instructive paragraph in the 'Personal Tit-Bits' column for 22 October 1892:

Amongst the many anecdotes that have been given of Tennyson, the fact has not been recalled that the poet was an amateur printer. In his earlier days he had a small hand-press of his own, on which he used to set up his poems in type, and take 'proofs', which he would correct and revise again and again. It was by this unsparing self-criticism and tireless revision of his work that Tennyson gained the perfection of his style.[31]

That Gosse saw *Tit-Bits* as the archetype of the new brazenly intrusive, commercialized culture was unsurprising, however. For many literary intellectuals, Newnes's enormously successful weekly had been a symbol of all that threatened 'pure and original literature' at least since 1889 when W. E. Henley's outspokenly avant-garde *Scots Observer* railed against the 'degradation of every-day literature in England'.[32] It conceded that *Tit-Bits* could be trying to educate the newly 'enfranchised Briton' – this is what Newnes's first major defender, E. G. Salmon, had argued three years earlier – but, for the *Observer*, such lofty aims were hopelessly at odds with its popular, fragmentary, and ephemeral format.

As he is whirled by omnibus or train from his suburban home to his office in the city he reads in his favourite journal – a kind of rag-bag in print – that Tennyson's *In Memoriam* is a great work. This statement he repeats ever afterwards with the conviction of one who has seen it in type. He finds it sandwiched in between a paragraph on 'Artists and their Models', and another on 'Beauty and How to Get it'. The three are of equal value to him.[33]

Like Gosse, then, the *Observer* insisted that the new 'popular culture' of the 1890s was eroding literate culture in the process of appropriating it; and, again like Gosse, it appealed to 'our recognized judges of literary merit' to control the damage.[34] Prefiguring the Modernists of the 1920s, the *Observer* looked to the 'Critic' as the saviour who would 'insist that books and poems are not to be esteemed, like loaves of bread or pots of ale, by the number of their purchasers; that popularity, save in such rare instances as Tennyson's, is the most fallible of tests; that literature exists of itself and for itself'.[35]

II

But what is the literary field and how might our understanding of it affect how we read these contemporary reactions to its transformation in the 1890s? In the *Introduction to the Critique of Political Economy* (1857), Marx, the most self-

9

critical of all Marxists, famously raised a problem for any material or socio-logical study of culture: 'It is well known that certain periods of highest development of art stand in no direct connection with the general development of society, nor with the material basis and the skeleton structure of its organization.'[36] The theory of the field is Bourdieu's answer to this methodo-logical challenge. It stands precisely at the perilous junction between culture and society, and it represents the focal point of his sustained analysis of their *indirect* connection. A literary field is, Bourdieu contends, a social 'microcosm' that has its own 'structure' and its own 'laws'; while writers, critics, and, indeed, publishers, printers, distributors, and readers are 'specialists' with 'particular interests' specific to that self-contained world.

It is this peculiar universe, this 'Republic of Letters', with its relations of power and its struggles for the preservation or the transformation of the established order, that is the basis for the strategies of producers, for the form of art they defend, for the alliances they form, for the schools they found, in short, for their specific interests.

Not that he wishes to deny the importance or the inevitability of the field's connection to the larger world. His analysis is intended only to put these broader issues in their proper secondary place. He recognizes that the literary field is embedded in, and indirectly affected by, changing social, economic, political, and technological conditions, and that its structure is never static. But, he claims, the field is relatively autonomous in respect to such influences. Instead of 'reflecting' outside developments, in any straightforwardly linear way, it 'refracts' them through its own changing structure, in the way a prism refracts light. This anti-reductive thrust of his argument is directed primarily at the more crude latter-day Marxists who claim that the literary world is part of the cultural superstructure 'determined' by the economic base, and sociologists who see social class as the decisive factor in any cultural analysis. For Bourdieu, by contrast, it is only once we know the field's 'specific laws of operation' that we can understand what is at stake in Gosse's diatribe or, for that matter, any act of writing or reading.[37]

The aim of this book is to demonstrate, through a detailed examination of three late-Victorian writers' careers, the power of the field as a theory of context, not only for cultural or book historians, but also for literary critics. Since the larger questions to do with its external determinants will emerge in the course of the book as a whole, I would like at this point to focus on Bourdieu's understanding of the field's internal organization and functioning. Most importantly, the theory presupposes a *structural* model of sociocultural relations. It is concerned not only with the actual interactions between, say, authors and publishers – the staple of pioneering studies like John Sutherland's *Victorian Novelists and their Publishers* (1976) – but with the implicit structures underlying such relations. This shift from an interactive to a structural perspective can best be explained by comparing Bourdieu's analysis with a more traditional model of cultural relations, like Robert Darnton's useful and influential 'communications circuit' which maps the networks of literary production and consumption. Darnton's purpose in formulating his circuit was to combat the blight of academic specialism, which he rightly identified as the main methodological weakness in the emergent field of book history. 'Some holistic view of the book as a means of communication seems necessary', he argued in 1982, 'if book history is to avoid being fragmented into esoteric specializations'. The circuit provides just that vantage-point. It encompasses the entire life cycle of the text from writing to reading, and through publication, material production, and distribution. But, as Darnton insisted, this is not simply a one-way system, since writing and reading are inextricable. Writers are not only themselves readers, they address implied readers and respond to explicit reviews. 'So the circuit runs full cycle.' As such his model gave a welcome outline of the 'whole' in relation to which the 'parts' examined by bibliographers, cultural historians, sociologists, economists, and literary critics, could take on their 'full significance'.[38]

For Darnton, the agents in the 'communications circuit' are defined primarily in terms of their *function* in the process of *material* production. Authors produce manuscripts, publishers and distributors provide services, printers and binders supply skilled manual labour, and readers are end-product consumers. Given his particular goals, this basic functionalist insight into the workings of the entire circuit has obvious methodological value. The trouble is it brings blindnesses of its own. In particular, it fails to reckon on the other ways in which a literary culture is organized and, as a consequence, it writes out a further dimension to the overall process of production. First, the agents' positions in the culture are defined not only horizontally, in terms of their *function* in the circuit, but vertically, in terms of their *status* in the intricately structured field. Though these two dimensions are, of course, intimately related – printers' abilities to fulfil their function as printers necessarily have an impact on their status, etc. – they are significantly distinct. As Leopold Wagner reminded literary aspirants in his handbook *How to Publish* (1898), an 'author cannot be too careful in his choice of a publisher'.

Assuming publishers to be all equally stable, and honourable as men of business, there is just the same subtle difference between them as exists between the Lyceum and the Gaiety, Exeter Hall and the Crystal Palace, the Royal Albert Hall and the Alhambra as places of public resort. A book may derive prestige from the imprint of one publisher, and be quite discredited by the imprint of another house in the same street.[39]

What is true for publishers is true for writers, printers, distributors, reviewers, and readers as well. Each has a changeable and, indeed, often precarious status relative to his or her immediate competitors and to the field of production as a whole. Moreover, this vertical ranking of agents has, as Wagner suggests, an important bearing on their function. Publishers not only issue books, they invest them with prestige; just as printers produce both material commodities and status objects. When rightly conceived, then, the communications circuit should be read both as a map of the tangible process of material production and distribution, as Darnton's analysis insists, and as an index of the more elusive process which Bourdieu calls 'symbolic production'.[40] For now we can take this to refer simply to the way a particular cultural *status* is conferred on any agent or text in the circuit. That Darnton fails adequately to address this second aspect of production should not come as a surprise, since it is directly related to the limitations of his interactive model. It is precisely at this point that Bourdieu's structural concept of the field acquires its methodological force. 'Symbolic production', he contends, is made possible only by the hierarchical structure of the field itself.

> What 'makes reputations' is not . . . this or that 'influential' person, this or that institution, review, magazine, academy, coterie, dealer or publisher; it is not even the whole set of what are sometimes called 'personalities of the world of arts and letters'; it is the field of production, understood as the system of objective relations between these agents or institutions and as the site of the struggles for the monopoly of the power to consecrate, in which the value of works of art and belief in that value are continuously generated.[41]

This account of the genesis of cultural status, which goes to the heart of Bourdieu's structural sociology of culture, is consciously directed against the common-sense views of someone like Wagner. Yet it is worth noting that Wagner's language belies his intuitively individualistic sense that renowned publishers can single-handedly make an aspirant's name. Prestige, he implies, is bound up with the large structural divisions within the culture, since, by analogy, the hierarchy of publishers is comparable to the hierarchy that set the West End theatre above the music hall.

Bourdieu might be a structural sociologist but he is no friend of the structuralists. While he accepts their critique of the New Critical idea of the literary work as a self-contained verbal text, and endorses their counter-ideal of intertextuality, he shares Darnton's distrust of any theory which remains exclusively preoccupied with textuality, however broadly conceived, and which evades the question of the material and sociohistorical conditions of writing or reading. None the less his concept of the field does make him an ally of the structuralists in at least one respect. By shifting the burden of analysis from celebrated individuals or works to the objective conditions that make particular ways of writing and reading possible, he reinforces their assault on the great man theory of cultural history. But, where the structuralists see only intertextual conditions – what Bourdieu calls the 'paradise of ideas' – he insists upon the social and material conditions of intertextuality itself.[42] For him, a writer's participation in an intertextual network (Foucault's 'field of strategic possibilities') simultaneously implicates him or her in a network of value, or disputes about value, which is ultimately grounded in the non-discursive, social structure of the field.[43] And, since this structure is specific to certain periods and countries, writing is always entangled in social history. This has some important methodological consequences, not only for Darnton's circuit or book history, but for literary interpretation. Given that texts are radically situated, for Bourdieu, as material forms with a specific status in the field, the first task of any literary analysis is not to interpret their meaning, but to reconstruct their predicament. Initially, this might involve tracing the text's journey through Darnton's circuit. Yet, since the full significance of what is happening in the circuit can be discerned only in terms of the field's particular structure, this stage of the analysis can only be provisional. The primary task, then, is to reconstruct the field.

The results of this larger project will depend on the specific period and country in question, but, as a general theoretical postulate, derived from his own analysis of the French literary world in the late nineteenth century, Bourdieu claims that the field is structured, in the first instance, around one 'fundamental' opposition. This is the division between what he calls the 'sub-field of restricted production' and the 'sub-field of large-scale production'.[44] This breakdown can itself be analyzed in two ways. Measured economically, in terms of audience size, capital investment, modes of production, pricing, marketing strategies, and the length of the profit cycle (short-term/long-term), it simply identifies two kinds of business enterprise. In the British literary field of the 1890s, this could be represented as the difference between a small, under-capitalized avant-garde publishing firm, specializing in limited editions of poetry and *belles lettres*, like John Lane and Elkin Mathews, and a large, public company like George Newnes, Ltd which specialized in cheap, mass-produced periodicals. Yet, for Bourdieu, any analysis that stopped here would run the risk of committing the fallacy of economism. In his view, cultural or book history cannot be reduced to business history, since these economic and organizational *differences*, important as they are, do not in themselves explain how the field comes to have its particular structure. They do not, in other words, account for the fact that these two sub-fields, which are in part two different communications circuits, occupy *rival* positions in the cultural hierarchy. This is where the irreducible stakes and laws of operation specific to the literary field enter the equation. The agents in the 'sub-field of restricted production' act according to the principles of legitimacy specific to the literary field. They measure value primarily, if not exclusively, in aesthetic terms; they concern themselves chiefly with the particular demands, traditions, and excellences of their craft; they respect only the opinion of peers or accredited connoisseurs and critics; and they deem legitimate only those rewards, like peer recognition, which affect one's status within the field itself. This is the relatively self-enclosed world of 'art for art's sake', or, to use Gosse's metaphor, the world inside Westminster Abbey. In the 'sub-field of large-scale production', by contrast, other, extra-literary principles of legitimacy pertain. Here value is measured in strictly economic terms; the agents see their craft, whether it is printing or writing, as a commercial enterprise; the opinion of the greatest number, expressed through sales, is all that counts; and rewards like money or fame which, by definition, are not specific to the literary field, are considered both acceptable and desirable. This is the relatively unbounded world outside Gosse's Abbey. These rival extremes, which give the field its hierarchical structure, set what I shall call the 'purists' against the 'profiteers'. For the former, the literary field exists in and for itself; for the latter, it is an instrument for achieving other purposes. The hierarchy arises, then, not only because of a superficial conflict of values, but because of a more profound dispute about the principles of valuation. To use a term from economics in a wider sense, the purists value strictly non-fungible goods (that is, art for art's sake, or peer recognition), while the profiteers value only the most fungible good of all, namely, money. This applies both to issues like rewards and to questions of competence (which are allied to audience size). The profiteers are discredited because the texts they circulate are valued for their accessibility to the greatest number, while a purist text demands the specialized competence of a reading elect. As Oscar Wilde, the master-purist of the 1890s, put it, 'they are the elect to whom beautiful things mean only Beauty'.[45] This question of competence also represents one of the crucial points of intersection between the field and the larger social world. To understand Gosse's belief that men constituted the only serious public, for instance, we clearly need to look beyond the narrow confines of the literary field into the gendered structures of late-Victorian society as a whole.

Of course, in practice, things are not as neat as this idealized opposition between the purists and profiteers makes out. Between these two extremes there are any number of positions which combine the two perspectives in various degrees. In some, value is measured not only economically, but in moral, political, or religious terms; the agents see themselves, neither as artists nor as money-makers, but as educators, prophets, political agitators, or entertainers; in various ways they target more specific readerships and markets; and they value less fungible, but still extra-literary, rewards like public honours, or political and social influence. Moreover, few agents are ever exclusively committed to a single position in the field. This is particularly true for the purists. In practice, most publishers and printers, like many avant-garde writers without a private or 'bread-and-butter' income, cannot subscribe only to the pure world of art for art's sake. Ordinary economic realities intrude. Some publishers, for instance, support avant-garde writers while ensuring their own economic survival by having a second list of best-sellers, just as some innovative novelists lead double lives as pseudonymous magazine serialists. In each period, moreover, historical contingencies add further complications. In the late-Victorian literary field, for instance, the Author's Society, founded by Walter Besant in 1883, put purists in a difficult position. Its agenda, like its first president, Tennyson, was eminently respectable. It was committed to consolidating international copyright, clarifying publishers' agreements, and defending authors' financial interests in an increasingly complex market. For someone like Gosse these were laudable objectives. Though he was himself protected from the insecurities of an avant-garde literary career by a regular salaried income – throughout the 1890s he was employed as a translator by the Board of Trade – he publicly supported the Society in its efforts to improve the legal and economic conditions of authorship. Characteristically, however, he claimed that the author's 'enemy' was not only the 'wicked publisher' – this was one of Besant's particular bugbears – but the 'wicked public', and he argued that 'the men and women whose property needed to be protected were those who were doing pure and useful work, which was at present appreciated only by a small circle'.[46] That was in 1887. In 1895 he complicated his relations with the Society still further when he defended publishers and booksellers and spoke out against the 'greedy author' by which he meant the modern novelist 'of great and sudden celebrity'.[47] Though this brought swift public censure from the Society, Gosse refused to yield. Not surprisingly, James, another testy member of the Society, took his friend's side in this dispute, but he noted in a letter:

I think the ventilation of the whole matter ought to do good – though it still leaves more to be said – I mean in the sense of the plea for a little simple silence about the too-iterated money-question. That's all one wants – for *in* it (in the silence) some little sound may at last get a chance to be heard on some other aspect of authorship, which is no more mentioned, mostly than if it didn't exist.[48]

These historical complications, typified by some writers' uneasy relations with the Author's Society, do not invalidate Bourdieu's model, however. Indeed, the complexities and dangers of the literary life (multiple careers, double lists, awkward allegiances, etc.) make sense only against the background of a structural analysis.

The objective structure of the field is not, however, only an effect of this primary opposition between the purists and the profiteers, and their rival principles of legitimacy. A second fundamental opposition, which Bourdieu unaccountably attributes only to the 'sub-field of restricted production', has less to do with the logic of the field and more to do with the accidents of history. This is, as he puts it, the opposition 'between *artistic generations*, often only a few years apart, between the "young" and the "old", the "neo" and the "paleo", the "new" and the "outmoded", etc.; in short, between the cultural orthodoxy and heresy'.[49] Here the distinction is more quantitative than qualitative. It points to the difference between, for instance, a well-established publishing house in the 1890s, like Macmillan, and a pioneering new firm, like Heinemann; or a fully accredited purist, like Tennyson, and a young avant-garde newcomer whose cultural standing was still uncertain, like Yeats. Bourdieu is no doubt right to stress the importance of this opposition within the restricted world of the literary elite, where intergenerational struggles are particularly fierce and frequent. In the context of the 1890s, this can readily be seen, for instance, in the antagonism between the Rhymers' Club and the Victorian literary establishment. The young group of poets who formed the Club in 1891 were self-conscious purists. This was the circle Yeats later praised for keeping 'the Muses' sterner laws', the 'companions of the Cheshire Cheese', like Lionel Johnson (1867–1902) and Ernest Dowson (1867–1900), who died young,

> But never made a poorer song
> That you might have a heavier purse,
> Nor gave loud service to a cause
> that you might have a troop of friends.[50]

As *aspirant* purists, however, their battle was not only against the seductions of money or social prestige. They also had to rescue poetry from the old guard. In their polemical 'revolt against Victorianism' – that is, the alleged scientific, religious, or political 'discursiveness' of Swinburne, Browning, and Tennyson – the new generation strove, as Yeats put it, to 'purify poetry of all that is not poetry' and to 'restore it by writing lyrics technically perfect' – indeed, the club's name emphasized their eagerness to put pure musicality before content. For them 'moral earnestness' was out, and Pater's 'pure and gem-like flame' was in (at least for the duration of the decade).[51] The Club's structural position was reinforced by their productive alliance with the young, innovative firm of John Lane and Elkin Mathews who published the only two volumes of *The Book of the Rhymers' Club* in stylish limited editions. Yet it is clear that comparable, if less definitive, generational struggles occurred at every level of the culture. Entrepreneurs, like Alfred Harmsworth and George Newnes who shaped the emergent mass market, also made much of their new, secular, but wholesome and instructive, brand of 'popular culture'. Periodicals like the *Strand* and *Tit-Bits* made the established religious monthlies and the more scurrilous working-class weeklies appear outmoded, because they were either too pious, too immoral, or too class-specific for the new homogeneous 'mass culture' of the 1890s. Clearly, the elite do not have a monopoly on the universal conflict between the young and the old. Moreover, while these two fundamental oppositions – the first based on principles of legitimacy, the second on generation gaps – are clearly different, they are also related in important ways. The generation game, after all, is often played out as a series of conflicts for and about legitimacy. Among the purists, newcomers, like the Rhymers' Club, tend to see themselves as restorers of the authentic avant-garde faith (Yeats spoke of poetry as 'a tradition like religion and liable to corruption'); while among the profiteers, a new generation distinguishes itself from the established by adopting different ideals of legitimacy altogether.[52] Generational struggles tend, that is, to be worked out in terms appropriate to each position: internal avant-garde disputes turn on specifically literary matters; while internal 'popular' contests centre on extraliterary issues, ranging from morality to commercialism.

In ideal terms, then, the field has a dual structure determined by two different but interrelated oppositions: the purists versus the profiteers, on the one hand, and the establishment versus the newcomers, on the other. For Bourdieu this structure represents a system of 'positions' according to which the various 'personalities' of the literary world are *objectively* situated in relation to others. And, more importantly, it is these objective positions, rather than the subjective dispositions of the agents, which give the field its hierarchical structure and make it a site of cultural contest. They constitute the impersonal framework of the personalities' specific interests and the foundation of their symbolic status.

In conclusion, I would like briefly to consider the ways this theoretical model, and the methodology Bourdieu attaches to it, not only challenge some of the assumptions underlying book history, but oblige one to rethink elements of literary interpretation and cultural history in general. In the first place, Bourdieu flies in the face of much literary theory since the 1960s by believing in the importance of authorship. Yet it has to be said that the Lazarus he revives is not quite the lofty fiction Roland Barthes dispatched, nor is it the unique individual cherished by the interviewer of the 1890s or the biography industry of the 1990s. An author's biography, for Bourdieu, has value only in so far as it adds a further external dimension to what is happening in the field. Just as outside events can affect the balance of power in the field – educational reforms, for instance, might produce a new mass readership and so bolster the position of the profiteers – so a writer's social origins influence his or her conduct as the holder of a specific position. This is where Bourdieu's concept of *habitus* (in part, the socially learned 'second nature') converges with his theory of the field. Very crudely, for the culturally and socially privileged, being a purist is like speaking a first language, while, for the more marginalized, it is like learning a second late in life. Biography or sociobiography, that is, affects how 'natural' a writer feels occupying a particular position in the field, and introduces a potential tension between positions and dispositions. This goes some way towards explaining the similarities between such diverse figures as Wilde, James, and Conrad, on the one hand, and Bennett, Wells, and Shaw on the other. In the 1890s, the former, who were all 'born' literary intellectuals, were relatively comfortable in their position as purists; while the latter, whose more modest backgrounds made them 'born again' members of the intelligentsia, were either aggressively against the purists or at least very ambivalent about the whole idea of art for art's sake. It is at this point, too, that a more detailed analysis of Gosse's reaction to the crowd outside the Abbey, as an established man of letters, would have to consider the special role literature played in his rebellion against his rigidly Puritan upbringing. His early admiration for the purists of the 1860s, especially Swinburne, and the energies at work in his vigorous defence of poetry in the 1890s, were bound up with his social and religious battle against his father. Indeed, as *Father and Son*

(1907) indicates, literary purism became his secular religion, in so far as it enshrined 'a human being's privilege to fashion his inner life for himself'.[53] His social background, in other words, had a bearing on the intensity of his feelings about the field's inviolability. Yet, if writers inevitably bring their social inheritance to the field, the field always comes between the 'life' and the 'work' complicating any simple cross-references.

The logical priority of the field and its positions, which makes the value of biography conditional, also obliges one to reconsider the process of literary composition. Like the structuralists and post-structuralists, Bourdieu dispels the mystique of the blank page, but, as I have suggested, he does so in a radically different way. For the former, the pre-condition of any act of writing is textuality. In Barthes memorable formulation, 'the text is a tissue of quotations drawn from the innumerable centres of culture'.[54] For Bourdieu, however, this has all the appearance of a blandly innocuous post-modern utopia in which all 'centres of culture' and all 'quotations' are equal and words are just words. In the Barthesian 'space of writing' transgression necessarily comes without cost or reward since that space is a fantastic realm of textuality without borders.[55] He makes writing a game without figural sticks and broken bones by ignoring the correspondence between the innumerable *spaces* of writing and the non-discursive structure of the field. In the abstract, each position is distinguished by its principles of legitimacy and the generational status of its occupants. The Rhymers' Club, for instance, was a group of young, aspirant purists. In practice, however, each position represents an horizon of textual and generic possibilities, according to which certain forms, genres, styles, and languages are deemed legitimate or illegitimate, new or dated. The Rhymers saw themselves both as the descendants of Swinburne, Browning, and Tennyson – that is, as the custodians of poetic form – and as the inheritors of a corrupted textual tradition which needed to be restored to its original purity – that is, as the discoverers or rediscovers of a genuine poetic language. At the same time, they were part of a much larger contemporary field in which, as Gosse insisted, purist poetry had a particular status. Indeed, it could be argued that the Rhymers' avant-garde poems represent one pole in the contemporary textual hierarchy, while 'sensational serials' and detective stories, the staple of the popular magazines, exemplify the opposite extreme. On this analysis, even Yeats's pure interest in the 'pure work' is part of a struggle 'for the monopoly of the power to consecrate', the ultimate basis of which is the field. To write, then, is not simply to participate in an intertextual network, but to enter a fray in which the stakes are always more than words.

For book historians, however, the most important implication of Bourdieu's analysis is that these contests between rival positions do not involve only writers. Each objective position in the structure is best thought of as a integrated network of communications circuits in which writers, publishers, printers, distributors, reviewers, and readers collaborate. What unites them is not necessarily a shared interest in specific styles or writers, nor indeed a network of personal or social ties, but rather a collective investment in common principles of legitimacy and, in some cases, a shared generational status. This means, somewhat perversely, that immediate commercial competitors are collaborators in the final analysis. By competing over the same markets, producing similar products, adopting the same marketing strategies, and drawing on a common pool of writers and artists, Newnes and Harmsworth, for instance, were economic rivals but cultural allies. Of course, in cases where a particular agent gains exclusive or significant control over one area of the circuit, cultural collaboration can be enforced through economic co-optation. This was clearly the case in the mid-Victorian period when Mudie made his circulating library into the 'Royal Academy of Literature', as one group of avant-garde detractors called it.[56] By creating a closed system of mutual economic advantage, among writers, publishers, and book borrowers, Mudie gained unprecedented and unsurpassed control over the book world and exercised a virtual monopoly of the power to define literary value in his own terms (which were primarily moral and commercial). The resentment this caused among avant-garde writers in the 1880s, like Hardy, George Moore, Gissing, and W. E. Henley is legendary – Gosse spoke of 'the disease which we may call Mudietis' – and, according to Bourdieu's model, unsurprising.[57] Every agent, from writer to librarian, publisher to reviewer, necessarily occupies a position in the field and, as such, is part of the ongoing struggle to determine literary value. This means that to reconstruct the predicament of a particular text we need to consider the entire production cycle from manuscript to book, not just as book historians concerned with the circuits of material production, but as literary critics occupied with symbolic production, and, indeed, with the way this dual process presupposes and manifests the structure of the field as a whole. (It should be noted, by the way, that the dissolution of the circulating libraries' monopoly in 1894, effected by W. H. Smith and Mudie himself, brought no comfort to the purists. As Keating points out, it effectively killed the three-volume novel and reduced the libraries' controlling influence, but it also unsettled the domestic market, gave new commercial importance to the book-buying public, and contributed significantly to the rise of the 'bestseller' phenomenon in the 1890s. In effect, it bolstered rather than moderated the market forces at work in the contemporary book world.)[58]

Finally, this framework of investigation enables one to overcome the intellectual restrictions imposed by conventional assumptions about cultural networks. Unlike informal literary coteries (the Rhymers' Club, for example), or more formalized literary organizations (like the Author's Society), these structural positions are not necessarily formed or reinforced by actual associations (dinners, parties, forums, etc.). For one thing, occupants of the same position can be cultural allies without meeting or sharing precisely the same views. As Gosse and Henley demonstrated, to give a simple example, structural equivalence does not preclude personal animosity. Indeed, for reasons Gosse never fully understood, his fellow avant-garde poet of the 1880s hated him intensely.[59] (The edition of Henley's poems in his library was not inscribed.) More importantly, the structural perspective not only enables, but requires, one to talk about the relations between the occupants of different positions. As Bourdieu puts it:

Perfectly illustrating the distinction between relations of interaction and the structural relations which constitute a field, the polar individuals may never meet, may even ignore each other systematically, to the extent of refusing each other membership of the same class, and yet their practice remains determined by the negative relation which unites them.[60]

Simply put, one cannot understand the new avant-garde culture of the 1890s, for instance, without considering its relations to the mid-Victorian purists, on the one hand, and the various more contemporary profiteers, on the other. In effect, this framework makes Darnton's methodological holism less a scholarly ideal than a theoretical necessity. To situate any agent or text, one is obliged to consider both the horizontal circuit of functional interactions, moving from writer to reader, and the vertical hierarchy of structural relations, encompassing the purists and the profiteers, the newcomers and the establishment. Again, unlike a more traditional sociology of culture which focuses on coteries, or groups of like-minded artists and writers, this structural sociology emphasizes the role of cultural intermediaries (publishers, printers, distributors, reviewers, etc.) and consumers. They are now not only functionaries in the circuit but symbolic brokers in the field. They write, print, publish, distribute, review, and read literary works, but, in the process, they also assert and defend specific principles of cultural legitimacy and generational imperatives.

Bourdieu's model of the field is the theoretical tool with which I set out to study the literary culture of late-Victorian Britain. Its power resides, I would argue, in its ability to articulate the mediating ground between textuality and social history, symbolic value and material production. It offers critics and book historians alike a sophisticated theory of context which obliges us to see writing and reading as thoroughly social practices. At the same time, Bourdieu's insistence on the relative autonomy of the field ensures that we do not collapse the text back into its context through a false reductionism, whether sociological or economic. Yet any simply theoretical exposition of such a concept, as I have offered in this introduction, runs the risk of obscuring what it sets out to illuminate. The field should act as the instrument by which a fine-grained cultural analysis can situate the text materially and socially, allowing us to enter into historical dialogue with the literatures and cultures of the past. Formulated in abstract terms, however, the concept threatens to become the very opposite: a series of ideal schemata and etiolated dualities suspended above history. That is why this book is constructed as a series of three inter-related case studies, each dealing with an exemplary figure of the period: Joseph Conrad, Arnold Bennett, and Arthur Conan Doyle. By a detailed analysis of the predicament, both literary and social, of these writers, this book endeavours to put the theory of the field to work. It is only by tracing their complex itineraries through a literary culture which they shared, but in which they assumed divergent structural positions, that the theory acquires its particular force. The aim of this book, then, is to demonstrate, by means of these three case studies, that the real interest of the field as a methodological concept lies, like the God of the mystics, in the details.

1 · MEN OF LETTERS AND CHILDREN OF THE SEA: JOSEPH CONRAD AND THE HENLEY CIRCLE

I ask myself sometimes whether you know exactly what you have given,
to whom, how much.
Conrad to W. E. Henley, 18 October 1898[1]

I

WRITING TO BARONESS JANINA DE BRUNNOW, a childhood friend, on 2 October 1897, Joseph Conrad (1857–1924) cast his mind back over the achievements and frustrations of the first three years of his literary career and reflected on his future prospects as an author.

I have some – literary – reputation but the future is anything but certain, for I am not a popular author and probably I never shall be. That does not sadden me at all, for I have never had the ambition to write for the all-powerful masses. I haven't the taste for democracy – and democracy hasn't the taste for me. I have gained the appreciation of a few select spirits and I do not doubt I shall be able to create a public for myself, limited it is true, but one which will permit me to earn my bread. I do not dream of a fortune; besides, one does not find it in an inkwell. But I confess to you I dream of peace, a little reputation, and the rest of my life devoted to the service of Art and free from material worries.[2]

By this time he had published two novels, *Almayer's Folly* (1895) and *An Outcast of the Islands* (1896), and three short stories had appeared in magazines: 'The Idiots' in the *Savoy* (October 1896), 'The Lagoon' in *Cornhill* (January 1897), and 'An Outpost of Progress' in *Cosmopolis* (June–July 1897). In addition, at the time of writing, the novella *The Nigger of the 'Narcissus'* was being serialized in the *New Review* (August–December 1897), and the short story 'Karain' was about to appear in *Blackwood's* (November 1897).

None of these publications had made him a popular author, a fact which was not, in his view, calamitous. He did not desire to write for the 'masses' – sometimes he defined his antagonists more narrowly as the 'beastly bourgeois', the 'Philistines', or the 'respectable (hats off) part of the population' – and he was not especially charitable towards those who apparently did.[3] Grant Allen, the author of the controversial but hugely successful anti-marriage novel *The Woman Who Did* (1895), was 'a man of inferior intelligence' whose work was 'not art in any sense'.[4] Sarah Grand, the influential 'New Woman' author of *The Heavenly Twins* (1893), was simply 'confused and stupid'.[5] While, in May 1902, a month after *The Hound of the Baskervilles* had finished its run in the

Strand, he felt particularly proud to defend his serious literary methods and intentions 'in a time when Sherlock Holmes looms so big'.[6] Marie Corelli, Hall Caine, and William Clark Russell were similarly beyond the pale, and often not because their style was commonplace or their characters puppet-like, but simply because they were popular.[7] After declaring that Allen, Caine, and Corelli were read only by 'philistines', he added that none of 'these writers belongs to literature'.[8] At this time – Christmas 1898 – those who did belong within his legitimate literary sphere were Kipling, Barrie, Meredith, Turgenev, George Moore, Wells, and Theodore Watts-Dunton.[9] In the *roman à clef*, *The Inheritors* (1901), this purist idea of cultural exclusivity – which Ford, his co-author, shared – lay behind his venomous portrait of Callan, a successful novelist based in part on Hall Caine.[10] Though this anti-populist outlook harmonized well with some of Conrad's explicit political declarations – for instance, when Joseph Chamberlain succeeded in getting the Third Reform Bill passed and the Liberals won the General Election of 1885, he lost no time in deriding the 'newly enfranchised idiots' and the 'rush of social-democratic ideas' – as a committed purist he also had specifically literary reasons for condemning the 'democracy' and especially its novelists.[11]

First, as he saw it, all popular novelists were profiteers. The likes of Corelli, Caine, and Allen succeeded partly because they were 'puffed in the press' and partly because they tailored their writing to meet the tastes and literary competence of the greatest number of readers. As he put it, 'they are popular because they express the common thought, and the common man is delighted to find himself in accord with people he supposes distinguished'. 'This,' he added, 'is the secret of many popularities.'[12] Cynically motivated or not, these writers failed to live up to his purist idea of the uncompromising artist, one of whose essential attributes was 'single-mindedness'. In the Preface to the *Nigger*, his first aesthetic manifesto, he defined legitimate literary writing as, among other things, 'a *single-minded* attempt to render the highest kind of justice to the visible universe'.[13] And again, in a letter praising some of Edward Garnett's prose sketches, he declared: 'I envy your writing – the *single minded* [sic] expression, without a thought for the deaf and blind of the world.'[14] 'Single-mindedness', in other words, referred primarily to the genuine writer's indifference to, indeed principled aloofness from, the established tastes of the public or the demands of a literary market. And so, in the letter to the Baroness, he presents himself as a writer who has to 'create a public' and who is disinterestedly devoted to the 'service of Art'. 'I would rather recall', he wrote later, 'Wagner the musician and Rodin the Sculptor who both had to starve a little in their day – and Whistler the painter who made Ruskin the critic foam at the mouth with indignation'.[15] The value of such austerity was only increased by its lack of appeal in what he disdainfully called 'the age of Besants, Authors' Clubs and Literary agent'.[16]

Yet, if he shunned worldly claims and rewards, there were compensatory attainments: in particular, the achievement of what he called a 'literary reputation'. As an earlier letter shows, achieving the recognition of a 'few select spirits' was his first priority as a newcomer to the literary field. On 10 March 1896, just before *An Outcast of the Islands* appeared, he told Karol Zagórski 'if I have ventured into this field it is with the determination to achieve a reputation'.[17] Later, recalling the exactions of his career as a seaman, and with the critical reception of the *Nigger* very much on his mind, he explained more precisely what this meant:

Only a small group of human beings – a few friends, relations – remain to the seaman always distinct, indubitable, the only ones who matter. And so to the solitary writer. As he writes he thinks only of a small knot of men – three or four perhaps – the only ones who matter.[18]

This idea of his new profession influenced his career in practical ways. It lay behind his early resistance to being published in popular monthlies, like *Pearson's Magazine* (1896), for instance. When *Pearson's* expressed an interest in publishing him in 1897, he refused to send them 'The Return', which he had considered submitting to the *Yellow Book* (1894–1897), on the grounds that it was 'much too good to be thrown away where the *right people* won't see it'.[19] His early choice of publishing venues suggests who the 'right people' really were. By October 1897 he had published two novels with T. Fisher Unwin whose imprint was enough to ensure that any writer new to his stable received long notices in such prestigious literary weeklies as the *Saturday Review* and the *Athenaeum;* and all his other work had appeared, or was appearing, in high-class literary and political magazines.[20] Of course, the 'right people' were not necessarily the readers of these magazines; they were the literary professionals who produced them. In Conrad's case, these included William Blackwood (*Blackwood's*), Arthur Symons (*Savoy*), Frederick Ortmans (*Cosmopolis*), J. St Loe Strachey (*Cornhill*), and W. E. Henley (*New Review*), the magazine editors; fellow writers and reviewers such as R. B. Cunninghame Graham, H. G. Wells, Henry James, and Stephen Crane; and, most importantly, Edward Garnett, Unwin's reader. In their own way, and with varying degrees of energy and involvement, this diverse group of 'select spirits' constituted the inner circle of Conrad's early peers who, by the process of what Bourdieu calls 'co-optation', established and confirmed his position in the literary field of the 1890s.

As a purist, Conrad valued the good opinion of recognized peers above all else, but, as he readily acknowledged, 'there is the problem of the daily bread which can not be solved by praise – public or private'.[21] Lacking as he did Gosse's regular salaried income or George Moore's landowning interests, the practical problem of how to make a living as an avant-garde writer preoccupied him from the outset of his second career. In January 1895, three months before *Almayer's Folly* was published, Garnett, then his closest literary confidant, advised him to 'follow his own path and disregard the public's taste'. To this Conrad replied emphatically: 'But I won't live in an attic! . . . I am past that, you understand?'[22] As a thirty-seven-year-old bachelor, with a taste for a gentlemanly life style, the attics of New Grub Street clearly had little appeal; yet, at this stage, his problems were not especially acute. As Najder points out, in 1894 he already had 'enough to give him a comfortable living for two or three years', and, moreover, in January 1895 he was a month away from inheriting £4,000 from his uncle Tadeusz Bobrowski's estate.[23] The real trouble started eighteen months later. For reasons that remain unclear, he lost most of his capital in July 1896 when a South African mining company, in which he had invested, seemingly collapsed.[24] By then he also had a wife to support – he had married on 24 March 1896 – and his prospects of finding another position at sea seemed to be fading fast.[25] So, by mid-1896, the need to make his literary work more profitable had acquired new urgency.

His first major move, after the financial disaster, was to try to negotiate a better deal with T. Fisher Unwin. In October 1896, when Unwin offered him the same £50 advance on royalties for *Tales of Unrest*, his first volume of short stories, as he had for *An Outcast of the Islands*, Conrad demanded double. 'I can't afford to work for less than ten pence per hour', he wrote, 'and must work in a way that will give me this magnificent income'.[26] When Unwin refused to comply, he began negotiations with other publishers under Garnett's discreet supervision: first with the reputable Smith, Elder; then, when that fell through, with the pioneering young publisher, William Heinemann. But making *all* his work more profitable by seeking better deals with publishers was only one of the strategies he pursued in 1896. Before the financial disaster, he had already decided to make *some* work more marketable as well. As he put it on 10 March 1896, 'it is therefore only a question of earning money – "Qui est une chose tout à fait à part du mérite littéraire"'.[27] On completing *An Outcast* in September 1895, he began his third novel, *The Sisters*. Its subject – the bohemian life of painters in Paris – represented a deliberate attempt to break away from the exotic adventure-story mode of his previous work. On Garnett's advice, however, he soon abandoned it, and took up adventure stories once again.[28] And so, in late March 1896, while on honeymoon in Brittany, he began work on the third part of the Lingard trilogy that was later to become *The Rescue*. Of all the novels he had difficulty writing – and he had difficulty with most – this was to prove the most intractable. He completed it only in 1919. In the first few months of 1896, however, his struggles with the novel precipitated what he was later to call the 'first crisis of my writing life'.[29] It was during this crisis that he began for the first time to produce short stories for magazines.

Before then he had been reluctant to publish any of his work in periodicals of any kind or quality. When Unwin suggested he would try to place *An Outcast* in a magazine or newspaper, Conrad remarked to E. L. Sanderson: 'I hate the idea but have given in to his arguments.'[30] His later objections to having his stories carved up into instalments go some way towards explaining this attitude.[31] Yet the exact reasons for his change of heart in early 1896 remain obscure. No doubt the desire to experiment with other modes and materials as well as his need to escape the horrors of *The Rescue* played a large part in it, but money also clearly came into it. This is especially true for the short stories written after the disaster. He began 'The Lagoon', for instance, during a particularly bad phase with *The Rescue*, remarking to Garnett on 5 August 1896 'I must do something to live.' Nine days later he reported that the new short story had 'the usual forests river – stars – wind sunrise, and so on – and lots of secondhand Conradese in it', but that sadly it was only 6,000 words long 'so it can't bring in many shekels'. Again, a few months later, when he was planning 'Karain', another 'Malay thing', he wrote: 'It will be easy and may bring a few pence.' No doubt it was not out of deference only to a friend's fiancée that he gave the story a 'hopeful', if not a 'happily-ever-after' ending. At the same time, too, he began to enjoy posturing, in some of his letters to Garnett, as a shameless profiteer. With mock cynicism, he remarked on hearing that no publisher would accept Garnett's London sketches, 'it is obvious that dishonesty (of the right kind) is the best policy: and henceforth my concern shall be to discover and steadfastly pursue a dishonest and profitable course'. Put this way his actions in no way contradicted his underlying cultural assumptions. He had always held that 'shallowness, imbecility, hypocrysy [sic]', not 'pure art', succeeded.[32] The only difference now was that he was prepared to enter the game.

The success of his strategy was soon apparent. Whereas he had received £20 for the full copyright of the 64,000-word *Almayer's Folly* (excluding French translation rights), and a £50 advance on a 12.5 per cent royalty for the book rights of *An Outcast* (115,000 words), he was now able to earn up to £40 10s for a short story of only 9,500 words (a rate of 1s for 12 words).[33] Even the average rate of 1s for 16 words for the magazine rights to the short stories published up to July 1897 was a tenfold improvement on the rate for *Almayer* (1s for 160).[34] Yet if this change in direction brought a significant relative increase in his earnings, it did not go very far towards improving his gross income. For work published up to July 1897, his total income amounted to only £158 6s, which averaged out at £5 16s per month over the twenty-seven-month period from April 1895 to July 1897.[35] That was 4s a month less than an average well-paid wage-earner could expect in the late 1890s.[36] If, as his letter to Garnett of 7 January 1898 suggests, he needed to maintain a cash flow of at least £20 a month at around this period, one can understand the urgency of his 'material worries' in early October 1897.[37] (It is worth recalling that in July 1902 he received a £300 grant from the Royal Literary Fund to bolster his dismal earnings. This was arranged by Gosse and supported by James.)

To begin with, then, his engagement with the magazine market was at best a qualified success. It should be noted, too, that his concessions, given the available options, were cautious. Unlike others who faced the same problem –

Arnold Bennett, Arthur Morrison, or Eden Phillpotts, for instance – he did not turn to producing genre fiction adapted to the requirements of the popular magazine market. Rather, he produced some new experimental work ('An Outpost') in the more lucrative short-story mode and some second-rate and less demanding versions of his more serious work ('The Lagoon' or 'Karain'). Though varied, all these stories still suited the more high-class and expensive magazines. Even within Conrad's own *œuvre* these early attempts at money-making were relatively low-key. By February 1904 he was dictating *The Mirror of the Sea* essays for Harmsworth's *Daily Mail*, among others, at the rate of 3,000 words in 4 hours and earning up to just under £4 an hour.[38] At the same time, he was also ready to write an 'imbecile short story' on commission for the *Strand*.[39] In the early years he would not willingly have produced such 'bosh', as he called it, and he would have resisted being seen in these publications.[40] As a newcomer, his need to produce more marketable work was in direct conflict with his more urgent need to establish his position in the field, and, in 1896, he was not yet confident in his literary self-image. The composition and serialization of *The Nigger of the 'Narcissus'* changed all this.

II

Conrad probably began the *Nigger* in June 1896.[41] It was initially planned as a short story, and, like others written at the time, it was a form of displacement behaviour. As he recalled its genesis later, he laid aside *The Rescue* in a fit of desperation, and with 'a sudden conviction that *there* only was the road to salvation', he began the *Nigger*.[42] If Garnett's recollection is correct, progress was not very rapid. When he returned from Brittany at the end of September, he had written only ten pages.[43] Yet by 19 October he had a clear sense that it would be a long short story of at least 25,000 words. Then, two weeks later, he wrote to Garnett: 'I am letting myself go with the *Nigger*. He grows and grows.'[44] On 17 January 1897, after what Garnett considered the 'most strenuous' weeks 'in the whole of his writing life', he finished what turned out to be a 53,000–word novella.[45]

What makes the *Nigger* unique among Conrad's work of this inaugural phase is that, early on in the process of composition, he expressed a desire to see it serialized in a magazine of his own choice, namely, Henley's *New Review*. 'The Idiots', a Naturalist story of madness and suicide, was sent by Unwin to the *Savoy* on Garnett's advice after both *Cosmopolis* and *Cornhill* had rejected it; 'An Outpost of Progress', a sardonic anti-Imperialist story, was written 'with the fear of *Cosmo[polis]* before my eyes', as Conrad put it, after the editor had asked to see another of his stories; and Conrad himself sent 'The Lagoon', an exotic story of betrayal, directly to the *Cornhill* at the editor's request.[46] By contrast, the *Nigger* was unsolicited and the choice of magazines was Conrad's alone. On 19 October 1896, when he still envisaged it as a short story, he wrote to Unwin saying with characteristically disingenuous modesty: 'I would like to try *W. Henley* with my *'Nigger'* – not so much for my own sake as to have a respectable shrine for the memory of men with whom I have, through many hard years lived and worked.' He made a similar remark to Garnett six days later.[47] If his subsequent statements to the chairman of the Provisional Committee of the Henley Memorial are accepted, then it seems Henley mattered from the start. Writing on 17 February 1904, Conrad claimed that the story was 'written with an eye on him – and yet with no idea whatever that it would ever meet his eye'.[48]

As it turned out, despite his hopes, the plan almost failed. During negotiations with Smith, Elder on 13 November 1896, he asked whether they would agree to serialize the *Nigger* in *Cornhill* as part of a larger deal he was trying to arrange.[49] Smith declined, saying it was too long for their purposes, and when he also failed to offer favourable terms for book publication, the negotiations fell through. At this point, Garnett contacted S. S. Pawling, a partner in the Heinemann firm who later became one of Conrad's keenest champions, and arranged to have the first two chapters of the manuscript shown to Henley.[50] Conrad was of course delighted, but, as usual, he also felt apprehensive. 'I sit tight now', he wrote to Garnett on 21 November, 'like a man with a lottery ticket; and hope for unheard-of fortunes'. As his letter to E. L. Sanderson on the same day reveals, the expected fortunes were not only, or even mainly, material:

One of the short stories (a pretty long one too – about half the lengtht [sic] of Almayer) is now under Henley's consideration for serial publication in the *New Review*. If accepted by Henley then Heineman [sic] will publish it afterwards in a small volume. I want £100 for serial and book rights and of course some percentage on the sales. Still I will take any offer (not absurdly low) they make because I do wish to appear in the *New Review*.[51]

By 25 November he had received the long-desired reply. Via Pawling and Garnett, Henley sent the message: 'Tell Conrad that if the rest is up to sample it shall certainly come out in the *New Review*.'[52] It was up to sample, and so, despite some further delays and uncertainties, the story eventually appeared in the review from August to December 1897, the last five months of Henley's editorship. (It was published in book form by Dodd, Mead & Co. in the United States on 30 November under the title *The Children of the Sea: A Tale of the Forecastle*, and by Heinemann in Britain on 2 December as *The Nigger of the 'Narcissus'*.)

Conrad rejoiced at the news. 'Now I have conquered Henley', he wrote to Garnett on 7 December 1896, 'I ain't 'fraid of the divvle himself.' To Unwin, a month later, he was more reserved: 'Of course if I had not supposed the thing tolerably good I would not have tried in that quarter – and I am very glad to see my own opinion backed by such a distinguished authority. I always had a great admiration for the man.'[53] He never forgot his success. On 18 October 1898, he gave a typically elaborate interpretation of its significance to Henley:

A chance comes once in life to all of us. Not the chance to get on; that only comes to good men. Fate is inexorably just. But Fate also is merciful and even to the poorest there comes sometimes the chance of an intimate, full, complete and pure satisfaction. That chance comes [sic] to me when you accepted the *Nigger*. I've got it, I hold it, I keep it, and all the machinations of my private devil cannot rob me of it. No man, either, can do ought [sic] against it. Even you, you yourself, have no power. You have given it and it is out of your hands.

This last reflexion is prompted not by impudence but by a less useful and a shade more honourable sentiment. I ask myself sometimes whether you know exactly what you have given, to whom, how much.[54]

Again, in 1904, he described it as 'the first event in my writing life which really counted', and spoke of its 'intrinsic value, as encouragement and recognition'.[55] And, just before his death in 1924, he recalled it again with undiminished satisfaction.[56]

But what exactly had Henley given him? And, more importantly, how is one to understand it? In his 1985 article on the serialization of the *Nigger*, Todd G. Willy outlines a number of suggestive answers to these questions. Besides describing the remarkable affinities between the politics of the *Nigger* and Henley's belligerent Toryism, Willy offers three explanations as to why Conrad might have desired Henley's approbation, and, as a corollary, why he might have accordingly rigged his text prior to submission. First, Willy speculates that Conrad might have 'had high hopes of emulating the popular success that had come to so many writers to whom Henley had given his imprimatur'.[57] For at least two reasons, however, this seems implausible. First, despite his straitened financial position, popular acclaim was not Conrad's primary objective at this point. Second, notwithstanding the success of some of Henley's authors – Stevenson and Kipling especially – one would be hard put to see such a fiercely purist editor as the gatekeeper to popular and commercial success.

Willy's second explanation is more convincing. As he points out, by the end of 1896 Conrad had a long-standing personal score to settle with Henley. Only two weeks after *Almayer's Folly* was published in April 1895, he sent the following manic note to Garnett:

Called on F[isher] U[nwin] who says Henley can't read more than 60 pages of the immortal work – after which he 'lays it down'. Despair and red herrings! Suicide by thirst on Henley's doorstep – no. Emigration to Champel and hydropathy when return with Alpenstock branded (untruthfully) 'Monte Rosa' and brain the sixty-page-power Henley.[58]

This was followed by a less than enthusiastic unsigned review in the *National Observer* of 14 September 1895, which criticized, among other things, the 'laboured and muddle-headed involution' of the novel's style.[59] To add insult to injury, the weekly followed this with an even more stinging review of *An*

Outcast of the Islands eight months later. Comparing Conrad unfavourably to Kipling and Stevenson, the anonymous reviewer accused the newcomer of the 'besetting sin of wordiness'; considered most of his characters a 'bore'; and, putting the boot in, observed that, despite its being a 'book of adventure', 'even schoolboys will probably have some difficulty in getting through it and we fear adults will find it impossible'.[60] Not surprisingly Conrad winced under what he called this 'wholesome "slating"'.[61] While Henley left the *National Observer* at the end of March 1894 – a detail Willy fails to mention – Conrad might have found it difficult to disentangle the public from the private assessments of his work.[62] Yet this consistent lambasting can at best be taken only as a partial explanation for his desire to seek Henley's endorsement specifically. Whether or not Henley wrote or approved the reviews, the *National Observer* was not alone in its criticism of Conrad's first two novels. The *World* and the *Athenaeum* made similar remarks about *Almayer*, and Wells criticized the wordiness of *An Outcast* at length in the *Saturday Review*.[63]

Willy's third, and most persuasive, explanation goes some way towards showing why Conrad might have singled out Henley. As Willy puts it, he desired, above all, 'to be accepted into that elite company of artists whose works Henley had published and championed in his monthly [and weekly] journals to the very considerable benefit of his own and their literary reputations'.[64] Useful though this observation is, Willy unfortunately takes his argument no further. One is still left wondering why Conrad wanted Henley's endorsement so badly. What was really at stake? And why did he make so much of his success?

To answer these remaining questions, I would argue, we need to shift the focus of the analysis from Conrad's actual relations with Henley to the implicit structures which informed them. We need to see Conrad as a purist newcomer and Henley as an elderly statesman among an emergent avant-garde, and we need to see both in the context of the field as a whole. This admittedly takes some of the verve out of Willy's compelling exposé. His central claim that Conrad contradicted his own avowed disinterestedness by consciously inflecting his text to gain Henley's approval still stands. Yet it can be argued that, at a more profound level, this strategic manoeuvring in fact reflected, rather than obscured, his purist convictions. It presupposed that the literary elect had exclusive control over literary value and that the only legitimate prize for writers, apart from the intrinsic rewards of the craft itself, was what he called a specifically 'literary reputation'. In this he displayed, as Bourdieu suggests, the characteristic beliefs and anxieties of an aspirant purist:

Few people depend as much as artists and intellectuals do for their self-image upon the image others, particularly other writers and artists, have of them . . . This is especially so for the quality of a writer, artist or scientist, which is so difficult to define because it exists only in, and through, co-optation, understood as the circular relations of reciprocal recognition among peers.[65]

That Conrad understood this aspect of the social process, particularly the aspirant's dependency on the image of others, is well-illustrated in *Under Western Eyes* (1911). The novel opens with an account of a young intellectual – Razumov, the central figure – whose sole ambition is to succeed in his chosen field, namely philosophy. As we discover, he has special reasons for his singleness of mind. Since his parents are unknown, he has, like a foreigner in an alien culture, no pre-established social position. He is, the narrator chillingly observes, 'as lonely in the world as a man swimming in the deep sea'. As a consequence, 'the word Razumov [is] the mere label of a solitary individuality'. To overcome this unendurable anonymity he channels all his energy into his studies, in the hope that 'distinction would convert the label Razumov into an honoured name'. At this point the narrator remarks in an aside:

There was nothing strange in the student Razumov's wish for distinction. A man's real life is that accorded to him in the thoughts of other men by reason of respect or natural love.[66]

The idea that one's 'real life' is somehow dependent on the esteem of others, or that there is a necessary reciprocity between the private and the public, informs much of Conrad's thinking about the nature of identity and especially its tragic possibilities, not least of all in *Under Western Eyes* itself and *Lord Jim*.

It also applies equally well to his own early literary career. At the outset his social and literary standing was as precarious as Razumov's. There were the inevitable obstacles of his objective circumstances – he was a newcomer to the literary field, a migrant in an alien culture, and he was constantly short of money – but there were also the added, and partly related, difficulties of his subjective dispositions. Besides the usual insecurities engendered by ambition and the vulnerabilities of being a late-starter – he was 39 in 1896 – he had, as his letters amply testify, a persistent, and at times immobilizing, lack of conviction as a writer. Undoubtedly his greatest fortune, given all of this, was to have come to Garnett's attention as early as he did. Though he was ten years younger, Garnett had, by 1896, already begun to establish himself, in his work for Unwin, as what Fritschner calls a 'prestigeful reader', that is, a publisher's reader who puts literary merit above commercial value, has direct contact with authors, and tends to act more as their broker than the publisher's assessor.[67] In terms of his values and patterns of social relations, Garnett was, in other words, a young purist reader, and, as his letters show, his relationship with Conrad is a study in 'co-optation'.[68] He offered him personal and critical support, advised him on how to deal with publishers, and, most importantly, he used his contacts to make Conrad's name known to others. Like Bourdieu's art trader, he became Conrad's first 'symbolic banker':

The art trader is not just the agent who gives the work a commercial value by bringing it into a market; he is not just the representative, the impresario, who 'defends the author he loves'. He is the person who can proclaim the value of the author he defends (cf. the fiction of the catalogue or blurb) and above all 'invests [sic] his prestige' in the author's cause, acting as a 'symbolic banker' who offers as security all the symbolic capital he has accumulated (which he is liable to forfeit if he backs a 'loser').[69]

Conrad acknowledged Garnett's role in more patriarchal language. He referred to him as 'my literary father' or 'my "Father in Letters"' and, in a characteristic act of reciprocal recognition, he dedicated the *Nigger* to him.[70] Yet, apart from a number of reviews, Garnett's part in the making of Conrad was acted out mostly behind the scenes.[71] To secure his position in the literary field in 1896, and to bolster his self-image as a writer, Conrad still needed the public endorsement of an older, more prominent and well-established peer. Of all contemporary 'symbolic bankers', Henley was the most spectacular and successful, so he chose to invest with him.

III

William Ernest Henley (1849–1903) was a commanding presence on the British literary scene in the mid-1890s. Though he had made a name in the previous two decades as a poet and dramatist in his own right, his high standing in the 1890s was more an outcome of what he considered his secondary career as a combative opinion leader and magazine editor. By the time he took on the *New Review* at the end of 1894, he had been a freelance for almost twenty years and he had edited three periodicals: *London*, a literary weekly (1877–79); Cassell's monthly *Magazine of Art* (1881–86); and the weekly *Scots Observer*, later renamed the *National Observer* (1888–94). The *New Review*, which he edited from January 1895 to December 1897, was his fourth and final venture. As an editor he rapidly became an outspoken and charismatic figure at the centre of the 1880s cultural avant-garde. While editing *London*, and during his controversial tenure at Cassell, he recruited an impressive band of writers, mostly in their thirties, including Andrew Lang (whom he came to despise), Robert Louis Stevenson (then his closest literary friend), George Saintsbury, William Archer, R. A. M. Stevenson (whose career as an art critic he launched), and W. H. Pollock (the editor of the *Saturday Review*). It was, however, during the final decade of his editorial career, first with the *Observer* and then with the *New Review*, that he emerged as, in George Meredith's words, 'one of the main supports of good literature in our time'.[72] Though he remained an advocate of established avant-garde figures like Meredith, Hardy, and Stevenson, he also began to foster a new generation. As Meredith put it, he 'gathered about him a troop of young writers who are proud in acknowledging their debt to him for the first of the steps they made on the road to distinction'.[73] Henley's circle now included Kipling, Wells, Arthur Morrison, Yeats, Kenneth Grahame, J. M. Barrie, G. S. Street, and H. B. Marriott-Watson, among the younger British writers; journalists and critics such as Charles Whibley, J. H. Millar, Francis Watt, G. W. Steevens, and George

Wyndham; and he also imported Marcel Schwob, Paul Verlaine, and Mallarmé, and championed the young Stephen Crane. By 1896, then, Henley, aged 47, was the senior figure in a prominent cosmopolitan literary circle.

This circle was neither as homogeneous nor as focused as a young avant-garde group like the Rhymer's Club. It emerged in the 1890s as a meeting point between the established avant-garde and the newcomers, it had no single aesthetic objective, and it represented diverse literary and political interests – both the *National Observer* and the *New Review* were ferociously Tory and Imperialist. What bound the disparate members of the group together, more than age, politics, or direct social contacts (men-only dinners at Solferino's and Verrey's were a regular event, however), were their shared principles of cultural legitimacy and their admiration for Henley's strident purism. For Kipling, Henley was 'a jewel of an editor, with the gift of fetching the very best out of his cattle'; and even Yeats, who saw Henley as part of the out-moded generation and disagreed with him about everything, none the less 'admired him beyond words'.[74] To Conrad he was a 'distinguished authority': the 'patron of Kipling and Stevenson' and the man to whom Wells dedicated his novels.[75]

If there was a single impulse underlying the various cultural attitudes of the circle, it was to defend the 'free estate' of the 'Republic of Letters' – 'once a fashionable phrase' – against the encroachments of commercial, political, and other extraliterary interests.[76] Of course, the virulent politics of some members, including Henley, often undermined this project from within – for various reasons, as we shall see, their purist aestheticism never went quite as far as Wilde's – but that did not invalidate the ideal, versions of which affected their views on every aspect of the writing, publishing, printing, distribution, and reading of literary texts. To gain access to the Henleyite Republic one had, in the first instance, to be worthy of the title 'man of letters'. This entailed following a strict code of writerly conduct:

The man of letters writes not for the many-headed monster; it is enough for him if he please himself and his friends. If once he listen to the voice of the great public, or yield to the tinkling of its shillings, he is a traitor to his art, and henceforth a stranger to literature.[77]

This did not mean that 'men of letters' could not look after their financial interests – the *Scots Observer* initially supported Walter Besant's efforts with the Society of Authors – but such concerns had to remain secondary. Forgetting this brought immediate disqualification. The Society, its founder, and its journal *The Author* (1890) lost credibility as soon as they were seen to be telling 'the world with painful persistency that the end of literature was the making of money'.[78] Henley's purists also (unfairly) blamed Besant for inventing that despised new breed of 'tradesman', the literary agent.[79] 'Even now,' the *National Observer* growled on 16 July 1892, 'Frankenstein shudders at his Monster.'[80] Yet, if 'men of letters' were expected to scorn the 'great public' and its rewards, they were also required to shun official honours and to resist any schemes for the 'aggrandisement of the author'.[81] The demand for titles, state subsidies over and above the Civil List, or a 'National Academy of Letters', voiced by the likes of Besant, Grant Allen, Mrs Oliphant, and William Watson, was dismissed as an unbecoming 'clamour for superfluous recognition'.[82]

Though keenly aware that in the 1890s 'men of letters' were under threat from all sides, as devotees of the cult of the solitary genius Henley's purists remained loftily unembattled:

Genius, which after all is the only permanent factor, will ever remain unaffected by the mob. We contemplate without apprehension the 'influence of the democracy upon literature', because we believe the democracy is powerless to exert such influence.[83]

It was unfortunate that the 'mob' no longer had prize-fighters as heroes – since 'the ring is dead, and Toynbee Hall rules in its stead, and the British 'Arry must needs pretend an interest in letters which he cannot feel' – but it was unimaginable that it could pose a serious danger.[84] Unlike Gosse, the Henley circle took a consistently hard line on the transformation of late-Victorian culture: 'Neither education nor the Democracy, neither a population fed fat on *Tit-Bits* nor a whole army of prigs, can hinder or advance the march of genius.'[85] Since the security of their position depended in part on this belief, any challenge to it was met with an immediate counterblast. When the first English translation of Max Nordau's *Degeneration* (1895) appeared, for instance, Charles Whibley, Henley's most vitriolic henchman, lost no time in attacking both it and its precursor, Cesare Lombroso's *Man of Genius* (1891). What he found particularly galling about the latter was the apparent popularity of the theory that intellectuals suffer from a form of insanity. Calling Lombroso 'the god of cheap culture', he explained why his 'rag-bag' theories 'had brought comfort to a thousand common homes':

When you realise the smug rapture wherewith the clerk or reporter murmurs, after studying his Lombroso, 'I thank God I am not a man of genius', you understand the popularity of this, the last of the sham sciences.

He then set about Nordau's attempt to explain the apparently degenerate tendencies of avant-garde art. Quoting the observation, made in Nordau's dedicatory preface to Lombroso, that 'degenerates' are 'not always criminals, prostitutes, anarchists, and pronounced lunatics; they are often authors and artists', Whibley remarked: 'And so he runs atilt at Ibsen and Tolstoi, Wagner and Verlaine, Rossetti and Swinburne, with an energy which is admirable, with an ignorance which is sublime.' Turning the theory back on the theorizer, he dismissed Nordau, on his own authority, as 'a mattoid, afflicted with graphomania and monotypism'.[86]

Not surprisingly, given these assumptions, the Henley circle's cultural black-list was extensive. But it was not neat. Popularity with the 'great mass of readers', especially when unsought, was not necessarily a disqualification, for instance. With Scott and Austen in mind, the *Observer* scorned 'petty newspaper' critics who would not accept that the popular 'romance of action' could flourish alongside more exclusive genres like the 'novel of analysis'.[87] Never as enthralled by Romance as Andrew Lang, who sniped at *Tess of the D'Urbervilles* but boomed *The Prisoner of Zenda*, the Henley circle none the less included Stevenson, Wells and H. B. Marriott-Watson, and they admired Rider Haggard (Henley himself had a taste for Dickens, Dumas, Scott, and Cervantes).[88] 'The public and the critical', they admitted, 'are but seldom of the same mind; when they do agree, their unanimity is wonderful'.[89] Conversely, when militant manly prejudice gave the lie to their aestheticism, even recognized 'men of letters' were not safe. If they praised Walter Pater, the 'high priest of aestheticism', and gave him a 'place apart' in English literature, they chastised him – and 'most of the antic figures begotten of him on his generation' – for his 'waywardness, his preciosity, his lack of virility'.[90] Henry James came in for a similar drubbing. Under protest, Henley, who privately called him 'Henrietta', was obliged by his less dogmatic board of directors to serialize *What Maisie Knew* in the *New Review*.[91] And earlier the *Observer* had conceded that James's 'style is never *bourgeois*', but, it went on, the 'vulgar is as far out of his reach as the heroic.' He was, it unnervingly lamented, 'not skilled to quicken the blood nor to marshal men of spirit and of war'.[92] So much for the coexistence of adventure and analysis. But it was Wilde who most famously fell victim to the importance of being virile. Whibley's venomous, short, and unsigned review of the magazine version of *The Picture of Dorian Grey* managed to avoid libel, but, given the references to the Cleveland Street homosexual scandal of 1889, the prejudice underlying its rancour was unmistakable. Wilde's story was 'plainly the work of a man of letters', but, he concluded, 'if he can write for none but outlawed noblemen and perverted telegraph-boys, the sooner he takes to tailoring (or some other decent trade) the better for his own reputation and the public morals'.[93] So much for the autonomy of the aesthetic.

These were the exceptions, however. As a rule Henley's 'men of letters' had few mixed opinions about who belonged in their republic. The 'sweet phrase "popular culture" is the sorriest contradiction in terms', Henley declared.[94] Throughout the 1880s, his publications had railed against conventional middle-class tastes and cultural institutions. Under his direction, the *Magazine of Art* had set itself against Ruskin and the Royal Academy – and the managerial board at Cassell – by defiantly championing the likes of Millet, Rodin, Manet, and Whistler, some of Conrad's model artists.[95] The *Observer* extended this quarrel to the circulating libraries, like Mudie's and Smith's, which it tellingly reviled as the 'Royal Academy of literature'. 'What the respectable gold frame is to the Academic pot-boiler, that also is the smug binding, thrice repeated, to the slab of commercial fiction.'[96] The libraries and their patrons were, in fact, the blight of the nineteenth century:

When a great and cultured aristocracy patronised literature in England, literature was great in style and in method; when a wealthy middle class pushed that aristocracy from its stool and took to buying books or borrowing them from libraries (and thus patronising literature), literature became *bourgeois*, concerned itself with *bourgeois* ideals, and grew gradually more and more smug and fat, more and more puritanical, more and more superficial, more and more insincere in matters of life and death.

By the end of the 1880s, however, two new developments had become the focus of their purist disdain: the 'New Journalism' and what they branded '*Drivel*: Weekly 1d.' Both were understood to be part of the emergent culture of the 'People with a big "p"', the 'democracy indoctrinated with the several R's of the School Board'.[97] The 'New Journalism', pioneered by the likes of W. T. Stead and T. P. O'Connor, both of whom Henley despised, had begun to dominate the newspaper press by the end of the decade. For Henley's 'men of letters', who traced their journalistic and Tory pedigree back to Lockhart, Maginn, and Aytoun, this new trend violated the 'bounds of good taste' with its 'easy personal style', its women's pages and interviews with 'second-rate burlesque actresses' who lived in 'palm-treed flat[s] with Liberty draperies', and its preoccupation with crime and the latest divorce court sensations.[98] A venerable tradition of newspaper journalism had been supplanted, they wrote, by mere 'snapshots with a Kodak' – in their vocabulary the new inexpensive camera became a symbol of all that was repellent about the modern leisure culture for the masses.[99] The other new tendency was as distasteful. Established popular papers, like the *Family Herald* (1842) and the *People's Friend* (1869), came in for their share of Henleyite contempt, but it was the new-style penny weekly, which had begun to spread itself 'abroad like influenza' in the early 1880s, that proved most offensive.[100] This was the culture of 'comic snippets, legal snippets, [and] "fictional" snippets' associated with George Newnes's *Tit-Bits* (1881) and the 'vulgar' cartoons of Gilbert Dalziel's *Ally Sloper's Half-Holiday* (1884).[101] In their view, the apotheosis of this new culture, the 'logical outcome of the Education Act of 1870' and the 'coster's own laureate', was George R. Sims.[102] This 'man of business' even had the effrontery to regard himself 'as a serious man of letters'.[103]

Avowedly popular writers and publishers, like Sims and Newnes, were easy to rule out; more serious pretenders within the republic were another matter. The antagonism between the Henley circle and the group of young avant-garde writers who gathered around the publisher John Lane in the early 1890s challenges any history that reduces the complexities of the period to a simple contest between, say, the 'intellectuals' and the 'masses'. This is not to deny that there was a cartoonish side to the rivalry between the two intellectual factions. In his mock 'letters to the editor' of the *Yellow Book*, Henry Harland's 'Yellow Dwarf' set out to distinguish the refined producers of 'Cat-Literature', who included Henry James, Hubert Crackanthorpe, Ella D'Arcy, and himself, from the 'Dogs of Bookland' beloved of the 'Average Man', such as Hall

Caine, Jerome K. Jerome, Marie Corelli, and Conan Doyle. But he began his comic tirade by saying:

The Cat is always a Princess, because everything nice in this world, everything fine, sensitive, distinguished, everything beautiful, everything worthwhile, is of essence Feminine, though it may be male by the accident of sex; – and that's as true as gospel, let Mr. W. E. Henley's lusty young disciples shout their loudest in celebration of the Virile.

He then proceeded to decry the 'Master's influence', especially his 'Brutality'.[104] Earlier, Richard Le Gallienne, Lane's first reader, the literary columnist for T. P. O'Connor's *Star*, and one of the 'Master's' pet hates, had, with some justice, taken Henley to task for dedicating a collection of critical essays 'To the *Men* of the "Scots Observer"':

Mrs. Graham Tomson, Mrs. Meynell, Miss May Kendall, and 'E. Nesbit' had, I suppose, already contributed some of their charming verses to the paper at that day, but, of course, they are of no account. It's the 'men', my boy (slap your chest), who pay the rent, damme; what are a few dainty window curtains? – all the women are good for.[105]

This was not just journalistic heckling. In the context of the 'New Woman' debate, as the Henley circle and their opponents well knew, crude manliness was a serious, and reactionary, sociopolitical position. Yet, even though Lane made a particular point of championing women and 'New Woman' writers, like 'George Egerton', Ella D'Arcy, and Grant Allen, these political differences were themselves only part of a more specific cultural rivalry. The primary contest was over status positions *within* the 'Republic of Letters' between majors and minors, the established and the newcomers, the 'real' and the 'apparent' men of letters.

There was, after all, much that united the two groups. They shared a common set of purist opinions, and both were known to promote new writers and avant-garde tastes. Moreover, Lane published Meynell, Grahame, Yeats, Wells, and Street; and James deigned to appear in both the *New Review* and the *Yellow Book*. Yet it was, of course, the differences that counted, and that the Henley circle stressed. The Bodley Head group was, in their view, a gathering of self-promoting minor figures with dubious commercial motives. The *New Review* insisted that John Davidson, William Watson, Norman Gale, Arthur Symons, and Le Gallienne were, at best, flawed, minor 'verse-writers'. 'Of all these younger writers', only Francis Thompson was 'worthy, and unquestionably worthy, of the name poet'.[106] In the *Observer*, however, their hostility went beyond literary criticism. There they questioned Lane's commercial ambitions and derided the 'coxcombry of limited editions':

Do you regard Mr. Le Gallienne and Mr. Norman Gale as supporters of English Letters? No! Not even if their collected works stand you in a hundred pounds. Why should we criticise in a spirit of seriousness the myriad poetasters who inflate their own value by shrieking that only two hundred and fifty copies of their works may be distributed among the clamouring public? The artifice is old and tiresome . . . They are here to-day, because their bookseller, who has influence with a morning paper, and understands the profitable planting of garbage, chooses to sell them.[107]

The first volume of the *Yellow Book* came in for a similar lambasting. Most of the matter, with the exception of contributions by older figures like Saintsbury and James, was 'nonsensical and hysterical'; the art ranged unevenly from Frederick Leighton's 'formal, academic, and frigid style' to Beardsley's out-rageous figures that 'resemble nothing on earth'; the overall design was distinguished by its 'audacious vulgarity and laborious inelegance'; and the whole production had been 'boomed into notoriety and an unintelligent circulation'. Yet it was, they felt, 'assured of a welcome from the obedient suburban populace'. Taking issue with a point made in Lane's promotional announcement for the new quarterly, they added 'we should like to know, by the way, what the promoters take to be the best sense of the word "popular", and how they imagine that anything concerned with art or letters can be at once popular (in the ordinary sense of the word) and distinguished'.[108] It is worth recalling, in this context, that Garnett, who brokered Conrad's relation-ship with Henley, also dissuaded him from sending 'The Return', an eminently suitable marriage problem story, to the *Yellow Book*.[109]

Henley's 'men of letters' were expected to follow a rigid code of conduct covering why they wrote and who they wrote for. While this inevitably had a bearing on what they wrote, their choice of themes, styles, genres, and forms was of course not prescribed. With equal enthusiasm, Henley championed Irish Revivalists (Yeats, Katherine Tynan, and Standish O'Grady), social and regional Realists (Kipling, Morrison, Pugh, Phillpotts, and Hardy), as well as manly adventure, scientific, and childhood Romanticists (Stevenson, Marriott-Watson, Grahame, and Wells). Yet, as we have seen, this did not mean that his circle lacked strongly held critical opinions. One of the most important of these, which had to do with a debate within the Realist tradition specifically (though it went further), was their vehement opposition to Naturalism. Here the enemies were Zola, 'the fiercest Realist of them all', and his doctrines of 'scientific realism'.[110] Though their quarrel with 'Zolaism' could sometimes degenerate into an anti-Decadent diatribe – they would, like the National Vigilance Association, protest about 'the strange and hideous dreams of Flaubert and Baudelaire, and the monstrous fancies of M. Zola and de Maupassant' – it was mainly a more elevated dispute over literary methods.[111] In their view, Zola's version of Realism was untenable largely because it dispensed with the 'master quality of the world', namely 'human invention'.[112] For defenders of the cult of genius, this was an especially damaging conse-quence. But, more importantly, in seeming to abolish genius, Zola threatened the very existence of specifically aesthetic values. By eliminating the author's shaping imagination in his quest for scientific objectivity, it was claimed he degraded the novelist to 'newspaper reporter', made literature analogous to mere 'photography' or 'cinematography', and reduced artistic truth to the documentary 'truth of science'.[113] Indeed, he transferred to literature the habits of the much-despised Pre-Raphaelite painters.[114] What this complex set of derogatory associations in the end meant is clarified by the remarks one of Henley's essayists made on first witnessing Lumière's cinematograph in 1896:

Both the Cinematograph and the Pre-Raphaelite suffer from the same vice. The one and the other are incapable of selection; they grasp at every straw that comes their way; they see the trivial and the important, the near and the distant, with the same fecklessly impartial eye.

He then went on to ask sardonically: 'Is not Zola the M. Lumière of his art?'[115] The contention was, then, that Zola, like journalists, scientists, photographers, cinematographers, and the Pre-Raphaelites, simply documented experience indiscriminately without shaping it in any meaningful or singular way.

To some extent the Henley circle's alternative versions of Realism followed a standard late nineteenth-century line. As Morrison insisted in his defence of *A Child of the Jago*, Realism simply reflected 'the artist's privilege to seek his material where he thinks well'. It was an expression of purist autonomy at the level of subject-matter in so far as it allowed him to discard 'the conventions of the schools' and to affront the 'merely genteel, who were shocked to read of low creatures, as Kiddo Cook and Pigeony Poll, and to find the page nowhere illuminated by a marquis'.[116] A similar respect for the individual talent was at work in the *Observer's* case against Sims. It criticized him for his 'battered and threadbare conventionalities', his lack of any direct 'acquaintance with the slang of the hawker or outcast' and his limited 'power of vision'.[117] Here literary Realism figured in the Art/Nature debate, where visual representation served as the model, and the Henley circle came down on the side of the direct and comprehensive observation of Nature. Yet this never, of course, led to Zola's documentary realism. If the artist's 'own eye' had priority over the 'eye of habit or tradition', Henley's 'men of letters' also wanted to distinguish the 'hungry eye', which seeks out mere 'copy', from a genuinely artistic vision.[118]

To this end they added two further refinements to their ideal literary method, the first of which was essentialist. Henley praised Meredith, for instance, for carrying out the artist's real task which was 'not to copy but to synthesise: to eliminate from that gross confusion of actuality which is his raw material whatever is accidental, idle, irrelevant, and select for perpetuation that only which is appropriate and immortal'. This was 'the merit and distinction of art'.[119] The same argument was used to defend Kipling against the charge of being merely an 'industrious servant of the Kodak'.[120] Their other related refinement was impressionist. In their art criticism they had had a long-standing feud with what they called the 'literary school of painting' and its promoters at the Royal Academy.[121] Committed as it was to 'the worship of commercialism and the cult of the Anecdote and the Christmas Card', they scorned narrative painting for its 'cheap romance and middle-class classicism'.[122] In direct opposition to this tradition, they held up Corot as the founder of Impressionism, and defended Whistler, Manet, and Monet.[123] Yet, like most avant-garde writers of the late 1880s, they were also keenly aware of the literary value of this new artistic development. Indeed, Henley's own poetry, specifically the sequence *In Hospital* (1888), had been praised for its impressionistic innovations. Wilde described the collection as 'a series of vivid concentrated impressions', while Arthur Symons thought it epitomized Verlaine's 'poetry of Impressionism'.[124] In 1892 *Punch* went so far as to identify Henley as a pioneer the 'New Poetry', but, as the self-appointed defender of conventional British taste, it added its own characteristically anti-avant-garde reflections:

There are perhaps some who believe that a poem should not only express high and noble thoughts, or recount great deeds, but that it should do so in verse that is musical, cadenced, rhythmical, instinct with grace, and reserved rather than boisterous. If any such there be, let them know at once that they are hopelessly old-fashioned. The New Poetry in its *highest* expression banishes form, regularity and rhythm, and treats rhyme with unexampled barbarity . . . That is really what is meant by 'impressionism' in poetry carried to its highest excellence.

It did, however, rightly point out that Henley's own 'New Poetry' also included 'the "blustering, hob-nailed" variety' and 'the "coarse, but manly" kind which swears by the great god, Jingo'.[125]

Henley's avant-garde impressionists preached what they practised. Whibley admired Maupassant, for instance, because his 'method resembles that of the most distinguished of the Impressionists.'[126] And, in January 1896, five months before Conrad began the *Nigger*, George Wyndham, Henley's prize 'pupil in letters', applauded Stephen Crane for the technical innovations in his novella *The Red Badge of Courage*. Contrasting it throughout with Zola's *La Debâcle*, he explained Crane's admirable 'new device':

In order to show the features of modern war, he takes a subject – a youth with a peculiar temperament, capable of exaltation and yet morbidly sensitive. Then he traces the successive impressions made on such a temperament, from minute to minute, during two days of heavy fighting. He stages the drama of the war, so to speak, within the mind of one man, and then admits you as to a theatre.

This method, he went on to argue, produced a more realistic account of war than could be found in Zola who merely gave the 'truth of science'.[127] Four months later, another essayist in the *New Review* argued that the 'eye of the true impressionist' was the antithesis of both Zola and the Cinematograph 'because it is never mechanical, because it expresses a personal bias both in its choice and its rejection.'[128] In other words, the impressionist aesthetic, like the essentialist, privileged the selective powers of the individual observer. It put genius back into the equation, and reinforced specifically aesthetic values.

If the 'Republic of Letters' had to be defended against extraliterary interests, and if literary modes of writing could not be collapsed into the 'documentary', then purist texts had also to be rescued from unliterary readers and modes of reading. As a letter of 18 October 1895 to Lord Windsor, then a contributor to the *New Review*, indicates, Henley's own attitude to the reading public was nuanced but disparaging. While recognizing that 'what is called *the* Public consists of many smaller publics' and that 'there are scores of mansions in the House of Fiction', he insisted that 'good work is never popular in the sense of commanding the largest number of readers'. The response to Stevenson's early work was 'most suggestive' in this regard, he thought:

He wrote *Treasure Island* [1881], *The Black Arrow* [1883], & *Kidnapped* [1886] for a rag called *Young Folk's Paper*. None of the three was a success; but the two first were steadily (& devilishly) imitated in the same paper, which lived for years on the rubbish thus produced. Stevenson's true public would have found it unreadable. Not so *this* public – a Board School public, one may call it. It's taste was all for hog wash.

If you could demand, in the manner of the middle-class reformers, that such reading be 'mainly non-poisonous', 'you cannot insist on literary quality, for, if you do, you disgust at once the *non*-(or even anti-) literary publics; which is as much to say, that you deprive two-thirds of the enormous mob of persons who can read of the only reading they can tackle & enjoy'. This anti-literary 'mob', it should be noted, did not only include the 'Board School' public: it ranged from the 'shop-girl' and 'errand boy' to the 'Sporting Bart.' and the 'serious Nonconformist'.[129]

In tone and style, these private remarks echoed the public position Henley's circle held throughout the last two decades of the nineteenth century. In the 1880s, the reading habits of the middle classes were their greatest concern. Chief among these was the practice of applying 'to art the standards of life'.[130] In this context, Henley's brand of muscular aestheticism, inconsistent as it was, dominated the debate. The conviction that 'Art is simply un-moral' was Henley's guiding principle, according to J. H. Millar.[131] Even for Whibley, Wilde's defamer, the 'Puritan' now figured as the foremost enemy: 'A lack of imagination compels him forever to confuse morals and print.'[132] This was in a review commending Henley's scholarly interest in slang. Their opposition to the moral mode of reading, which judged art by ethical standards and focused on *what* was represented rather than the *manner* of representation, contributed to their taste for literary Realism and Impressionism. It led them to defend the likes of Hardy, Meredith, Maupassant, and even Zola's translator and publisher, Henry Vizetelly, and it also made them the unlikely champions of the 'penny dreadful'.[133] In the early 1890s, when it was 'the fashion to talk in pompous tirades against the romances of the people', they felt compelled to argue that 'it is falsity of tone and corruption of style rather than any vice of subject which makes the penny novel dangerous'.[134] Such convictions inevitably made them decry the 'standard of Mudie' and the 'reign of the Young Person', and to attack writers, like Besant, who defended 'Average Opinion' in censorship debates and suggested 'no remedy' because they saw 'no disease'.[135] Genteel moralism was not the only problem, however. Politics, as the case of Ibsen indicates, also threatened to infiltrate the 'neutral zone' of reading.[136] Ibsen was, in their view, a 'man of genius', a 'vivesector of the existing social body', who had regrettably been co-opted by the Radical 'New Journalists' for whom he was 'a compendium of the seven names of the prophet'.[137] (Their caricature 'New Journalist', who bore an unusual resemblance to Le Gallienne, could, according to Whibley, always be identified by his 'long waving locks', 'Liberty tie', 'soft felt hat', and 'pocket Ibsen'.[138]) Against those readers and critics who focused on the 'Problem' or the 'Lesson' in Ibsen's plays – the Liberal *Daily Telegraph* was specially blamed – G. W. Steevens praised his technical 'workmanship'.[139] Formalist aestheticism could, after all, be politically interested.

By the 1890s, however, the cultural transformations signalled by the 'New Journalism' had raised other issues about reading and given new urgency to the question of who constituted the 'general public':

It is not the hundreds who know of one Mr. George Meredith, nor the thousands who read Mr. Payn and Mr. Besant, nor the tens of thousands who glory in Mr. Rider Haggard. The general public is now to be counted in millions, for it includes nearly all the mill-workers, tradesmen, domestic servants, errand-boys, and strikers. To these add the innumerable clerks of our great cities, and we have some notion of the public whom our novelists miss and Snippets catches.

The men of this new mass public, especially the suburban commuters, apparently read *Tit-Bits* and *Ally Sloper*, while the women had their 'penny novelettes'.[140] As we have seen, Henley's 'men of letters' were initially untroubled by the rise of this readership. This was partly because, in their view, the new 'general public' hardly experienced reading as a mental act. Their 'Bits' papers were at best a 'mental pabulum', and for them reading was merely 'consumption'.[141] 'The democracy invented George R. Sims, and his works are as stimulating and as little concerned with letters as so many glasses of mild and bitter.'[142] Their composure did not survive the decade, however. By the turn of the century Henley, for one, felt they had underestimated the threat of this emergent culture. Two years before his death, he remarked in a letter of 1 January 1901 to Marriott-Watson:

Yes: the old landmarks are disappearing one by one. Harmsworth, Pearson & Co. are doing their work. And there is none to say 'To your tents, O Israel!' . . . But, O, by God, I'd give – sometimes – ten years of the few that remain to me to have the old flag floating, and the old riders round me, once again! It is as though we'd come too soon, and missed our true attack on the gross and fatuous indecency of to-day.[143]

As I have suggested, Henley was not simply the driving force behind an unusually vociferous pressure group in the literary field: his circle also represented an equally extreme set of political interests. Indeed, these wider concerns offended some members – Yeats, for one, deplored 'that propaganda whereby Henley . . . turned the young men at Oxford and Cambridge into imperialists' – and repeatedly clashed with his attempts to preserve the neutrality of culture.[144] When his purism was not being undermined by his manly prejudices, it came up against the anti-democratic elitism which the *Observer* and the *New Review* espoused. On some occasions, they considered the gradual attempt to move away from 'privilege, oligarchy, class government', by extending the franchise, to be simply a 'Great Democratic Joke'. Comparing the membership of the Cabinet in 1886 and 1892, the *New Review* declared, with smug satisfaction, that the 'Government of Britain is still an aristocratic oligarchy, largely tempered by plutocracy'.[145] In a less complacent mood, however, it acknowledged that the enfranchisement of urban and rural workers in 1867 and 1884 had in fact brought about some unfortunate changes in the political life of the nation. In particular, given the apparent intellectual inadequacies of the new electorate, democracy had inevitably led to demagoguery: since the 'vast majority of adult men are mere grown-up children, physically mature, but intellectually undeveloped', and, since the 'multitude do not know what they want', they were 'the natural prey of demagogues who buy [their] vote by fawning flattery, by loathsome lying, by abominable appeals to [their] meanest motives, by profligate promises made in reckless profusion, and incapable of performance'.[146] Among the worst offenders were such diverse personalities as Lord Randolph Churchill and Joseph Chamberlain who, like all demagogues, seemingly lacked any party loyalty, sought votes like canvassers for advertisements, and habitually resorted to 'inflammatory rhetoric' to achieve their ends.[147] What these unprincipled individuals lacked, in particular, was the necessary manliness which the new democracy had sadly eroded. Adding a political dimension to Henley's 'Invictus', the *New Review* looked back nostalgically to the time when politicians still held 'their heads high and remain[ed] "captains of their souls"'. 'Compare this manliness with the average vote-hunting of today.'[148] The 'demagogues' were, in effect, the popular authors of the political field.

To those who suggested that the only way to overcome the possible shortcomings of democracy was to educate the new electorate, Henley's political commentators were as unaccommodating as they were to the 'demagogues'. At their most charitable, they simply asked: 'But of what avail is this so-called "education", or of any instruction which the masses can possibly receive, for the task of governing an empire?'[149] More generally, however, their hostility to the educational reforms of the last three decades of the century was more acrimonious, not least because these new policies represented, in their view, the first victory of 'State Socialism'. Referring to the Education Act of 1870, which both Liberals and Conservatives supported, the *Observer* argued:

We started on the precarious slope about twenty years ago, when we made elementary education compulsory: that was the first mistake of the Socialistic series we seem committed to. We shall probably continue, and some years hence discover (what many have discovered long since) that the education which we have made compulsory, and propose to make free, is a commodity that is dear at any price: that it is not merely a superfluity, but an actual obstruction.[150]

The Board Schools were part of the problem. Equally objectionable were such projects as Toynbee Hall, the largely Christian–Socialist educational 'settlement' in London's East End, and the university extension scheme which was both Socialist and anti-Socialist.[151] They were also sharply critical of the public library system which they, and many others, claimed had failed to achieve its primary purpose, namely, to supply 'the poorer classes generally with books which would prove useful to them in their work, and helpful in the development of better citizens'. By 1895, twenty-seven districts of London had established 'free libraries' in accordance with the Public Libraries Act of 1850, but, as the *New Review* survey of their borrowing records revealed, these well-intentioned institutions had merely become purveyors of popular fiction.[152]

Yet for Henley's commentators, these redistributive projects, whether political or cultural, were merely symptoms of a more pervasive malady within late-Victorian society. 'Now is the Golden Age of the sentimentalist', the *Observer* declared on 29 November 1890.[153] And, in Henley's first issue of the *New Review*, one essayist quoted the following 'profound remark of Carlyle': 'The deepest difficulty which presses on us all is the sick sentimentalism which we suck in with our whole nourishment, and get ingrained into the very blood of us, in these miserable ages.'[154] Though apparently an index of modernity, in so far as it lay behind the calls for greater social justice, sentimentality was really a form of atavism. The 'result of centuries of retarded evolution', it was still manifest in the behaviour of 'Celts', 'negroes' and women: 'Few women are stupid; but all (politically speaking) are uninformed, uneducated, sentimental, and "unevoluted".' Anglo-Saxon men, though higher on the evolutionary scale, were not necessarily safe: 'when sentiment forces itself into the place of intellect, the result is Radicalism'.[155] Many individuals and groups were alleged to have succumbed, including W. T. Stead, William Booth, Cardinal Manning, all philanthropists, the Liberal Party, and the New Journalists, but the Socialists were singled out as the most dangerous Radical sentimentalists. These were not only the 'red-revolutionaries', like Karl Pearson, Belfort Bax and William Morris, or 'rose-water revolutionists', like Alexandre Dumas fils, they were also the 'apostles of violence' who corrupted legitimate trade unions, like Keir Hardie and R. B. Cunninghame Graham.[156] In general terms, the sentimentalist was characterized as a 'shameless bleater' who had a 'fine contempt for facts' and who was, like the demagogue, 'a loyal servant of words and phrases'.[157] They were the 'Radical Fadmongers' who championed everything 'silly and weak', such as giving women the vote, pampering the unemployed, sympathizing with strikers and cadgers, protecting the sick or infirm, and treating blacks as equals.[158] Under their influence, it was claimed, the Liberal Party had lost direction and become demoralized, and the 'whole community [had] become far more soft, far more gentle, far more thoughtful of distress'.[159]

To combat this unpleasant trend towards an atavistic feminization of culture, the *Observer* promoted a counter-ideology called 'Common Sense' which it figured, without irony, as a militant woman:

Those who are not 'good' with the 'goodness' of the New Journalist and the gospel-sharp look forward with a vague hope to the blessed time when Common Sense shall set her hobnailed heel on the neck of gross and ignorant and infamous Sentimentality.[160]

As it turned out, 'Common Sense' was an idiosyncratic ideological blend of Tory individualism, Social Darwinism, and manly self-assertion. Unlike the 'common Radical', and 'General Booth', the 'Common-Sense' man never ignored the 'facts of Nature'.[161] When Booth published *In Darkest England* (1890) and set about launching his scheme to rescue the 'Submerged Tenth' in England and Wales, the *Observer* offered the following retort:

It is a physiological fact that, relieved from the rude checks of Nature in a barbarous or semi-civilised society, mankind shows a constant and incorrigible tendency to revert to low types ... Modern sanitary and medical arrangements – (it is the merest commonplace) – are such that the weakliest have chances of life they never had before, and of which they have made such use that one has but to look upon our populations in street, workshop, and factory to see that the puny and low-class Briton is rapidly outnumbering the larger and finer types.

If Booth and his co-sentimentalists, like Stead, carried out their project, they forecast that 'Britain would have lapsed to semi-barbarism, and would be overrun with black dwarfs and idiots' within fifty years.[162] 'Common Sense' of this kind was also used to justify severe treatment of the unemployed. British cities were overpopulated with 'casuals', 'cadgers', and the 'unfit', 'all because philanthropy is not wise nor kind nor courageous enough to permit the useless to perish in their sloth'.[163] Here the guilty sentimentalists like Booth were joined by such politically diverse figures as the militant Socialist, H. M. Hyndman, and the Fabian, Bernard Shaw. What was needed 'For England's sake', as one of Henley's poets put it, was 'War righteous and true' and the 'discipline of pain', 'Ere the tricks and arts of peace / Make our manliness to cease'.[164]

The assumption that some were *naturally* predisposed to be ruled by others was easily transposed from domestic politics to the international sphere. In the *New Review*, Mrs J. (Weston) Campbell, signing herself either 'Colonial' or 'C. De Thierry', was the most seductive of Henley's Imperial rhapsodists. Though she had the usual misgivings of a Henleyite Conservative, claiming that England had been in decline ever 'since the ship of State has come to be guided by a captain, whose master is the shifting majority', her patriotic faith was always restored by the conviction that for 'over three hundred years this little Isle has been the sheet-anchor of Europe: the light of the moral, social, and intellectual world'.[165] This conviction, coupled with ideas of *natural* superiority, lay behind the Henley circle's contempt for Little Englanders and their uncompromising views on Irish Home Rule, India, South Africa, and especially the black colonies in Africa and the West Indies. The blacks of the West Indies, for instance, were 'the idol of the Anti-Slavery Society' and the 'spoiled child of our Colonial Empire'.[166] But the *Observer* saw things differently.

The black will not become a civilised being according to our standard, even the humblest we can make. On the contrary he will, Nature having so provided, continue to be what he has been for countless centuries in his native Africa. Under compulsion which sets him a task, gives him rules of life, and keeps him to them by nose-bag and whip, he may be made a good servant.[167]

'Men of sense' could see for themselves how this applied to Ireland and the Indian Native Congresses.[168] Yet it was Henley himself who gave the most unnerving expression to his political commentators' belief in the pre-eminence of the Anglo-Saxon male in the Darwinian struggle for racial dominance. In his very unimpressionistic collection *The Song of the Sword* (1892), he spurred his fellow countrymen on to fulfil their destiny by 'Sifting the nations, / The slag from the metal, / The waste and the weak / From the fit and the strong'.[169]

This cluster of prejudices, which set the stoical adult Anglo-Saxon Tory male above the child-like sentimentalists – the masses, blacks, women, Radicals, and the Irish – frequently cast a shadow over the Henley circle's purist aestheticism. Relieved that the 'monotonous whine of the sentimentalist is inaudible in his work', the *Observer* praised Hardy because 'he looks on rustic life very much as Millet did – Millet to whom it was "true humanity and great poetry"'.[170] (Earlier, Henley had celebrated Millet as a painter who 'liked nothing that was not strong and sincere', and for whom 'affectation, corruption, falsehood, effeminacy were eminently displeasing'.[171]) Furthermore, the idea of the rustic as hero, upon which Hardy's work was allegedly based, had a peculiarly political appeal:

When the rustic mind meets one of the more distressing problems of life it makes a homely aphorism and leaves it. 'Where the pigs be many the wash runs thin', dismisses the whole question of surplus population. There is no criticism there – only a statement of fact.[172]

To this extent, the rustic, as celebrated by Hardy and Millet, embodied Henleyite 'Common Sense', and appeared as the heroic alternative to the sentimentalist. Though the same could not be said of the urban figures in Morrison's *Tales of Mean Streets* or *A Child of the Jago*, his Realist fiction about the East End itself represented a direct affront to the 'sentimental cocksure': not only the 'genteel' middle classes, but more especially the 'blindly self-confident' philanthropists 'in their committee-rooms'.[173] In the novel, Morrison described the sordid life and times of Dicky Perrott, the child of the title, who inhabits one of London's most notorious East End slums, the Old Nichol (the Jago of the story). The first thirteen chapters, which were published in the *New Review*, included accounts of violent faction fights between the Ranns and the Learys, as well as details about the practice of coshing, the neglect of infants, alcoholism, and the self-perpetuating cycle of poverty and crime. The ideological aim of the story was to expose the apparently hopeless incompetence of philanthropic organizations like the 'East End Elevation Mission and Pansophical Institute'. With Toynbee Hall in his mind, Morrison derided the 'young men . . . with the educational varnish fresh and raw upon them' who came to the East End as 'Missionaries' 'to struggle – for a fortnight – with its suffering and its brutishness'.[174] As the biblical epigraph published at the head of every serialized part in the magazine suggested, the philanthropists were the story's primary target. They were the 'foolish prophets' in Ezekiel xiii, 3, x–xii, who 'follow their own spirit, and have seen nothing!'[175] Taking up the allusion, Morrison explained why the philanthropists objected to his story: 'Your professed philanthropist, following his own spirit, and seeing nothing, honestly resents the demonstration that his tinkering profits little.'[176] Given this, it comes as no surprise to find that Henley was among the first editors in England to publish articles exposing the greatest philanthropic sham of the 1890s: King Leopold's International Association of the Congo.[177] But Realist fiction, of the kind Hardy and Morrison produced, was not only another way of unmasking philanthropists and sentimentalists: it also served Henley's 'men of letters' well in their taste war against the middle classes and 'scientific realism', in their cultural struggle against the new phenomenon of mass culture, and in their political battle against Liberals and Socialists.

IV

Both Henley's major editorial ventures led double lives. They were, in the first instance, belated mid-Victorian reviews. The *Scots Observer* was established in the tradition of the weekly *Saturday Review* (1856) with the initial intention of reasserting Edinburgh's cultural and intellectual prestige. Though Walter Blaikie, the innovative Scottish printer and one of the weekly's co-founders, gave it a modern look, using durable high-quality paper, and bold, unfussy type, seen in the late-Victorian context its format was resolutely old-fashioned. The dense two-column layout, as well as the lengthy 'leaders' and 'middles' themselves, stood as a typographical rebuke of the modern taste for the 'spasmodic' 'New Journalism' which, in Henley's view, signalled the 'degradation of the newspaper' with its 'blatant headline' and 'sensational paragraph'.[178] Never narrowly regionalist, by the time the *Observer* changed its name it had a national reputation as 'the most slashing of the sixpenny weeklies' and it was considered to have outdone its precursor as the 'literary man's bogey'.[179]

Despite its title, the *New Review*, under Henley, was no less traditional in style and format, though this was not how its founding editor Archibald Grove, an Oxford-educated Liberal, had originally conceived it. When he launched it in June 1889, he had set out to democratize the mid-Victorian review by maintaining the traditions of the *Fortnightly* (1863), the *Contemporary* (1866), and the *Nineteenth Century* (1877) in a cheaper format.[180] Instead of the usual 2s 6d charged by the old-style monthly reviews, his at first cost only sixpence, the same as the successful *English Illustrated* (1883) and popular religious monthlies like *Leisure Hour* (1852), *Good Words* (1860), and *Sunday at Home* (1854). It was, his prospectus implied, to be the print version of the University Extension Scheme. His object was 'to place within the reach of all a critical periodical of the first order.'[181]

It is true that with the easy methods of transmission through the post office, railroads, etc., the old quarterlies have been in a great way replaced by the monthly reviews. But they have been, for the most part, too expensive, frequently too 'special', and only occasionally sufficiently attractive to appeal to the enormous reading public that has grown up out of a liberal legislation in educational matters.[182]

Not unexpectedly, the Henley circle dismissed Grove as a Radical 'consumed with anxiety to procure pecuniary and other advantages' for himself and 'working men'.[183] Though initially successful, Grove was compelled steadily to increase the cover price until, by 1892, it had doubled. Despite his faith in his 'growing and intelligent audience', which he justifiably supported by pointing to the success of W. T. Stead's sixpenny *Review of Reviews* (1890) – their two projects were significantly related – competition from the new and hugely successful illustrated monthlies, like the *Strand* (1891), *Idler* (1892), and *Pall Mall* (1893), soon began to alter the dynamics of the market.[184] While he always condemned these new arrivals – in his view they contained 'the mere "interview" and personal gossip sandwiched between ephemeral fiction, and illustrated by cheap process' – by January 1894 he had to concede.[185] To 'widen the scope' and 'modernise' his review, he added illustrations, news items, and a chess column, improved the 'general get-up', and had the pages cut 'in order to facilitate the reading of the magazine for those who are travelling'.[186] All this, he hoped, would make it appeal 'to popular tastes of the day in the very best sense of the word'.[187] Advertisements now declared that the review appealed to 'two large and distinct publics; on the one hand, to that which seeks first-class and dignified literary matter, and on the other, to that which buys a magazine primarily to be entertained'.[188] Yet, having started out to challenge such hierarchical divisions, Grove now fell victim to them. With such items as the 'Secrets of the Court of Spain' (May–December 1894) and 'Some Noteworthy Hands' (June 1894) appearing uneasily alongside Keir Hardie's 'The Case of an Independent Labour Party' (June 1894) and poetry by Paul Verlaine (May 1894), the illustrated review fell between its two publics; and, by the end of 1894, with monthly circulation below 5,000, Grove was willing to sell.[189] Henley, of course, shared none of Grove's political ideals, and he certainly made no bid for a popular market. When he took over at the end of 1894, he promptly eliminated the populist articles, chess columns, and illustrations – not to mention the essays on Liberal and Labour politics – and, though he kept the price at a shilling, in all other respects the monthly reverted to the traditions of the old-style reviews. As George Wyndham put it, they were determined to 'compete with the "Fortnightly" and "XIXth Century" on equal terms'.[190]

As Keating notes, the mid-Victorian reviews 'appealed to a largely middle-class and university-educated readership', and they were designed 'to establish between themselves and their readers common principles and standards on the major political, moral, religious, and cultural issues of the day'.[191] In this respect, too, Henley's *Observer* and *New Review*, at least in their guise as reviews, maintained the mid-Victorian traditions. Indeed, since neither succeeded commercially, they were not only founded but massively subsidized by prosperous, university-educated, middle-class Tories. The *Observer* was under-written by R. Fitzroy Bell, Robert Hamilton Bruce, and Walter Blaikie, all of whom belonged to Edinburgh's wealthy, professional classes; and the *New Review* was purchased by Sir Herbert Stephen, MP, George Wyndham, MP, and Henry Cust. Indeed, Henley, the erratically educated son of an impover-ished Gloucester bookseller, was the *arriviste* in these circles. Though largely set up for Henley, whose name figured prominently on the cover of each issue, the monthly was, in fact, edited by a board comprising Lord Windsor (as chair), Wyndham (the driving force), Stephen, and the Cambridge-educated Charles Whibley. Most of Henley's contributors came from the same elite circles, and many were Oxbridge men. Some, like Whibley, David Hannay, and P. Anderson Graham, were full-time journalists; but most were members of the higher professions, principally barristers. Though notoriously excluded from the circle's official self-image, a small group of women did occasionally contribute to both the weekly and the monthly, albeit sometimes under neutral pseudonyms like 'C. de Thierry' or 'C. E. Raimond'.

In theory, the circle's readership was not as limited as Keating suggests. The *Observer* was sold at the 'principal English Railway Stations' by W. H. Smith and at 'numerous Newsagents'; and though Smith was, according to Wyndham, initially 'more obdurate than the adder to [their] publisher's advances', the *New Review* was eventually distributed through his network of bookstalls as well.[192] (As part of a campaign in early 1896, Wyndham sent 25,000 copies of a promotional circular to Smith's clerks at 650 railway stations.) In practice, however, both the weekly and the monthly appealed to the review's traditional readers who, not surprisingly, resembled its producers. If the new mass-circulation periodicals of the 1890s (and Grove) targeted the commuter, Henley's reactionary journals focused on the clubman. Though advertisers were told the *Observer* was 'a valuable medium for reaching the Wealthy and Cultured Classes', clubmen represented the core of its intended readership – during a promotional drive in October 1891, 3,000 free copies were issued to the metropolitan 'political clubs'.[193] As the advertisements suggest, this was also true for the *New Review*. Publishers' Lists were the staple – Heinemann, its publisher, was particularly prominent – as were announcements of other periodicals targeted at a similar readership. In April 1896, these included *The Quarto*, a 5s quarterly of Art, Literature, and Music; and the *North American Review*, also published by Heinemann. Among the few consumer commodities advertised, the major patent medicine companies (Boots and Eno, for instance), who figured prominently in the sixpenny illustrated monthlies, were noticeably absent, while more expensive items, such as 'Lundberg's Famous Perfumes' (2s 6d or 4s), 'Durand & Co. Quality Champagnes' (54–60s a dozen), and 'Labrador Watches' (50s), featured regularly, as did products or services for the bookish, including 'Remington Typewriters', 'John Browning' (an 'Ophthalmic Optician'), 'Stone's Filing Systems', and the 'Library Bureau Rotary Bookcases'.[194] Though the circulation figures imply that the actual readership was extremely select – the *Observer* had an average weekly circulation of only 1,900 copies, and Stephen reported that the *New Review* never went above 1,000 – the club readership suggests that the actual figures could have been as high as 10,000.[195]

Yet, largely owing to Henley, neither publication was simply a traditional mid-Victorian review that targeted the 'Wealthy and Cultured', advocated particular political interests, and provided a public platform for 'gentlemen of letters'. Both were also avant-garde coterie magazines that appealed to literary intellectuals, championed 'uncommercial' writers, and defended purist interests in the literary field. They were, in effect, early modernist 'little magazines' in mid-Victorian clothing. This double set of interests, though sometimes at odds, did not necessarily create difficulties. Avant-garde art, reactionary politics, and a social animus against the 'masses' were for the Henley circle (and for many of their modernist successors) integral parts of their self-understanding as literary purists. This happy alliance of interests was visibly displayed in the only series of illustrations they ever published. From June to December 1897 the *New Review* included seven woodcut portraits, on a separate leaf in each issue, by the avant-garde artist William Nicholson. As an editorial note in the July 1897 issue put it, they were intended to form 'a gallery representative of the most unique and influential personalities of our time'.[196] These were, in order, Queen Victoria, Sarah Bernhardt, Lord Roberts, Whistler, Kipling, Cecil Rhodes, and Prince Bismarck. But, in other respects, the magazines' dual function created irreconcilable tensions, particularly between the 'gentlemen of letters' and the literary purists. Though some of the former, like Whibley and Wyndham, were enthusiastic Henleyites, others, like J. H. Millar and Herbert Stephen, had their doubts. Millar, an erudite Scottish barrister who contributed regularly to both the *Observer* and the *New Review*, was unwilling, for instance, to accept Henley's official – albeit equivocal –

aestheticism. And he was certainly reluctant to share his circle's enthusiasm for Maupassant.

Take, for instance, a book like *Bel Ami*: unexceptionable in execution, a masterpiece of French prose, a triumph of all that Mr. Henley admits on paper to constitute art. Yet he and his disciples would, we suspect, feel compelled, not only as honest men but also as good critics, to admit that by reason of some quality – present or absent – which finds no place in their category of art, that most vile and abominable work – written, if any book ever was, by a 'bounder' for 'bounders' – indisputably falls short of being perfectly and truly artistic.[197]

Stephen, on the other hand, found *The Nigger of the 'Narcissus'* difficult to take. As one of the directors of the *New Review*, he felt bound to read each instalment, but 'found it intolerably depressing, and was haunted by a nightmare fear that it would never end, and that [he] should have to go on reading it all [his] life'.[198] No doubt many of his, and Millar's, fellow clubmen concurred. Such differences in taste and opinion were, however, relatively harmless. The real damage was done only when they involved more serious questions of control. Both the monthly and the weekly were repeatedly threatened by conflicts of interest. In fact, Fitzroy Bell, the *Observer's* principal backer, who had paid out an astonishing £18,000 over five years (over £65 a week), complained that Henley's combative tone scared away advertisers, and eventually cut his losses in early 1894.[199] He was not simply looking for any excuse to rid himself of a liability. Popular perceptions bore him out. As Arnold Bennett, then a rising 'New Journalist', told readers of 'Marjorie's' weekly gossip column in *Woman*, the paper had earned 'the sobriquet of the "National Snobserver"' for its 'cynical, contemptuous, self-assertive style, that affects an exaggerated culture and superiority, and finds nothing to praise'. The fact that it had failed to prove 'sufficiently remunerative under its late editor' – 'one of the most cultured scholars of the day' – afforded an 'interesting object lesson', and he hoped Henley would take this 'to heart and take a brighter, more liberal view of humanity and life in the future'.[200]

The *Observer* lasted five years under Henley, and though the *New Review* went on for three, it barely survived its first. By December 1895, sales were declining, and, according to Wyndham, the 'situation was complicated by the foolish quarrels and jealousies that mar so many brave enterprises; editor, publisher, directors and shareholders having no feeling beyond mutual recrimination'.[201] At times Henley, who generally found the editing unrewarding, thought Heinemann 'too bloody cultured' and accused him of wanting 'to edit the magazine – not to sell it'.[202] Yet, as Stephen recalled, the editor was the main problem: 'My recollection of the board meetings is principally of our crowding round Henley and beseeching him not to be indiscreet.'[203] That it survived another two years was largely due to Wyndham's efforts, or what Whibley sympathetically called his 'unfailing zeal' and 'simple faith'.[204] In January 1896, he persuaded the directors 'to spend money on a dashing policy for 5 months', won the support of W. H. Smith, and arranged with *McClure's Magazine* in America to share the costs of highly paid articles.[205] Undoubtedly his greatest success was to obtain the exclusive rights to a pro-Imperialist article on the crisis in South Africa by F. Rutherford Harris who had been secretary of Rhodes's Chartered Company for seven years.[206] Though the *New Review*, like most monthly reviews, seldom figured in *Bookman's* 'Monthly Report of the Wholesale Book Trade', it was now reported that this essay, and others on the causes and consequences of the Jameson Raid, had boosted sales considerably.[207] This relative boom lasted only from April to September, however. Indeed, by July the 'dashing policy' was encountering problems of its own. Though the issue for that month announced Kipling's potentially very popular new serial *Captains Courageous*, by September the promise had to be withdrawn. Charitably claiming that Kipling considered the novel 'unsuited to the tastes of readers of the "New Review"', the editor declared he had decided 'to cede [its] purchase to the proprietors of "Pearson's Magazine"'.[208] In fact, competition for the serial rights to the story had been fierce: English editors, including Henley, had offered £500, £800, and £1,400 for the 50,000-word novel. In the end, however, the British serial rights went to *Pearson's* for £2,500 (1s per word), while *McClure's Magazine* in America bought the American serial rights for £3,000.[209] Referring to the *Pearson's* offer, an advertisement in the *New Review* proclaimed that this was 'the highest price ever paid to any Author for a Magazine Story'.[210] Though this usefully confirms Kipling's exceptional status as a popular literary intellectual, and demonstrates that the cultural divisions between the high-class reviews and the illustrated monthlies were not always as rigid as might be supposed, it also shows how competition among magazines benefited marketable authors and threatened less commercially successful ventures like Henley's *New Review*. It is worth bearing in mind that Henley could afford to pay Wells only £100 for the serial rights of *The Time Machine* (the still reasonable rate for a first novel of about 1s for 20 words).[211]

Stephen blamed the *New Review's* eventual demise on Henley's stridently avant-garde literary tastes. After the publication of a story in which the seduction of a housemaid was described too explicitly, he claimed the circulation 'which had slowly and laboriously crept up to four figures, dropped like a stone'.[212] The offending story may have been Edwin Pugh's 'The Mother of John', published in May 1896, which contains a detailed description of an argument between a man and his former mistress who is a domestic servant.[213] Whether or not this was the decisive factor – the fact that *Bookman* reported sales to be good as late as September 1896 suggests that Stephen's record cannot entirely be trusted – after September the review no longer appeared in *Bookman's* trade reports. As Stephen diplomatically admitted 'our taste and Henley's was no more that of any paying public than it had been when offered to them weekly.'[214] Whibley, however, placed the blame for the failure squarely on the public. It was, he claimed, neither Wyndham's nor Henley's fault 'that readers of the 'nineties found things better suited to their taste than *The New Review*'.[215] Finally, an insert in the issue for December 1897 announced Henley's resignation on the grounds of 'uncertain health and the necessities of his own literary work.'[216] It also advertised Wyndham's new venture: a threepenny weekly called *The Outlook and New Review* which, he hoped, would maintain the high literary standards and Tory Imperialist traditions of its precursor, while also appealing to a wider audience. On 9 April 1898, the new weekly published Conrad's first piece of literary journalism – 'an inconceivably silly thing' about Alphonse Daudet. 'I've gone and done it', he cried, 'I write for the press!!!!!!'[217]

V

The Nigger of the 'Narcissus' would not have helped the *New Review* survive beyond 1897. Before the manuscript was complete, Conrad himself predicted it would not be a popular success. Writing to Garnett on 29 November 1896, he confessed:

Of course nothing can alter the course of the 'Nigger'. Let it be unpopularity if it *must* be. But it seems to me that the thing – precious as it is to me – is trivial enough on the surface to have some charms for the man in the street. As to lack of incident well – it's life. The incomplete joy, the incomplete sorrow, the incomplete rascality or heroism – the incomplete suffering. Events crowd and push and nothing happens. You know what I mean. The opportunities do not last long enough.
    Unless in a boy's book of adventures.[218]

As it turned out, his worries were well founded. When the novella first appeared as a 6s book in Britain on 2 December 1897, it was not among the fast-moving items in the wholesale book trade. The season's favourites, according to *Bookman*, included *Captains Courageous*, *What Maisie Knew*, Hall Caine's *The Christian*, and Sarah Grand's *The Beth Book*.[219] And, over the short term, sales showed no signs of improving. Though 1,500 copies were sold in Britain in the first month, the next 2,500 took just over two years to move, and in May 1910 Conrad was still calling it 'an impossible book' as far as sales were concerned.[220] While sales are not a reliable indicator of readership – as Conrad was happy to report, the *Nigger* was in great demand at the library of Galsworthy's Conservative club, the Junior Carlton – he none the less began to fear his novels were showing a tendency to 'drop into the past like a stone into water'.[221] By 19 May 1900 he could claim to have earned only £200 in royalties.[222]

Yet if the book-buyers' response was not impressive, the critics were more reassuring. On 7 January 1898, he reported to Garnett:

I had 23 reviews. One indifferent (The Standard) and *one bad* (the Academy). Two or three of a hesitating kind in the prov[incial] papers. The rest unexpectedly appreciative.[223]

To add to the prestige of serial publication in the *New Review*, he now had, in Garnett's words, a 'general blast of eulogy from a dozen impressive sources' including James Payn and A. T. Quiller-Couch.[224] For all the critical praise, however, even the most favourable reviews confirmed Conrad's own early predictions. Speaking for most, the *Spectator* concluded: 'Mr. Conrad is a writer of genius; but his choice of themes, and the uncompromising nature of his methods, debar him from attaining a wide popularity.'[225] For many, the novella's unconventional narrative structure proved particularly baffling. Though constructed within broadly recognizable patterns, such as departure/ arrival, mustering/paying-off, or storm/calm, the story is, in fact, a series of *thematically* related impressionistic episodes. Unlike, say, a detective story which follows the relatively predictable generic pattern of effects (corpses, crimes, etc.) leading to discoverable causes (the criminals and their motives), the *Nigger* is constructed as a series of ethically and politically charged moments, the relations between which are often neither causal nor explicit. For instance, in the course of the mustering in chapter 1, the preoccupation with authority and its challengers is established by means of a complex series of mutually significant episodes beginning with Belfast's unreliable account of his act of insubordination, then leading to Donkin's talk about seamen's rights, and finally to Wait's more threatening and ambiguous confrontation with Baker, the chief mate. This strategy is repeated more elaborately in the final two chapters which, like the closing section of *Heart of Darkness*, focus on the ethics of truth-telling. Here the four main episodes all centre on Wait as the narrative moves from Donkin's self-interested complicity with Wait's self-deception, to Podmore's 'altruistic' desire to confront him with the truth and save his soul, to the Captain and crew's variously motivated decisions to bolster his life-lie, and finally to Donkin's 'perfidious desire of truthfulness' which precipitates Wait's death.[226] For many reviewers the problem lay, not so much with the complexities of this ethical vision, but with the more immediate difficulties posed by the oblique and impressionistic structure in which it was expressed. Much to Conrad's dismay, the *Daily Mail* told its vast readership that the 'tale is no tale at all, but merely an account of the uneventful voyage of the *Narcissus* from Bombay to the Thames'.[227] Zangwill, writing in the *Academy*, put it more bluntly: the tale, he declared, 'has no plot'.[228] Exasperated by these criticisms, Conrad advised Cunninghame Graham to ensure that all his stories have a clear narrative line: 'If you haven't, every fool reviewer will kick you because there can't be literature without plot.'[229]

The novella's unorthodox structure was not the only impediment to its popular success. Seen in the tradition of the popular sea tale associated with Marryat, Clark Russell, and Kipling, it was, for most reviewers, either a puzzling or a pleasing anomaly. As *Literature*, the anti-populist precursor to the

Times Literary Supplement, observed, with the exception of the storm and the attempted mutiny, Conrad's story thankfully ignored most of the genre's stock events and characters:

there are no adventures, beyond the supreme and continuous adventure of the sea; there is no stale resetting of horseplay at the line; the incident of the weevilled biscuit does not recur, nor does the 'old man' unflinchingly taste rotten salt-pork and declare it fit for a lord, let alone a set of &c., &c.[230]

More bemused, the *Daily Chronicle* added: 'There is no pirate in it, no wreck, no desert island, no treasure trove.' Most surprising, however, was the total exclusion of love interest, or, as many reviewers put it, 'petticoats'. According to the *Glasgow Herald,* Conrad did not 'seek any adventitious aid by the introduction in mid-ocean of beautiful but athletic young ladies who have been yachting with their papa, and have suffered some extraordinary ill-fortune at the whim of Father Neptune'.[231] Instead, readers were offered only a brief glimpse of the second mate's romantic dreams, and some talk of prostitutes among the crew.[232] Otherwise, the *Daily Mail* commented, it was an exclusively 'masculine narrative'. Finally, according to the *Spectator,* the story had 'practically no hero'. Some suggested Wait was the 'central figure', some focused on Singleton, while others claimed that the main 'interest is thrown on the play of character in a crew of sailors'. Summing-up the opinions of those reviewers who defended popular tastes, and echoing some of Conrad's own predictions, the *Daily Mail* complained: 'There is no plot, no villainy, no heroism, and, apart from a storm and the death and burial, no incident.' This led the *Academy* to conclude: 'We are grateful for the author's cleverness, yet we venture to remind him that the first duty of a writer is to interest.'[233]

As both Conrad and Henley's 'men of letters' would have responded, the question was not so much *that* writers should interest but *whom* they should interest. If the *Nigger* did not attain wide popularity, as Conrad expected and the reviewers and sales confirmed, it did appeal to the 'small knot of men' for whom it was primarily devised.[234] Though its success in this quarter depended in part on its conspicuous disregard for the protocols of popular fiction and for the expectations of the majority of readers, other strategic elements were also at work. The narrative begins, for instance, by repudiating the tradition of nineteenth-century popular fiction the Henley circle condemned: the *'bourgeois'* library novels that were 'insincere in matters of life and death'.[235] After the initial scenes in which the 'tipsy seamen' begin to assemble on the forecastle, 'swearing at every second word', the narrator focuses on Singleton who is sitting apart from the others and reading Bulwer Lytton's *Pelham* (1828). This prompts the following convenient aside:

The popularity of Bulwer Lytton in the forecastles of Southern-going ships is a wonderful and bizarre phenomenon. What ideas do his polished and so curiously insincere sentences awaken in the simple minds of the big children who people those dark and wandering places of the earth? What meaning their rough, inexperienced souls can find in the elegant verbiage of his pages? What excitement? – what forgetfulness? – what appeasement? Mystery!

Following this line of thought, he then distinguishes between the 'resplendent world' projected in Bulwer Lytton's fiction, and the world of 'infamy and filth', 'dirt and hunger', 'misery and dissipation' which is the 'only thing' the seamen 'know of life' ashore. By implication, his narrative promises to concern itself with this other world which is inhabited by those who 'exist beyond the pale of life' and beyond the pale of Lytton's fiction.[236] Drawing on another of Henley's preferences, Conrad asserted in a letter of 23 December 1897: 'it has been my desire to do for seamen what Millet (if I dare pronounce the name of that great man and good artist in this connection) has done for peasants'.[237] While none of this would have been lost on Henley's 'men of letters', Conrad's commitment to 'unvarnished realism', as the *Glasgow Herald* called it, was not universally appreciated. In particular, many reviewers regretted he had allowed his aversion to Lytton's 'elegant verbiage' to influence his own literary practice. Calling Conrad an 'unflinching realist' and a 'latter-day "naturalist"', W. L. Courtney, the Liberal *Daily Telegraph's* prestigious reviewer, objected to the racism of the tale's 'ugliest conceivable title', and, like many others, went on to lament that the characters talked 'as undoubtedly they ought to talk, and would have talked, without any squeamishness on the part of the author in deference to our sensitive and refined nerves'.[238] Courtney, of course, did not realize he was in fact reading an already partially sanitized version of the text. As Conrad reported on 11 October 1897:

Heinemann objects to the *bloody's* in the book. That Israelite is afraid of women . . . So I struck 3 or 4 *bloody's* out. I am sure there is a couple left yet but, damn it, I am not going to hunt 'em up.[239]

It had appeared in Henley's review 'bloody's' and all. Despite his cavalier tone on this occasion, Conrad himself acknowledged that certain aspects of his virile style might repel women readers. To Helen Watson he remarked that there 'is much in the book in need of your forgiveness', but declared that 'the intention was blameless'; he was also sure Minnie Brooke would not like the story because 'it is too salty and tarry'.[240] The coarse slang of the seamen was, however, not the real reason why Conrad needed to apologize to his women readers.

The *Nigger's* aesthetic appeal for the Henley circle went well beyond its obvious conformity to the ideals of 'manly Realism' and to the terms of the broader cultural debate within which those ideals figured. Conrad also recognized Henley's position within the Realist tradition itself, particularly his attack on Zola's naturalism. Referring to Zola, George Moore and the 'naturalistic school', he wrote in a letter of Christmas 1898: 'Tout ça, c'est très vieux jeu.'[241] Moreover, his manifesto, which first appeared as an 'Author's Note' after the last instalment in the *New Review* – Heinemann refused to include it in the first book edition – is an attempt to define specifically aesthetic values in terms no Henleyite would have found unfamiliar. To begin with, it contrasts the aims of the writer, on the one hand, with those of the scientist and thinker, on the other. The latter, whose domain is constituted by 'ideas' or 'facts', are, it claims, concerned with 'weighty matters': with physical and mental well-being, and with 'our precious aims' and the 'perfection of the means' by which they might be realized. In this last objective, the thinker/ scientist is directly opposed to the writer, one of whose impressionist aims is to 'arrest . . . the hands busy about the work of the earth, and compel men entranced by the sight of distant goals to glance for a moment at the surrounding vision of form and colour'. But, more importantly, the artist's *domain* is also significantly different from that of the scientist or thinker. Rather than engross himself in 'ideas' or 'facts', the artist 'descends within himself, and in that lonely region of stress and strife . . . finds the terms of his appeal'. In an image which draws on Millet's painting and the ideals of the cult of the genius, he is figured as a solitary labourer toiling in a vast landscape. Though the manifesto is clear that this lonely inner domain, which Conrad generally referred to as the artist's 'temperament', is the basis and origin of all art, there is some confusion about the ways in which it guides literary practice. At times, the claim appears to rest on an essentialist conception of the artistic method when he defines art 'as a single-minded attempt to render the highest kind of justice to the visible universe, by bringing to light the truth, manifold and one, underlying its every aspect'. Then again it seems to be idealist, since all temperaments possess a 'subtle and resistless power' which 'endows passing events with their true meaning'. The most consistent conception, however, which encompasses both the methods and the effects of art, is impressionist. Here the claim is that, since all art, including painting and music, must 'be an impression conveyed through the senses' to be effective, the 'artistic aim when expressing itself in written words must also make its appeal through the senses'. Directed by his or her temperament, the artist holds up a 'rescued fragment' from the 'remorseless rush of time' and shows 'its vibration, its colour, its form'. With this impressionistic method, the artist is in a position to realize the preferred end of legitimate art. Challenging the majority of readers who, Conrad claimed, read fiction in order to be 'edified, consoled, amused' or 'improved, or encouraged, or frightened, or shocked, or charmed', and, by implication, the profiteers who responded to these expectations, he identified the purist writer as one whose object was 'to make you hear, to make you feel . . . [and] before all, to make you *see*!'[242]

Echoes of the Henley circle's purist ideals can be heard throughout the manifesto, but its discussion of literary impressionism is specifically indebted to Wyndham's remarks about Crane's *Red Badge of Courage*. In the essay, published in the *New Review* in January 1896, Wyndham indicated what resources could best be drawn upon to give an authentic account of war, and, by extension, to produce effective Realist fiction of any kind:

The sights flashed indelibly on the retina of the eye; the sounds that after long silences suddenly cypher; the stenches that sicken in after-life at any chance allusion to decay; or, stirred by these, the storms of passion that force yells of defiance out of inarticulate clowns . . . these colossal facts of the senses and the soul are the only colours in which the very image of war can be painted.

As we have seen, Wyndham went on to argue that Crane had discovered a 'new device' for achieving this – what would now be called a restricted third-person narrator. As Wyndham put it, the 'book is not written in the form of an autobiography: the author narrates'.

Yet in all his descriptions and all his reports he confines himself only to such things as that youth [the central figure] heard and saw, and, of these, only to such as influenced his emotions. By this compromise he combines the strength and truth of monodrama [he cites Tennyson's *Maud* and Browning's *Martin Relf*] with the directness and colour of the best narrative prose.

This narrative method enabled Crane to present the 'truth of experience', rather than Zola's 'truth of science', and it left 'such indelible traces as are left by the actual experience of war'. By such means, Wyndham concluded, war stories like Crane's, as well as all good sea stories, made it possible for one to 'recognize all life for a battle and this earth for a vessel lost in space'.[243]

Conrad read and endorsed Wyndham's appraisal. Towards the end of his life, in a preface to a new edition of the *Red Badge* which appeared in 1925, he recalled the commotion the novella had caused in the mid-1890s, and observed that one of the 'most interesting, if not the most valuable, of printed criticisms was perhaps that of Mr. George Wyndham, soldier, man of the world, and in a sense a man of letters'.[244] He then proceeded to quote passages from it and to rehearse its main arguments in his own essay. And, indeed, as the *Nigger's* innovative narrative technique suggests, the Crane/ Wyndham ideal also influenced his literary practice. In terms of the technical questions of narrative point of view, the *Nigger* marks a transitional point in Conrad's *œuvre* between the more orthodox unrestricted third-person narratives like *Almayer* (1895) and *An Outcast* (1896), and the framed self-conscious first-person narratives of *Heart of Darkness* (1899) and *Lord Jim* (1900). Like the *Red Badge*, it attempts to foreground Wyndham's 'colossal facts of the senses and the soul'; yet, while Crane had achieved this by the device of a restricted third-person narrator, Conrad adopted a more flexible strategy. Much of the narrative is recounted from the limited perspective of an unselfconscious first-person plural narrator ('we' and 'our'), who functions as a spokesman for the crew, as a commentator on their shifting collective emotions, and as a central filtering consciousness. In the last few paragraphs, he emerges as a first-person singular narrator ('I'). But when this perspective proves too limiting – when, for instance, Wait's thoughts or his private conversations with Donkin need to be recorded – the narrative modulates easily into the more conventional unrestricted third-person mode ('they').[245] Among other things, this dual strategy enabled Conrad to remain faithful to his impressionist methods and to his sophisticated ethical vision at the same time. Most early reviewers did not detect this duality and many found the impressionistic style either bewildering or tedious or both. Zangwill, who reported that the 'tale is told in the first person' only, complained that the novella's 'tense, exaggerated, highly poetic diction' was not appropriate for a seaman-narrator.[246] Others objected to what *Bookman* called the tale's 'over minute method' and its 'fragmentary conversations'.[247] Yet it was Courtney who first pointed out the technical similarities between the *Nigger* and the *Red Badge*. Though he preferred Conrad's style to Crane's, he regretted that both novellas shared the 'same jerky and spasmodic quality', and that they were written, 'even to the verge of the wearisome', in the same 'spirit of faithful and minute description'. In the end, he confessed, 'we are left with only the vaguest idea of what the story has been all about.'[248] In a letter to Crane, Conrad dismissed Courtney as 'that ass' and called his review the 'most *mean-minded* criticism I've read in my life.' About the comparison between them, he remarked: 'if it was true I would be well content to follow you but it isn't true and the perfidious ass tried to damage us both.'[249] Later, as we shall see, Conrad himself pointed out certain similarities between the two novellas.

The *Nigger's* narrative methods and implicit aesthetic guaranteed it would not be popular, but they ensured its success with Henley's purists. Yet, as Conrad insisted, it was not simply a literary experiment: 'I also wanted', he confessed in a letter of 9 December 1897, 'to connect the small world of the ship with that larger world carrying perplexities, fears, affections, rebellions, in a loneliness greater than that of the ship at sea'.[250] This analogical and interpretative impulse is reiterated in the novella itself. The *Narcissus*, for instance, is seen as a 'small planet' and, more dramatically, as 'the last vestige of a shattered creation . . . bearing an anguished remnant of sinful mankind'; or, in a patriotic reversal of the analogy, England is seen as 'a mighty ship bestarred with vigilant lights' and as 'the great flagship of the race'.[251] As the rhetoric of these multi-purpose analogies implies, the connections between the small and the large worlds are complex and various. At times the ship can be read metaphorically as an image of the entire planet seen from a late-Victorian perspective. On this reading, the earth becomes Wyndham's 'vessel lost in space' – the image of a world from which God has withdrawn and which, the novella claims, is redeemed only 'by the vast silence of pain and labour'.[252] At other times, however, it can be read metonymically as a representative fragment of the whole, where the whole is understood to be late-Victorian England. On this reading, the *Nigger* becomes a condition of England novel, and the condition, as Conrad claimed, was characterized mainly by the advent of mass society with all its attendant ethical and political ills. Drawing a parallel at the level of subject-matter between the *Red Badge* and the *Nigger*, he observed:

Stephen Crane dealt in his book with the psychology of the mass – the army; while I – in mine – had been dealing with the same subject on a much smaller scale and in more specialized conditions – the crew of a merchant ship, brought to the test of what I may venture to call the moral problem of conduct.

This shared interest made him think Crane 'eminently fit to pronounce a judgement' on his own novella.[253] Also, it suggests that, if the *Nigger* was not written for (or bought by) the 'masses', it was written, in part at least, about them, and from a sociopolitical perspective Henley's 'men of letters' would not have found uncongenial.

Unlike a 'documentary realist' such as Arnold Bennett, Conrad was not concerned about precise historical detail in his fiction. His interests lay elsewhere. Yet, if one reads the *Nigger* as a condition of England novel, it is clear that it rests on one important, though imprecise, historical assumption; namely, that everything changed sometime around the 1860s. As the narrator indicates in the first chapter, the *Narcissus* is manned by two generations of seamen who differ not only in age, but in their social and political assumptions. The older generation, represented by Singleton, was born around the 1820s. The sixty-year-old seaman was 'old enough to remember slavers' and he had 'sailed to the southward since the age of twelve'.[254] In Britain, the slave trade was formally outlawed in 1807, though it continued until the abolition in 1833. Given this, Singleton's birth date can be fixed, on the most generous view, at sometime in the early 1820s. If one assumes that the fictional voyage from Bombay to London takes place at about the same time as Conrad's voyage from Bombay to Dunkirk on the actual *Narcissus* in 1884, then this approximation, given Singleton's age, again seems plausible. From this it follows that the younger generation – most of the other crew members – was born sometime in the 1850s and 1860s, and for those like Young Charley, who is probably still in his teens, even as late as 1870. The precise dates, however, are less important than the one dominant idea: the older generation spent their formative years in a time before the advent of mass society. As the allusion to slavery suggests, it was a time not only before the political and educational reforms or the 'New Unionism' and 'New Journalism' of the late-Victorian period, but also before the humanitarian attitudes that fostered the abolition movement had gained a wider currency. Though the third-person narrator observes early on that 'a truth, a faith, a generation of men goes – and is forgotten, and it does not matter', his stoical indifference to inevitable historical change is qualified by the rhetoric and dramatic logic of the novella.[255] If the *Nigger* does not mourn the loss of Singleton's generation, neither does it celebrate the advent of modernity.

From the outset, the two generations are symbolically juxtaposed and unequally valued. Though both are figured as 'children', following the late-Victorian conception of the masses which the Henley circle and others shared, they are, as the narrator insists, at different stages of 'development' and they have been nurtured under different conditions: the older generation are the 'everlasting children of the mysterious sea', while its successors are the 'grown-up children of a discontented earth'. The implications of these differences go well beyond a superficial loss of innocence, however. The older generation, for instance, existed, as Singleton still does, 'with a vast empty past and with no future', and as a consequence did not experience the torments of life in time. They 'knew how to exist beyond the pale of life and within sight of eternity'; and they 'had been strong, as those are strong who know neither doubts nor hopes'. Whether as a consequence or a cause of this, they also inhabited a world allegedly uncorrupted by the treacheries, or even the necessities, of language. They were 'voiceless men', 'strong and mute', 'inarticulate and indispensable'. Their silence should not, of course, be taken to mean that they were literally incapable of speech, but rather that they were capable of living without an articulated or formulated conception of how to live, and without the need for such a conception. As such, these 'unthinking' men embody the narrator's idea (and ideal) of a robust ethical and political innocence. Though they 'knew toil, privation, violence, debauchery', and though they mutinied because they wanted 'to broach the cargo and get at the liquor', they were also 'effaced, bowed and enduring', without fear and without a 'desire of spite in their hearts'. Moreover, this virile innocence made possible a particular kind and quality of rustic wisdom. Singleton, who has 'steady old eyes', is, for instance, the 'incarnation of barbarian wisdom serene in the blasphemous turmoil of the world', and, as we shall see, he offers significant pronouncements on the events and characters of the story. As one figure implies, this generation's innocence had advantages for the society to which they belonged: they were 'like stone caryatides that hold up in the night the lighted halls of a resplendent and glorious edifice'. Their stability, selflessness, and reliability are demonstrated in the course of the narrative by Singleton's conduct during the storm. Throughout the time that the ship is on its side, he remains dutifully at the wheel, and, once it is righted, he steers 'with care' into the 'tumult of the seas'.[256]

By contrast, the younger generation is 'less naughty, but less innocent; less profane, but perhaps also less believing', and as such, the novella implies, they have become less reliable members of their profession and society. More importantly, their lives are acted out within the 'weary succession of nights and days' and they have 'learned how to speak'. Though the novella's stance towards them reflects the kind of conservative perspective on mass society the Henley circle espoused – they are still 'children', they are easily swayed by the words of demagogues, and, during the attempted mutiny, it becomes clear that, despite their loquacity, they cannot articulate what they want – it does not consider them to be beyond redemption, albeit redemption on its terms, not theirs. Their time-bound lives are 'tainted by the obstinate clamour of sages, demanding bliss and an empty heaven' – that is, false forms of redemption whether religious, social or political – but they are none the less among those who can be 'redeemed at last' by the 'dumb fear and the dumb courage of men obscure, forgetful, and enduring'.[257] In effect, though they are victims of modernity and its ills, they can, despite themselves and under special conditions, be redeemed as their predecessors had been. To this extent the novella retains some sympathy for most of the crew, but, when it comes to the irredeemable Donkin, the severity of its attack on modernity is unbounded.

Donkin is one of the ideological demons that haunted the Henley circle: he is, in their view, modernity in its most repellent incarnation. This 'East-end trash', with his 'long and thin' neck, his 'big ears', and his 'inefficient carcass', is immediately recognizable as one of the unfit whom the Henleyite Social Darwinists would happily have seen exterminated or phased out. Yet, as the narrator adds, probing one of the Social Darwinists' central assumptions, he is also 'an ominous *survival* testifying to the *eternal fitness* of lies and impudence'. This lying shirker is the novella's 'votary of change': he is the self-styled guardian of the younger generation's Socialist-inspired rights-based culture and the greatest exponent of the 'filthy loquacity' by means of which it is allegedly articulated and sustained. Throughout the novella, this new articulate culture is associated with the earth – Donkin first appears on board covered in mud – and opposed to the older, unformulated, manly culture of the sea. As the narrator remarks, Donkin is:

The sympathetic and deserving creature that knows all about his rights, but knows nothing of courage, of endurance, and of the unexpressed faith, of the unspoken loyalty that knits together a ship's company. The independent offspring of the ignoble freedom of the slums full of disdain and hate for the austere servitude of the sea.

While the older manly culture is celebrated in terms that echo the purist's literary values, the new generation's ideals are doubly repudiated: first by association, and second by their alleged impact on their constituency. By making Donkin, the rapacious opportunist and cadger, the *only* labour representative, the novella reduces any concern for rights to personal *ressentiment*, fuelled by feelings of inferiority, laziness, and spite. Yet, displaying a greater political insight than the Henley circle generally achieved, and challenging some of their own views, the novella shows that many of these feelings also fuel Donkin's vicious nationalism ('damned furriners should be kept under') and his equally untempered racism (he calls Wait a 'vulgar nigger'). Lacking any genuine public spirit or even a wider sense of solidarity, the profiteering Donkin ensures that Socialism and the Labour movement – the distinction is blurred in the novella – are given a bad press. But, to further strengthen the case, he is also shown to be a *failed* agitator. This is the second repudiating strategy. During the calm, the crew are seduced by his 'hopeful doctrines' and by his skilful transformation of Wait into a symbol of labour's defiance against capital and authority – he convinces them (and Wait) that Wait is a justified and politically motivated malingerer, not a dying man, and encourages them to follow his example. Yet his impact is only temporary. He is soon silenced by Knowles's story about a myopic philanthropist who wrongly persuaded a crew to defy its officers, and by his question 'If we all went sick what would become of the ship, eh?' After this, the conversation turns to prostitutes, and Donkin is left feeling 'severe and disgusted'. Again, during the attempted mutiny, which in the end has nothing to do with Donkin, when he throws a belaying pin at the captain and incites the crew to violence, they turn on him and declare 'We ain't that kind!' By implication, the crew (and the labouring masses they represent) are apparently neither really interested in or convinced by Donkin's Socialism, nor are they inclined to adopt militant means to bring about the 'time when every lonely ship would travel over a serene sea, manned by a wealthy and well-fed crew of satisfied skippers'. The final indictment of Donkin would have set the seal on the Henley circle's case against him and all he represents. At the paying-off, he talks animatedly to the 'pasty-faced' Board of Trade 'clerk'; and, after 'dropping h's against one another as if for a wager', the clerk, who had called Singleton a 'disgusting old brute', considers him 'an intelligent man'.[258]

Donkin serves as the focus of the novella's attack on Socialism and the Labour movement; Wait, his occasional ally, is the vehicle for its onslaught against sentimentalism, the more pervasive malaise in late-Victorian society according to Henley's 'men of letters'. In this context, Donkin's repudiated aspirations become merely a symptom of the general malady, and, at this point, the convergence between the novella's political assumptions and those of the Henley circle is complete. As the British title emphasises, Wait, a black West Indian, poses the greatest threat to the social stability and order of the ship. His 'deep, ringing voice' has a more insidious and lasting hold on the crew than Donkin's 'squeaky voice'. His predicament is simple enough: he is dying, most probably of consumption, but he is terrified by the prospect of death. His effect on the crew and his subtle game of seeming deception and real self-deception are, however, much more complex. For the crew, he poses two interrelated problems. First, because of his subtle game, he makes it difficult for them to maintain a consistent moral stance towards him. Never certain whether he is malingering or really dying – their ambivalence is vital to Wait's self-deception – and torn as they are between Donkin's and Singleton's views on the matter, they cannot tell 'the meaning of that black man'. Their blindness is, of course, not helped by their susceptibility to rumour, their narcissism, or their lost innocence. Whereas Singleton lives 'untouched by human emotions', they oscillate 'between the desire of virtue and the fear of ridicule': 'We wished to save ourselves from the pain of remorse, but did not want to be made the contemptible dupes of our sentiment'. Yet their ambivalence is, in a sense, only a superficial problem: its more damaging cause is their sentimental concern for Wait's real or feigned suffering. In this way the crew serve to dramatize the novella's central question: how ought one to act towards the suffering of others, whether its origins are physical, moral or sociopolitical? As numerous allusions to the wider concerns of late-Victorian society suggest, this question goes well beyond the ethical problems enacted on the *Narcissus*. With Henleyite vigour, the novella in fact sets out to demonstrate that the philanthropists, humanitarians, Socialists, and religious charities of late-Victorian society, who concerned themselves with the alleviation of suffering or questions of social and economic injustice, had got it wrong: they were, it claims, more often than not blind, self-interested, or both. While Donkin, that 'pet of philanthropists and self-seeking landlubbers', undermines the Socialist cause, Podmore provides an opportunity for reviling Christian charity. Though the value of the cook's heroic and selfless act of coffee-making during the storm is not questioned, it is significantly qualified by his self-righteous proclamation of his own 'virtue and holiness' after the fact: 'Like many benefactors of humanity, the cook took himself too seriously, and reaped the reward of irreverence.'[259]

Despite the many allusions to the problems of late-Victorian society as a whole, the central question of the novella is finally worked out according to its own dramatic logic, particularly in the final two chapters which centre on the ethics of truth-telling. Donkin and Podmore – and all they represent – are, for instance, thoroughly repudiated in so far as they both force Wait to confront the truth about his imminent death. Donkin is the worst, since he is motivated by a 'desire to assert his importance, to break, to crush; to be even with everybody for everything; to tear the veil, unmask, expose, leave no refuge – a perfidious desire of truthfulness!' His utter lack of remorse leads directly to Wait's death and gives him the chance to steal the dead man's money. Yet Podmore, who wishes to save Wait's soul, is only slightly less reprehensible. Taken up by his own religious fervour, the experience of which is likened to the time he became 'intoxicated at an East-End music-hall', his heart overflows 'with tenderness, with comprehension, with the desire to meddle'; and, finally, with his head full of 'shining faces, lilies, prayer-books, unearthly joy, white shirts, gold harps, black coats, wings', he 'prayerfully' divests himself 'of the last vestige of his humanity' and terrifies Wait into action.[260] This precipitates the mutiny.

The crew, by contrast, are in a more complex ethical position. Though they laudably bolster Wait's life-lie, their motives are wholly condemned. In their case, falsehood triumphs 'through doubt, through stupidity, through pity, through sentimentalism'. Echoing the Henley circle's anti-decadent diatribes against the effects of sentimentalism on English society, the first-person narrator observes:

He was demoralising. Through him we were becoming highly humanised, tender, complex, excessively decadent: we understood the subtlety of his fear, sympathised with all his repulsions, shrinkings, evasions, delusions – as though we had been over-civilised, and rotten, and without any knowledge of the meaning of life.

Worst of all, by allowing this to happen, the crew have, according to the novella's gendered vision of the world, all but forfeited their manhood. Unlike the older generation who had been 'men enough to scorn in their hearts the sentimental voices that bewailed the hardness of their fate', the new generation, and the Irish Belfast in particular, have become 'as gentle as a woman, as tenderly gay as an old philanthropist, as sentimentally careful of [their] nigger as a model slave-owner'. By this set of associations, the novella implies that modernity, with its concern for the rights of labour, the weak, blacks, and women, entailed decadence, and that this was, in part at least, due to an unwelcome feminization of culture. This underlies the irony of Donkin's cry 'I am the only man 'ere' and the pathos of Belfast's final emotional outburst 'Jimmy, be a man!'[261] In this respect, too, the novella fully endorses the Henley circle's anti-decadent cult of manliness.

The only characters who manage to retain their cherished manhood, and, at the same time, respond justly to Wait's suffering, are Singleton and Captain Allistoun. But again a distinction can be drawn. Singleton, the custodian of primitive wisdom and the novella's equivalent of the Henley circle's 'rustic hero', is admirably clear-eyed and direct in his response to Wait. Shocking all the others, he simply asks him: 'Are you dying?' When Wait says he is, he replies 'with venerable mildness': 'Well, get on with your dying . . . don't raise a blamed fuss with us over that job. We can't help you.' He then leaves Wait alone to die in his own way. Though this matter-of-fact attitude is validated by the dignified manner in which Singleton contemplates his own death – like the rest of his generation he had never given a 'thought to his mortal self', but, when he realizes he will not live much longer, he simply confronts the sea without evasion or fear and listens to 'its impatient voice calling' – there is also a suspicion that his directness is an expression of racist indifference. The old man, who remembers 'gruesome things, details of horrors, hecatombs of niggers', and who has seen blacks 'die like flies' on the slave ships, is amazed by the concern the rest of the crew feel, and for 'a black fellow, too'. There is little in the novella to gainsay such racism, except in so far as Singleton shares his views with Donkin, and yet his conduct can be contrasted to Allistoun's which is approved unambiguously. After Wait is terrified into wanting to resume his duties by Podmore, the captain forces him to lie-up, on the grounds that he has been shamming sick: 'you choose to lie-up to please yourself – and now you shall lie-up to please me'. As he later reveals, this is a lie: he sees clearly enough that Wait is 'in a mortal funk to die', but decides to 'let him go out in his own way'. Though the crew misunderstand this, and so attempt the confused mutiny, he explains his actions to his officers who are left 'more impressed than if they had seen a stone image shed a miraculous tear of compassion over the incertitudes of life and death'.[262] In the end, then, the Scottish captain alone is capable of manly justice. For the producers of the Tory *Scots Observer*, the wider political implications of *that* would not have been easily missed.

With *The Nigger of the 'Narcissus'* Conrad made a determined bid to secure what he reckoned to be his 'natural' position in the literary field of the 1890s, and, as such, part of its purpose was to certify his credentials. He produced an avant-garde, impressionistic novella and a reactionary political allegory oriented to a specific purist literary circle, review, and, above all, editor. To this extent, his text illustrates with particular force the complex non-discursive interests, some of which are specifically literary, at stake in any act of writing, and it testifies to the power of the field's structural determinations. Yet, as an example, it is also unfortunate in so far as it implies that the affinities between texts and their initial publishing contexts are always a consequence of conscious connivance on the author's part. True, in this instance the evidence permits such a worldly reading, since even Conrad's assertions of disinterested-ness seem designing. It was no coincidence, for example, that he appended to his conspicuously inflected text a manifesto which made explicit his purist views on writing and reading, and, most importantly, asserted his belief in the idea of the writer as solitary, struggling genius:

Realism, Romanticism, Naturalism, even the unofficial sentimentalism (which like the poor, is exceedingly difficult to get rid of), all these gods must, after a short period of fellowship, abandon [the artist] – even on the very threshold of the temple – to the stammerings of his conscience and to the outspoken consciousness of the difficulties of his work.

In this 'uneasy solitude' even the Aesthete's 'supreme cry of Art for Art itself' lost the 'exciting ring of its apparent immorality', though it was, he added, 'at times, and faintly, encouraging'.[263] As we have seen, this image of writing as a strenuous private act of supreme integrity, staged in a sanctified space like Gosse's Westminster Abbey, was not only belied by Conrad's own public manœuvring, but was itself one of the complex cluster of legitimizing ideals that bound together the purists of the 1890s. Among the members of Henley's circle, it was part of the code of practice expected of all those worthy of the honorific title 'man of letters'. To this extent Conrad's manifesto reveals in the act of concealment: its assertion of his solitary dedication was simultaneously an expression and a denial of his social ambitions as a writer. It is (perhaps not by chance) an appropriate preface to Wait's story. Conrad, in fact, remained a special case throughout his career, since calculated self-concealment became something of a habit with him. In his reminiscences, he consistently played down the strength of his determination to become a 'man of letters'. As Najder argues (following Baines) he 'always insisted that he became a writer by chance, that literature was not a matter of conscious choice nor even the result of some strong inner need'. Najder claims this reinforces the hypothesis that for Conrad writing was both a covert 'act of compensation, of correcting, perfecting, or at least complementing his own pre- and extraliterary life', and an implicit 'moral act on the purely personal plane' which embodied his struggle against what he felt to be his own dangerously romantic and/or nihilistic tendencies.[264] Like all purely psychological or biographical explanations, however, this underestimates the social dimension of writing which brings other, less personal, pressures to bear on individual authors, the texts they produce, and the public image they present. As a prospective 'man of letters' in the literary field of the 1890s, Conrad had, as we have seen, a special interest in insisting upon his purist disinterestedness. Yet, in all this, he was more an exception than a typical case. Though the theory of the field recognizes that such deliberate manœuvring is not uncommon among newcomers, it does not presuppose that every act of writing involves connivance. Rather, conscious calculation is only a possible development of the ordinary, and less motivated, business of being part of a field. Membership of a specific field is achieved and shown by mastering an extensive body of local information about literary fashions (all Conrad's -isms), publishing venues, specific personalities, contemporary cultural debates, possible positions, etc. This can be gathered through numerous channels of communication ranging from periodicals (Conrad's reading of Wyndham in the *New Review*, for instance) and books to formal lectures and gossip (Garnett was vital for Conrad in this), and it might be acquired by deliberate effort or simply by being part of the right social circles. As Bourdieu argues, this 'practical mastery', which is always incomplete, 'gives its possessors a "nose" and a "feeling", *without any need for cynical calculation,* for "what needs to be done", where to do it, how and with whom, in view of all that has been done and is being done, all those who are doing it, and where.' Whether bolstered by careful manœuvring or not, this primary competence informs a writer's decisions about how to play the contemporary field. Of all these 'choosing the right place of publication' is, according to Bourdieu, 'vitally important because for each author, each form of production and product, there is a corresponding *natural site* in the field of production, and producers and products that are not in their right place are more or less bound to fail'.[265] By writing the *Nigger* with an eye on Henley and the *New Review*, Conrad did all he could to safeguard his place in the field, and, when the gamble paid off, he entered his major phase.

2 · PLAYING THE FIELD: ARNOLD BENNETT AS NOVELIST, SERIALIST AND JOURNALIST

'What horrible dangers you ran!' she said.
'But look at the reward!' replied he.
Ah!' she breathed. 'Money! Is it worth – ?'
Bennett and Phillpotts, *Sinews of War*, 1906[1]

I

In 1894 ARNOLD BENNETT (1867–1931) did not think he was destined to be a literary author. 'You must remember', he wrote on 28 October to George Sturt, then his closest literary confidant, 'that in order that a man sit down deliberately to be artistic, & be damned to every other consideration – he must have some inward assurance that there is a brilliant or at least pleasant conclusion to the dark tunnel which he is entering'.[2] At that point he felt he had no such assurance. For one thing, his social background – he came from a family of provincial shopkeepers – had taught him to see literary authors, especially metropolitan ones, as 'beings apart and peculiar' who 'belonged to the weird tribe of Benjamin'.[3] Though he escaped the 'excessively irksome', 'pietistic-religious' cultural environment of Burslem in 1889, his early experiences in London as a solicitor's clerk and journalist did little to ease this sense of alienation.[4] Not that he lost any time in his metropolitan cultural apprenticeship. Guided by a fellow London clerk, John Eland, he continued to develop his already keen taste for French literature and he became something of a bibliophile; then, in 1891, he moved to Chelsea where he was 'dazzled'. He began moving in a new 'circle of painters and musicians' and felt 'compelled to set to work on the reconstruction of nearly all my ideals'. It was as if he had to learn a new language. In Methodist Burslem, the word 'beautiful' was 'scarcely heard': 'modern oak sideboards were called handsome, and Christmas cards were called pretty; and that was about all'. His new Chelsea friends, however, 'talked of beauty openly and unashamed'. They also persuaded him that 'caricature' was a 'legitimate form of art' and then encouraged him to enter a *Tit-Bits* competition for the best condensation of Grant Allen's prize serial *What's Bred in the Bone* (1891).[5] After he won the twenty-one guinea prize, he began freelancing for *Tit-Bits*, T. P. O'Connor's half-penny evening paper the *Sun* (1893), and sixpenny monthlies like *Cassell's Family Magazine* (1853) and the *English Illustrated* (1883).

68

This freelance phase of his career, which lasted till the end of 1893, was 'not precisely a triumph', he later recalled – he made little more than £15 a year from his writing, though his annual earnings as a clerk went up from £65 in 1889 to £200 in 1893.[6] In January 1894, however, he became assistant editor of *Woman* (1890), a cautiously 'advanced' penny weekly whose motto was 'Forward! But Not Too Fast!' At first, he was less comfortably off as a full-time journalist than he had been as a clerk. While he had more time to himself – he was working only four half-days and one full day a week – his annual salary from *Woman* for the first two years was only £156.[7] He made up for this by continuing to do piecework for newspapers and magazines. With frequent contributions to *Woman*, the *Sun*, *Pall Mall Gazette* (1865), *Westminster Gazette* (1893), and *Daily Chronicle* (1855), he earned an additional £55 5s 5d in 1894 and £98 15s 7d in 1895.[8] He also started to make something of a name for himself as a popular satirist. By late 1894 his 'topical fantastic' short stories were being accepted by 'the more exclusive, the consciously superior, penny evening papers'.[9] To him his place in the literary field seemed clear. He was to be designated a successful 'caricaturist of passing follies', not an artistic 'producer of "documents humains"', a status he found congenial enough. His more populist 'line of business' had its rewards. It meant he might be 'read with zest' by the 'man in the street', mix with 'fellows whose names shine on the foreheads of the magazines' and, above all, live a life of 'semi-luxurious competence'. Reciting his favourite defiantly self-satisfied line from Walt Whitman's *Song of Myself*, he concluded, in another letter to Sturt, 'I exist as I am: that is enough.'

Like most of Bennett's new circle of literary friends, Sturt bought none of this. He branded him an intellectually confused 'fatalist' and thought his assumed 'indifference' to 'Art' concealed a fear of failure. Not that Bennett ever seriously denied this. When he was not ridiculing the ideals of 'art for art's sake', which his more purist friends espoused, he admitted that a large part of his problem was that he got 'no encouragement to be deliberately & exclusively artistic'. By late October 1894 the 'best thing' he had yet done had been 'refused by half the Editors in London'.[10] This was his first self-consciously 'literary' short story 'A Letter Home' which he had written the previous summer. It was neither topical nor fantastic. It was a grim Naturalistic tale about the death of a provincial down-and-out in London which he described as 'a *conte* – exquisitely Gallic as to spirit and form'.[11] A month later, however, all this changed. On 27 November he wrote eagerly to Sturt:

You may perhaps be glad to hear that I have already sold ten stories to appear in the first quarter of 1895, one in the *Yellow Book*. I should like you to see this one; the others have no importance whatever, except fiscal.

The exacting Sturt saw the page-proofs of the story the following July, and commented: 'It *is* good. And its goodness is at least a partial vindication of the stuff I have before found fault with – the potboilers which up till now you have palmed off upon me as specimens of your work.'[12] 'A Letter Home' appeared in John Lane's five-shilling *Yellow Book* in July 1895 alongside Henry James's short story 'The Next Time' which, fittingly, told of a purist literary author's failure to write what James called 'vulgar' fiction.[13] For Bennett, the publica- tion of *his* tale in *that* periodical radically altered his sense of his position, or potential position, in the literary field. 'I . . . discovered that I could write – and when I use the term "write" here, I use it in a special sense, to be appreciated only by those elect who can themselves "write", and difficult of comprehension by all others.'[14] This public authorization, not by the 'man in the street' or the editors of popular papers, but by admired literary peers and a prominent avant-garde periodical, gave him the private assurance he needed to enter the 'dark tunnel'. In mid-April 1895, he began what he called a 'conscientious novel' which was to be 'art, with a water-tight fire-proof A'.[15]

If creditable difference is a condition for access to any cultural avant-garde, Bennett's first novel is a minor but exemplary 1890s-style avant-garde text. It flaunts difference at every point. As any well-informed aspirant novelist in London then knew, being distinctive mostly meant one had to reject the canonical mid-Victorian English authors and learn from what the French literary intelligentsia had been doing since the 1860s. This, at least, is what James had announced – not without his usual reservations – in his pioneering essay 'The Art of Fiction' (1884), what George Moore had demonstrated in his novels of the 1880s, and what the *Yellow Book* had made part of its cultural mission. Bennett duly set out to flout the 'accepted canons' of fiction laid down by Dickens, Thackeray, George Eliot, and Mrs. Henry Wood.[16] His novel was 'to be entirely unlike all English novels' but very like his 'favourite masters & models' who were, in order, Turgenev, Maupassant, *les frères* Goncourt, and George Moore.[17] Of course, his choice of allegiances was as much a social as a literary act of resistance. In distancing himself from the established English authors, he acknowledged he was also repudiating the 'estimable' tastes of his immediate public, principally the middle-class subscribers to Mudie's circu- lating library.[18] This was itself a required attitude for any prospective member of the 1890s avant-garde.

The cosmopolitan literary avant-garde set out to purify the novel form. At one level, this involved rescuing it from the traditional reticences of English fiction still safeguarded by the likes of Mudie. It licensed Bennett, for instance, to represent the 'glittering vices of the metropolis', like prostitution at West End music halls, and the sexual underlife of his clerk-hero.[19] These were fashionable topics in the *Yellow Book*, but ones which offended Bennett's more populist reviewers.[20] Yet it was not simply a question of *what* could now legitimately be represented. Technically, the new order, as Bennett saw it, dispensed with the 'moralizings' of an intrusive narrator; gave at least equal weight to 'subject' and 'words as words'; and replaced the 'startling events', 'ingenious combinations' and 'coincidences' of the conventional plot with 'rhythmic contour'.[21] As we have seen in the case of the *Nigger*, this last device, which was bound up with the literary impressionist vogue, entailed that the narrative be constructed as a series of short evocative episodes or vignettes. Bennett learned this mainly from the Goncourts, but it had also been a prominent feature of John Lane's radical 'Keynotes Series' since 1893, and he later recalled it was 'a precious distinction in those Yellerbocky days'.[22] As he warned readers of *Hearth and Home* in his self-promoting review of the novel, this new form posed another challenge to popular expectations. While he was understandably eager to have the paper's predominantly female middle-class readership believe his novel was 'clean, healthy, and powerful', he also insisted it was not like the 'sensational serials' with which they were most familiar: 'there is no journalistic attempt to bring about "good curtains" at any hazard of veracity, or to write "bright pages" at the cost of true character-drawing'.[23] Yet, as he said to Sturt, an appropriately distinctive debut text was not only meant to *be* legitimately different, but to *look* different. He was writing, not for the discerning 'intellect only', but 'for the eye', the 'eye which reads a whole page in a flash, as it were'.[24] Following the layout of the Goncourt's *Renée Mauperin* (1864) in particular, he divided the single-volume text into thirty-two 'complete' and 'detached' scenes each of about 2,000 to 3,000 words; and, in keeping with his stylistic effort towards the Goncourts' 'austere simplicity' and against the 'damnably Mudiesque', he ensured there would be 'no poetical quotations' and 'no titles to the chapters' (just bare Roman numerals).[25] Stylistically and visually he adopted the new anti-Literary literary practice. Again echoing the visual effects of the Goncourts, he strove to exploit 'vague but tremendous' ellipses at the end of sections and to make the most of long, block-like paragraphs divided by short lines.[26] The result was a conspicuously 'exotic' 50,000-word *roman documentaire*, entitled *In the Shadow*, about a provincial clerk's attempts to affront his social destiny by making his name as a metropolitan author and by marrying a 'New Woman' of the 1890s, 'an artist of some sort, absolutely irreligious, broad in social views, the essence of refinement'.[27] Given the 'naturalistic' conventions Bennett then followed – and the force of his title – the commonplace hero of course fails in both quests and is doomed to unliterary anonymity in a 'suburban doll's-house', married to a 'typical matron of the lower middle-class'.[28]

Half way through the difficult process of composition, which involved two manuscript drafts and a final typescript, he began to feel increasingly confident about his chosen course. On 11 November 1895 he wrote to Sturt:

I feel more sure than ever I did in my life before, that I can *write* in time, & 'make people care', too, as Hy. James says – though praps only a few people. Still, to have made fellow artists care – that is the thing! That is what will give ultimate peace of mind. Do you ever suddenly stand still and ponder: 'Suppose, after all, I am an artist, rather a fine one!'[29]

Yet he was still uneasy about ascribing this honorific to himself, not simply because he had yet to complete the draft, but because he sensed that 'Artists' as such were, in principle, not self-defining. 'Dared I utter this great saying ['The man's an artist'] to my shaving-mirror? No, I repeat that I dared not.'[30] The title, with all it entailed in the 1890s, could, he realized, be conferred legitimately only by recognized guarantors. To acknowledge his new position and prospects fully, he required not only the sanction of 'fellow artists' (Sturt, Eden Phillpotts, Wells, and Conrad were to play important roles here), but also the *imprimatur* of the right cultural intermediaries, including critics, and above all, publishers. 'When I have read my first novel in print', he told Sturt, 'I think I shall know.'[31]

He completed the final draft on 15 May 1896, and sent the typescript to John Lane, at the Bodley Head in Vigo Street, four days later. There were pragmatic reasons that made this an obvious initial move. He was, as we have seen, already on good terms with Lane's firm. His short story had appeared in the *Yellow Book* a year earlier, and, in the interim, he had established friendly relations with Lane's respected manager, Frederic Chapman. Moreover, he knew Lane was one of the most likely publishers then in London to accept a self-consciously unconventional, even slightly *risqué*, first novel by a young writer. As Leopold Wagner wisely informed aspirants in 1898, ' "sexual" fiction should not be sent to the S. P. C. K, nor a temperance story to Mr. Heinemann or Mr. John Lane'.[32] By 1896, Lane's first fiction series, the 'Keynotes Series', which had largely earned him this reputation, ran to thirty volumes, half of which were first novels by unknown young authors. Yet choosing Lane was not only a prudently pragmatic move on Bennett's part. It was also the final phase in a carefully timed but still bold effort to reinvent himself culturally. Seen in this way, his decision had less to do with connections or Lane's policy towards new writers, and more to do with the position the Bodley Head occupied, or was seen to occupy, in the literary field in 1896.

Bennett had clear ideas about what the firm represented. In his view, Lane had created, particularly with the *Yellow Book*, a 'theatre for experiments in technique, an enclosure where the literary artist may snap his fingers at commercialism and write as he would, not as the world bids'.[33] His stable of writers, some of whom also served as his manuscript readers, comprised an 'elect', a coterie of 'fellow artists' capable of appreciating what it meant to 'write' in a 'special sense'.[34] They were 'young lion[s] of the people-despising kind' who condemned 'popular taste', and Lane's name was 'a household word wherever the English language is written for posterity.'[35] At a time when the emergence of large-scale firms, like George Newnes, Ltd., heralded the arrival of mass culture, the Bodley Head possessed, for Bennett, all the credentials of an exclusive small-scale press. It promoted artistic autonomy; it was above 'commercialism'; it championed a new generation of select writers; and, rather than cater to known tastes and the immediate public, it created taste by publishing for 'posterity'. In short, according to Bennett, Lane had established himself in the field as a leader of a new avant-garde generation and as a recognized arbiter whose imprint was not merely a sign of legal ownership but a classificatory cachet. As such, he had not only the means to transform manuscripts into published books, but the power to create 'literary artists'.

This glamorous reading of Lane's position was not merely convenient for someone with Bennett's ambitions. It was a widely, but not universally, accepted view. In a decade that saw the emergence of such pioneering publishers as Heinemann, Fisher Unwin, and Grant Richards, 'no one will deny', wrote Holbrook Jackson in 1913, 'that the Bodley Head was the chief home of the new movement'.[36] And, according to Lewis May, one of Lane's employees in the early 1890s, the premises in Vigo Street were 'more like a club than a place of business. It was a sodality, a confraternity of which Lane was the abbot.'[37] Yet this image of the firm was less a testimony to its founder's courageously disinterested avant-garde ideals than it was a product of his talent for managing resources, collaborators, and opinion. It was the outcome of the first six years of his publishing career which represented a sustained, and increasingly ambitious, effort to manufacture his own cultural credibility, to make, as one of his advertisements proclaimed, the Bodley Head 'imprint' into a 'guarantee of the worth' of what he published.[38]

Lane was another provincial on the make. He had left his yeoman family in Devonshire for London in 1869, done the usual stint as a clerk, and, like Bennett, become caught up in the rare book craze. In 1887 he set up an antiquarian bookshop in Vigo Street with Elkin Mathews, a bookseller from Exeter and the brother of a fellow clerk, and two years later they modestly set out as small-scale specialist producers of select poetry, drama, and *belles-lettres* for fellow bibliophiles and connoisseurs.[39] It was an unhappy alliance. Lane was always the driving force. This imbalance, and Lane's sometimes under-hand initiatives, in fact led to the dissolution of the partnership in 1894. Yet, even before ditching his less ambitious partner, Lane had begun to make his name with more high-profile, controversial projects like the *Yellow Book* and the 'Keynotes Series' that appealed to a wider market. His goal throughout (but particularly in the second phase from 1893 to 1895) was to achieve rapid distinction at a discount. His bohemian stable of 'uncommercial' writers and artists, which Richard Le Gallienne described as 'only accidentally a group', were the foundation of the firm's avant-garde image.[40] They were young rebels with various religious, political, social, sexual, and aesthetic causes, who, like Ella D'Arcy, saw 'Art and Literature' as an affront to the 'comfortably prosaic circles of suburban grocers' from which so many of them came.[41] But they were also, for the most part, cheap, minor, young unknowns, a junior elite many of whose reputations did not survive the decade. Even then their standing, and Lane's, was contested. Some established figures, like Gosse, were encouraging, but others held the newcomers in contempt. As we have seen,

Henley, who had his own stable of select 'young men', regarded the Bodley Head group as a gathering of questionable minor figures, a view which James and Mrs Oliphant shared. As *Blackwood's* anonymous 'Looker-on', Mrs Oliphant remarked that, while the first number of the *Yellow Book* had 'shocked many good people', the second 'betrayed how the shock had been transferred from the people who read to the people who wrote'. The 'young gentlemen' or 'their capitalist' had got 'frightened' and so 'all the flash and fury of youthful genius was served up to us discreetly concealed within a sandwich of respectability'.[42] Though James contributed to the new venture and praised it in public, privately he, too, put the newcomers in their place. In a letter to his brother, he claimed he was contributing only 'for gold and to oblige the worshipful Harland', the quarterly's young American literary editor. For the rest, he declared, 'I hate too much the horrid aspect and company of the whole publication.'[43]

The reasons for Lane's equivocal position lay partly in the way he conducted business. To begin with, there was something doubtful about his books. Produced in collaboration with enterprising fine printers in Britain and America, and innovative artists like Beardsley, Ricketts, and Shannon, the typical Bodley book was intended to be the material expression of the Bodley text and a symbol of the firm's antagonism to what Le Gallienne called the new 'evil' of 'over-production'.[44] Yet, unlike William Morris, Lane was as concerned to market commercial commodities as he was to produce symbolic goods. Rather than initiate the 'Revival of Printing' in the 1890s, he capitalized on it to create distinctively modern products that cost no more than the average new book. The production of Bennett's first novel provides a good example of his usual practice. The final product was a 'fine book' in what Susan Thompson has called the 'Aesthetic format' of the 1890s. Its simple red binding, elegantly unadorned title page, wide margins, and laid paper with deckle edges, not only reinforced Bennett's textual effort towards 'austere simplicity', but looked back to Ruskin's revolt against 'superfluous ornament' and, more particularly, to the uncluttered book design Whistler and Walter Blaikie had developed in the 1880s.[45] Yet, at every point in the production process, Lane strove to economize. First, he had copies for both the British and the American markets set and printed in the US, thereby exploiting a discrepancy in international copyright law and avoiding double production costs. This was a cost-cutting measure he pioneered.[46] Second, he contracted the book out to John Wilson and Son in Cambridge, Massachusetts, one of the leading fine printers in America. It was no coincidence that William Orcutt, who had become head of the firm in 1895, shared Lane's commercial and cultural ideals. As a printer, he believed his job was to 'build low-cost volumes upon the same principles as *de luxe* editions, eliminating the expensive materials but retaining the harmony and consistency that come from designing the book from an architectural standpoint'.[47] Finally, Lane limited the edition size and cut binding costs (of the 750 copies produced for the British market only 600 were bound), and, as we shall see, he paid Bennett what was at best a charitable royalty.[48] The result was a symbolically purist book, in terms of its design, edition size, and textual content, that could be sold at a relatively inexpensive 3s 6d. (It is worth recalling that Morris's Kelmscott books retailed at between 30s and £15 15s.)

Yet the ambiguities of Lane's position are most clearly evident in his particularly modern attitude to marketing. Though Margaret Stetz overstates her case by suggesting he 'devised the first modern sales campaign in publishing', the primary aim of which was 'to create and to sell an image of the firm itself', he did bring a new enthusiasm for marketing to the gentlemanly world of publishing which further complicated his cultural position. Using posters, prospectuses, his contacts in the press, and extensive advertisements bound into his own books, he pursued a purist image with the energy of a profiteer, particularly after breaking with Mathews. As Stetz puts it, he set out to present his 'increasingly mass-market firm, which enjoyed a wide distribution in both England and America, as though it were a private press'. Like the Henley circle, Stetz finds this eager self-promotion, combined with Lane's cost-conscious anti-commercialism, a little suspect. She compares him to Arthur Liberty, the contemporary London retailer who believed that the 'aesthetically acceptable could be combined with the commercially viable', and concludes that 'in a decade filled with social poseurs and literary masqueraders, the "Bodley Head" itself was a bit of a fraud'.[49]

Yet such suspicions, as much as Bennett's trusting credulity, underestimate the complexity of Lane's position. There is no doubt, as Lewis May admitted, that Lane, himself a former clerk from the provinces, had a reputation as an upstart 'arriviste' and a 'tuft-hunter'. But this was, May implied, as much a matter of structural as of social forces:

The great fixed stars in the publishing firmament, Macmillans, Longmans, John Murray, Blackwoods, Smith Elder, had each a sort of magnetic or gravitational attraction and drew all the clients they needed into their respective orbits. But a new-comer had to fend for himself, had to make himself known, had to go forth into the world conquering and to conquer. He *had* to push his way, or go under.[50]

Added to this, Lane was also a seriously under-capitalized newcomer. Henry Harland was, for instance, required to produce his emblematically purist quarterly on a budget of £200 per issue for contributor's costs.[51] This inevitably meant he had to make do with more tales by unknowns like Bennett which, at a guinea per thousand words, cost almost four times less than James's satires attacking modern 'commercialism'.[52] Lane's dilemma, then, was to find ways of establishing a reputable name, which in the age of mass culture entailed a visible refusal of 'commercialism', while safeguarding his own economic survival. Stylishly produced limited editions, combined with vig-orous marketing, represented one viable strategy, but it was also too transparent and too specialist. Cultural daring, however, was cheap, it generated its own publicity, and it had a wider impact. The only problem was it was also dangerous. So, to counteract the risks, Lane adopted a number of self-protective tactics as well. If the *Yellow Book* carried Beardsley's provocative drawings and designs, Lane (as Mrs Oliphant rightly surmised) ensured that it also published sketches by the eminently respectable Sir Frederick Leighton, P. R. A.; or, if he issued Grant Allen's stridently anti-marriage novel *The Woman Who Did* (1895), he also put out 'Victoria Crosse's' pro-marriage reply *The Woman Who Didn't* (1895).[53] And, when controversy began to look less like good publicity and more like commercial suicide, he lost no time in adjusting to the new conditions. After Wilde's arrest in 1895, when the firm came under threat both from within and without, he instituted what 'George Egerton' called the 'new Bodley Head policy'.[54] He removed Beardsley from the *Yellow Book*; took Wilde's volumes off the list; and adopted a more cautious editorial policy which included censoring some of his more radical 'Keynotes' authors (like 'Egerton') and inaugurating two more tame series ('Lane's Library' (1896) of lighter fiction, and the 'Arcady Library' (1896) of keepsake verse).[55] In short, he was neither a fraud nor a principled cultural pioneer, but rather a shrewd entrepreneur, with a flair for public relations, who collaborated with affordable avant-garde authors, editors, artists, and printers to create a prestigious brand name. Moreover, his energetic networking and marketing reinforce Bourdieu's contention that cultural status exists only 'in relationship with the field of production as a whole'.[56] Lane understood he was neither a sovereign arbiter nor the ultimate source of cultural value. He knew his position was dependent on the writers and artists in his stable; on the readers, printers, and book-designers he employed; on the good (or bad) opinion of other publishers as well as reviewers; and ultimately on the book-buyers who did or did not see the appeal of his name. In effect, his position as an important mediating agent among the junior purists presupposed a complex interplay of social, legal, economic, and cultural factors, all of which ultimately had their roots in the whole literary field of the 1890s.

Bennett sent his novel to a cultural icon called 'John Lane, At the Bodley Head', but, as he soon discovered, he had to do business with an actual entrepreneur. Initially things went well enough. Lane forwarded the typescript to his new reader, the twenty-one-year-old John Buchan, then an impoverished undergraduate studying Classics at Oxford. Buchan, a typically young, displaced, and needy Lane employee, was no doubt part of the new 1895 policy. He had sophisticated literary tastes, but, unlike Le Gallienne, his predecessor, he was not overly radical. While he admired Pater and Ibsen, read Nietzsche, and had a taste for French novelists (especially Flaubert and Maupassant), he saw himself at that time as a robust pastoral Aesthete and an Arnoldian Scholar-Gypsy.[57] He was fiercely opposed to what he termed the 'ravings of a vitiated decadence', and, as the son of a Scottish Presbyterian minister, he had no time for the ' "sex" novels' in Lane's 'Keynotes Series' which Le Gallienne had championed.[58] He was also an exacting critic. Only 17 per cent of his surviving reader's reports recommend acceptance (or 29 out of 172).[59] To Bennett, he had all the right credentials, however. He was admittedly a 'very young', 'most modest, retiring man', but he was also someone 'to compel respect; one who "counts" '.[60] Buchan's report, submitted a week after Bennett posted the typescript, was cautiously approving. He thought the 'inadequate' title *In the Shadow* should be changed; recommended that a 'certain amount of journalistic detail' be 'left out'; and added that he did 'not think it likely to be a striking success'. However, he concluded, it was 'an honest and creditable piece of work, quite creditable to any firm'.[61] According to Bennett's account in *The Truth about an Author*, Lane muttered about first novels being 'too risky'. When Bennett pointed to one of his 'notorious successes', no doubt 'George Egerton's' first novel *Keynotes* (1893) which ran to five editions and over 6,000 copies in its first six months, Lane conceded, but still insisted his profits were not 'so much as you think'. However, making 'an honest attempt not to look like a philanthropist' and on the strength of Buchan's recommendation, he finally offered to publish it on strictly limited terms.[62]

This was on 28 May 1896. By 6 October, Bennett had made the necessary minor revisions and come up with the new title *A Man from the North*.[63] He also noted in a letter of that date that the novel was to be printed in America. Yet it was to take another twenty months for him to pressurize Lane into signing a formal contract. (He was understandably unimpressed when Lane processed his second book, *Journalism for Women*, a potentially more profitable little handbook, in a matter of weeks.[64]) When this was finally done on 15 December 1897, the agreement was for a five per cent royalty on the first 2,000 copies sold in Britain, and two-and-a-half per cent on the American sales.[65] Given that Lane most probably had only half that number printed – while 750 copies were produced for sale in Britain, it is unlikely that as many were prepared for the American market – this meant Bennett stood to earn at most around £7 from a 3s 6d book. In fact, in 1900 he reported that, after covering the costs of having the manuscript typed, the book had earned him 'the sum of one sovereign'. This was nothing to 'grumble' about, however. 'Many a first book has cost its author a hundred pounds', he noted later. 'I got a new hat out of mine.'[66]

Not that money had ever been part of the plan; indeed, it had been consciously ruled out. He had set out to reinvent himself by writing a 'deliberately & exclusively artistic' text that could serve as his passport to the metropolitan literary avant-garde.[67] His choice of publishing venue was the final phase in this project, and he selected Lane as an accredited but accessible gatekeeper. Only when the text finally appeared on 23 February 1898 as a Bodley Head book, bearing Lane's imprint and coded bibliographically as

'Art', did Bennett allow himself to record modestly: 'I was no longer a mere journalist; I was an author.'[68] Yet it is important not to see this outcome in narrowly individualistic terms as a successful transaction between an ambitious aspirant seeking a 'reputation' and an inspired publisher in search of affordable 'talent'. With the publication of his first novel, Bennett crossed a border and gained access to an objectively defined position in the literary field, which we might call that of a junior purist or, in Bennett's own terms, 'literary artist'. Like any institutionalized status, this *de facto* position had its selection procedures, its approved jury (in this case, publishers, critics, and 'fellow artists'), and it acquired meaning only in relation to other relevant status positions (for example, 'established purist', 'journalist', or 'popular author'). It also imposed practical claims on its incumbent. These included a delimited horizon of possible texts a purist could produce, codes of writerly conduct (for example, 'Artists' could not 'write for money' or 'to entertain'), and restrictions on acceptable associations (including publishing venues). This is worth noting because, having achieved this position, Bennett spent the remainder of his career challenging the rules of the game and the restrictive assumptions underlying the hierarchy. This began in September 1898 – seven months after his first novel appeared – when he decided to write 'sensational serials' for money.

II

In his journal entry for 12 September 1898 Bennett noted:

Partly owing to the influence of Phillpotts, I have decided very seriously to take up fiction for a livelihood. A certain chronic poverty had forced upon me the fact that I was giving no attention to money-making, beyond my editorship, and so the resolution came about. Till the end of 1899 I propose to give myself absolutely to writing the sort of fiction that sells itself.[69]

The remark about the influence of Eden Phillpotts was genuine enough. Recalled now chiefly for his longevity (1862–1960), his prolific and diverse output (225 titles), and his contribution to the British regionalist novel (many stories were set in Dartmoor), Phillpotts had followed a very similar social and professional trajectory to Bennett – provinces, London, clerking, editing – but since he was seven years older, Bennett looked to him less as a confidant like Sturt and more as a literary mentor. Indeed, not being Sturt was one of Phillpotts's greatest virtues for Bennett. What interested him was his new friend's determinedly professional attitude to authorship. When they first met in May 1897, Phillpotts was himself beginning to explore the serial market and to challenge established codes of literary conduct. As he explained later that year in letter to his agent William Morris Colles: 'A man can do work on different planes and there is no sin for a poor man like myself to spend a month of his time in writing a tale of adventure.'[70] For many reasons, this outlook appealed to Bennett. Yet, at the end of 1898, it was not simply a matter of poverty. On 9 January the following year he admitted to the more fastidious Sturt that he was at the time 'actually earning ample for all purposes'. This was despite the fact that, in February 1898, he had moved from the shared Chelsea house to his own place at 9 Fulham Park Gardens which cost 'a hell of a lot to keep going in a generous way'.[71] Besides his salary from *Woman,* which was by then most probably somewhere between £300 and £400 a year, he had a regular income from contributions to the *Academy, Hearth and Home,* and *Woman* itself. In 1899, for instance, he earned just over £590 from 228 articles and stories.[72] 'Chronic poverty', then, seems at best to have been opportune overstatement.

As it turned out, his decision was motivated less by the desire for money than by an increasingly keen longing for a more independent life style. Soon after his welcome promotion to editor of *Woman* in November 1896, he began complaining about the added responsibilities it involved. On 9 December he noted: 'the office dogs me everywhere, night and day'.[73] Though he did not resign until late 1900, this sense of frustration persisted. His journal entry for 12 September 1898 continued:

To write popular fiction is offensive to me, but it is far more agreeable than being tied daily to an office editing a lady's paper; and perhaps it is less ignoble, and less of a strain on the conscience. To edit a lady's paper, even a relatively advanced one, is to foster conventionality and hinder progress once a week. Moreover I think that fiction will pay better, and in order to be happy I must have a fair supply of money.[74]

To Sturt, on 5 January 1899, he was more blunt: 'I am sick of editing *Woman,* & of being bound to go to a blasted office every day'.

I want to work when I feel inclined, & to travel more. I saw only one way of freeing myself of official ties, namely fiction. If other people can hit the popular taste & live on magazine & newspaper fiction, why not me?[75]

As he made clear later that month, he could not expect to earn a living from fiction if he continued to 'turn out psychological treatises like *A Man from the North*'.[76] True, he had been writing more profitable short stories since the beginning of his career, but they hardly represented a decent income. In 1894, the *Sun* paid him up to £1 1s for 1,500-word 'storyettes', which was the same rate as the *Humanitarian* had offered for 'Faust and Marguerite' and *Tit-Bits* for 'The Artist's Model' (1s for 71 words), while in 1895 the *Yellow Book* paid a relatively handsome £3 3s for the 2,700-word story 'A Letter Home' (1s for 43 words).[77] The seemingly more lucrative popular serials were, then, intended primarily to be a means of escaping the routines and pressures of editing, and, more positively, to provide an income that would make possible the independent country-house life style to which Phillpotts had also introduced him. As Drabble notes, and as some of Bennett's articles in *T. P.'s Weekly* testify, he was never a devotee of the growing cult of the simple life, with its plain-living, country-cottage ideals.[78] Yet, when a checklist of the 'foremost writers' in

Britain revealed that 'nearly all lived in the country' – by then Conrad was living in Kent, and James in Sussex – he did come to believe that a more dignified country house was an important accessory for the 'literary artist'.[79] And so, after visiting Phillpotts at his house in Torquay in February 1899, he reaffirmed his resolution to make serials the means by which to realize his 'desire to live in a large house in the country with plenty of servants, as he does, not working too hard, but working when and how one likes, at good rates'.[80]

The practical knowledge he had gained as an editor acquired new value when it came to putting his resolution into practice. While editing *Woman*, he discovered that serial fiction was 'sold and bought just like any other fancy goods': it had its 'wholesale houses, its commercial travellers – even its trusts and "corners"'.[81] As an editor, he did most of his business with the pioneer 'wholesale house', Tillotson's 'Fiction Bureau', the Bolton-based fiction syndicators who had been supplying the provincial and London press since the early 1870s. From them he bought 'important "names"', the 'names one sees on the title-pages of railway novels', at a 'moderate price': 'Christmas stories in March, and seaside fiction in December, and good solid Baring-Gould or Le Queux or L. T. Meade all the year round'.[82] Though he did not have a particularly high opinion of James Lever Tillotson (1875–1940) who took over the 'Bureau' in 1893 – privately he was struck 'by the man's perfect ignorance of what constitutes literature, and by the accord which exists between his own literary tastes and those of the baser portion of the general public' – he believed that his syndicate, and others like the Northern Newspaper Syndicate and the National Press Agency, performed a 'useful function'.[83] They generally sold editors the British or English serial rights to a story, which could be further restricted to a particular city, district, or region (with the price varying in a direct ratio to the size of the area served), and further classified as either primary or secondary (the former, being the rights to first publication, were more expensive). In this way, 'all editorial purses are suited, the syndicates reap much profit, and they are in a position to pay their authors, both tame and wild, a just emolument'.[84] As a potential Tillotson supplier, rather than customer, it was this last fact which most attracted him in 1898. In January, James Tillotson had let him in on what some of the major names were making:

Thomas Hardy is being outstripped by some of the younger men. He stands now only equal with H. G. Wells, at 12 guineas per thousand, which is also the price of the blood-and-thunder William Le Queux. Stanley Weyman, because of his large following in America, can only be bought at 16 to 18 guineas per thousand. Kipling stands solitary and terrible at £50 per thousand, £200 being his minimum for the shortest short story.[85]

These were, of course, the exceptions. At the same time Phillpotts was earning only just over £300 for a standard 60,000-word serial, or less than half what Wells, Hardy, and Le Queux were getting; and, as Bennett noted in 1903, the majority of aspirants could expect as little as £60, or, if lucky, £90, while serialists with a reputation generally earned up to £360.[86] It was no doubt this latter figure, and Phillpotts's earnings, that he had in mind when he thought of substituting his editorial salary with an income from serials.

Towards the end of October 1898, after testing the market with a few short stories in the popular mode, one of which described a passionate romance involving a secret society, intricate disguises, and a suicide, he laid aside the manuscript of what was to become *Anna of the Five Towns* (1902) and began *Love and Life*.[87] In letters he called it 'an uncompromising high-coloured blood & thunder sensational serial'. For a story of professional and romantic jealousy that contains multiple murders, a ghost, a train crash, and a shipwreck, that was fair enough. Though he found the writing difficult at first, by the fourth instalment he 'seemed suddenly to conquer the trick of the thing'. What pleased him most was the increased facility the act of writing seemed to induce. By 5 January 1899, he could boast to the disapproving Sturt: 'I believe I could fart sensational fiction now.'[88] When he eventually finished, on 23 January, he noted with less bravado:

I found the business, after I had got fairly into it, easy enough, and I rather enjoyed it. I could comfortably write 2,500 words in half a day.[89]

The final product took him a total of twenty-four half-days spread over three months to complete. Yet, as he learned on 19 January, it was not quite the sort of thing James Tillotson wanted. He had got the form right: it divided into twelve 5,000-word parts, each of which had the required 'curtain'. And he had also managed to say 'nothing against Trades Unionism', the syndicator's only political worry. But he got the setting and some of the narrative apparatus wrong. It was supposed to be set 'wholly in Great Britain & Ireland' and there was meant to be 'no supernaturalism'.[90] He had set it in London and Paris; and the main mystery, and so the armature of the plot, centres on the inexplicable torments inflicted on the heroine's suitors, who are, as it turns out, being harassed by the ghost of her possessive ex-lover. Tillotson was not too fussy, however. He offered to take it for £60, and, after Bennett asked for £80, he agreed to settle on £75.[91] The syndicate then sold what were most probably the primary serial rights to *Hearth and Home* where it eventually appeared, with illustrations by J. H. D. Bonnor, from 17 May to 2 August 1900. (It was published as a book entitled *The Ghost* in a substantially revised form by Chatto and Windus in 1907.) Though the 'lingering remains of an artistic conscience' prompted Bennett to use a pseudonym – he thought of calling himself 'Sampson Death' – it appeared, after Tillotson persuaded him against the idea, under the bold signature 'E. A. Bennett'.[92]

At the rate of 1s for 40 words, or just over £3 for half a day's work, his income from the debut serial was not inconsiderable – in half a day he earned more than he had in a week as an assistant editor four years earlier. Yet, despite his remark to Sturt that there were 'loftier heights yet to conquer' – he was inspired by the news that an unnamed woman writer could produce 40,000 words a week and make £3,000 a year – he found it difficult to keep his resolution to write only 'the sort of fiction that sells itself' for the rest of 1899, though he did produce a short 30,000-word serial entitled *The Gates of Wrath* that summer.[93] The following April, however, after being prompted by Colles who was then acting as his agent, he did think of trying to write a 40,000-word serial 'about the masses for the masses' for *Lloyd's Newspaper*. Cathing, the editor, was more discriminating than Tillotson. He was willing to accept anything that was 'good literature' (like Gissing, Colles reported, though not so 'pessimistic') so long as it did not contain anything about 'sexual relations'.[94] Though the deal would have given Bennett useful exposure in his home territory – the paper was then specially targeting the North and Midlands, and claimed to have a circulation of half a million there alone – for whatever reason the idea sadly never came to anything. Instead, that summer, just prior to his resignation from *Woman*, he began to work seriously on his second major serial, *The Grand Babylon Hotel*.

From the start, he intended it to be more ambitious than the first. Recalling the phenomenal impact of the mid-nineteenth-century French *feuilletoniste* Eugène Sue, whose works, like *Les Mystères de Paris*, had 'excited a nation by admirable sensationalism', he dreamed that this time he would have 'the whole of London preoccupied with [his] serial instead of cricket and politics', and that it would become a topic of discussion among 'dandiacal City youths' on the Underground. This time he excluded any element of the supernatural: it was to be 'of the earth earthly'. Then, as part of his plan to lavish every 'material splendour of modern life' on it, he chose to set the bulk of the action in an expensive West End hotel, comparable to the Savoy, and incidental scenes on a luxury yacht and in Ostende, the most accessible holiday resort on the Continent. Finally, to capture his audience's attention, he began it 'with a scene quite unique in the annals of syndicates': in the first instalment, the fashionable young American heroine affronts the hotel management and British society by rejecting the chef's set menu, which includes *Consommé Britannia* and *Saumon d'Ecosse*, and ordering beefsteak and a bottle of Bass instead; when the disdainful head waiter refuses her request, her millionaire father buys the hotel for £400,000. As it turned out, however, his careful planning resulted in one of his worst blunders. After producing the fifteen instalments in as many days, which admittedly left him feeling a 'wreck', he submitted the manuscript to Tillotsons, and in the subsequent negotiations, conducted this time by Philip Gibbs who took over as editor of the 'Fiction Bureau' in 1899, he made one of the 'greatest financial mistakes' of his career. When Gibbs offered him the same flat rate for the 70,000-word serial as he had been given for the first (£75), he understandably turned it down. Clearly eager to get a good story, Gibbs then took him to lunch and asked him to name his price. 'I ought to have known, with all my boasted knowledge of the world of business', Bennett later recalled, 'that syndicates do not invite almost unknown authors to lunch without excellent reason'.[95] He misjudged his position and apparently accepted £100 for the entire rights.[96] Though this was, as he claimed, a 'good price for me then' (1s for 35 words), it turned out to be a disastrous deal.[97]

Tillotsons sold the primary serial rights to the *Golden Penny*, a popular London-based national weekly issued by the proprietors of the *Graphic*, which then launched a vigorous publicity campaign. In the weeks leading up to publication, the editor targeted the all-important commuter readership and posted the following billboard in 800 railway stations:

HOTEL

MYSTERY!

- - - - - - - - - - -

DEEP INTRIGUES!!

STRANGE

DISAPPEARANCES!!

- - - - - - - - - -

THE BEEFSTEAK AND BASS

THAT COST £400,000!!

A Serial Story, so original, amusing, and thrilling that it is sure to create a sensation. Nothing like it has appeared since 'The Mystery of a Hansom Cab' made such a stir about fifteen years since. The author, Mr. E. A. Bennett, has certainly produced a most remarkable book.[98]

Bennett was impressed by this 'whirl of adjectives' and especially flattered by the allusion to Fergus Hume's bestselling mystery story which first appeared in 1888.[99] The editor also contracted Reginald Cleaver, who had done work for *Punch*, the *Graphic*, and the *Daily Graphic*, to illustrate each episode; and, finally, in the week before the serial began, the paper carried a publicity interview with the author and a short biographical sketch of the illustrator. After running 'with great éclat' in the *Golden Penny* from 2 February to 15 June 1901, it 'overran the provincial Press like a locust storm', and then went on to become a bestseller in book form.[100] Tillotsons sold the world book rights to Chatto and Windus for £80, and, when the volume appeared in 1902, it received critical praise from such authoritative reviews as the *Spectator* and the new *Times Literary Supplement*, and immediately went into a second edition.[101] By 1904 it had appeared in French, German, Italian, and Swedish, and, in Bennett's lifetime, it went on to sell over 50,000 hardback copies.[102] It was, in short, a 'boom', the profits of which, as Bennett sadly admitted, went mainly to the 'astute syndicate'.[103] According to Philip Gibbs, Tillotsons 'made quite a bit of money by spotting a new literary lion . . . before he knew his own value'.[104]

Contrary to Bennett's initial hopes, then, popular serials on their own did not provide a sustainable or even adequate alternative to editing. Yet the project he set himself at the end of 1898 did not end in failure. While he was breaking into the serial market, he was also exploring other, sometimes more profitable, sources of income, the most important of which was the theatre. Once again, he followed Phillpotts's lead. In February 1899, after Phillpotts mentioned he was earning up to £50 a year from 3,000-word one-act plays that took him a month to write, he began experimenting with dramatic duologues for private entertainment, and the following year he considered a career as a popular dramatist more seriously.[105] As he admitted from the start, his aim was 'strictly commercial': 'I wanted money in heaps, and I wanted advertisement for my books.'[106] Having earned £275 in 1900 for two plays that were never performed, by 1902 he claimed that a 20,000-word drawing-room melodrama, which he could invent, compose, and revise in three months, would bring him at least £200 (1s for 5 words) even if it was unsuccessful.[107] Though the theatre appeared to be the most lucrative option, he decided at the same time to enter the publishing world. In March 1900, he arranged to act as literary advisor for Pearsons, a job which he never enjoyed, but which brought him on average just over £50 extra a year.[108] It was these two new developments, combined with his career as a journalist, serialist, and novelist, that made it possible for him to leave *Woman* in September 1900, and, a month later, to move into Trinity Hall Farm in Bedfordshire, the long-desired country house. If his own record of his income for 1901, his first full year as an independent professional, is complete, it was not an easy transition. His recorded earnings for that year, mainly from Pearsons, Tillotsons, the *Academy*, and *Hearth and Home*, came to only £300, which was a substantial reduction on the previous year's unprecedented total of £620.[109] But by the following year the situation had improved significantly. His total income for 1902 was just over £800.[110] Though he was still four years away from reaching his early goal of 'fame and a thousand a year', he was now, as a bachelor, comfortably installed among the professional middle classes.[111]

The success of *Grand Babylon* made his name as a serialist, but as soon as it began to appear he considered abandoning the form altogether. He admitted in a letter of 21 February 1901:

I have now attained to the lordly eminence of declining commissions for serials. I hope not to do any more, but unless Julia [his theatre manager] sharpens up, I shall have to.[112]

Serials were now only a surety against any set-back in his career as a dramatist, and, a year later, having found plays 'more amusing and more remunerative', he pronounced himself 'a serialist no longer'.[113] This was premature. As it happened, making his mark in the theatrical field turned out to be more difficult than he had imagined – he had to wait until 1908 before he actually had a play produced – and so serials continued to form a significant part of his total literary output.[114] From 1902 to 1914, he produced nine serials (and one series of popular short stories), as against ten novels, three collections of short stories, and six plays. Yet, until 1906, it was still not clear how remunerative the serials really were. Between 1902 and 1904, his expected total income from a standard serial – that is, from British serial and book rights as well as translation rights – was around only £300 (1s for 10 words).[115] Of this, well over half was to be covered by the serial rights: at this stage, he was ambitiously demanding just under £190 for the British serial rights of a 60,000-word story (1s for 16 words).[116] As he discovered, however, most editors were unwilling to accept his rates. *T. P.'s Weekly* turned him down at the end of 1902 and again in 1904, and, when *To-Day* made an 'extremely depressing' offer for *Hugo*, his fifth serial, in April 1905, he decided he would not produce any more unless on commission.[117]

Then, in 1906, three factors changed his mind: collaboration, his agent's astute negotiations, and the American market. On 7 December 1905, he wrote to Pinker who had been his literary agent since 1900:

Phillpotts has got a great notion for a mystery story of 60,000 words, & he has asked me to collaborate with him in it some time next year . . . He has arrangements which enable him to make sure, in England & America, of at least £900 out of such a story, of which he did one last year. He offers me halves and personally guarantees me a minimum of £450. He will draft the entire book, & I shall write it.[118]

The money, even shared, was as inspiring as the tribute from the more established writer. His sixth serial, *The City of Pleasure*, which he wrote in the spring of 1905, had been his most profitable so far. In competition with the Northern Newspaper Syndicate, Tillotsons had increased their initial offer of £175 for the serial rights to £200, and, though he expected the usual £75 advance from Chatto and Windus, they eventually bought the book rights outright for £200 (in all 1s for 7.5 words).[119] Now it appeared that even his half-share in the new serial, *The Sinews of War*, would bring him just over 1s for 7 words. As it turned out, this was a massive underestimate. When the initial negotiations with the *Tribune* fell through, Pinker sold the British serial rights to *T. P.'s Weekly* for an unprecedented price. Though Bennett was extremely unhappy about the editor's demand that, for the price, the story should be 100,000 words – they eventually settled on a compromise – he was pleased the deal went through.[120] He had been writing articles and reviews for the popular literary weekly since its inception in 1902, and, as we have seen, he had from the start also been trying to negotiate with its editors for a serial. They had turned him down in late 1902; and in July 1904, when he tried to sell them the rights to *Hugo*, the deal fell through once again. As usual rates were the main issue, but the chief editor, T. P. O'Connor, also objected to a *risqué* scene in which the unaccompanied heroine goes to visit her prospective fiancé in his flat in order to prevent him from committing suicide.[121] When the editors were dragging their feet during the final stage of the negotiations for *Sinews*, Phillpotts wrote loftily to Pinker:

I don't think *T. P.'s* quite know their company, but, as Bennett is specially anxious for this show, we'll say £450, if they will rise to that. Won't consider less.[122]

After some skilful negotiations on Pinker's part, they agreed, and in its final form the contract, as confirmed on 19 January, was for an 80,000-word mystery story in twenty instalments, at £450 (or 1s for 9 words), with the first three instalments to be delivered by 20 February.[123] Pinker then made arrangements for T. Werner Laurie to publish the book version in Britain, and Curtis Brown, then Phillpotts's agent, did the same for serial and book publication in America.[124] With all these contracts in the offing, and another for the Tauchnitz edition, the authors now expected to make £1,000 a piece; though, as it appears Brown could sell only the American *book* rights to McClure, Phillips of New York, Bennett noted on 18 June that his total earnings had by then come to £775.[125] At this point, in other words, they were assured of at least £1,550 in all, or just over 1s for 3 words, with the British serial rights representing only a third of the total.[126]

Though the earnings were shared equally, the advantages were all on Phillpotts's side. According to Bennett, his collaborator sketched the 'scenario' (basic plot and cast of characters) in four days which meant he was ultimately going to get 'about £250 a day for his trouble'. In the end, Phillpotts did write 'one or two descriptions of scenery', just as Bennett contributed one element to the plot – he introduced the Russo-Japanese war at the end – but by far the greater share of the work was still Bennett's.[127] Even so, his earnings, calculated at a weekly rate, were still substantial. Writing in Paris, where he had moved to in March 1903, he produced the first instalment of 4,000 words in two days, and then worked steadily, finishing half by 1 March, and the whole thing by 7 April. In all it took him ten weeks to complete, at an average rate of 8,000 words and just over £77 a week. When half was done, he noted modestly: 'I have kept my contract with myself, and the stuff is good of its kind; but I am slightly overworking.'[128] Throughout the process, Phillpotts, who was at the time roughing it at the Hotel de la Terrasse in Cannes, wisely kept him well-fuelled with praise. On 23 February, after seeing the first three instalments, he admitted to being slightly uneasy about the many 'queer names': the heroine is called Giralda, and other characters include Oxwich, Varcoe, Sir Anthony Didring, Mrs Upottery, and Captain Pollexfen:

You have woven such a marvellous air of vraisemblance over the narrative & made everybody in it so intensely alive & real that names like those you have chosen seem not worth while. But I admit they grow upon one.

This was his only quibble. For the most part the letter contained effusive compliments. He compared the plot, characters, and style to Stevenson; and assured his co-author that he 'could equal Gaboriau at a crime story & leave our own Conan Doyle & Co hopelessly & utterly in the rear'. He was especially impressed by Bennett's ability – he called it his 'real Gaboriau instinct' – to 'weave character into a sensational story' and so, unlike most serialists, avoid reducing the narrative to mere incident. Of all the characters, Coco, the pidgin-speaking West Indian sailor, who remains devoted to his master, the murder victim, and eventually kills the villain and himself, struck him as the most apt: 'nothing could be truer – so far as I know the niggers.' '*The Sinews of War*', he concluded, 'is Art & has just as much human nature in it as any Gaboriau'.[129]

At the same time, *T. P.'s Weekly* announced their 'new and intensely interesting Serial Story':

What kind of story is the 'Sinews of War'?

Briefly, it is a story of today; it is laid on land and sea; it deals with men and money; it has a strong love interest; and it is full of action and character.

So up-to-date is the 'Sinews of War' that it opens with certain happenings in Kingsway, the great new road from Holborn to the Strand, recently opened by King Edward VII.[130]

As the copy-writer carefully insisted, it was topical, of special interest to London readers, and appealing to both men and women. It ran from 2 March to 13 July 1906, and, as Pinker reported to Bennett, it was an immediate success.[131] The same could not be said of the book which appeared in November. Though the *Spectator* called it a 'first-class detective story', and thought it 'extremely well done', most other leading reviews shared the opinion of *Bookman* which called it 'a tale of crime and mystery, so frankly and unblushingly impossible that it defies all criticism'.[132] As the *Athenaeum* astutely added, it even failed to live up to this generic classification which the pre-publication billing had also rashly assumed to be accurate. The publisher's advertisement read:

A romance of love and strange crime, moving with breathless speed through scenes as vivid as a dream. The book completely conquers and subdues the reader in its interest. Nothing will he allow to interrupt him. HE SIMPLY MUST LEARN THE GUILTY PERSON. And until at the very end that secret is won a cannon could not distract his attention.[133]

The *Athenaeum* soberly pointed out that 'halfway through the book the authors reveal their mystery, which is disappointing, and thenceforward we are dependent upon the graphic narration of incident'.[134] It was, the *Academy* concluded, 'a failure', but the kind of failure which, 'we surmise, took very little time to perpetrate, and paid exceedingly well'.[135] While this was true for the authors, it was not the case for the book publishers. Demonstrating that popular fiction did not necessarily benefit all those involved in the publication process, Werner Laurie claimed that, with the dismal sales, they lost £150 on the book.[136]

The success of *Sinews*, at least as far as its authors were concerned, had two important consequences for Bennett. First, at the end of 1906, he was able to record that he had reached his initial goal of a thousand a year for the first time. His receipts, which included £900 from Pinker (mainly from *Sinews*) and £138 12s from *T. P.'s Weekly* (mainly for his thirty-two *Savoir-Vivre Papers*), amounted to £1,136 6s 10d, though he noted that his total earnings for the year were about £1,350.[137] Second, his income from the story convinced him that serials continued to be worth writing. Though his second and last collaboration with Phillpotts, entitled *The Statue* (1908), was not as successful as the first – it was never placed serially, and disputes over the contract ended their amicable relations – he used it to justify his continued commitment to the genre.[138] When Pinker attempted to persuade him to abandon his serial-writing in 1907, he argued that, even if the serials failed, as *The Statue* had done, they could still bring him £500 for five weeks' work. As he insisted a year later when Chapman and Hall advanced only £150 for the 200,000-word *Old Wives' Tale*, which took him eight months to produce, 'it is a good thing for me that I can work very quickly indeed on smaller things'. By 1911, *Harper's* were offering him £3,000 for the serial rights and a further £1,000 advance on royalties for one of these 'smaller things' – *The Price of Love* – and a year later Bennett 'staggered' himself by calculating that his minimum earnings from book and serial rights for 1912 would be £11,000.[139] His actual earnings amounted to £16,000, and that year he bought the *Velsa*, a large yacht with cabins for guests, a Cunard-style bedroom, a saloon, a piano, and an encyclopaedia, for £550, as well as a country house in Thorpe-le-Soken, Essex.[140]

III

Bennett was not unique in choosing to lead a double life as a profiteering serialist and an avant-garde literary novelist. Many writers in similar circumstances did the same. Some, like Phillpotts, discreetly used pseudonyms; while others, like Arthur Morrison, were candid but low-key. What made Bennett unusual was that he made his private decision part of a public offensive against the literary purists of the 1890s. As an outspoken contributor to the *Academy* and then to the *New Age* he transformed his teasing exchanges with Sturt into a larger cultural debate and established himself as the literary professional's *agent provocateur*. Among the various energies that drove him to take this adversarial line, his prickly sense of himself as an outsider to the metropolitan literary establishment, and particularly his perception of himself as a robustly self-sufficient man from the north, played a prominent part. Writing of his family in a journal entry for 9 December 1896, he noted revealingly: 'We are of the

North, incredibly, ruthlessly independent; and eager to say "Damn you" to all the deities at the least hint of condescension.'[141]

The *Academy* he joined in 1896 was not quite what it had been. Originally founded in 1869 by the Oxford don, Charles Appleton, it had been designed for university men, and it was largely produced by them. It was sub-titled *A Monthly Record of Literature, Learning, Science and Art.* In 1896, however, it was purchased by John Morgan Richards, a wealthy American patent-medicine merchant, who installed the young professional journalist and art critic, C. Lewis Hind, as editor.[142] The Fabian, Wells, saw the satirical side of this transaction. In *Tono-Bungay*, Edward Ponderevo, his own patent-medicine tycoon, hijacks the *Sacred Grove*, 'that representative organ of British intellectual culture', as part of a relentless campaign to promote his cure-all products. The result, according to George Ponderevo, the tycoon's nephew and the acerbic narrator of the story, is a bizarre weekly remarkable for the unhappy disparity between the 'aggressive brilliance' of its advertizing and the 'quiet conservatism' of its contents and editorial tone. Appearing on the cover alongside the fictional list of contents, which includes 'A Hitherto Unpublished Letter from Walter Pater' and 'The Dignity of Letters', are advertisements for '23', Uncle Ponderevo's new American liver pills. For George, this distasteful blend affords a clear political lesson: it illustrates the 'hopeless condition' of a country which leaves its literary criticism 'entirely to private enterprise and open to the advances of any purchaser'.[143] Historically, the effect of the takeover was, in fact, more dramatic than Wells allowed. For one thing, under its new management, the review as a whole became far more populist than Ponderevo's *Sacred Grove*. Seeking a broader appeal, and responding to the competition from new literary reviews like *Bookman* (1891) – as Keating points out, William Robertson Nicoll's more progressive monthly soon gave the older weeklies like the *Athenaeum* (1828) and the *Academy* an 'irretrievably out-of-date' appearance – Hind now changed the title to *The Academy: A Weekly Review of Literature and Life*, and introduced literary prize competitions for readers, lists of the bestselling books in various English cities, as well as literary awards for the 'Crowned' books of each year.[144] He also gathered round him a like-minded staff of contributors, including E. V. Lucas, Wilfred Whitten, and Bennett.[145] With this staff, and under Hind's regime, which lasted until 1903, the review continued to be aimed mainly at metropolitan literary circles, but it was now more lively, more comprehensive, and at times more combative than it had ever been.

Hind invited Bennett to join his new staff after spotting some of his reviews in *Woman*. No doubt these were the articles on literature, theatre, and the arts Bennett later described as 'so advanced' that they might have ruined the paper 'had they been read'.[146] While the bulk of the weekly was taken up with paragraphs of society gossip, advice on fashion, servants and household management, and serials with titles like *The Lost Prima Donna*, as 'Barbara' in the regular 'Book Chat' column, Bennett encouraged readers to keep up with the avant-garde fiction in Henley's *New Review* and Lane's *Yellow Book*.[147] Hind liked the novelty of this and Bennett's 'sledge-hammer manner'. He was also more than impressed by his efficiency as a contributor: he called him 'that dynamo' and admitted to having never altered a word in his proofs. Encouraged by his new editor, Bennett reinvented himself for the refashioned *Academy*. Whereas he had been the champion of avant-garde culture in *Woman*, a penny weekly, he now became a strident populist in the sixpenny review, and, according to Hind, 'the most valuable member of the staff'.[148] Besides the book reviews, which he did regularly from 1896 to 1902, he also contributed two extended series, both of which specifically targeted literary purists. The first was a series of twenty 'Enquiries' which appeared irregularly from 1 July 1899 to 4 May 1901 – most were subsequently collected in *Fame and Fiction: An Enquiry into Certain Popularities* (1901). Though it included laudatory discussions of the likes of George Gissing, Turgenev, and George Moore, some of Bennett's own literary idols, its chief concern was with the purists' attitudes to such bestsellers of the day as Silas Hocking, Marie Corelli, and Mary Cholmondeley. The second series had the same general aim, though the issues were more specific. As he later recalled, Hind commissioned the autobiographical essays that eventually formed *The Truth About an Author* as a 'sensational serial', with the intention of enlivening the review and causing a commotion in London's literary circles. Like the first book edition, the serial, which ran from 3 May to 2 August 1902, was published anonymously partly from 'discretion' and partly to keep the 'London world of letters' guessing. Once again Bennett delighted in the task: 'I took a malicious and frigid pleasure, as I always do, in setting down facts which are opposed to accepted sentimental falsities'.[149] The result was as much a spirited, and faithful, chronicle of a writer's development – it covered Bennett's life from the early 1870s to 1901 – as it was a studiedly outrageous narrative of a maverick's progress.

He opened the first series with a specially challenging piece on Silas Hocking, the Methodist minister turned bestselling novelist. Having ascertained from Frederick Warne that by July 1899 Hocking had sold over a million copies of his novels, which included *Her Benny* (1879), *Ivy* (1881), *For Abigail* (1888), *God's Outcast* (1898), and *The Day of Recompense* (1899), he announced that this astounding fact enshrined 'a dazzling and marvellous secret'. Hocking's achievement, Bennett argued, was that he had managed to appeal to a resistant readership. His enormous following was drawn not from the metropolis, but from the Nonconformist 'trading and industrial classes' of the Midlands and the North whose general attitude to literature was, Bennett claimed from experience, 'at once timid, antagonistic, and resentful'. With his admirable 'tact', however, Hocking had won them over. The trouble was that his success was bound up with a regrettable strain of plodding didacticism in his work. In *The Day of Recompense*, Bennett noted with dismay, 'the intellect and the intelligence are treated as invalids, waited on hand and foot'. This was the perspective Bennett maintained throughout the series: he granted the bestsellers a measure of legitimacy by judging them worthy of an uncondescending critical evaluation. For the purists of the 1890s, this critical strategy was controversial enough. Yet Bennett was not willing to leave it at that. Taking a more direct approach, he also made the purists' anti-populist discourse central to his attack by talking about specific readerships, rather than the 'masses', and by challenging their Henleyite prejudices against popular authors. As he repeatedly insisted, bestselling authors represented an engaging cultural phenomenon precisely because so few were calculating profiteers. Hocking's 'tact', for instance, was not 'acquired': he succeeded simply because he was 'the Methodist million made vocal'. 'I have no doubt', Bennett added provocatively, 'that he expresses himself in these books of his as sincerely as any Meredith or Henry James who has sacrificed popularity to the artistic conscience'.[150] Similarly, when it came to the enormous success of Mary Cholmondeley's *Red Pottage* (1899) – it sold 12,000 copies in its first week with Mudie's alone taking 2,000 – he refused to 'utter a jeremiad upon the decadence of taste' on the grounds that it would be 'absurd'. Melodramatic bestsellers, like Cholmondeley's, were, in his view, a 'legitimate form of literary art' which occupied only a particular sector of a complex market, a sector characterized by large sales, a rapid turnover, and quick but generally brief popularity.[151]

Bestsellers were not the only topic of his series, however. He also turned his attention to the new popular magazine industry of the 1890s, and here his revisionist attack on purist dogma was more direct:

It is a common saying of literary reactionaries that this is an era of 'bits', 'cuts', and 'snippets', that the taste of the reading public is fatally impaired, and that the golden ages which began with Chaucer are for ever closed. Our bookstalls (they lament) 'groan' with 'trash' that can appeal only to the half-instructed, while serious productions of an improving and solid nature ask in vain for attention.

Challenging this indictment, he argued that the 'praisers of times past' had overlooked two important phenomena, namely, the 'Education Act of 1870 and the growth of commercial enterprise'. The former, he claimed, had 'created a new reading public' which, not surprisingly, 'had no tradition of self-culture by means of books'. Though it found itself with the 'mechanical power to read', this new public had 'neither the habit of reading nor the disciplined intellect which are both necessary to render that mechanical power effective'. This was the need innovative entrepreneurs, like George Newnes, had set out to meet with papers like *Tit-Bits* which had been welcomed not only by the 'public of the Education Act', but by 'a large section of the older public which had hitherto sought fruitlessly for what it wanted'. These 'two masses' constituted a market as 'gloriously dazzling to the commercial instinct' as India was to the Lancashire industrialists. In the process of discovering these new markets, Newnes had also re-defined the relationship between producers and consumers. He saw that the 'reproach against England that the British merchant always seeks to dictate to the buyer what he shall buy' applied 'in a peculiar degree to English journalism'. Unlike the 'old autocrats of *Maga* and *Cornhill*', who apparently offered readers what they *ought* to want, Newnes had 'elevated' *his* readers 'to a throne' and studied their needs 'as patiently and thoroughly as a German manufacturer'.[152] This new commercial practice was no less evident in the market for sixpenny illustrated monthlies which Newnes had revolutionized with the *Strand* (1891).[153] For Bennett, these developments did not prove that 'the general taste had declined', but rather that the magazines were now its 'truer mirror'. While he was once again not prepared to deny that the reader of popular magazines was usually a 'frail creature' who required undemanding reading, or that the magazines themselves could, if judged by an 'absolute standard', be a 'compact of offence to nostrils delicate enough to appreciate the virtues of comeliness, quietude, and austerity in art and culture', he was also unwilling to leave it at that. 'Most questions are questions of degree', he argued.

Is it not better that the man in the street, a creature scorned but nevertheless admirably unaffected, should read an English sixpenny magazine than that he should read, say, the Sunday edition of the *New York Journal*? And is it not better that he should read the Sunday edition of the *New York Journal* than he should read nothing?

Indeed, in the end, the 'crudest excitement of the imaginative faculty is to be preferred to a swinish preoccupation with gross physical existence'. For this reason, he concluded, the purists could do well to cast off the 'mere dandyism of art' and to recognize in the bestsellers and the popular magazines the 'germ of a tremendous movement'.[154]

In the more polemical second series *The Truth About an Author*, where special effects generally came before the whole truth, he focused more narrowly on the purists' self-image and capitalized on his decision to write serials. In keeping with the archly anti-purist image the autobiography was intended to project – there is a more than passing resemblance between its implied author and the audacious, money-making hero Bennett created in *The Card* (1911) – he now claimed to have 'entered into a compact' with himself to 'keep the novel-form unsullied for the pure exercise of the artist in me':

What became of this high compact? I merely ignored it. I tore it up and it was forgotten, the instant I saw a chance of earning the money of shame. I devised excuses, of course. I said that my drawing-room wanted new furniture; I said that I might lift the sensational serial to a higher plane, thus serving the cause of art; I said – I don't know what I said, all to my conscience.

As this final evasion suggests, the private realities of his decision were, in this public context, less important than the defiant posture his decision enabled him to command: 'I, apprentice of Flaubert et Cie, stood forth to the universe as a sensation-monger.' The point was to shock, but he was also careful to draw distinctions. If he knowingly confessed to 'have never once produced any literary work without a preliminary incentive quite other than the incentive of ebullient imagination', he also insisted that 'when I am working on my own initiative, for the sole advancement of my artistic reputation, I ignore finance and think of glory alone'. On this occasion, his targets were the Henleyite proponents of the cult of genius – the inhuman 'geniuses with a mania for posterity' – but, as he later admitted in the *Evening Standard*, the literary purists were not the only ones to outlaw 'commercialism'.[155] The reading public itself seemed equally committed to a Romantic image of the unworldly artist which had been revitalized in the 1890s by such popular works as George du Maurier's *Trilby* (1894), Puccini's *La Bohème* (1896), and, to some extent, in the Sherlock Holmes stories.[156] By the 1920s, however, he was happy to goad everyone who believed 'This "Bosh" About Art For Art's Sake'.[157]

Money was not the only contentious issue, however. As he announced in *The Author's Craft* (1914), the 'same dilettante spirit which refuses to see the connection between art and money has also a tendency to repudiate the world of men at large, as being unfit for the habitation of artists'.[158] Recalling the brief lives of 'exotic periodicals' like the *Yellow Book* (1894–7), the *Savoy* (1896), the *Dial* (1889–1897), the *Anglo-Saxon* (1899–1901) and the *Neolith* (1907–08) – he might well have included the slightly less exotic *New Review* – he warned of the dangers underlying 'the inevitable tendency to disdain the public, and to appeal only to artists', and argued that 'artists, like washerwomen, cannot live on one another'.[159] By this stage he had left behind the avant-garde newcomer who had eagerly contributed to the *Yellow Book*, and written *A Man from the North* primarily for 'fellow artists'. The professional writer, he now urged, should 'contrive while pleasing himself to please the public, or *a* public'.[160] This argument about the scope of the writer's 'legitimate' public served his purposes in two ways. It justified his willingness to oblige magazine readers who wanted 'love, beauty, luxury, adventure, thrills, heroism, simply and perhaps crudely presented, in its literature' on the grounds that sometimes 'our chief purpose in reading magazines is not to enlarge our minds and to save our souls, but to kill time'.[161] It also underwrote his responsiveness, as a literary novelist, to the book-reading public. Though he went on to produce novels, like *The Old Wives' Tale*, which contained elements he knew would 'shock the prudes', such as the young provincial heroine's elopement or the *Yellow Book*-style scenes in Paris with the old prostitute Madame Foucault, he came to believe that even avant-garde novelists should 'mingle with the public'.[162] Not that he had any illusions about the frustrations this might involve. Writing in the *New Age* in 1909, he acknowledged that the chief purchasers of his novels were the circulating libraries which included Mudie's, the *Times* Book Club, and W. H. Smith's. Their patrons, he guessed, came mostly from the 375,000 income-tax payers of 1908 who represented an estimated one million members of the 'prosperous' middle class. He recognized a much vaster 'potential public' in the lower-middle class, but he thought the 'great majority of my readers must be somewhere in this million'. Characterized by political conservatism, 'temperamental dullness', and a lofty sense of their own social superiority, these readers were simply 'the enemies of art and progress'.[163] But they were also undeniably part of the literary field, he claimed, and, for the avant-garde novelist, they were 'a great actuality, like war'. This made him a reluctant advocate of pragmatic self-censorship.

The sagacious artist will respect basic national prejudices. For example, no first-class English novelist or dramatist would dream of allowing to his pen the freedom in treating sexual phenomena which Continental writers enjoy as a matter of course. The British public is admittedly wrong on this important point – hypocritical, illogical and absurd. But what would you?[164]

This did not prevent him from denouncing these prejudices as a critic, or defending more aggressively controversial authors like Wells, George Moore, Lawrence, and Joyce.[165] As a 'wily' novelist, however, he felt the need to temper his avant-garde French tastes, and his keen (but private) interest in sexuality, to keep his novels in print and on local 'library counters'.[166]

This controversial view of the writer's position in the literary field created a well-documented tradition of indignation among purists. As Drabble and Carey have recorded, Bennett was all too readily made into a useful foil against which such exclusive modernists as Ezra Pound, Virginia Woolf, Wyndham Lewis, Clive Bell, and T. S. Eliot could define their own emergent positions in the field.[167] Yet, as the critical reception of *The Truth About an Author* makes clear, the modernists were pre-empted by the purists of the 1890s. Though Bennett recalled that the success of the serial was 'terrific – among about a hundred people' (Wells, for one, thought particularly highly of it) – most 'respectable and dignified organs' were 'embittered' by it.[168] The *Athenaeum* was alarmed by its 'unblushing pages', and *Blackwood's*, with the assistance of the 1890s most eloquent literary reactionary, Charles Whibley, took the bait and issued a high-toned counterblast.[169] Though Whibley acknowledged its humorous intention, in his view it none the less demonstrated 'to what a pass of ignominy "authorship" has come, that such a book as this should have been written even in jest'. According to his alarmist reading, it reduced authorship to 'a trade like any other' and plainly asserted that 'only one end justifies its pursuit – money'. Worse still, the author's claim about not wishing to be paid under ten shillings an hour for 'piecework', suggested 'a brand-new trades union, with secretaries, blacklegs, and pickets complete'. Recalling the grand old days when 'Lockhart stung in "The Quarterly" and Jeffrey thundered in "The Edinburgh"', he concluded:

In those days the few books which got into print were conned at leisure. Now the syndicates and agents contrive that every one who can hold a pen shall write a novel, and send it, bad spelling and all, to the publishers. Of course the older fashion was better, and, alas! we shall never return to it. But is it too much to hope that the next time an 'author' condescends to enlighten the people concerning his craft, he will rise, at least for a page or two, above the till?[170]

Not unexpectedly, the *Author*, the official publication of the Society of Authors, called it an 'admirable piece of invective', which was useful and instructive unlike the many 'silly and serious guides that profess to teach the literary art', and it praised the author for being 'one of that admirable and daily increasing class which frankly, with no aesthetic pretensions to the contrary, provides sustenance for the melodramatic appetite of the English reader'.[171]

IV

Yet Bennett was not quite the ally the *Author* made him out to be, nor was he simply the populist whose career amounted to what Carey has called 'a systematic dismemberment of the intellectuals' case against the masses'.[172] This is not simply because he was less concerned about the intelligentsia's general social prejudices than he was about the purists' position in the literary field, but because he was also equally antagonistic to the masses' anti-intellectualism. Signs of this more complex set of attitudes were already present in his contributions to *Woman*, but it was once he began to write regularly for *T. P.'s Weekly* that he showed himself to be neither a populist nor an elitist, but a maverick committed to revolutionizing the literary field. At the end of 1902, in an effort to concentrate more fully on his literary novels, he cancelled his contracts with both *Hearth and Home* and the *Academy*. As a journalist, he continued writing only for T. P. O'Connor's new penny paper which he had joined, along with Wilfred Whitten, another emigrant from Hind's *Academy*, at its inception on 14 November 1902. Though his declared reason for his loyalty was that O'Connor paid well – Bennett had left the *Academy* in part because of a pay dispute – his interest in the new paper no doubt went beyond money.[173] After all, it embodied many of his most cherished convictions. It was designed primarily to educate the new generation of readers which had, he claimed, 'no tradition of self-culture by means of books' and to carry out his call, first expressed in the *Academy*, for the democratization of culture.[174] O'Connor, who was always as much an English Radical journalist as he was an Irish Nationalist MP, saw the new venture as an extension of his reformist ambitions. As a pioneer of the 'New Journalism' in the late 1880s, and the founding editor of the half-penny evening *Star* (1888), the *Sunday Sun* (1891), and the *Sun* (1893), he had long been a political advocate of the new democracy. Yet, from the start, he understood this in broader cultural terms as well. In an attempt to go beyond the preoccupation with 'mere politics' shared by most metropolitan dailies, and following the well-established practice of the provincial press, he promised readers of the *Star* he would occasionally publish 'a short, dramatic, and picturesque tale'.[175] While,

95

in the *Sun*, he went some way towards fulfilling his ambition 'to bring literature to journalism'. Along with two columns of society and celebrity news, which he insisted would be 'genial, impartial and kindly', the front page of each issue included a 'good short story' which appealed to him 'as a fine piece of literary work – as a human document – as something that suggests a moral or draws a noble picture'.[176] Among those stories that met his standards in 1893 and 1894 were seven of Bennett's early efforts, some of which described the difficult lives of ambitious artists, while others satirized the 'New Women' (not especially gently). Justifying this literary element of his policy, O'Connor remarked: 'I have never seen any good reason why the daily journal should not administer to that desire for good literature – whether in fiction or criticism or essay – which is now universal in the first School-Board-taught generation of Englishmen and Englishwomen.'[177] His interest in this new audience and its media remained with him throughout his career. He went on to establish other popular periodicals, including *M. A. P.: A Popular Penny Weekly of Pleasant Gossip, Personal Portraits, and Social News* (1898), *P. T. O.* (1906), and *T. P.'s Magazine* (1910); in 1907 he issued a reprint series of popular novels with Hodder and Stoughton entitled 'T. P.'s Sixpennies'; and in 1917 he became the first president of the Board of Film Censors.

The principal idea behind *T. P.'s Weekly* which, he claimed, 'had been haunting [his] imagination for years', was to bring 'to many thousands a love of letters'.[178] This consciously elevated aim – note that key word 'letters' – did not make him a democratic literary purist, however. True, he rejected the 'old-fashioned Puritan' idea, cherished by his parent's generation, that 'novel-reading was perilous to the young'. But he simply replaced religious condemnation with moral affirmation. 'To others I wish to teach the lesson I myself have learned – that in all moments of life, even the blackest, literature is the Consoler.'[179] He had learned this, he pointed out, from reading George Eliot when he was an impoverished young Irish provincial trying to make his way as a journalist in London. After the paper's first year, however, he emerged as a less rhapsodic Samuel Smiles of Edwardian self-culture:

My ideal is to make a paper to be regarded by every parent in the country as a necessary complement to the education of his boy and girl . . . and that it may, at the same time, represent to the adult lover of letters a constant and close tie between him and the thought and expression of his day and generation.[180]

In 1909, this same ideal led him to found, allegedly on the appeal of his readers, the '*T. P.'s Weekly* Correspondence College', an educational scheme, offering courses in writing, reasoning, business, art and French, designed primarily for school-leavers and dedicated to the cause of 'self-culture'.[181] Given these aims, Keating's claim that the paper represented the 'chatty' mood of literary criticism at the turn of the century – as compared to the 'austere' *Times Literary Supplement* (1902) and the 'belletristic' *Bookman* (1891) – misses the mark.[182] Though a comparison with the *TLS* in particular is valid –

the papers represent two divergent attitudes to the rise of 'mass culture', the one exclusive and defensive, the other inclusive and educative – it is clear O'Connor did not intend his paper to keep such company. Rather, it was meant to be a more literary and instructive version of *Tit-Bits, Answers,* or *Pearson's Weekly*. Though it never matched their massive circulation – at best it sold between 120,000 and 175,000 copies a week (at least four times less than *Tit-Bits*) – it reached an estimated half a million readers, chiefly among the culturally aspiring urban working- and lower-middle-classes.[183] It was also used as a teaching-aid in schools. As Bennett put it in his survey of the periodical market in 1903, it appealed 'to a slightly higher order of intelligence than the *Tit-Bits* class' and contained 'rather superior' fiction.[184] Besides regular book reviews, it included columns like 'Cameos from the Classics' (including extracts from Byron, Carlyle, Scott, Wordsworth, Shelley, Browning, De Quincey, Plutarch, Keats, Dickens, Emerson, and Poe), as well as serials and short stories by the likes of Bennett, Haggard, Conrad, Gissing, Jack London, Katherine Tynan, Edwin Pugh, and Ernest Rhys. And, as O'Connor liked to advertise, it came with recommendations from Wells, Hardy, Meredith, Phillpotts, W. M. Rossetti, and A. T. Quiller-Couch. Its favourable reception convinced him that 'the education, the refinement, and the readiness for higher intellectual things among the masses' had reached a point few but the most acute observers had realized.[185]

As was the case with the Hind's *Academy*, Bennett proved to be O'Connor's greatest asset. This time he emerged as the *arriviste* among the aspirants, presenting himself, with a self-mocking glance at Grant Allen's controversial novel *The Woman Who Did* (1895), as 'The Man Who Does', a master of cultural *savoir-faire*. In what turned out to be his seven-year career with the paper, he ranged widely in a total of 162 signed articles which offered practical advice to young provincials trying to make their way in London; hints to city clerks on how to get a cheap lunch; ideas about how to conduct oneself in the company of modern women; attacks on 'superior people' who scorned halfpenny papers or popular novels and who espoused separatist, vegetarian, country-cottage ideals; criticisms of the intellectual limitations and lack of realism of popular British magazines; as well as tips on marriage, on how to bring-up children more liberally, and on spending holidays in Belgium.[186] Yet, from the start, two themes, both central to O'Connor's enterprise, dominated this miscellaneous assortment: self-improvement and self-culture. They recurred frequently in the early series, and then formed the basis of two complete features on their own: self-improvement in the *Human Machine* series (20 March–3 July 1908), and self-culture in *Literary Taste: How to Form it* (2 October 1908–15 January 1909).[187] As both concerns proved to be of special interest to O'Connor's readership, Bennett rapidly established himself as the paper's most popular and most frequently discussed contributor.

As the champion of self-improvement, he took as his model the bodybuilder and late-Victorian expert in 'Curative Physical Culture', Eugen Sandow, whose health and exercise programmes were regularly advertised in *T. P.'s Weekly*, and presented himself as a 'Sandow of the brain' offering instruction in 'mental efficiency' and 'mind callisthenics'.[188] He always insisted that self-improvement was more important than self-culture. In the *Human Machine* series, he remarked that 'a large amount of what is known as self-improvement is simply self-indulgence', and compared those who were exclusively preoccupied with their literary tastes to an 'automobilist' who worried only about the gleam of his motor-car's 'acetylene lamps'.[189] Earlier he had told anxiously aspiring clerks that 'there are more important things in life than literature'.[190] Yet, if self-culture did not necessarily entail self-improvement, it did comprise one of the finest 'embroideries' of life.[191] At times this simply meant that reading literature was one of the more agreeable forms of leisure. Some literature, he willingly conceded, was simply 'a pastime, like golf, only a better one.' Though he claimed to 'take reading seriously', he emphasized this point as he was 'not one of those who speak of it with bated breath'. In the same way, he advised the 'apprentice to reading' to avoid the 'assumption of a too serious "pose" in regard to literature' on the grounds that 'his taste is *his* taste, and he has no right to scorn it'.[192] Tolerance did not entail relativism, however. A certain class of literature, he always insisted, was the '*sine qua non* of complete living'.[193] This included works by Gogol, Dostoyevsky, Tolstoy, and Turgenev; Balzac, Sand, Flaubert, Stendhal, Hugo, and Dumas; Meredith, Hardy, Conrad, Kipling, James, George Moore, Arthur Morrison, Phillpotts, and Wells; as well as the British 'classics'.[194] Whereas he had argued in defence of bestsellers in the *Academy*, he emerged in *T. P.'s Weekly* as a no less ardent champion of this cosmopolitan canon in an attempt to overcome the attitudes of 'fear', 'distrust', or earnest dutifulness the 'average decent person' had towards it. He presented himself as a mediator between the 'passionate few', whose tastes and enthusiasms, he insisted, alone determined which texts belonged in the canon, and the 'majority' who at best enjoyed a 'rattling good story' in the *Strand Magazine* or 'newish fiction', and at worst appreciated only gross 'artistic pleasures' comparable to the 'joy of Worcester Sauce on the palate'.[195]

In this role, he spent much of his time giving practical advice to the Leonard Basts of Edwardian England – young, urban, lower-middle-class readers whose annual salary of £120 left only £4 for literature – on how to make major literature, and books in general, part of their everyday lives.[196] He made suggestions about how to form book clubs; offered hints on how to store and shelve books; instructed potential book-buyers about rare editions and the value of such physical details as bindings, paper quality, and publisher's imprints; pointed out the bargains that could be got from East End book-barrows or Mudie's and Smith's secondhand catalogues; and, most notably, gave a detailed and itemized account of how a respectable library of 228

British classics from Chaucer to Gissing could be purchased for as little as £28 or sixpence a day spread over three years. This last proposal, he pointed out, was made possible primarily by of the advent of the cheap reprint series, the 1890s publishing initiative which he called one of the latest 'beneficent effects of the Education Act'. His library included many volumes from, among others, Newnes's 'Thin-Paper Classics' and 'Pocket Classics' series, Grant Richard's 'World's Classics', as well as Dent's 'Everyman' and 'Temple Classics'.[197] Along with this practical advice, he provided a scheme on how to read classics – he stressed the importance of knowing the author's biography, cautioned against reading for style alone as form and content were inseparable, advised beginners not to be distracted by abstract questions of genre, and recommended they start with Lamb – and he attempted to justify the pursuit of literary taste and to explain its value. Though always keenly aware of the social significance of books, he stressed that reading the classics ought not to be a means of status distinction, an 'elegant accomplishment', or a 'certificate of correct culture', but an activity taken up for its intrinsic aesthetic, intellectual, and ethical rewards. The 'greatest makers of literature', he explained, were the ones whose 'vision' disclosed the 'miraculous interestingness of the universe' and the 'true savour of life'. Taking as an example Shakespeare's sonnet XXXIII ('Full many a glorious morning . . .') – he also quoted from Whitman, Marcus Aurelius, and Wordsworth – he demonstrated how the poem could transform one's perception of 'the sun over the viaduct at Loughborough Junction of a morning'. By this 'disclosure of beauty' great literature enabled one to 'awake oneself', to 'be alive', and to 'intensify one's capacity for pleasure'. It also promised ethical and intellectual gains in so far as it promoted 'moral wisdom by the tracing everywhere of cause and effect' and so increased one's capacity 'for sympathy, and for comprehension'. It was, in short, 'a means of life' and, as such, 'the enterprise of forming one's literary taste' was, when rightly conceived, 'an enterprise of learning how best to use this means of life'.[198]

Though *T. P.'s Weekly* found an appreciative audience for fifteen years, the response to its cultural mission, of which Bennett was chief advocate, was not always cordial. Many readers were, of course, eager initiates: a twenty-one-year-old male mill worker from Lancashire, for instance, claimed that 'if I thought I could not escape by self-culture the daily ten hours' deadening grind, week in, week out, year after year, until I became an old man, I should go on the tramp'; while the daughter of a businessman wrote in to say that reading classical authors like Ruskin, Carlyle, Browning, and Whitman had made life in an Irish provincial town 'not merely bearable, but worth living'.[199] And one clerk, who spent much of 1904 visiting various branches of his bank around the country, eagerly reported that 'practically every bank clerk' he met read *T. P.'s Weekly*.[200] Others, however, pointed out the price of self-culture in tones ranging from the mildly dissatisfied to openly resentful.

Another bank clerk, himself an enthusiastic reader of *T. P.'s Weekly*, confessed that many of his colleagues did not 'rise beyond current sport and police news' and that some thought it a 'lamentable waste of time to read anything besides a newspaper or an occasional new novel'.[201] Even the willing had their complaints. 'Thanet', a City man, married with a family, and living in a northern suburb of London, argued that he simply could not 'find the time to read classical works': he worked a twelve-hour day during the week, a halfday on Saturdays, and spent most of Sunday at church. Bennett responded sympathetically, but added that the 'average City man, principal or clerk, but especially clerk, does *not* work really hard'. With a well-organized 'programme of hours' – he compared it to Mr Lewisham's 'schema' – he suggested even 'Thanet' could find at least a spare two hours for self-culture a day: if taken up for only four days a week this meant one could read the whole of Elizabethan drama, Tennyson, the French Symbolists, or the Eighteenth-Century essayists in six months. Even more progress would be possible if he read Plato's *Republic* on the train every day instead of the newspaper.[202] Though time was also a problem among the working classes – one woman declared that 'conditions of life for working women leave very little time for ease or pleasure, much less culture' – their most frequent complaint was that self-culture isolated them from their peers and made them the butt of 'jeers and scoffs', as a young Scottish miner put it.[203] Speaking for many, one worker declared that as soon as 'a working man' set out on 'the higher life he [became] incomprehensible to his associates' who were interested mainly in 'football gossip, racing and betting news' and read only a halfpenny paper, *Tit-Bits*, or a 'Home Weekly'.[204] 'Even in these days of free education and cheap literature', another observed, 'a book-case or book-shelf is by no means a common article of furniture in working-class homes'.[205] Such feelings of social dislocation were not exclusive to the working class, however. A twenty-year-old daughter of an army officer recounted that reading the classics, or what her friends called 'dry' authors like Meredith, Browning, and Hardy, made her 'out of sympathy with every single member of [her] family' and made men think her a 'blue-stocking'. 'Was the game worth the candle', she asked.[206] If some of the devotees felt dissatisfied, the heathens were unreservedly hostile. Speaking as someone engaged in a 'commercial position', H. R. J. of Birmingham remarked that reading 'good literature' inevitably made a man of his class discontent with 'the narrowness of his daily round' and rebellious in 'an environment where "culture" is neither understood nor held to be of any utility'.[207] This led H. H. C. of Brook Green, who believed that the 'most ignorant are the most content', to chime in: 'Let the cobbler stick to his last.' Pat Gordon of Regent's Park agreed and invoked Wells in a bitter indictment of the likes of Bennett and O'Connor: 'I hate the word culture and all that the Chester Cootes' and Walsingham's have complacently and condescendingly stuck on it.'[208]

V

What bearing does this analysis of Bennett's multiple positions in the field, as novelist, serialist, and journalist, have on our reading of his literary novels? Carey has suggested one answer to this central question. He has shown how the cultural satires like *A Great Man* (1904) and *What the Public Wants* (1909) and the literary novels like *A Man from the North* (1898), *Anna of the Five Towns* (1902), *The Old Wives' Tale* (1908), *Clayhanger* (1910), and *Hilda Lessways* (1911), reinforce Bennett's case against the social prejudices of the literary intelligentsia. The novels' preoccupation with the disregarded, marginalized or despised, be they women, servants, provincials, or suburbanites; their levelling and anti-elitist concern with such universal themes as the conflict between youth and age, and the time-bound life of the body; and their humanist celebration of the 'absolute singularity of each person' – all these, Carey claims, reflect Bennett's overall imaginative ambition to rescue 'the world from intellectuals'. Yet, as I have argued, this reading, which is sociological but blind to the specific sociology of the field, relies on a partial understanding of Bennett's position. It overlooks his early ambitions to be a John Lane author, focuses exclusively on the populist figure of the *Academy* and the *New Age*, and, more surprisingly, given Carey's own generously anti-elitist sympathies, ignores the popular serials altogether. A less reductive reading is possible, I shall argue, if one sees the novels as a manifestation of Bennett's more tangled interests as a turn-of-the-century literary maverick. Though they still reflect his desire to goad the 'apostles of art', they do so indirectly by reducing the literary purists to one sociocultural group among many.[209] They generalize the phenomenon of exclusivity and show how contests over status pervade social life. If they still address the narrow literary world, they also focus on the 'world of men at large' – in particular, the Edwardian book-reading public – while tactfully respecting some 'basic national prejudices'. At the same time, they make claims on the magazine-reading public by turning the world of the serials upside down.

Following John Buchan's advice, Bennett tried to find a more apt title for his first novel, and in the process he discovered where his central interests as a literary novelist lay. The version Buchan and Lane wanted changed – *In the Shadow* – was obscure and misleading. True, it hinted at the 'grey, sinister, and melancholy' atmosphere the novel was intended to evoke, but it was really a relic of an undeveloped idea bred of Bennett's short-lived regard for the 'scientific' doctrines of French Naturalism.[210] As we have seen, his novel was not, in the end, an exercise in Naturalist theory. Part self-ironizing auto-biography, part fashionably avant-garde fiction, it describes a provincial clerk's woeful failure to get on in the metropolitan world. The explanation for this unhappy outcome is, however, strictly Naturalist, though it is dramatically implausible. As we are told in the final paragraphs, but never shown in the course of the narrative, the hero's failure is an inevitable consequence of biology. He 'had been born in the shadow' of his weak-willed father, that 'mysterious, dead transmitter of traits' he never knew.[211] If this first title alluded to Zola, the second looked to the Goncourt brothers whose influence Bennett always felt more acutely. In the tradition of *Renée Mauperin* (1864), *Germinie Lacerteux* (1864), and *Mme Gervaisais* (1869), he gave the novel the name of its central figure *Richard Larch*. This transformed the narrative into a portrait of an ordinary young man and made 'character' its principal concern. Yet, if this version was less oblique and theory-laden than the first, it was at best drearily accurate. The more alluring final version, *A Man from the North*, not only shifted the focus once again, it pointed Bennett towards his own literary territory. Like all his major novels, *A Man from the North* describes the social as much as the geographical journey of an obscure individual. In this case, the dismal trajectory goes from the backwaters to the centre and back; or from the provinces to the metropolis and finally to the metropolitan provinces, the suburbs. Here the social journey entails a spatial one, but, as Bennett indicated in a figure like Constance Povey, the stay-at-home heroine of *The Old Wives' Tale*, one did not have to move about to be socially mobile. Constance journeys through time, and, therefore, through an ever-changing social landscape. This was Bennett's subject: the fate of individuals in a complex, dynamic and hierarchically structured social world.

Not that he ever lost his early Naturalist-inspired interest in biology. He always recognized that outside this network of social relations human beings are merely solitary and dehumanized 'organisms' – his favourite term for the biological base upon which the social superstructure is built. As this suggests, he considered biology foundational – hence the preoccupation with bodily disease Virginia Woolf derides – and death, its ultimate end, the law under which all were equal.[212] Yet, unlike the French Naturalists, he was not a strict determinist. Though prior, biology never caused or explained sociology in his view. Rather, these two planes of existence were caught in a fatal and always unequal conflict which biology inevitably won. What preoccupied him was the unerring human tendency to deny the biological base by constructing a fantastic, but not necessarily less cruel, counter-world comprised of labyrinthine social hierarchies. His attitude to this pervasive habit was ambivalent, however. As we shall see, the novels consistently contest the prejudices on which these hierarchies are built and expose their perverse logic in a generous spirit of rationalist humanism. But he also responded to the pathos they implied, as the portrait of Mr Baines in *The Old Wives' Tale* suggests. Old Mr Baines has been incapacitated by a stroke for eleven years. He is, the narrator claims, a 'ruined organism'. Yet, 'by habit of years', his wife has 'built up a gigantic fiction that the organism remained ever the supreme consultative head of the family'; and his friend, Mr Critchlow, has 'obstinately continued to treat' him as 'a crony'. Together these two devotees have sustained this 'mass of living and dead nerves' by 'indefatigably feeding his importance and his dignity'. They have, in short, nurtured the dying man's humanity (and protected their own) by ignoring a biological fact and fostering a social fantasy. 'The feat was,' the narrator observes, 'a miracle of stubborn, self-deceiving, splendidly blind devotion, and incorrigible pride'.[213]

This concern with the prison-house of biology served as a tragic counterpoint to Bennett's often comic preoccupation with the ways individuals, families, classes, genders, generations, and regions established hierarchies of status distinction among themselves. His special fascination, however, lay in the part culture and questions of taste played in these serious social power games. This is made immediately clear in the opening chapter of *The Old Wives' Tale*. There the young heroines, Sophia and Constance Baines, are shown to inhabit an intricately structured social world. Just as their county, where 'excess is deprecated', defines itself in opposition to the surrounding counties and the rest of England, so their district, their town, their square, and their family establish and defend their respective positions by fierce or subtle gestures of distinction. St Lukes's square, for instance, which is the centre of the town's retail trade, scorns the manufacturing sector 'as something wholesale, vulgar, and assuredly filthy'; while, among the various retailers, the drapers 'undoubtedly' constitute the 'aristocracy'. The grounds for these lofty claims vary, of course. The Five Towns district, though an 'insignificant stain on a county, considered geographically,' disdains the rest of Staffordshire because of its economic superiority as the centre of England's pottery industry; the retail traders distance themselves from the manufacturers, just as the drapers look down on the other retailers, because of their more refined trade and life style; while pre-industrial Bursley ignores the manufacturing towns in the district because it has the 'honours of antiquity'.[214] Whether driven by economic, social, cultural or historical factors, or all four at once, the logic was the same. Indeed, Bennett's point was that every self-understanding, from the regional to the individual, evolved only in relationship. As he recognized from the first, this had a paradoxical consequence: the logic of status distinction, which governed this network of self-understandings, inevitably made the superior dependent on their inferiors. Society was a hall of simultaneously flattering and demeaning mirrors. His literary spokesman in *A Man for the North*, Mr Aked, makes this clear. After sketching his scheme for a book entitled 'The Psychology of the Suburbs', which is designed to break down anti-suburban prejudices, Aked adds:

We could show how the special characteristics of the different suburbs exert a subtle influence on the great central spots. Take Fulham; no one thinks anything of Fulham, but suppose it were swept off the face of the earth the effect would be to alter, for the seeing eye, the character of Piccadilly and the Strand and Cheapside. The play of one suburb on another and on the central haunts is as regular, as orderly, as calculable, as the law of gravity itself.[215]

This was Bennett's first law of interdependence. It described how social life worked at any historical moment, or, in narrative terms, at any point in the episodic but linear story. Yet his argument, conducted partly at the level of narrative form, was always that the logic of status distinction operated both synchronically and diachronically. From the diachronic perspective, then, the complex social world the young Sophia and Constance inhabit in 1862 is doubly fragile. It is not just that the grand claims to distinction entail various specular distortions, but that they are all subject to the indignities of relentless historical change. This was Bennett's second law. The hall of mirrors is constantly being assembled and disassembled. Crucially for him, the changes involved in the second law were not necessarily part of the grand, national, orchestrated histories of political revolutions and wars. He was always impressed by the fact that the Sophias of the world often exist outside the sphere of official history. As we learn later, his lower middle-class heroine lives in Paris during the Franco-Prussian War and the Commune of 1871 without being fully aware of, or especially interested in, these great 'determining' events. She spends most of her time concerned with mundane, private matters, like getting adequate supplies for her boarding house. Bennett's populism attracted him to unofficial, local history that centred on small material changes and their devastating, often unintended effects. His novel shows, for instance, how in the space of forty years Bursley's civic pride, the prestige of St Lukes's Square, and the lofty superiority of its drapers – the girls' mid-Victorian public world, in short – are all undone by nothing more grandiose than the advent of electric trams.

This outlook, which encompassed history and sociology as well as the form and content of the fiction, applied equally to the public and to the private spheres. Sophia and Constance, for instance, the teenage daughters of Mr Baines, the invalid but respected Bursley draper, reinforce their private self-understanding through their mutual disdain for Maggie, the Baines's middle-aged domestic servant. Maggie is a mid-Victorian 'drudge'. She works seventeen hours a day in an 'underground kitchen', she goes out only on Sundays, and she is allowed visitors only once a month. One of Bennett's secondary concerns in the novel will be to explore the diachronic dimension to status distinction through the changing relations between masters and servants from the 1860s to the 1900s, but at this point Maggie's interest lies in her synchronic relation to the girls and particularly in her astonishing love life. Demonstrating Bennett's tactful sensitivity to what he called 'basic national prejudices', she is a discreetly censored reincarnation of the Goncourts' maidservant, the model for Germinie Lacerteux, who led a stormy but secret sex life. She has been engaged eleven times in seventeen years; in fact, 'engagements and tragic partings were Maggie's pastime'. When the two girls observe her from the shop window, she is on her way to her latest tryst. Partly out of class prejudice, but mainly out of 'the profound, instinctive cruelty of youth', they 'positively grudged' Maggie her 'tender yearnings', and, pointing to the material minutiae the will to distinction magnifies, they snobbishly criticize her for not wearing gloves and deride her new clothes. Importantly, though the girls consciously relish this derision – watching Maggie go off to her lovers is a favourite custom of theirs – their cruelty is 'instinctive'. Just as they 'had never been conscious' of the 'manifold interest of their situation' – the intricately constructed social world they inhabit – so their hostility is neither fully conscious nor overt. Outwardly, the narrator sardonically notes, they are 'nice, kind-hearted, well-behaved, and delightful girls!' This duplicity, combined with the fact that their venomous feelings are largely pre-verbal, inevitably created narrative difficulties. Bennett's solution was to have the text work on numerous levels simultaneously. At one level, the girls are merely focalizers. The narrator sees through their 'relentless eyes' that Maggie is 'ugly and soiled'. Since these perceptions are pre-verbal, they could not, of course, realistically be rendered as free indirect discourse. The narrator's function, then, is not simply to give the girls' point of view, but to articulate it, to translate what they 'obscurely thought' by putting words in their minds. Through the fiction of the narrator's ventriloquism, they 'think' it is 'unnatural' that Maggie should even 'desire to take the air of a Thursday', and they 'feel' her romantic yearnings are 'offensive and wicked'. Finally, their perspective is made manifest as such through juxtaposition. In contrast to the girls, the less socially interested narrator observes that Maggie harbours 'mysteries'.[216] This device of positive evasion implicitly undermines the girls' perspective, but it leaves open the question of the 'real' Maggie, or 'Mrs Brown' as Woolf would have it, without obtrusively insisting on any privileged answers. Though these narrative devices went against the modernist grain, they enabled Bennett to keep his central interest in focus and to emphasize that the energies driving distinction are largely subterranean.

For all their shared animosity to Maggie, Sophia and Constance are not, of course, exactly alike. Constance, the timid stay-at-home who will remain satisfied with her lot as a dutiful provincial daughter and then wife, uses patronizing benevolence to mask her derision. When Sophia openly criticizes the gloveless Maggie, her older sister comments in her 'foolishly good-natured' way that 'you can't expect her to have gloves'. The implication is that Sophia at least has the courage of her unconsciously cruel convictions. Later, her unashamed hauteur, and her discontent with her prescribed social status, drive her to become a schoolteacher, then to run off to Paris with the abject but temporarily alluring commercial traveller, Gerald Scales, and, finally, to establish herself as a successful hotelier. At this point, though, the more profound differences between the two girls are signified by their divergent tastes. Constance likes dutifully embroidering floral designs for her mother, while Sophia prefers defying social rules by dressing up in her mother's new skirts and dreaming of the Parisian 'princesses' in *Myra's Journal*, a popular fashion magazine. These differences are partly an effect of such physical, but always also social, factors as age and looks – Constance is 'agreeably' plain, while the younger Sophia is 'beautiful and handsome at the same time' – but, again, they are sharpened by the logic of distinction. As we soon discover, Sophia's rebelliousness is fuelled by resentment, another psychological by-product of status distinction. She senses she is inferior to her sister in the family hierarchy, since, 'in some subtle way, Constance had a standing with her parents which was more confidential than Sophia's'. Her 'secret resentment' at this is then intensified by her growing awareness that Samuel Povey, the Baines's shop assistant and Constance's future husband, is usurping her rightful place in her sister's affections. Like a political revolution on a national scale, this small-scale redistribution of status disrupts 'the order of the world' for the two girls and leads to the second eruption of 'something sinister and cruel' into their otherwise 'innocent' lives. We should also note that, in the passage describing those 'preposterous' fashion sketches that attract Sophia, another significant turn in the narrative occurs. In a bold move, comparable to a Brechtian 'alienation effect', Bennett shifts the burden of his theme beyond the narrative frame, and makes his postulated Edwardian middle-class reader the narrator's focalizer. He brings the 'world of men at large' into the text. The description of the 'ridiculous and out-moded fashions', like the following claim that the girls could not 'foresee the miraculous generation which is us', simultaneously voices and controverts the Edwardian readers' seemingly complacent belief in progress and their own superiority to the 'dark and backward' mid-Victorian world.[217] This is the force of Bennett's characteristic irony: a phrase abruptly betrays what it seductively affirms. By disrupting the fictional frame in this way, he shattered the flattering mirror of Whig history, brought the themes of identity and distinction closer to home, and glanced beyond the page to his *hypocrite lecteur*.

As this turn towards the reader implies, Bennett saw his novels as a form of social criticism targeted not simply at the literary purists but at the Edwardian middle-classes, the same readers whose specific prejudices about the place of sex in fiction he prudently chose to respect. The often disappointing fictional journeys of his heroes and heroines across social borders were an inverted figure for his reader's ideally more rewarding excursion through the text. If the act of reading did not put pay to status distinction – it was, as he knew, inextricably entangled in the process – it might at least make manifest its remorseless logic and mitigate some of its effects. One of his clearest statements of his emancipatory hopes as a novelist is the long short-story 'The Death of Simon Fuge' (1907). Its first person narrator, Mr Loring, represents Bennett's model reader. The story is about high art – in this case the paintings of Simon Fuge – and its apparently low origins, but it centres on Loring's journey to the Five Towns and his unusually positive encounter with the seemingly vulgar provincial world that produced the painter. A self-declared metropolitan 'man of taste', Loring is an antiquarian at the British Museum, a reader of Words-worth (notably *The Excursion*) and a London evening *Gazette*. He is also a Fuge connoisseur. Happy in the knowledge of his cultural eminence, he appreciates the fact that his evening paper is produced by 'an ironic, understanding, small band of men for just a few thousand persons' like him, and that, unlike the English public, it knows and proclaims Fuge's true stature.[218] At first Loring is shocked to learn what little regard the rough, unceremonious inhabitants of the Five Towns have for Fuge and his art – they are more interested in football results – and yet, in the course of his stay with Mr Brindley, his host who is a local architect, he is gradually compelled to revise his perceptions. As he discovers, this provincial world is itself an elaborate network of social and cultural distinctions, and it includes some, like Brindley, who display unex-pected talents and sophistication. Not only does Brindley have a warm and flourishing family life, unlike Loring who is a bachelor, he teaches the Londoner to appreciate hand-rolled cigarettes, the *Manchester Guardian*, and the unintended humour of advertisements; he also shows himself to be a keen appreciator of Rossetti's limericks, an authority on rare books, and a more than passable pianist. By the time Loring returns to London, he has not only demystified the *Gazette's* romantic obituary of Fuge, he has also managed to rise above sectarian differences and to acquire a new sense of the diversity and complexity of his society and its cultures.

Reading Mr Bennett was, in short, intended to be as liberating as a stay with Mr Brindley. By uncovering the buried dynamics of status distinction, and exposing their capacity for real and symbolic cruelty, Bennett hoped to disinter, if not dismantle, the myriad social prejudices by which his readers defined themselves and their place in the world. To this extent his novels were self-conscious acts of social defamiliarization. This, at least, constituted the affirmative, often comic but never utopian, side of his humanism. When he looked beyond the social world, however, he saw a bleak natural wasteland populated by dying 'organisms'. This was his version of the tragic. He was, in other words, neither an English 'realist' or 'naturalist' or 'materialist', nor simply a 'regionalist', but rather, as he implied in his manifesto *The Author's Craft* (1914) and in his contributions to *T. P.'s Weekly*, a literary idealist for whom 'observation' was both a creative and a 'moral act' that disrupted conventional language as much as ordinary social prejudice, and stimulated 'charity – not the charity which signs cheques, but the more precious charity which puts itself to the trouble of understanding'.[219]

Yet the novels were not simply a social critique directed at purist intellec-tuals and middle-class readers: they were a literary challenge to the canonical English authors and, as importantly, to the popular serialists and their readers. For literary critics, this is where the value of Bennett's own serials lies. Like the less prestigious London suburbs he mentioned in his first novel, their value is not so much intrinsic as dialectical. As a genre, they embody one of the poles in the contemporary field against which the new avant-garde novelists of the 1890s defined their own cultural position and literary practice. Morever, as the products of considered – if never infallible – calculation, unhampered by any seriously declared expressive intention, they represent a significant record of what a well-informed writer understood to be the preferences of the syndicates, newspapers, and popular magazines; and, by extension, of what the editors perceived to be the tastes of the new mass readership. How far these perceptions (and so the serials) actually reflected a clear and distinct idea of 'popular taste' is another question, and one Bennett characteristically preferred to leave open:

The great public is so various, and its predilections so subtly and mysteriously instinctive – so personal and intimate, that it may not be said to have a secret; it has a thousand secrets, all interwoven, and none to be fully interpreted till the last of all is found.[220]

As he knew from experience, the editors of popular magazines were neither masterful impresarios nor omniscient arbiters of taste. They were harassed, on the one hand, by the difficulties of constructing 'that mysterious "policy"' for their proprietors out of stories, articles and illustrations; and, on the other, by 'that thrice-mysterious "public taste" which has to be aimed at in the dark and hit!'[221] In the absence of any reliable knowledge and in an age before market surveys, they had, like the aspiring serialist, to rely mainly on their wits and experience in the field, and, where possible, on a vague idea of what the tastes of some 'average reader' might be. With due reservation Bennett suggested this nominal reader possessed four broad expectations: a desire for an 'imposing plot' which developed 'obviously and leisurely' towards an inevitable happy ending and which did not 'embrace the whole of life'; an interest in unmistakable 'heroes and heroines' not 'ordinary people, astoundingly revealed by art in an extraordinary light'; a preference for stories with a 'dominant love-interest' and set in 'various contrasted scenes' of which a good proportion displayed 'the luxury of wealth and the most elaborate forms of social ritual'; and, finally, a negative expectation, expressed as a tendency to eschew anything 'really subversive of that vast fabric of prejudices and misconceptions which the worthy reader would call his philosophy'.[222] Not surprisingly, as his analysis indicates, these were the expectations he set out to sabotage with his impressionistic avant-garde novels about unglamorous lives.

The generic form of the serial was clear in his view: 'a popular serial must have horror and mystification; horror and mystification mean crime, and crime means the detection of crime; therefore, the typical serial must be, in essence, a detective story'.[223] As in all such stories, plot, or the tension between the 'surface' story and the 'real' order of events, is the focus of narrative interest. In his serial mysteries, the unsuspecting heroes, who are seldom professional detectives, are propelled into the middle of things, so that they are entangled in the crime as it occurs and even become targets for the criminals.

Though the ultimate objective is to uncover the 'real story' – the actual aims and motives of the plotters and their relations to the victims – this method had the advantage of increasing suspense (and padding) by allowing for plenty of incidental mystification and demystification along the way for both hero and reader. In the course of the narrative, the meaning of events and actions can be strategically neglected or obscured under misleading interpretations, astonishing disguises can suddenly be unveiled, alleged corpses revived, and putative criminals or victims cleared. In the more technically successful serials, like *The Grand Babylon Hotel* and *The City of Pleasure*, the resolution of these incidental mysteries coincides with the end of each instalment making the narrative as a whole a series of minor puzzles and solutions within the major one.

Though the 'real stories' play only a minor part in the surface narrative, they determine one important feature of the Manichaean world of the 'sensational serial'; namely, the status and motives of the villains. In Bennett's view, the system of character typologies demanded by the genre and its readers rested on one exclusive assumption: no members of the English working or middle classes could be cast as villains. The criminals had to be either wealthy, untitled figures with foreign-sounding names, like Mrs Cavalossi and her accomplice Dr Colpus in *The Gates of Wrath*; or they had to be foreign aristocrats, like Lord Clarenceux in *Love and Life* and the shadowy King of Bosnia in *Grand Babylon*, or, if they were English, they had to be exceptionally rich and repellent, like Simon Lock in *Teresa*, Louis Ravengar in *Hugo*, and Mrs Ilam in *City of Pleasure*. The only story to depart from these conventions is *The Sinews of War*. Here the villain, Walter Pollexfen, whose name suggests he has Irish origins, is not wealthy – he lives in the East End – though he has led a singularly displaced and dissolute life: he has been a revolutionary in Uruguay, a circus-master in Yokohama, he has murdered his wife and brother, and, more importantly it seems, he has had a career as a well-respected actor. As the hero muses at one point, this last fact alone sets Pollexfen apart from ordinary wholesome Englishmen like himself: 'all actors', he declares, 'have something *bizarre* in their composition'.[224] In keeping both with their exclusive status and with the average reader's alleged preference for 'glaring tints' rather than 'fine shades', the villains are all driven by spectacular passions.[225] While their aims and motives differ, all are figured as zealous and unscrupulous monomaniacs. The beautiful and ruthless widow, Mrs Cavalossi, for instance, who uses her innocent daughter as a lure to entrap rich men, takes delight in moulding events with her 'powerful, unscrupulous hand'; while Louis Ravengar, a 'great scorner of scruples', suffers from a 'species of monomania'.[226] Clearly, in this fictional world, there is no place for the insidious psychology of the miserly and despotic Clerkenwell bookseller of *Riceyman Steps*, nor is it possible for an ordinary excursion by a maidservant to inspire the comment that 'probably in human activity there is no such a thing as a single motive'.[227] Similarly, no serial characters display that complex blend of resentment and disdain, innocence and cruelty that lives in the young Sophia Baines. The conflicts that underlie the simple but grandiose obsessions are, however, consistently small-scale and domestic. Unlike spy stories, or Emile Gaboriau's detective stories on which Bennett modelled his own, these mysteries do not draw together the 'threads of a vast and complicated politico-social intrigue': they remain modest dramas of romantic love and family values.[228] At most national or international affairs form only a decorative and topical frame, as in *The Sinews of War* where the treasure turns out to be money stolen from the Czar's navy by Russian revolutionaries during the Russo-Japanese War. Even the villains' violations of statutory criminal laws are given less weight when compared to their transgression of chivalric codes or the laws of 'natural' familial affection. The worst criminals in this folkloric realm are murderous rivals and jealous lovers like Lord Clarenceux and the king of Bosnia, bigamists like Simon Lock, ruthlessly possessive or exploitative mothers like Mrs Ilam and Mrs Cavalossi, and vengeful brothers or step-brothers like Walter Pollexfen and Louis Ravengar. One of Bennett's most overworked domestic themes, in stories that constantly recycle a limited set of character types and dramatic scenarios, was that of parental treachery and irresponsibility among the social elite. Sir Cyril Smart, a leading opera impresario, turns out to be the negligent father of the heroine in a sub-plot of *Love and Life*; Arthur Forrest, the hero of *Gates of Wrath*, incidentally discovers (after Mrs Cavalossi) that he is the illegitimate son of a millionaire bigamist; Simon Lock, another millionaire bigamist, emerges as the double-crossing father of the heroines in the 'real story' of *Teresa*; and again in the 'real story' of *The City of Pleasure*, the self-styled Jetson, Mrs Ilam's stepson, returns to reclaim his rightful inheritance when he learns that his possessive and ambitious stepmother had attempted to murder him when he was a child.

As this catalogue of misdemeanours suggests, the serials wage a not so surreptitious symbolic war against the privileged and governing classes. Yet for all this – and despite Bennett's personal beliefs and the tendencies implicit in his novels – they conspicuously avoid any suggestion of real social or political discontent. The contrast of extremes in British society typical of Dickens's serial-mysteries, which had exercised the consciences of the mid-Victorian middle-class public and reformers, has no place in the social topography of these late-Victorian variants. All are chiefly set in contemporary London, for instance, yet their glossy map of the city systematically excludes both the underworld of the East End and the newly developed suburbs. All focus on the glamour and opulence of the West End, and especially on the splendours of the late-Victorian leisure and consumer culture: the lavish hotels on the Embankment, the grandiose department stores, the West End theatres and opera houses, and the new Earls-Court-style exhibitions which provided mass entertainment and celebrated technological progress. This is not the 'city of very rich and very poor' Bennett described in his journals, and its splendid department stores never afford glimpses of 'mad luxury floating on that uneasy sea of dissatisfied labour'.[229] It is, by contrast, a fabled 'City of Pleasure' rich in Babylonian luxuries and ruled by a corrupt elite. If the narrative requires additional settings, as most usually do, this general atmosphere is preserved by relocating the action to glamorous resorts on the Continent (Bruges and Ostende were among Bennett's favourites) or to the Caribbean. Though *Sinews*, the most Dickensian of all, includes a satirical account of Mr Hilgay's shabbily tasteful hotel for the 'distressed respectable' (modelled on Lord Rowton's new poor man's boarding-houses), and though it tarnishes the mystique of the privileged in its portrayal of the new 'Physique Club' devoted to the 'cult of the body' and in its portrait of the upper-class twit Sir Anthony Didring, it none the less makes only a brief and wary excursion beyond the confines of the West End. The hero, who faces the prospect of sliding into the 'Abyss' himself, regards the East End as a 'foreign land', 'strange, exotic, and full of sinister romance', and finds himself turning 'westward, as a horse will turn towards a stable, even when the manger is empty'.

At the heart of the metropolitan splendour are the late-Victorian entrepreneurs, the hoteliers, American millionaires, exhibition promoters, financiers, department-store owners, and newspaper barons, who appear not only as villains, but also as heroes or bit-players. Frequently compared to Napoleon, these commercial empire-builders, whose wealth and power are sedulously itemized, constitute a dominant group in the serials' pantheon of prestige. The account of Lord Nasing, the newspaper baron who appears briefly in *Sinews*, is typical. From his office that is 'an exact reproduction of Napoleon's Council Chamber at Fountainbleau' he directs three dailies, twenty-nine weeklies, and three monthlies; a huge and complex network of employees; and a company that uses the latest printing and linotype technology and boasts annual profits of over £250,000.[230] While the prerequisite for membership of this elite was usually wealth, the cultural prestige of celebrities, especially actresses and opera singers, was also accepted currency, since cultural distinction and refined tastes were themselves part of the complex social apparatus of glamour. Here the fictional world of the serials reproduced and embellished the fashionable world documented in the gossip columns and portraits of celebrities that dominated most of the popular magazines. The predominantly lower-middle-class and middle-class women readers of *Hearth and Home*, for instance, could turn from a flattering front-page portrait of Madame Albani, the 'gifted Canadian prima-donna' and personal friend of the queen, to the on-going adventures of Rosa Caro, the famous soprano and heroine of *Love and Life*.[231] In keeping with their sociology, and with the dominant ethos of the magazines, the stories are also profoundly elitist in their cultural assumptions. With some self-irony, Bennett opened his first serial *Love and Life* with a satirical, and entirely ornamental, portrait of Sullivan Smith, a composer of popular musical comedies who makes £7,000 a year, no doubt a caricature of

Arthur Sullivan. A relentless self-advertiser, Smith despises 'high art', which in this story means Wagner's operas, as 'all rot', and explains his pragmatic ideals to the narrator-hero who happens to be a Wagner enthusiast:

I'm a man of business, I am, Adrian. Give the public what they want, and save half your income; that's the ticket. I am a swell. I'm a celebrity. I get two pence apiece royalty on my photographs.

His social-climbing wife, Emmeline, who has a 'trace of a Cockney accent' and a 'Jewish caste' and who had once been 'Sissy Vox', the star of the music halls, also hates opera and conveniently feels that the soprano-heroine should be killed.[232] In contrast to these caricature vulgarians, the heroes and heroines of the serials display impeccable tastes. Hugo's allure, for instance, is as much a function of his wealth, his splendid department store and his power over 3,500 employees as it is of his 'Tripoli carpets', his 'turquoise-blue and gold' apartment, his 'paintings of the Barbizon school', his 'Louis Quatorze screen', and his preference for Boswell, Montaigne, Wagner, and Chopin.[233] Though Charles Carpentaria, the managing and musical director of the eponymous 'City of Pleasure' exhibition and the hero of the story, is a popular composer and orchestra leader, he is given all the qualities and tastes of an authentic artist and contrasted throughout with his business partner, Josephus Ilam, the apparent villain. Carpentaria is tall, red-headed, single-minded about his art, and passionate about the aesthetic splendour of his exhibition; while Ilam is stout, with grey-black hair, eyes 'like a pig's', and he is exclusively preoccupied with money and advertisement. Moreover, Carpentaria conducts only 'national hymns', his own compositions, and 'as a superlative concession, Wagner and Beethoven'.[234] In short, whether it was through the metropolitan *topos*, fashionable 'Society', or 'high art', the serials fed those social fantasies of status distinction Bennett set out to dispel in his novels.

Clearly, then, the serials display what might at best be considered an ambivalent attitude towards the glittering elite: on the one hand, they demonize some aristocrats, celebrities, and plutocrats; and, on the other, they capitalize on their glamorous life style and metropolitan milieu. The tension between these two perspectives is resolved, however, by a third that centres on the relations between the heroes and heroines. Bennett did not favour a narrow approach to the mystery genre. Poe, for instance, was 'overpraised as a mystery novelist' because 'the interest of his tales is too exclusively limited to detection'. Instead, he preferred a hybrid of genres, including the sea story (*Love and Life* and *Grand Babylon*), the exotic adventure story (*Sinews*) and, most especially, the love-story:

I want more than mere detective ratiocination in my mystery stories. I want love, romances, and all sorts of things besides.[235]

So his serials trade on two kinds of narrative uncertainty – detection and courtship – and their plots are directed towards two satisfying resolutions: the disclosure of the 'real story', which involves the punishment and/or death of the villains, and marriage. Most importantly, the love story provides a means by which both the anti-elitist assumptions of the narratives and the glamour of 'Society' can be preserved. In all the serials the love story is also a Cinderella fable in which social (and usually economic) boundaries are crossed and eventually eliminated. In *Love and Life*, a young middle-class doctor from Devonshire defeats his ghostly aristocratic rival, inherits a fortune and marries the wealthy and world-renowned opera soprano, Rosa Caro; in *Gates of Wrath*, a young art critic, with an income of £400, becomes a millionaire overnight, outwits his treacherous mother-in-law, and then lives happily with his charming 'Society' bride; in *Sinews* the indigent middle-class hero, who is lavishly rewarded by the Russian authorities when he recovers their money, marries the heroine, a famous actress; while in *Hugo* and *City of Pleasure*, the young heroines, who are typists and milliners, marry millionaire entrepreneurs. The only exception to this general rule is *Grand Babylon*, but, here, cultural and social borders are still crossed in that the American millionaire's daughter, the heroine, marries a German aristocrat and saves his impecunious family from financial ruin. Of course, in this fairy-tale world, none of the characters is tormented or doubtful about their sudden change in status, and their external obstacles, the nasty rivals or corrupt parents, are always overcome. None experiences the ordinary frustrations of characters in a *Bildungsroman* as Richard Larch or Edwin Clayhanger do, just as none manifests the comfortable inertia of Constance Povey; nor do any suffer acute feelings of dislocation when they encounter unfamiliar social and cultural territories as Bennett had observed of a young clerk and his wife: 'Both were skilful, experienced, alive in the things which lay within their own segment of life's circle, and lost and awed, like babes in the wood, if they happened to stray outside that segment.'[236] He noted this on 30 January 1897, adding that one of the dazzling things beyond their horizon was the *Yellow Book*. In the always optimistic serials, however, the complexities of the self in society and the cruelties of status distinction are easily erased, since selfhood, reduced to a few unchanging traits, a slim biography, and an array of external signs, is all but obliterated. The young bachelor-heroes, of whatever class or status, who embody the ideals of chivalry and English fair play, are all as 'imperturbable and resourceful' as Richard Redgrave in *Teresa*, and all, like him but unlike Richard Larch, see and experience life as an 'avenue of adventure and of success'; similarly, all display the audacity and *savoir-faire* of Philip Masters, the down-and-out hero of *Sinews*, who thinks nothing of negotiating a tough contract as a novice journalist with Lord Nasing and then inviting the august proprietor to lunch.[237] Such intrepidity is, according to the gender code of the serials, an exclusively masculine trait. Though the heroines are sometimes eager, but never directing, accomplices in the heroes' adventures, and though some, like Nella Racksole in *Grand Babylon*, occasionally lead the way, they never occupy centre stage nor do they display the enterprise and fortitude of a Sophia Baines or a Hilda Lessways. Their job is primarily to be demure objects of masculine desire and damsels in various forms of distress. Even Nella keeps her place in relation to her lover Prince Aribert. After he rescues her from the clutches of the villains, they begin to fall in love, and the narrator comments: 'She, in his eyes, surrounded by the glamour of beauty and vast wealth; he, in her eyes, surrounded by the glamour of masculine intrepidity and the brilliance of a throne.'[238] As Bennett remarked about the female figures in the fashion sketches in *Woman* in the 1890s, the heroines display 'the curves of a certain stock figure' and they are 'all taller than life and slimmer than life, with hands and fingers longer than life'.[239] They are the 'princesses' in *Myra's Journal* who awaken Sophia's dreams of a world beyond Bursley and shopkeeping.[240] Above all, any qualities that do not contribute to a general aura of allure in the eyes of the hero are ignored. While beauty, youth, elegance, and charm are the heroines' most conspicuous attributes, the added hint of an obscure or even non-existent southern European inheritance always provides a necessary measure of covert sexual appeal. The betrayed mother of Juana and Teresa Craig, the young heroines of *Teresa*, for instance, had 'some aristocratic Spanish blood in her veins through her mother's father'; while Camilla Payne, the English heroine of *Hugo*, who serves as a representative type, is made to fit the ideal in the following elaborate rigmarole:

Camilla was beautiful, and supremely beautiful; she was tall, well and generously formed, graceful, fair, with fine eyes and fine dark chestnut hair; her absolutely regular features had the proud Tennysonian cast. But the coldness of Tennysonian damsels was not hers. Whether she had Latin blood in her veins, or whether Nature had peculiarly gifted her out of sheer caprice, she possessed in a high degree that indescribable demeanour, at once a defiance and a surrender, a question and an answer, a confession and a denial, which is the universal weapon of women of Latin race in the battle of the sexes, but of which Englishwomen seem to be almost deprived. 'I am Eve!' say the mocking, melting eyes of the Southern woman, and so said Camilla's eyes.[241]

Though this coded description reveals some of Bennett's animosity against English sexual attitudes, it relies mainly upon the conventional ideal of the young, alluring heroine he wanted banished from his novels. As he put it in the preface to *The Old Wives' Tale*, he had 'always revolted against the absurd youthfulness, the unfading youthfulness of the average heroine'. So, for that novel, which he modelled on Maupassant's *Une Vie*, he consciously chose to relate the 'entire life-history' of the sort of women 'who would pass unnoticed in a crowd'; while in *Leonora* he 'staggered' reviewers by having a heroine of forty.[242]

The serials conclude, then, with the reassuring culmination of two male adventures, one ending in the detective-hero's exposure of the 'real story' and the other in the lover-hero's conquest of the appealing young heroine. Sudden wealth is a fringe benefit of one or both of these successes. Most importantly, however, the triumphant resolution of the second quest and the resultant happy marriages provide an especially consoling testimony to the fact that typists, milliners, provincial doctors, and clerks are equal to the glamour of metropolitan 'Society'. In *Hugo*, the millionaire hero marries Camilla, a young lower-middle-class milliner, but, in a concluding conversation with a male confidant, he lightly dismisses the marvels of all this.

'She must have the best blood in her veins. With that style, that carriage, she surely must be – '
'My dear fellow,' said Hugo, 'beauty has no rank. It bloweth where it listeth.'[243]

It could be argued that this egalitarian impulse marks a point of convergence between the values and perspectives of the author of *The Old Wives' Tale* and the author of *Love and Life*. In fact, it represents their most radical disjunction. Of all the magical sleights of hand that sustain the world of the serial this is perhaps the most mesmerizing. It bypasses the complexities of the self in society and projects the utopian fantasy of a world beyond the logic of status distinction in which everyone is in the end equally and effortlessly elite. In effect, the serials assuage their readers by naturalizing the social hall of mirrors while rendering its specular distortions harmless. They proffer a fantasy freedom in which social positions are interchangeable and self-transformation is possible without friction or struggle. They are therapeutic and uplifting but only in a fairy-tale mode. By contrast, the novels confront their readers antagonistically by revealing that the social is an ever-shifting mirage in the wasteland of common biological mortality. They offer a paradoxical emancipation through a literary unveiling of human bondage. They are bleakly salutary in a muted, democratized, documentary mode.

As a literary maverick Bennett attempted to negotiate the treacherous dialectic that divided the purist from the profiteer, avant-garde from popular culture. And as an adversarial journalist he eagerly exploited, and even insisted upon, the inconsistencies of his multiple careers as a serialist and a novelist. Yet, in private, he also tried to smooth over the disjunctions this involved. This was shown partly in his occasional exasperation with the serial form, and partly in his view of his long-term position. If dealing with the book-borrowing public as an avant-garde novelist entailed self-imposed subterfuge, he recognized that writing for the magazine public demanded outright subjection to external censorship. As he knew from experience, the serial, and especially its representations of women and courtship rituals, was rigorously policed by sharp-eyed magazine editors keen to defend their own positions in the field. For some, like T. P. O'Connor, these were defined in terms of moral (his audience, as he knew and intended, included children) and commercial interests. When he rejected *Hugo*, for instance, these considerations, rather than simple prudishness, as well as other managerial questions, lay behind his decision. He objected to a scene in chapter 5 in which Camilla had apparently changed into a new costume, a gift of her former lover, in the *cabinet de toilette* of his apartment. At Pinker's request, Bennett willingly revised the scene for other editors: he introduced a housekeeper, emphasized her presence throughout the exchange, altered the *cabinet de toilette* into the housekeeper's room, and suppressed the change of costume, making the lover give Camilla a hat and cloak as a present instead. As he admitted to Pinker, he had certainly not intended any offence:

What is the matter with me is that my mind is too pure. It never occurred to me for a moment that anyone could twist that chapter into an indecency. However, there is no doubt that it can be so twisted. I can see it when it is pointed out.[244]

On other occasions, however, editors were clearly motivated by larger ideological commitments. This was certainly the case when the *Strand* turned down his mildly pro-suffragette story, *The Lion's Share*, in 1915.[245] These factors, as well as a general sense of frustration at having to tailor his writing to the magazine market, led him to remark on completing *The Card*: 'Good honest everyday work, vitiated by my constant thought of a magazine public'. Conversely, when released from the demands imposed by the various generic and sociopolitical strictures of serial fiction, he felt a joyful sense of emancipation:

In three days I have written nearly 6,000 words of a long short story called 'The Death of Simon Fuge', *not* destined for any magazine. I enjoyed writing this more than I have enjoyed writing anything for a long time. Not to have the fear of the unperceptive stupidity of the magazine public before your eyes is certainly a wonderful release.[246]

Moreover, while he defended the right of professional authors to work for money – and experience the rewards and frustrations of doing so – and while he considered the serial a legitimate literary form, he never gave his own serials more than their due and he remained resolutely protective of his own literary status. As he remarked to Pinker on 24 April 1904:

It cannot be too clearly understood that though one may do lighter work for the sake of a temporary splash etc. & for relief, it is the *Leonora* type which is & will be the solid foundation of the reputation. It is *Leonora* & *Anna* which will be talked of 20 years hence, when people will wonder why they attracted so little notice at the time.

This understanding lay behind his judicious management of his literary output. He arranged his work into three exclusive and hierarchical categories: 'realistic novels', 'satiric novels', and 'fantasias'. He then insisted to Pinker that the serials be published in book form under the last category, sometimes with an explanatory note attached, and that the three genres be carefully marketed so that no year would 'elapse without a serious book being issued'.[247] To critics, like Edward Garnett who praised *The Old Wives' Tale* but chastised him for frittering away his talent 'in pleasing the fourth-rate tastes of Philistia', he lost no time in making clear his ranking of the three categories: he gave the novels first place, defended the satires, and claimed that he did not value the ephemeral serials 'at all'.[248] Yet it was not only his immediate status that concerned him. He was also anxious about his long-term prospects of being canonized as a 'serious' literary novelist. Posterity was, he hoped, a world without ephemera, a purist utopia beyond the hazardous polarities of the contemporary field.

History has generally borne him out. Though his reputation as a literary novelist has never quite recovered from the battering it received at the hands of his modernist successors, most of the major novels are still in print, and some, like *A Man from the North*, are being rehabilitated as part of the publisher Alan Sutton's alternative canon of minor classics. Of the serials, only *The Grand Babylon Hotel* is still widely available outside second-hand bookshops. History, after all, has literary critics, librarians, academic syllabus-makers, publishers and film-makers on its side who supervise the process of cultural survival and who have, for the most part, colluded with Bennett by reading his career as he wished it to be read. If we take the field as our object of study, however, we are obliged to read against Bennett's own designs upon posterity and the history of his subsequent reception. It means looking beyond the sanitized and simplified version of events embodied in the canon, and rescuing the fractured, mobile figure of the author in the process of making a career. In Bennett's case, it means we must, above all, reclaim the serials he would happily have had suppressed, not as enthusiasts of 'popular culture', nor as complacent defenders of the canon, nor only as historians of the literary field, but as readers concerned to recover the dialectical energies of the major novels.

3 · LIGHT READING AND THE DIGNITY OF LETTERS: GEORGE NEWNES, LTD. AND THE MAKING OF ARTHUR CONAN DOYLE

Your duty is at home, and with good pure leaven to raise the tone of the popular taste and feeling.
Mary Foley Doyle to her son, Arthur Conan Doyle, December 1899[1]

I

TWO FACTORS NEATLY ILLUSTRATE the tensions implicit in Arthur Conan Doyle's (1859–1930) position in the literary field of the 1890s. While he respectfully attended the service held for Tennyson in Westminster Abbey on 12 October 1892, the purists of the period, young and old alike, placed him firmly outside Gosse's imagined Abbey. For Henry Harland, the *Yellow Book's* archly acerbic 'Yellow Dwarf', he belonged with Marie Corelli, Jerome K. Jerome, and Anthony Hope, all of whom showed themselves to be 'the very Dogs of Bookland' in 'their violation of the decencies of art, in their low truckling to the tastes of the purchaser, in their commonness, their vulgarity, in their total lack of suppleness and distinction'. There were, Harland conceded, different breeds within the species. Whereas Corelli's 'gushing' best-sellers were like a 'formless, unclipped white Poodle, with pink eyes', and Jerome and his 'School' – the *Idler* (1892) group that included J. M. Barrie, Robert Barr, and Israel Zangwill – performed like the 'Dog of the Public House', Conan Doyle had produced 'a litter of assorted Mongrels, going cheap – *regardez moi leurs pattes!*'[2] By this stage – Harland was writing in July 1896 – Conan Doyle's already diverse and popular output included four historical novels, *Micah Clarke* (1889), *The White Company* (1891), *The Great Shadow* (1892) and *The Refugees* (1893); *Round the Red Lamp* (1894), a series of short stories about medical life; *The Stark Munro Letters* (1895), a fictionalized autobiography; *The Exploits of Brigadier Gerard* (1896), a series of comic war adventures set in the Napoleonic era; as well as four volumes in the Sherlock Holmes saga, *A Study in Scarlet* (1888), *The Sign of the Four* (1890), *The Adventures of Sherlock Holmes* (1892) and *The Memoirs of Sherlock Holmes* (1893).

For once, Henley's observers agreed with Harland. For them, however, Conan Doyle's sorry status was reflected as much in the bibliographical form of his books as in his populist choice of genres. In their estimation, the first English book edition of *The Adventures of Sherlock Holmes*, published in a run of

10,000 copies as volume one of George Newnes's new 'Strand Library' in October 1892, told its own damning story. With its gilt edges, its light-blue cloth cover and heavily bevelled boards, its illustrations, its Royal octavo format and its 6s price, it was consciously marketed as a *de luxe* book-version of the *Strand Magazine* itself. For the *National Observer* the cultural meaning of this brand image was self-evident. Its witty parody of the stories, entitled 'The Real Sherlock Holmes', which appeared on 29 October 1892, concluded with the 'real' Holmes making the following bookish deductions:

You see this book is large and expensively brought out; moreover it is issued by a publisher who caters for the million. Why? Because the book is supposed to contain a popular element, and that popular element is myself. Now, it follows that Dr. Doyle must have heard of me, through Watson or the police; that he saw I should suit his game (which is money); and having invented spurious stories about me he hit upon a publisher similarly unscrupulous.[3]

Henley's *New Review* followed this piece of playful bibliographical vilification with a more serious denunciation. Given Conan Doyle's literary ideals and political beliefs, there is little doubt that he was one of the main undeclared targets of its Whibleyesque attack on popular authors who considered novels to be a 'means of conveying moral and historical information'; who believed 'invention' to consist in the 'contrivance of an ingenious embroilment'; and who felt it was part of their business as celebrities to involve themselves in political affairs, not least by openly declaring their 'august sympathy' towards the United States during the Anglo-American diplomatic crisis of the mid-1890s.[4] Though Conan Doyle's long and energetic public career had barely begun when this article appeared in September 1897 – in the ensuing years he would figure as a progressive champion of Divorce Law Reform, an outspoken critic of Belgian atrocities in the Congo, a patriotic defender of national honour in the aftermath of the Boer War, and a Spiritualist missionary – he had from early on proclaimed his belief in the value of strong Anglo-American relations which rested on his equally vigorous faith in the global mission of the preeminent Anglo-Saxon race. As he put it in an interview with Raymond Blathwayt in 1892:

I believe in time that every Saxon will be united under one form of government. Home Rule, with a centre of authority, and the Anglo-Saxon will swing the sword of justice over the whole world. We will not permit then the horrors of Siberia or the like. America and England, joined in their common Anglo-Saxonhood, with their common blood, will rule the world.[5]

During the diplomatic crisis to which the *New Review* alluded, he wrote a more measured letter to the *Times* calling for the establishment of an Anglo-American Society to strengthen bilateral relations.[6] In short, given his choice of literary genres, his association with the new large-scale publishing firms of the 1890s, the bibliographical form of his texts, his celebrity status and his aspirations to political influence, Conan Doyle was an easy target of purist disdain and a useful tool in their struggle to dominate the literary field of the 1890s.

Though this idea of him as an unscrupulous profiteer was, of course, an invention of the purists' self-interested discourse, on one reading he can readily be seen to exemplify what his avant-garde detractors (and one of his recent biographers) understood to be the 'Philistinism' of the late-Victorian educated middle class from which he came.[7] On this view he figures as a hearty middle-class patriot and sportsman – cricket was his particular passion – who, according to his daughter, preferred 'well-known music, hundred-best tunes music' – she mentions 'Cavalleria Rusticana', 'How Beautiful they are the Lordly Ones', 'Samson and Delilah', and 'some opera' – not 'Bach or music like that', and whose tastes in painting were restricted to the 'Old Masters'.[8] Indeed, this idea of him as, in short, the antithesis of the avant-garde intellectual, was a lasting part of his own self-understanding. While a clerk turned *arriviste* like Bennett was championing Wagner's operas as the epitome of 'high art' and castigating Londoners for their provincial reaction to the Post-Impressionist exhibition of 1910, Conan Doyle, the former provincial doctor, noted in his unpublished journal in July 1912 that 'one of the singular characteristics of the present age is a wave of artistic and intellectual insanity breaking out in various forms in various places'.[9] He was thinking of Strauss's *Electra* (1909), the Italian Futurists, and the Post-Impressionists, the last of whom he had already derided in a volume of poems entitled *Songs of the Road* (1911). In the sardonically titled 'A Post-Impressionist', a Realist painter who despairs of ever achieving fame, as only 'decadent forms of Art / Drew the patrons of the mart', one rainy night throws his latest work 'Isle of Wight from Southsea Pier' out of the window of his studio. The next morning he finds it lying in the dustbin:

> Mud-bespattered, spoiled and botched,
> Water sodden, fungus-blotched,
> . . .
> Fluids of a dappled hue,
> Blues on reds and reds on blue,
> A pea-green mother with her daughter,
> Crazy boats on crazy water
> Steering out to who knows what,
> An island or a lobster-pot?

Of course, a renowned critic then sees the 'spoiled' painting, extols it as a masterpiece, and claims that the artist has 'Out Monet-ed Monet'.[10] Compared to the 'madness' of all this, Conan Doyle considered the artistic aberrations Max Nordau had pointed to in *Degeneration* (1895), such as the Pre-Raphaelites, Wagner's operas, and the French Symbolists, examples of mere 'queerness'.[11] Though he had a high opinion of Henley as a poet, critic and patron – tellingly, however, he also thought he belonged to the 'roaring days of Marlowe of the mighty line and the pothouse fray' – these attitudes, particularly his endorsement of Nordau, clearly set him apart from the Henley circle.[12] If he happened to share Henley's distaste for the Pre-Raphaelites, his motives were manifestly different. Similarly, his cultural attitudes, and especially his strong aversion to Nietzsche, reflected his distance from the values endorsed by avant-garde magazines like the *Savoy* and the *New Age*.[13] Whereas Havelock Ellis, writing in the *Savoy* in April 1896, echoed many other literary intellectuals, including Yeats, Shaw, Symons, and George Moore, in describing Nietzsche as 'an extraordinarily interesting figure' and representing him as an exemplary antagonist to mass culture, Conan Doyle considered Nietzsche's 'philosophy' to be 'symptomatic' of the modern malaise: 'it is openly founded in lunacy for the poor fellow died raving'.[14] Two years after this private remark, in his self-consciously propagandistic pamphlet *To Arms!* which appeared in August 1914, Nietzsche resurfaced as a nightmarish spectre whose 'doctrine that the immorality of the superman may be as colossal as his strength and that the slave-evangel of Christianity was superseded by a sterner law' had, with the help of 'scolding Professors', betrayed the German public and undermined the 'strong, deep Germany of old, the Germany of music and of philosophy'.[15] Conan Doyle's proposed remedy for this avant-garde scourge was no less characteristic of his cultural position than his alarmist diagnosis. The most he could say for the new trends was that 'perhaps in art as in history a sort of French Revolution is due from time to time, odious in itself and yet inaugurating a new and better era formed rather as a reaction against it than as a consequence of it'. Yet, for all his stoicism, he was not willing merely to endure this inevitable upheaval nor to wait passively for the new era. Speaking no doubt as a representative of the British middle class, he argued that Nietzsche, Post-Impressionism, and Strauss threatened to 'submerge us' and advised that 'one should put one's shoulder to the door and keep out insanity all one can'. To validate his cause, he invoked Tennyson who was 'so great' because 'he was strong, original, and always sane'.[16] In the light of these assumptions, his association with the new popular magazines of the 1890s, like the *Strand* and the *Idler*, amounted to a mutually beneficial cultural alliance.

Yet this reading of Conan Doyle as the embodiment, and indeed champion, of middle-class cultural values reflects at best only one element of his complex position in the contemporary field. Neither a purist nor a profiteer, he occupied a more uncertain position between these two extremes as a populist with high aspirations who became increasingly anxious about his own literary standing. The characteristic precariousness of his position can initially be seen in his attitude to the various styles of literary Realism prevalent in the 1890s. Believing that issues of literary taste were best considered in a 'broad and catholic spirit', he welcomed and, at times, vigorously supported, avant-garde experimentation despite his own less radical aesthetic and generic preferences.[17] If he considered controversial New Women novelists like Hardy and 'Lucas Malet' 'extreme men' – he had in mind *Tess of the D'Urbervilles* (1891) and *The Wages of Sin* (1891) – he granted them their 'mission', which was to 'pave the way', and hoped they would help break the 'spell of Puritanism' that had, in his view, prevailed in England for too long.[18] Similarly – albeit even more prudently – in late 1889, when the controversy surrounding Henry Vizetelly's publication of Zola was still very much in the air, he described Zola's Naturalist novels as 'careful and candid' and noted their influence on George Moore's *A Mummer's Wife* (1885).[19] Four years later, when W. H. Smith and Son withdrew *Esther Waters* (1894) from their bookstalls and circulating library after complaints from Bishop Walsham How, he issued a more forthright defence of Moore's Realist fiction. The suppressed novel, he argued in a letter to the *Daily Chronicle*, was 'a good book – good in literature and in ethics – and if it is to be placed outside the pale of legitimate fiction, it is difficult to say how any true and serious work is to be done within it'. Like any accredited purist, he insisted that W. H. Smith had acted outside their jurisdiction as booksellers: their duty was simply to distribute books not to act as their 'illegal and unauthorised censor'.[20] His impatience with over-zealous moralists can also be seen in his appraisal of *The Picture of Dorian Gray* (1891) as 'a book which is surely upon a high moral plane.'[21] Yet it could be argued that these avant-garde sympathies cut two ways for him. While some clearly narrowed the gulf between him and the intelligentsia, others indicated how removed he was from their aggressive polemics. After all, few staunch Aesthetes would have been satisfied with his blithe or mindful disregard of the ethical implications of Wildean Aestheticism, and the Henley circle would have taken him to task for his tolerance of Zola and Wilde himself.

This ambivalence is less pronounced in some of Conan Doyle's other cultural attitudes, however; notably in his commitment to a particular version of the late-Victorian cult of manliness. While this constellation of attitudes still set him apart from the feminist members of John Lane's junior elite, it harmonized well with some of the more reactionary views cherished by the Henley circle. To his lasting credit, his manly ideals bore no trace of Henleyite rancour: they were rooted in the chivalric tradition of the gentleman, rather than in a complex amalgam of social, cultural and political aversions. Officially a Liberal Unionist until his conversion to Home Rule in 1911, and by inclination a paternalistic Imperialist, his broad, often conservative, socio-political tendencies are best revealed in his respect for the 'charming gentlemanly tone, the broad, liberal outlook, the general absence of bigotry and of prejudice' he claimed to have found in Macaulay, one of his earliest literary mentors.[22] Yet this is not to say his manliness had no darker undercurrents. These surfaced in the martial themes and values of his historical novels, in his Imperialist and patriotic verses that rivalled Henley at his most strident, and in some of his personal remarks on war. Few readers of his post-1919 autobiography, *Memories and Adventures* (1924), would, for instance, pass unflinchingly over his contemptuous description of pacifists in the First World War as 'half-mad cranks', nor would they readily overlook his remark, apropos the 'wonderful' atmosphere of war, that 'when the millennium comes' the world will 'lose its greatest thrill'. But manliness did not entail only militarism, since, as he put it, 'two white lies are permitted to a gentleman': if one was 'to get into a fight when the fight is a rightful one', the other was 'to screen a woman'. Always a model of gentility in his personal conduct towards women, he was never sympathetic to the suffragettes' political cause, and in social life he cherished the exclusive clubland atmosphere of male-only dinners: 'I have never heard more interesting talk than at these male gatherings, for it is notorious that though ladies greatly improve the appearance of a feast they usually detract from the quality of the talk.'[23]

Some of the cultural ramifications of this manly perspective are revealed in his attitude to Stevenson who was among the most significant influences on his literary career. In an early self-defining article, which included a strong endorsement of Meredith's refusal to be 'fettered by conventionalities', he hailed Stevenson, in terms that no member of the Henley circle would have disdained, as a pioneer of the 'modern masculine novel'. He praised him for representing the 'rougher, more stirring side of life', but, above all, he admired him for his refusal to follow the view of 'nine books out of ten' published in Britain that 'love and marriage' are 'the be-all and end-all of life', and for his recognition of the fact that a man is 'swayed by many strong emotions' encompassing 'his business, his ambitions, his friendships, his struggles'.[24] In this respect, Conan Doyle's Stevenson shared some of the virtues of his Scott and Macaulay, his other major influences, whom he admired for their 'love of all that is manly and noble and martial!'[25] Yet, unlike Scott, or indeed most of 'our greatest authors', Stevenson also commendably avoided the British novelist's 'traditional national sins': 'digression and want of method and order'.[26] In effect, Stevenson not only served as an exemplary technician and a useful resource for Conan Doyle in his formative years – among many other things he frequently reworked what he termed Stevenson's idea of the 'mutilated villain' in the Sherlock Holmes saga – he also offered him, in conjunction with Scott, a broad and ambitious literary orientation.[27] In all his fiction, but most famously in the Holmes saga with its celebrated male friendship, he showed himself to be what could be termed, in contrast to Henley's manly Realists, a manly Romantic in the tradition of Stevenson and Scott. (He was in fact approached without success by Stevenson's executors, one of whom was Charles Baxter, a prominent member of Henley circle, to complete the unfinished *St Ives*).[28] Beyond its obvious significance for Conan Doyle, this detail of his literary inheritance has at least two wider cultural implications. First, by establishing some common ground between him and the Henley circle, it brings into question any strict partition of 1890s literary culture into elitists versus populists; and, second, by drawing attention to the manly Romantics, as well as the popular literary intellectuals like Stevenson and Kipling, among the ranks of the manly Realist and anti-populist Henley circle, it emphasizes the actual complexities of their cultural position which their own polemic for the most part concealed.

If some of Conan Doyle's literary aspirations brought him closer to some members of the avant-garde, his attitudes to the literary profession, and his conception of the relationship between writers and their public, once again marked out some critical points of difference. For one thing, unlike most purists, but like his critical guide Walter Bagehot (1826–1877), he believed in the primary value and authority of the 'collective voice of the reading public'. In the article on Stevenson, which appeared in Alfred Austin's *National Review* in February 1890, he quoted with approval Bagehot's observation that 'experience shows that no man is on all points so wise as the mass of men are after a good discussion, and that if the ideas of the very wisest were, by miracle, to be fixed on the race, the certain result would be to stereotype monstrous error'. Coupled with his disgruntled belief in the 'extreme fallibility of contemporary criticism', this populist conviction underscored Conan Doyle's faith in 'public opinion' as the 'final court of appeal' in questions of literary value.[29] Similar anti-elitist sentiments dominated his rare reflections on the theory of narrative fiction. More perplexed than preoccupied by the subtleties of the many literary 'methods and schools' prevalent at the turn of the century – he mentions 'romance and realism, symbolism and naturalism' – he assumed the role of an ethically concerned pragmatist when it came to matters of aesthetic theory. In his preface to the Author's Edition of his works, written in 1901, he argued that, within the 'bounds of morality', any mode of writing was valid and legitimate in so far as it attained the 'one object' of all narrative art which was to 'interest':

Every school is right in claiming that it is justified, and every school is wrong when it tries to prove that its rival is unjustified. You are right to make your book adventurous, you are right to make it theological, you are right to make it informative or controversial or idyllic, or humorous or grave or what you will, but you *must* make it interesting. That is essential – all the rest is detail.

If the individualist spirit of Conrad's earlier manifesto is dimly apparent here, Conan Doyle's underlying eagerness to defuse cultural tensions, his defensive tone, and his banal conclusion make this more an apology for populism than a determined assertion of artistic autonomy. Yet the real force of his argument, which revealed the extent of the gulf between him and the purists, lay in his reply to his invisible opponent's retort: 'You say "interesting" – interesting to *whom*?' Here, he claimed, the 'difficulty is not really a great one'. First, the 'work which is the cult of a clique, too precious for general use, must be wanting in some quality'; and, second, the 'most honoured names in our literature' – he mentions Scott, Thackeray, Dickens, Reade, and Poe – 'do not interest one or other social stratum, but they appeal equally to all educated readers'.[30] This second point about the appeal of the Victorian classics served him in a number of ways. It confirmed his hostility to 'narrow esoteric schools' and his faith in the opinion of a broad-based reading public, while it also validated his sense of his own cultural position as reflected in the response he received from readers.[31] In May 1892, when the first series of Holmes adventures had almost completed its run in the *Strand* – the event that established Conan Doyle's enormous popularity for the first time – he claimed to have received numerous letters from an extensive range of readers, including schoolboys, commercial travellers and lawyers.[32] Ardent Imperialist and Anglo-American as he was, he hoped to build on this response and to reach, and no doubt unite, a constituency – he called it a 'tribe' – that encompassed the 'hundred millions' of the 'great English-speaking race' who, like him, cared little for the 'bickerings of cliques'.[33] Underscoring this anti-elitism, he also insisted that, as a writer, he ministered to ordinary human needs, rather than special or uniquely 'aesthetic' emotions. He wrote for 'the sleepless man worn with insomnia, the watcher beside the sick-bed, the man of business whose very sanity depends upon getting his thoughts out of one weary groove, the tired student, the woman whose only escape from an endless sordid life is that one window of imagination which leads out into the enchanted country', and he did so with the unpretentiously Utilitarian aim of leaving 'others a little happier than he found them'.[34] Though the 1901 preface represented his most detailed account of his ideas about literary practice, he had first outlined his position in an after-dinner speech at the Author's Club on 29 June 1896 where his views were reportedly received with the 'highest enthusiasm'.[35] On that occasion, in the absence of Walter Besant, Anthony Hope presided.

None of this would have improved Conan Doyle's standing among the literary purists. Yet, once again, he anxiously rejected their anti-populist stereotype of the profiteer. About the commercial side of the literary profession he was, for instance, nothing if not fastidious, particularly after he had achieved some measure of success. If he openly acknowledged in his speech at the Author's Club that money had been an important consideration in the first phase of his literary career which lasted from 1879 to 1891, his implied attitude to this fact was significantly apologetic: 'I should like to say that I was led into the field of letters by a cheering ambition, but I fear it is more correct to say that I was chased into it by a howling creditor'.[36] Though this was only partially true – 'cheering' ambitions had their place in his early career – his claims about the 'howling creditor' were not wholly exaggerated. For the first eight years of his career, his principal income as a part-time writer was from short magazine stories which he was publishing at the rate of six a year in 1883 and 1884.[37] He later claimed these sold for an average of £4 each and brought him an estimated £10 to £15 a year (though, on his own reckoning, in a good year like 1883 they would have earned him closer to double that).[38] At a time when his income from his 'ill-paying practice' in Southsea was gradually improving from £154 in 1882 to his ceiling of £300 a year in 1885, this often represented an additional, and much needed, 10 per cent on his total annual earnings.[39] On occasion, when things were particularly difficult, a considerate editor, like James Hogg of *London Society*, would double his usual rate per story from £5 to £10, and so enable him to keep the rent-collector at bay for another quarter.[40] Yet, if money had been an incentive in his early years as an amateur, by the end of his long professional career he was eager to correct any misunderstandings of his conduct as a writer. In 1927 in a contribution to a symposium on writing organized by Herbert Greenhough Smith, the managing editor of the *Strand*, he set out his position in anxiously unequivocal terms:

From the time that I no longer had to write for sustenance I have never considered money in my work. When the work is done the money is very welcome, and it is the author who should have it. But I have never accepted a contract because it is well paid, and indeed I have very seldom accepted a contract at all, preferring to wait until I had some idea which stimulated me, and not letting my agent or editor know until I was well advanced with the work.[41]

This change of outlook, made possible mainly by a greater sense of financial security, coincided surprisingly with his decision in May 1891 to give up medicine for good and to become a professional writer. 'I was determined', he recalled, 'now that I had no longer the excuse of absolute pecuniary pressure, never again to write anything which was not as good as I could possibly make it'.[42] This implied disdain for profiteering reflected some of his most cherished professional ideals. While he believed that 'every man with a drop of artistic blood in his veins' shared his high principles, his attitudes were informed less by a Henleyite idea of artistic genius, than by the values he embraced as a middle-class professional.[43] As he made clear in August 1897 in his public criticism of Hall Caine, he viewed literature as a 'high profession' comparable to 'law, medicine, [and] the Army'. It followed that, like other professionals, authors were (or ought to be) bound by 'unwritten laws' of 'gentlemanly etiquette' according to which commercialism, such as Caine's habitual and inappropriate self-publicizing, was deemed 'unworthy' of the 'dignity' and 'tone of the profession'. Though he hoped that the Society of Authors would deal with future violations of this code, 'as legal or medical societies enforce a high standard of professional etiquette', he felt he had to protest against Caine's degrading 'wire-pullings and personalities' as 'every body of men is the guardian of its own honour'. He was, he insisted, not acting on 'narrow individual grounds', but out of concern about the example set for the 'young aspirant', respect for the 'honourable traditions' handed down by 'great men', and in the interests of the profession as a whole.[44] Though he was himself never diffident about promoting his own work – he discreetly financed advertisements for the book edition of *The Adventures of Sherlock Holmes*, for instance – after this incident Caine became synonymous in his mind with dishonourable self-promotion.[45] In 1902, when attempting to explain his reluctance to accept the offer of a knighthood to his insistent mother – he called it the 'badge of the provincial mayor' – he invoked both Caine and Alfred Austin, then poet laureate. Citing 'black ancestral pride' as the main reason for his stubbornness, he went on to remark:

Fancy Rhodes or Chamberlain or Kipling doing such a thing! And why should my standards be lower than theirs? It is the Alfred Austin and Hall Caine type of man who takes rewards.[46]

On this occasion his formidable mother got her way, though he slyly reasserted himself in 'The Three Garridebs' (*Case-Book*) when he made Holmes, the exemplary though many-sided Doylean gentleman and purist, decline a similar offer.[47] As a victim early on in his career of American piracy and unscrupulous publishers, he was equally critical of profiteering in other areas of publishing. In May 1899, for instance, provoked by a personal injury, he publicly attacked the 'crying evil' of multiple-reviewing.[48] In this campaign he found a passionate, but less focused, ally in Charles Whibley and, not unexpectedly, a cavalier opponent in Arnold Bennett, unashamed multiple-reviewer *extraordinaire*.[49] In *The Truth About an Author* (1902), Bennett concluded the account of his prodigious, but sadly never very lucrative, career as a reviewer for the *Academy*, *Woman*, and *Hearth & Home*, with a swipe at the 'carping' 'minority' who 'demand the scalps of multiple-reviewers as a terrible example and warning to the smaller fry'.[50] Anxious as he was about his own cultural dignity and credibility, Conan Doyle was never capable of such high-spirited provocation.

Respect for the 'dignity of letters' and for the 'honourable traditions' handed down from the past was not only manifest in Conan Doyle's values and attitudes, it was also displayed in the practical strategies that determined the shape of his literary career. Most importantly, despite both his anti-elitist belief in the primary value of public opinion and his claims about his initial commercial motives, ambition, in the form of a determined bid for cultural prestige, lay behind many of his early tactical decisions. While contributing a number of articles to the *Lancet* (1823) and the *British Medical Journal* (1842) as a young doctor making his way in his new profession, he was also, as an aspirant writer, seeking out reputable literary magazines in a similar attempt to establish his credentials.[51] During the initial phase of his 'long and trying' literary apprenticeship, from 1879 to 1887, he published only short stories, most of which were exercises in the mystery and adventure genres.[52] Varying in length from 3,000 to 14,000 words, and most often written in the form of a first-person or first-person framed personal memoir, they ranged from accounts of greed and superstition at the edge of the Empire, as in his first story 'The Mystery of Sasassa Valley' (1879), to political intrigues involving secret revolutionary organizations, such as 'A Night Among the Nihilists' (1881) and 'An Exciting Christmas' (1883); and from gothic romances like 'The Winning Shot' (1883) to early, detective-style pieces such as 'The Cabman's Story' (1884). These appeared chiefly – though often despite his best efforts – in established and respectable middle-class shilling monthlies like *London Society* (1862) and *Temple Bar* (1861); in a larger circulation sixpenny magazine like *Cassell's Family Magazine* (1867); and in popular weeklies like *Chambers's Journal* (1832), *All the Year Round* (1859) and the Religious Tract Society's *Boy's Own Paper* (1879). Yet, throughout this period, he regularly began by first submitting stories to the more prestigious *Blackwood's* (1817) and *Cornhill* (1860) mostly without success. He began sending manuscripts, along with suitably deferential covering letters, to the editor of the former, then William Blackwood III, as early as 1880. Apropos 'The Actor's Duel', for instance, he wrote in early 1882: 'However defective the working out may be I am conscious that the denouement is both original and powerful, worthy, I hope of the traditions of your magazine.'[53] Like many others, it was rejected and so 'in disgust' he sent it to *Boy's Own Paper*, only to have it rejected once again. He had to wait until 1890 before he crossed the 'stout Scottish barrier' of *Blackwood's* for the first and last time when the editor accepted 'A Physiologist's Wife', a story Conan Doyle claimed was written under the influence of Henry James. With the *Cornhill*, then under James Payn (1830–98), he was more fortunate. In July 1883, Payn agreed to publish 'J. Habakuk Jephson's Statement', his fictional resolution to the riddle of *Mary Celeste* which had been found mysteriously abandoned by its crew in 1872. This was his first major conquest, and he recalled it in characteristic terms:

What gave me great pleasure and for the first time made me realise that I was ceasing to be a hack writer and was getting into good company was when James Payn accepted my short story 'Habakuk Jephson's Statement' for 'Cornhill'. I had a reverence for this splendid magazine with its traditions from Thackeray to Stevenson and the thought that I had won my way into it pleased me even more than the cheque for £30, which came duly to hand.[54]

He did not seem perturbed that the magazine had by this time lost some of its cultural allure. Payn, a former editor of *Chambers's Journal*, and, like Walter Besant, a popular novelist and an advocate of the new professionalism, took over the editorship of *Cornhill* from Leslie Stephen in January 1883.[55] He was installed as part of a new, more populist editorial policy in an attempt to boost circulation, which had dropped under Stephen's editorship from 20,000 to 12,000 a month, and to compete with the more successful sixpenny family magazines like *Cassell's* (1867).[56] He lowered the cover price from one shilling to sixpence; and replaced Stephen's stable of authors, which had included Hardy, James, Gosse, and Stevenson, with, among others, Grant Allen, Stanley Weyman, Sabine Baring-Gould, Rider Haggard, and Conan Doyle himself. Of course, given the policy of authorial anonymity still maintained by most magazines in the 1880s, including *Cornhill*, Conan Doyle's early successes were largely private rather than public. For someone with his aspirations, this inevitably became a source of frustration, and, after seven years as an anonymous magazine author, he realized that 'a man may put the very best that is in him into magazine work for years and years, and reap no benefit from it, save, of course, the inherent benefits of literary practice'.[57] This dissatisfaction lay behind his next major career decision: to write a novel that would be published under his own name and preferably by a well-established house.

II

The next episode in the making of Arthur Conan Doyle happened by chance to coincide with Sherlock Holmes's inauspicious public debut. *A Study in Scarlet* was Conan Doyle's fourth attempt at writing the novel that would give him the entrée he required, but it was his first to be accepted for publication.[58] He had settled on the title and briefly sketched some initial thoughts about the main protagonists by late 1885.[59] His early notes indicate that the new novel was planned as a detective story – his first in that more specialized mystery genre – to be set in '221 B Upper Baker Street', the lodging shared by the two principal characters, then called 'Ormond Sacker' and 'J Sherrinford Holmes'. It was also intended to be self-consciously revisionist. In the initial sketch, an indeterminate first-person narrator, most probably the Holmes figure, 'petulantly' tosses aside a 'volume' and declares 'I have no patience with people who build up fine theories in their own armchairs which can never be reduced to practice'. He then goes on to denounce Emile Gaboriau's (1832–73) detective-hero Lecoq as a 'bungler', and to praise Poe's (1809–49) Dupin as an 'analytical genius' who was, however, sometimes 'more sensational than clever'.[60] It was an ambitious choice of literary opponents. Poe was, in Conan Doyle's view, the 'originator of the detective story', and his tales were second only to Macaulay's *Essays* on the list of books that had most influenced his 'life' – he also said Dupin had been one of his childhood heroes.[61] Gaboriau, by contrast, was in 1885 one of the most prominent contemporary detective fiction writers in Britain. A popular *feuilletoniste* in France in the 1860s, his posthumous British success, mainly the result of a publishing initiative by the controversial Henry Vizetelly, contributed to the enormous popularity of the detective genre in the 1880s. As the *Saturday Review* commented on 4 December 1886, 'if the abundance of supply affords any accurate test', detective novels 'must surely be counted amongst the greatest successes of the day'. This new fashion was not the product of 'native talent', it noted, since the 'stories apparently most popular with the British public are of French or American origin'. The anonymous reviewer then went on to cite in particular the successful 'reprints' of Anna Katherine Green's *The Leavenworth Case* (1878) and

A Strange Disappearance (1884) as well as the 'not always irreproachable translations of Gaboriau and Du Boisgobey' published by the 'enterprising' Vizetelly
in his 'Popular French Novels' series.[62] Given that Conan Doyle claimed to
have been reading Gaboriau's *Lecoq, the Detective* (1881), *The Lerouge Case* (1881),
and *The Gilded Clique* (1884) in the mid-1880s, it is likely that the 'volume' the
proto-Holmes throws aside is one of these three novels.[63] The early notes also
included some preliminary ideas about the two main protagonists. While
Sacker was, at this point, simply said to live with Holmes and to have come
from Afghanistan, Holmes, clearly the hero, was already a more fully
developed figure. He was to be a 'reserved', 'sleepy eyed young man'; working
as a 'Consulting detective' and living on £400 a year; and he was to be a
'philosopher', a connoisseur – he is a 'Collector of rare Violins . . . An Amati'
– and a scientist associated in some way with a 'Chemical laboratory'.[64] As
Conan Doyle later recalled the genesis of the story, both his revisionist
objectives and his idea of Holmes were partly inspired by his medical mentor,
the Edinburgh surgeon Joseph Bell whom he had already alluded to in one of
his earliest stories.[65] When he considered writing a story along the lines
suggested by Poe and Gaboriau, he immediately thought of his charismatic
teacher's 'eagle face, of his curious ways, of his eerie trick of spotting details'.[66]
He described his subsequent thought process in an interview for *Tit-Bits* in
December 1900:

I began to think, suppose my old professor at Edinburgh were in the place of one of
these lucky detectives, he would have worked out the process of effect from cause just as
logically as he would have diagnosed a disease, instead of having something given to
him by mere luck, which . . . does not happen in real life.[67]

His plan was, then, to rewrite the detective genre by investing it with a new
aura of plausibility and scientific rigour and by devising an alluring but
credible intellectual hero.

By the time he returned to these initial ideas in March 1886, after
completing his third novel *The Firm of Girdlestone*, he had made some emenda-
tions and designed a narrative, composed largely of borrowed fragments,
around which to develop his innovative plan. For the 'real story' to be
uncovered by Holmes, he adopted the conventional mystery genre device of
the vengeance plot familiar to him in the stories of Mayne Reid, Wilkie
Collins, and Stevenson.[68] For the background to this plot and to his villains, he
exploited, often unduly, the notion of the Mormons as a ruthlessly oppressive
secret society found in one of his favourite Stevenson stories, 'The Destroying
Angel'.[69] He also settled on a new, more mundane name for Sacker as well as
a more imposing first name for his hero; and he defined more clearly the
nature of the relationship between the two – Sacker/Watson was to be a first-
person narrator who would play a commonplace Boswell to Holmes's charismatic Johnson. At the same time, while keeping to his revisionist scheme, he
slightly modified his initial conception of his hero, and so created an

ambivalent first portrait of Holmes. At some points in the final text, Holmes is figured simply as an exceptional, if idiosyncratic, man of science, rather than a versatile late-Victorian savant. In the opening scenes, for instance, he is shown working in a chemical laboratory (as planned, though for the first and last time in the saga), and this is followed by a chapter in which he elaborates his views on detection, first developed in his Bell-like article 'The Book of Life', as an exact science of observation and analysis (again as planned).[70] Yet no doubt to emphasize his revisionism – the attacks on Poe and Gaboriau, though slightly modified, are still there – Conan Doyle also made Holmes seem for the most part a learned, but narrow, specialist.[71] In Watson's catalogue of the hero's accomplishments, Holmes is shown to have no knowledge of literature, philosophy, or astronomy, and little of politics; but he is well versed in some aspects of botany and geology and in all aspects of chemistry, anatomy, British law, and 'Sensational Literature'. More specifically, he is shown to be ignorant of Copernicus and Carlyle. Yet, at the same time, remnants of the polymathic proto-Holmes still remain, since he is, among other things, a skilled but eccentric violin player (he is also a connoisseur, rather than collector of violins) who knows about Darwin's theory of music; a bibliophile; and an expert at combative sports.[72] In *The Sign of the Four*, any tension between these two aspects of Holmes was resolved when Conan Doyle settled on the final conception of his hero.

He went on to write the final 43,000-word draft in record time: whereas his third novel had taken him almost two years to complete, his fourth took a matter of weeks. He finished it sometime in April 1886. On 7 May, Payn, the first editor to see the manuscript, returned it with an apology for having 'kept your story an unconscionably long time'. Payn's letter was also the first of many disappointing rejections. Though he thought highly of the story, saying it was the 'best of the "shilling dreadfuls" – except Stevenson's', he turned it down on the grounds that Smith, Elder did not cater to the shilling market and that it was both 'too long – & too short' for publication in *Cornhill*.[73] After Payn, Conan Doyle proposed it to Arrowsmith, who had recently had a major success with 'Hugh Conway's' detective best-seller *Called Back*, which first appeared in *Arrowsmith's Christmas Annual* in 1883.[74] They returned it unread in July, and when it was also rejected by his third choice, Frederick Warne & Co., he wrote to his mother: 'Verily literature is a difficult oyster to open.'[75] When *The Firm of Girdlestone*, which he never rated highly, was repeatedly refused he felt 'grieved but not surprised'. But when *A Study* also began to do the 'circular tour' of magazines and publishers he admitted he was 'hurt'. This time he felt confident the 'book was as good as [he] could make it' and that it 'deserved a better fate'. Finally, having accepted that his only chance lay with publishers of what he disdainfully called 'cheap and sensational literature', he sent it to Ward, Lock & Co. in September.[76] On the indirect recommendation of their chief editor's wife, Mrs Bettany, who was herself an aspiring novelist and a contributor to *Temple Bar*, *The Argosy*, and *Belgravia*, they agreed to publish it, but only on two conditions: first, that it should be held over for a year, as the market was 'flooded at present with cheap fiction'; and second, that they could buy the British copyright outright for £25 (or 1s for 86 words).[77] Conan Doyle hesitated to accept the proposal and attempted unsuccessfully to secure a royalty. 'It was not merely the small sum offered', he later recalled, 'but it was the long delay, for this book might open a road for me'.[78] After his 'repeated disappointments' however, and given his professional goal, he reluctantly accepted the terms and the deal was completed by 20 November.[79]

As planned, the story first appeared a year later in Ward, Lock's popular *Beeton's Christmas Annual* (1859) for November 1887, alongside two drawing-room plays and with illustrations by D. H. Friston.[80] The first book edition, which never sold particularly well, was then published as a 'shilling dreadful', with illustrations by Conan Doyle's father, in July 1888.[81] It had white paper covers, an appropriately red title, and it carried advertisements for Pears' Soap, Ridges's Food, and Sir James Murray's Pure Fluid Magnesia. As the price, publishing format, and early reception suggest, the story was first marketed as popular literary entertainment suited to established middle-class tastes. Though all favourable, the few reviews of the shilling *Annual*, which appeared mostly in provincial papers, considered it only an impressive variant of the customary Christmas fare. According to a reviewer in the *Hampshire Post*, the detective genre, of which Conan Doyle's story was a 'brilliant example', was simply the latest development in the long tradition of 'bloody tragedies' – encompassing tales of the supernatural; accounts of sea, mine, and railway accidents; and murder mysteries – that appeared annually 'for our Christmas enjoyment'.[82] The first book edition entered a similarly well-established popular market. In their promotional 'Publishers' Preface', Ward, Lock made much of Charles Doyle's illustrations and laid particular emphasis on his being the younger brother of Richard Doyle, the 'eminent' *Punch* (1841) illustrator.[83] Yet, as the *Saturday Review* made scrupulously clear, the success, and so the status, of the detective genre was largely an effect of its modes of publication and distribution: 'It is a book-stall success, so to speak; that achieved by extensive, sometimes phenomenal, sales at low rates, and meaning a widespread dissemination far exceeding anything the circulating libraries could accomplish.'[84] *A Study*, which was sold chiefly at railway bookstalls, like W. H. Smith's, was part of the general trend. It was shrewdly singled out from a 'flood of new books' by the distinguished critic Andrew Lang – as an advisor to Longmans, Green, & Co., he had recently accepted *Micah Clarke* for publication – and recommended to readers of *Longman's Magazine* (1869) as an excellent 'railway story, to beguile the way'.[85] Indeed, as Conan Doyle had assumed, most of his first readers would, like him, have been in a position to appreciate a parody of the more popular, but still broadly middle-class, morning papers which formed part of his pantomime story.[86] In the fictional newspaper reports covering Drebber's murder, the old-style Liberal *Daily Telegraph* (1855) blames the Socialists, the Conservative *Standard* (1827) blames the Liberals, while the more progressive Liberal *Daily News* (1845) blames Continental despotism.[87]

Though Conan Doyle had the satisfaction of realizing his revisionist goals in *A Study*, his first published novel was, from a professional point of view, a double disappointment: to gain access to the field he had chosen a particularly fashionable genre but he had been obliged to sign away all the British rights and accept a less than dignified publishing format. His next venture into the book world was to be more ambitious. In mid-1887, 'determined to test [his] powers to the full', he began *Micah Clarke*, the historical novel he had had in mind since 1885. His reason for adopting the new genre at that point was, he later recalled, that it seemed 'the one way of combining a certain amount of literary dignity with those scenes of action and adventure which were natural to my young and ardent mind'. As some of his other remarks indicate, however, this idea of the genre as a useful compromise between his 'natural' tastes and his professional goals was not borne out in practice. The 'literary dignity' of historical novels always counted most in his book. This was partly an effect of his attitude to the 'honourable traditions' handed down by his more revered literary mentors, Walter Scott and Macaulay, and his own secret ambition to be the Scott of the 1890s; but it was also rooted in his understanding of the genre's status relative to detective fiction. He had various reasons for this critical opinion. Historical fiction was, in the first place, superior to the detective story because it put character before plot. While the detective genre demanded only 'the use of a certain portion of one's imaginative faculty, the invention of a plot', historical novels left plenty of 'scope for character drawing'.[88] Then again, detective stories, like most popular genres, made too much of the single heroic figure. As he put it in the preface to the 'Author's Edition':

To me it always seems that the actual condition of a country at any time, a true sight of it with its beauties and brutalities, its life as it really was . . . are of greater interest than the small aims and petty love story of any single human being.[89]

As the reference to 'life as it really was' suggests, this claim about the scope of the two genres was bound up with his ideas about their relative mimetic potential. In his view, historical fiction was always more earnestly informative than playfully fictive; whereas detective stories belonged firmly in what he called the 'fairy kingdom of romance'.[90] Not that his contemporary readers necessarily agreed with this categorization. Much to his dismay, critics insisted on praising *The White Company* (1891), which he thought 'made an accurate picture' of the 'great age' of Edward III, as a stirring adventure yarn.[91] In a dejected letter to his mother he commented, 'it seems to me most critics don't know the difference between good work and bad'. His primary intention, he claimed, had not been to tell a good action story, but 'to draw the exact types of character of the folk then living'.[92] As he grandly declared in an interview in 1892, 'I really think I have succeeded in reconstructing the fourteenth century.'[93]

This was not simply bravado. For him there were serious ideological issues at stake in writing historical fiction which made its mimetic powers indispensable. Part of the distinct value of these supposedly authentic literary reconstructions lay in their serious political purpose. From the outset he saw his novels about the past as a means of bringing about the future world order which, as we have seen, depended in his view on a strong Anglo-American alliance. In 1891 he dedicated *The White Company*, 'To the Hope of the Future / The Reunion of the English-Speaking Races' and called the novel a 'Chronicle of Our Common / Ancestry'. And, two years later, he wrote to his mother about *The Refugees* (1893), which centred on the fate of a Puritan New Englander and a New York woodsman in the court of Louis XIV:

If I, a Britisher, can draw their early types so as to win their approval I should indeed be proud. By such international associations nations are drawn together, and on the drawing together of these two nations depends the future history of the world.[94]

These assumptions make sense of his lofty prediction, made in October 1894, that 'the age of fiction is coming – the age when religious and social and political changes will all be effected by means of a novelist'.[95] These were not the views of a literary purist, but they were those of a writer with an ambitious extra-literary mission for whom the historical genre was not mere entertainment. This scheme of literary values, which generated many of Conan Doyle's positional anxieties, had a significant impact on the rest of his career.

Unlike *A Study*, *Micah Clarke* was not a fluent version of a popular genre. It took a year to research and five months to write. When it was completed in early 1888, he recalled, 'I thought I had a tool in my hands that would cut a path for me.'[96] This time his hopes were rewarded. After being refused by Payn and Blackwood, among others, it was finally published, on Lang's advice, by the equally well-established firm of Longman, Green, in February 1889, in an elegant 6s first edition of 1,000 copies, bound in dark blue cloth with no advertisements for soap or patent medicines.[97] With Lang's endorsement, which Conan Doyle called his 'first real opening', as well as Longman's imprint, good reviews, and impressive sales, he felt he had, ten years into his career, 'the first corner-stone laid for some sort of literary reputation'.[98] With a new sense of direction, in Easter 1889 he began the extensive background research for *The White Company*, his second historical novel, and by 19 August he was ready to write.[99] The novel would eventually consolidate his position as an historical novelist, and give him the satisfaction of a coveted *Cornhill* serialization and the sober respectability of a 31s 6d three-volume first book edition by Smith, Elder – when it was accepted, 'in spite of' Payn's low opinion of historical novels, Doyle remarked that he had 'fulfilled another ambition by having a serial in that famous magazine'.[100] But its composition was inauspiciously interrupted by his first major commission. In late August that year, Ward, Lock, who had recently become the British publishers of the Philadelphia-based *Lippincott's Magazine*, and the monthly's American managing editor, Joseph Marshall Stoddart, were commissioning British authors for the 'Special English Edition' of the magazine which was to begin publication in January 1890.[101] Ward, Lock duly recommended one of their few recent discoveries to Stoddart, and so Conan Doyle was invited to London for a business dinner at the Langham Hotel, along with Stoddart's friends, Oscar Wilde and Thomas Patrick Gill, a former associate editor of the *North American Review*.[102] It was, according to Conan Doyle, who was then still a little-known provincial doctor, 'a golden evening' for him which marked his advancement in the literary field. To his 'surprise' Wilde, the 'champion of aestheticism', had apparently read *Micah Clarke*, and 'was enthusiastic about it, so that I did not feel a complete outsider.' He also reported that Wilde's conversation, as well as his 'delicacy of feeling and tact', left an 'indelible impression' on his mind.[103] At this meeting both authors accepted a contract to write a story for *Lippincott's* – Wilde went on to produce *The Picture of Dorian Gray* while Conan Doyle wrote *The Sign*. In a diary entry for 30 August, Conan Doyle noted: 'Agreed to write Story of 45000 words for £100 for Lippincott'.[104] After his bad experience with Ward, Lock, he safely ensured that the agreement, which included the full American rights, covered only three months' serial rights in Britain.[105] For these limited rights alone he was now earning at the rate of 1s for 22 words. As he was probably left free to choose the genre and subject for the commission, he decided on his own initiative to 'rig up' Holmes once again, and so, unwittingly, allowed his detective-hero to preside over another change in his professional status.[106] As he remarked in 1896, there 'comes a day when, instead of sending a story, a story is ordered, and that day marks the turning point in an author's career'.[107]

Like *A Study*, the final text, this time 44,000 words, took only weeks to produce. Though the manuscript was to be delivered only before January 1890, his diary entry for 30 September 1889 notes: '"The Sign of the Four" finished & dispatched.'[108] He wrote to Stoddart the next day:

I think it is pretty fair, though I am not usually satisfied with my own things. It has the advantage over the *Study in Scarlet* not only as being much more intricate, but also as forming a connected narrative without any harking back as in the second part of the *Study*. Holmes, I am glad to say, is in capital form all through.[109]

Like its predecessor, though to a lesser extent, the rapidly assembled narrative was composed of many derivative elements. Among other things, the 'real story', or the object of Holmes's investigation, is a variation on the familiar vengeance plot; Jonathan Small, the sympathetic murderer, is figured as one of

Stevenson's 'mutilated villains'; and the central crime, the murder of Bartholomew Sholto, is a re-working of the 'sealed-room' mystery taken from Poe's 'The Murders in the Rue Morgue' (1841). There were, however, also a number of innovations and developments. Besides making the technical improvements outlined in the letter, and shifting the love interest from the background of the vengeance plot to the foregrounded detective quest, he also reinvented Holmes as a sophisticated, and philosophically inclined, virtuoso, thereby settling the ambiguities of *A Study* and, as Roden suggests, tailoring his hero for a 'wider and more reputable readership'.[110] In a letter to Ronald Knox of 5 July 1912, Conan Doyle noted that, while Holmes 'never shows heart', he

changed entirely as the stories went on. In the first one . . . he was a mere calculating machine, but I had to make him more of an educated human being as I went on with him.[111]

In *The Sign*, Holmes's humanizing education took two forms. First, Conan Doyle dropped the idea of him as a narrow specialist, and gave him the cultural credentials of an educated member of the late-Victorian middle class. In this new incarnation, Holmes is able, for instance, to explain Carlyle's indebtedness to German Romanticism, to quote philosophical maxims from Goethe, and to recommend Winwood Reade's 'daring' secularist work *The Martyrdom of Man* to Watson.[112] Here Conan Doyle simply projected his own educated tastes onto Holmes. In the 1880s he had himself discussed Carlyle and Reade in letters to local Portsmouth newspapers and at meetings of the Portsmouth Literary and Scientific Society.[113] His second approach was less directly personal. Writing in the month after his dinner with Wilde, and his first brush with the 1880s avant-garde, he decided to incorporate a comic portrait of an aesthete into his story in the figure of Thaddeus Sholto. Though the fictional aesthete bears some slight physical resemblance to Wilde, his 'very high head' and bald scalp, his luxurious Oriental decor, his collection of European wines and paintings, and his suburban address, make him more like a popular caricature than the real thing.[114] In a less satirical spirit, Conan Doyle at the same time chose to emphasize Holmes's bohemian tendencies by investing him with the borrowed prestige of advanced and mildly decadent culture.[115] While *A Study* had opened with an imposing portrait of the Bell-like hero as an eccentric man of science, its sequel begins with an equally dramatic image of him as a Wildean Aesthete. At the outset, he is figured as a world-weary cocaine (and morphine) addict, who abhors the 'dull routine of existence', and later, during a dinner with Watson, he is shown to be a 'brilliant' conversationalist.[116] Though the solitary and reserved specialist-Holmes of *A Study* had been 'communicative enough' at times, he is now able to 'talk exceedingly well' when he chooses on a wide range of arcane subjects, including 'miracle plays', 'medieval pottery', 'Stradivarius violins', 'the Buddhism of Ceylon' and 'the warships of the future'.[117] (In his autobiography,

Conan Doyle recalled that at the Langham dinner Wilde had spoken of, among other things, the 'wars of the future').[118] Against this background, too, his gentlemanly attitude to his profession and his pure interest in the 'work itself', which had been there from the start, begin to acquire additional significance, prefiguring the Holmes of 'The Copper Beeches' (*Adventures*) who 'loves art for its own sake' – the art, of course, being detection.[119] As Conan Doyle had shown with Bell, Holmes was in part a caricature of all the charismatic purists his author had met. In *The Sign*, then, Holmes became the more fully developed and composite mythic hero of the saga, at once a Doylean gentleman, a languid aesthete, a rigorous scientist, a learned scholar, and a daring man of action.

The Sign was published in three distinct formats in 1890: as a complete magazine story in the British and American editions of *Lippincott's Magazine* (February); as a book in an American edition by J. B. Lippincott (February) and in a British edition by Spencer Blackett (October); and as a serial in three provincial British newspapers (May–September).[120] As such, it was clearly a financial success for Conan Doyle, and it was also professionally useful. Holmes was now keeping better company in Spencer Blackett's attractive 3s 6d 'Standard Library' and in *Lippincott's*, than he had been in *Beeton's Christmas Annual* or Ward, Lock's 'shilling dreadful' format; he was also reaching a wider national and international readership and being noticed, albeit critically, by such prestigious metropolitan literary reviews as the *Academy* and the *Athenaeum*.[121] One indication of Conan Doyle's response to these developments is that, early the following year, under very different personal circumstances, he decided on his own initiative to return to the detective genre and to repackage his hero in a series of short stories suitable for popular magazines.

At the end of November 1890, on the advice of a Harley Street dermatologist, he decided to give up his never very lucrative position as a general practitioner in Southsea and to train as an eye specialist in Vienna, then capital of the Austro-Hungarian Empire which included Bohemia.[122] His long-term plan, he wrote to his sister, was to learn '*all* there is to know about the eye' and then to 'come back to London and start as an eye-surgeon, still of course keeping literature as my milk-cow'.[123] As a London-based specialist he hoped to increase his income and to give himself more time for writing. The excursion to Vienna, which lasted from 5 January to 24 March 1891, was, however, less than successful as far as his medical career was concerned. According to Green, 'his knowledge of technical German proved inadequate and most of the time was given over to the pleasures of Viennese society, skating and writing'.[124] He spent the first three weeks, for instance, working on *The Doings of Raffles Haw*, a 34,000-word serial, on commission for *Answers* (1888), Alfred Harmsworth's new penny weekly.[125] On his return, he none the less set about establishing himself as an eye specialist and by 1 April he had acquired professional premises near Harley Street.[126] Yet, within the first week of his arrival, he sent A. P. Watt, whose literary agency he had been using since late 1890, the manuscript of 'A Scandal in Bohemia'.[127] In a letter dated 31 March, Watt wrote:

I am in receipt of yours of today's date and will take the story which has also arrived to the 'Strand Magazine', as none of the other periodicals can use more than 7000 words at the outside. I note that you propose to write a series, and that you will entrust the sale of it to us.[128]

Though the allusion to 'a series' and the word length suggest that the story referred to is most likely 'A Scandal in Bohemia' – it came to just over 8,660 words – Watt's next letter, dated 11 April, written the day after he received the manuscript of the second story 'A Case of Identity', clarifies matters:

You will remember I offered the first story of Sherlock Holmes to 'The Strand'. They have accepted it and expressed a wish to have the remainder of the series, and I shall, therefore, with your permission, offer them the second instalment.[129]

Conan Doyle's pocket diary for 1891 indicates that he produced the new Holmes adventures in his usual brisk manner – in 1892 it was reported that it took him 'about a week' to get one done, and that he could write 'some three thousand words a day'.[130] Having dispatched 'A Case of Identity' on 10 April, he sent Watt 'The Red-Headed League' on the 20th, followed by 'The Boscombe Valley Mystery' on the 27th.[131] Then there was a brief hiatus of two weeks, followed by a longer one of over two months. On 4 May he went down with influenza, and so the fifth story reached Watt only by the 12th. In a letter dated the following day, Watt offered sympathies about the illness and acknowledged receipt of the 'fifth [i.e. not the last] in the Sherlock Holmes series' – 'The Five Orange Pips' – which he said he would 'deliver to the "Strand Magazine" at once'.[132] The sixth story followed some months later. In August, when Conan Doyle had fully recovered, and once he finished writing *Beyond the City*, a serial for *Good Words*, he dispatched 'The Man with the Twisted Lip'.[133]

The Watt correspondence casts new light on the composition and serialization of these first six stories, and clears up some of the confusion caused by Conan Doyle and Herbert Greenhough Smith, the *Strand's* managing editor.[134] In the first place, the letters reveal that the idea for a series was there from the start and that it came from Conan Doyle. This is again implicit in Watt's letter of 22 April in which he requests the 'exact wording' for the 'collective title of the Sherlock Holmes series'.[135] Thus far the correspondence simply confirms the version of events outlined in Conan Doyle's autobiography. There he claimed that the idea of a 'single character running through a series' of short stories struck him as an 'ideal compromise' between the two staples of the magazine market – the serial and the 'disconnected' short story – and that 'I believe I was the first to realize this and "The Strand Magazine" the first to put it into practice.'[136] Though the idea was no doubt inspired in part by Stevenson's *New Arabian Nights* (1882) and *More New Arabian Nights* (1885), as well as by Poe's Dupin stories, Conan Doyle did create an influential narrative form particularly suited to the conditions of the monthly magazine market. Writing in the *Academy* for 24 February 1900, Bennett noted that the form most favoured by the illustrated sixpenny monthlies was 'the connected series of short stories, of five to six thousand words, in which the same characters, pitted against a succession of criminals or adverse fates, pass again and again through situations thrillingly dangerous, and emerge at length into the calm security of ultimate conquest'. In his view, Conan Doyle 'invented it, or reinvented it to present uses', Mrs L. T. Meade was its 'most popular current practitioner', and Grant Allen and Kipling were among its many other adherents – including Bennett himself who produced *The Loot of the Cities* (1905) series on commission for *Windsor Magazine*.[137] Yet the Watt files also suggest that Conan Doyle most likely conceived of the initial series in *six* parts himself. On 14 April, just after receiving the second story, Watt wrote to S. S. McClure, the New York syndicator: 'I . . . understand that you are willing to give the sum of £50 (fifty pounds) for a series of six stories of a detective nature relating to the experiences of a Mr. Sherlock Holmes.'[138] There is no evidence in the correspondence to suggest that Watt or McClure wished Conan Doyle to make it a six-part series, and, though the *Strand*, as we have seen, was eager to take the whole series, at this early stage the editor did not commission more stories. Smith's only request was for a minor textual addition to 'A Scandal'. In a letter of 11 April, Watt wrote to Conan Doyle:

I have the pleasure of herewith sending per book post proofs of 'A Scandal in Bohemia'. With regard to this story, the editor said to me the other day when calling that he would be glad if you could insert a few lines at the beginning of the story, in order to make the character of Sherlock Holmes intelligible to those who have not had the pleasure of reading 'The Sign of Four'[sic]. Perhaps you can insert a few lines in the manner suggested.[139]

Interestingly, it appears from Green's collation of the MS and the printed editions, that Conan Doyle's only response was to remove the single reference to *The Sign of the Four* (1890) which had appeared in the second paragraph of the MS (and presumably in the proofs as well). Thus, in the MS, and the 1993 Oxford edition, the opening sentence of the second paragraph reads: 'I had seen little of Holmes since the singular chain of events which I have already narrated in a bold fashion under the heading of *The Sign of Four* [sic].' In the *Strand*, and the subsequent book editions taken from it, the 'revised' sentence says simply: 'I had seen little of Holmes lately.'[140] Not surprisingly, Conan Doyle did not lose much time over this revision. Watt wrote to Smith on 14 April: 'I have the pleasure of herewith enclosing proofs corrected by the author of "A Scandal in Bohemia".'[141] No doubt Conan Doyle thought this fudge would be the easiest way to remove any confusion in the mind of the reader and to get Smith off his back. It should be remembered, however, that he did not remove the reference to *A Study* which appears in the next paragraph. The phrase 'the dark incidents of the Study in Scarlet' stands in the MS, the *Strand*, and the Oxford University Press edition.[142] Apparently it was more important to please Smith than to appease bewildered readers. The stories began to appear in the *Strand* in July 1891, and it was only after their initial success that its editor commissioned more.

The claim that Conan Doyle was responsible for the first six-part series is strengthened if we consider the record of payments included in the Watt correspondence. Watt had negotiated a rate of £4 per thousand words for the British serial rights of the entire first series, a useful seventeen-shilling improvement on Conan Doyle's standard 1890 rate of three guineas.[143] The six stories were, in effect, treated as a single commercial transaction. In Watt's account for 'A Scandal', dated 28 April, he noted 'By cheque recd from "Strand Magazine" [£]36' (the length was no doubt rounded up to a neat 9,000 words).[144] Things evened out with the next payment, however. For the 'British serial use' of 'The Red-Headed League' (this time 9,300 words), Watt's account for 23 May gave another £36.[145] But in a letter of 20 May to Miss Conan Doyle – most probably one of Arthur's sisters was helping to nurse him during his bout of influenza – Watt wrote: 'I find that "The Strand Magazine" owes Dr. Doyle for the 2nd, 3rd, 4th and 5th stories of the "Sherlock Holmes" series the sum of £134:8:0.'[146] This figure again confirms the general rate of £4 per thousand which is the rate Watt also negotiated with the *Illustrated London News* for 'A Question of Diplomacy'. At this relatively early stage in his career, then, Conan Doyle was financially in the same league as a well-established figure like Mrs Oliphant, and just below the equally reputable Mrs Lynn Linton.[147] In all, he would have grossed just over £200 for the first six-part series in the *Strand*. This was before Watt's commission which varied from £5 8s for 'A Scandal' (15 per cent) to £3 12s for 'Red-Headed' (6 per cent). If the difference reflected Watt's changing estimate of the value of his services once the first story had been placed, and if it remained consistent, then Conan Doyle would have been left with a net total of around £184 from the British serial rights (a net average of £30 10s per story). To this, of course, he could add the £50 (gross) from McClure's American serial rights, a rate of roughly £1 per thousand. Though this was a relatively meagre bonus – at this time William Clark Russell was earning the same rate from American serial rights, but Kipling was getting an astounding £5 per thousand – Conan Doyle once again had his agent to thank.[148] As Watt informed him on 22 April, he had ensured that the stories would begin their *Strand* run only with the July issue, once the Chace Act had come into effect, 'so that the American copyright will be quite safe'.[149]

The initial negotiations for the first six-part series coincided with Conan Doyle's decision, taken in May 1891 while he was recovering from influenza, to abandon his medical career altogether and to become a professional writer. It

was, he said, 'one of the greatest moments of exultation of my life'.[150] By the
end of June, he and his wife and baby daughter had moved from their
temporary lodgings off Russell Square into a suburban villa in South
Norwood.[151] Though he had, at that time, no inkling of the enormous success
awaiting the new Holmes stories, his confidence as a writer and his commercial
standing had been steadily improving since the publication of *Micah Clarke*
(1889), and by 1891 he had the added assurance of regular commissions and of
a potentially significant income from the newly regulated American market.
From the British serial rights to *The Doings of Raffles Haw*, *Beyond the City*, and
the first six Holmes stories, all written in 1891, he received just under £500
alone (in 1890, it should be remembered, he accepted £450 for the serial and
book rights of *The White Company*), and, according to Pearson, his total income
for the year came to 'about £1,500' (or five times what he had been earning as
a family practitioner in Southsea in 1890).[152] He was now in a position to
afford an annual rent of £85, and by November he was listed, along with
Grant Allen and J. C. Eno, as among the more prominent individual shareholders in George Newnes, Ltd., one of the newest 'Joint Stock Publishing
Companies'.[153] By the end of that year he had invested a total of £529 10s in
the company.[154]

Though 'A Scandal in Bohemia' was not Conan Doyle's first *Strand*
publication – 'The Voice of Science', which Watt had sent to the editor in
January, had appeared in the March issue – its appearance in July 1891
marked the beginning of his long and close association with the magazine. By
October, after the first four stories had appeared, Smith clearly had no doubt
about the value of the series for his magazine. On 14 October, Conan Doyle
wrote to his mother, '"The Strand" are simply imploring me to continue
Holmes.' On the same day he sent the editors what he called a 'high-handed'
reply saying he would do so only if they paid £50 for each story, irrespective of
length.[155] They readily complied, and he then went on to produce the first five
stories in the new series in under a month – a total of just under 44,500 words,
for which he earned on average one shilling for 9 words from the British serial
rights alone. On 11 November he wrote to his mother:

I think that they are up to the standard of the first series, & the twelve ought to make a
rather good book of the sort. I think of slaying Holmes in the sixth & winding him up
for good & all. He takes my mind from better things.[156]

He was at this time planning *The Refugees*, his next historical novel, which he
began writing in December 1891. It appears, however, that his mother
dissuaded him from killing off his hero – as Green points out, he in fact used
one of her plot suggestions for the sixth story, 'The Copper Beeches' – and so
Holmes lived to be commissioned once again.[157] The second half of the
Adventures series ran in the *Strand* from January to June 1892, and by February
the editors were already, as Conan Doyle put it, 'bothering me for more

Sherlock Holmes tales.' Again he tried the deterrent of high rates. As he wrote to his mother: 'Under pressure I offered to do a dozen for a thousand pounds, but I sincerely hope that they won't accept it now.'[158] Though he was now demanding an average of one shilling for 5 words, or three times his initial rate, the *Strand* again accepted the terms without hesitation and the new twelve-part series, *The Memoirs of Sherlock Holmes*, eventually ran in the magazine from December 1892 to December 1893. As these stories also circulated in the New York edition of the *Strand*, as well as in other American publications, including *Harper's Weekly*, *McClure's Magazine*, and major city newspapers, by the time Conan Doyle finally resolved to send Holmes over the Reichenbach Falls in 'The Final Problem', his hero had evolved into an international myth with enormous appeal. In Britain he had an eager following of at least a million *Strand* readers alone.[159] Though Conan Doyle wrote to his mother on 6 April 1893, saying 'I am in the middle of the last Holmes story, after which the gentleman vanishes, never never to reappear', it was, as Green has argued, only later that year, sometime in December, that he decided, as an afterthought, to give the series a more dramatic sense of closure with 'The Final Problem'.[160]

Without Conan Doyle knowing or intending it, his detective-hero had by the end of 1893 forged an alliance between him and the *Strand* that would dominate his literary career for the next 37 years.[161] Yet if the character had a consistently unplanned influence over the course of his author's career, and a mythical life that went far beyond his creator's intentions, we cannot reduce this to a cartoonish postmodern struggle between a helpless creator and his mythopoeic creation. The contest was, more plausibly, between a strong, albeit never omnipotent, author and the new conditions of literary production in the 1890s. For one thing, Conan Doyle ensured that the terms of his association with the *Strand* remained strictly informal – he turned down Smith's offer to pay a retainer for the first rights to anything he wrote – and his loyalty to the magazine was not unconditional.[162] When Smith felt some of his prices for the later Holmes stories were excessive, Conan Doyle replied:

I could have obtained that price elsewhere, and though I am anxious that my work should appear where it has always appeared it would hardly be fair that I should make actual pecuniary sacrifice for this.[163]

This particular dispute centred on the British serial rights to 'The Second Stain', one of many final Holmes stories, for which Conan Doyle had been asking £1,000 in America.[164] Three years earlier he had successfully persuaded Smith and the *Strand's* directors that, if *The Hound of the Baskervilles* was to have Holmes as its hero, he would have to be paid double his usual rate of £50 per thousand words for the British and American rights (he earned just under £6,000 for it).[165] At other times, however, he resisted submitting stories he considered unsuitable for the *Strand*, even if doing so cost him financially.

About *A Duet with an Occasional Chorus* (1899), the controversial love story that inspired Robertson Nicoll's multiple outraged reviews, he told Smith:

I did not think it would be to your interest to publish this thing – no incident – and so I forbore to offer it, much to my own financial loss. I could not see it cut into lengths either. The most expensive luxury in life is even so limited an artistic conscience as mine.[166]

As this discreetly evasive justification implies, he had, despite his natural concerns about his independence and rates, a lasting sense of obligation to Smith and the magazine. When C. A. Pearson, Ltd. and Harmsworth Bros., Ltd. attempted unsuccessfully to undercut the Newnes-dominated sixpenny magazine market by launching threepenny illustrated monthlies, respectively, the *Royal Magazine* (October 1898) and *Harmsworth's Monthly Pictorial* (July 1898), he wrote reassuringly to Smith:

I hope your old ship is weathering the storm caused by all these cheap imitations. I observed that the *Royal* stole the very print of your table of contents. They are always pestering me, but I do not even answer their letters now. My ambition is always to stand by the old craft.[167]

Over the next three decades, he kept his word. While he often changed British and American book publishers, and maintained no fixed loyalty to any one American magazine, all the Holmes stories, as well as all his longer fiction and most of his short stories written after 1898, first appeared in the *Strand*.

Yet, despite persistent efforts, after 1893 the magazine no longer had a major influence over the production schedule of the Holmes saga. Conan Doyle decided on his own initiative to re-use (but not revive) Holmes in *The Hound of the Baskervilles* if the *Strand* was willing to pay handsomely (August 1901–April 1902); Colliers of New York paid him at least £7,200 (American serial rights only) to revive Holmes in the final series planned as such, *The Return of Sherlock Holmes* (October 1903–December 1904); and from 1908 to 1927 Conan Doyle returned, at irregular intervals, often when inspired by new drama or film productions of the saga, to write the occasional post-retirement stories that eventually appeared as *His Last Bow* (September 1908–September 1917), *The Valley of Fear* (September 1914–May 1915), and *The Case-Book of Sherlock Holmes* (October 1921–April 1927).[168] Though Smith's direct involvement was reduced, he remained throughout an attentive critic, champion, and, of course, investor. Never afraid of being critical, he bolstered his leading author's often flagging morale, while insisting he maintain his high standards. In early 1903, during the production of the *Return* series, when Conan Doyle was expressing his 'intense disinclination to continue these stories' and complaining about the impossibility of avoiding 'a certain sameness & want of freshness', Smith persuaded him to sharpen up 'The Solitary Cyclist' and remained unenthusiastic about 'The Norwood Builder'. Conan Doyle took this all appreciatively, saying in reply: 'You never will offend me, my dear chap, by saying what you think.'[169] Smith also clearly kept up the pressure for more Holmes, or at least, more detective stories. When he attempted to package the *Round the Fire Stories*, many of which appeared in the *Strand* in 1898 and 1899, as a new series in the detective genre, Conan Doyle responded firmly:

'Detective Stories' would not fairly characterize them, and I want to give myself a very free hand so that in case any tap runs dry I can turn on another. I should therefore not say anything about Detectives or Holmes in the announcement.[170]

Given this, Smith was no doubt delighted to receive Conan Doyle's letter, dated 4 March 1908, saying 'I don't suppose so far as I see that I should write a new "Sherlock Holmes" series but I see no reason why I should not do an occasional scattered story under some such heading as "Reminiscences of Mr Sherlock Holmes" (Extracted from the Diaries of his friend, Dr James [sic] Watson).'[171] This led to the stories in *His Last Bow*, most of which Conan Doyle obligingly produced in time for the *Strand's* special Christmas numbers. On another occasion he remarked sardonically:

You will be amused to hear that I am at work upon a Sherlock Holmes story. So the old dog returns to his vomit.[172]

Though Smith never carried out Conan Doyle's plan to run a competition in the magazine for the best mystery plots, when his author's resources were particularly low he offered suggestions of his own, most conspicuously in 'Thor Bridge' (*Case-Book*) for which Conan Doyle used Smith's idea, based on an actual case, of a suicide made to look like a murder.[173] This was only the most direct case of the *Strand's* influence on the saga however, since, as Green has shown, Conan Doyle frequently borrowed ideas for plots and other smaller details from both the *Strand* (especially its 'Curiosities' page) and *Tit-Bits*.[174] Expressing his general indebtedness to Smith, and perhaps showing his gratitude for another plot suggestion, Conan Doyle gave him the manuscript of 'The Golden Pince-Nez' in February 1916 with an inscription reading 'A Souvenir of 20 years of collaboration'; and in 1921 he summed-up their productive partnership by saying of Holmes, 'if I am his father, you were the "accoucheur"'.[175]

III

George Newnes (1851–1910), the founder of the *Strand,* and its chief editor from 1891 to 1910, entered the magazine trade relatively late in life. The son of a Congregationalist minister, he had initially embarked on a commercial career, as a clerk apprenticed to a London-based haberdashery firm, at the age of sixteen.[176] Though clearly successful in his chosen path – in 1875 he married and settled in Manchester as the firm's local branch manager – in late 1881, aged 30, he decided to try his luck in the publishing business with a new-style popular paper. His initial idea, which had been in his mind for 'about a year', was to create a penny weekly composed of short humorous, anecdotal, and informative excerpts from other published sources; or, as his full title put it, *Tit-Bits from All the Most Interesting Books, Periodicals and Newspapers in the World*.[177] His aim was to appropriate available material and to repackage it in a more accessible format. The first issue, which appeared on Saturday, 22 October 1881, contained sixteen closely printed pages including a front page of two-line jokes, some longer anecdotes in the inside pages, and a section entitled 'Tit-Bits of Information'. This rudimentary format, which none the less remained part of the paper's standard repertoire throughout its long history, constituted the essence of his editorial innovation and went some way towards making the paper, as Keating remarks, a 'pioneering late Victorian periodical'.[178] Within months there were eleven imitations on the market, and by 1891 Newnes's venture had given rise to a new class of popular weekly which included such titles as *Rare-Bits* (1881), *Scraps* (1883), *Great Thoughts* (1884), *Wit and Wisdom* (1886), *Spare Moments* (1888), *Snacks* (1889), and, most importantly, *Answers* (1888) and *Pearson's Weekly* (1890).[179] The last two, the most successful imitations, were founded by Alfred Harmsworth and C. A. Pearson, respectively, both of whom started out on the *Tit-Bits* staff in the mid-1880s.[180]

After the first issue, which sold 12,000 copies (5,000 were taken in Manchester alone), Newnes immediately started to refine his initial policy.[181] Starting on 6 May 1882, he added a series of excerpts from selected writers including Bulwer Lytton, Thackeray, George Eliot, Scott, Trollope, Macaulay, Carlyle, Oliver Wendell Holmes, Poe, Emerson, Ruskin, and Lamb. He also began to introduce features, such as 'Tit-Bits of Legal Information' (19 November 1881), an 'Answers to Correspondents' column (10 December 1881), and a 'Tit-Bits Enquiry Column' (25 February 1882), that had been staples of the penny weeklies at least since Wilkie Collins explored the reading of the 'Unknown Public' in 1858.[182] Newnes added serial fiction, another staple of the established penny papers, only in 1889. To this extent, despite the novelty of his original editorial idea, the new-style penny weekly, as it developed into its standard format, retained some measure of continuity with the traditions of the popular mid-Victorian penny press, not only in terms of its contents, but also, as Collins's essay again suggests, in its underlying editorial ideals. Collins's five selected 'penny-novel Journals' displayed 'an intense in-dwelling respectability in their dullness'; and, as Newnes noted in an interview for the *Idler* in March 1893, his own aim was to create a popular paper that was less dull but as respectable:

When I came out with *Tit-Bits* there was not a single popular paper containing fun or jokes or anything of the kind – except the illustrated ones [such as *Judy* (1867), *Fun* (1861), *The British Working Man* (1875), and *Moonshine* (1879)] – but what relied more or less upon prurient matter to tickle the fancies of prurient minds.[183]

Though, as Collins's remarks indicate, there clearly were some eminently respectable, albeit not especially humorous, penny weeklies available at the time – the *Family Herald* (1842) was one of the most popular – Newnes made decency both his primary selling point and his chief defence against the charge of profiteering.[184] On another occasion, he claimed his more 'wholesome' publication helped keep 'an enormous class of superficial readers' away from the 'so-called sporting papers', the most notorious of which was the *Sporting Times* (1865, otherwise known as 'The Pink 'Un').[185] As an advertisement for *Tit-Bits* in 1891 insisted, it published 'nothing that will bore, nothing that will pollute – only that which will brighten, amuse, and instruct'.[186] With these carefully chosen words, which permitted amusement without neglecting the moral demands for self-improvement, Newnes created space for his product in a competitive market and defended his position in the literary field as a socially responsible entrepreneur. Like his main rivals, Pearson and Harmsworth, he appealed to the new 'masses' of the 1890s by quietly casting off the piety of the mid-Victorian religious press while loudly capitalizing on the middle-class moral panics about juvenile crime and the 'penny dreadful', or gambling and the 'sporting papers'.[187] In a tribute of 1902, Conan Doyle observed that Newnes had responded with 'extraordinary sagacity and foresight' to the new post-1870 generation 'who were anxious for something to read, and who were not sufficiently educated to study the deepest and thickest volumes' by providing 'just that class of literature which at the same time interested them, elevated them, and did them good'.[188]

In terms of its contents, format, and editorial policy, *Tit-Bits* has only a partial claim to being a pioneering venture. Yet, if one considers the way it was marketed, and especially the vigour with which promotions were pursued, its phenomenal rise in circulation, and its impact both on society and on the magazine trade, its status as an instrument for revolutionary change in late-Victorian culture is indisputable. At the outset, Newnes was the paper's sole owner and editor – when no one was willing to support him, he raised the £500 capital he needed to get it started by opening a vegetarian restaurant in Manchester – and from the start he energetically pursued two principal marketing strategies in order to make it a success.[189] Taking the more conventional line, within weeks he had made arrangements for W. H. Smith's to sell the paper at their railway bookstalls, and he had begun advertising it, at 'great expense', in London and the provinces.[190] When some readers in Newcastle misunderstood the title, and thought it was another indecent publication unsuitable for female readers, he organized a parade through the town by a group of sandwichmen bearing placards on which he had written '*Tit-Bits:* I like it, my wife likes it, my daughter likes it, my mother likes it.'[191] In conjunction with these promotional campaigns, he immediately sought to establish a direct relationship with his readers by encouraging what could be termed participatory journalism. From the first issue, readers were invited, with the prospect of winning a guinea (then a weekly wage for many skilled labourers), to enter a weekly competition for the 'Prize Tit-Bit' submitted.

This was the beginning of a long series of lucrative competitions, most of which had a literary aspect and so often attracted both established and aspirant writers. In 1890, Grant Allen, who was already a published author, won a £1,000 prize for *What's Bred in the Bone*, one of the first serials published in the paper; and, the next year, Bennett, then a young clerk in London, went on to win a twenty-guinea prize for the best condensation of the story. As a struggling provincial doctor, Conan Doyle was a less successful, but equally eager, participant in these competitions. He lost the best Christmas-story contest he entered in November 1883, the prize for which was a £400 house called '*Tit-Bits* Villa'. (Feeling done down, he challenged Newnes to take the original story he sent in to an impartial judge, preferably James Payn; but Newnes, who had 22,000 other hopefuls to contend with, did not respond. The prize was actually won by Private William Mellish of the 8th Hussars who chose a villa in Dulwich. As the competition rules did not require an original story, he had sent in a piece by Max Adeler.)[192] Then, to attract his all-important commuter readership, Newnes introduced a Railway Insurance Scheme, inaugurated in 1885, in which he offered £100 to the next of kin of anyone who died in a railway accident with a copy of *Tit-Bits* in their possession. As he noted in 1899, though the paper 'caught the public fancy on the instant', it was also 'well nurtured and cared for, and new ideas were brought into it, which, though not really costly, attracted public attention'.[193] With these various marketing schemes, all of which became a standard feature of the penny weeklies in the 1890s, its circulation increased spectacularly. From an initial 12,000 it went to 200,000 a week in 1883; then, after a promotional drive designed to boost circulation in 1889, it rose to a weekly average for that year of 430,318; and in 1897 it attained what was then the highest weekly rate of 671,000 copies.[194] Yet, by December 1889, most newsagents already regarded it as the most saleable weekly on the market. They ranked it well above popular mid-Victorian weeklies like the *Family Herald* (1842), *Reynolds's Weekly* (1850) and *Lloyd's Weekly News* (1842) – its closest rival was the equally new illustrated weekly *Ally Sloper's Half-Holiday* (1884).[195]

Tit-Bits was launched as a national weekly intended chiefly for a broad lower-middle-class and middle-class family readership. In the third issue, Newnes represented his ideal audience as the model 'Tifkins' family – a husband, wife, and two daughters, all of whom live in a suburban 'villa'.[196] Much of the paper's success was clearly the result of his familiarity with, and responsiveness to, the needs and interests of this readership. The first Christmas issue, for instance, carried a 'Prize Tit-Bit' giving advice on the rituals of respectable courtship for men and 'unmarried ladies', as well as details about home entertainments for the festive season; and, during the following summer, each weekly issue offered practical information about numerous English and Welsh seaside resorts, including details about rail fares and timetables, the climate, costs, and local attractions.[197] Lower-ranking, urban white-collar employees, such as typists, clerks, and shorthand secretaries, no doubt formed a significant proportion of his readership, since, starting in October 1890, he put out a monthly 'Shorthand Edition' of the paper, priced at twopence, in conjunction with Isaac Pitman and Sons. Yet, if the weekly's intended and actual audience was broadly middle class, its price also kept it within the budget of many working-class homes; and, as Lady Bell's 1907 study of the reading habits of skilled labourers in North Yorkshire shows, it did find its way into this class, competing with the traditional Sunday papers, such as *Reynolds's Weekly* and *Lloyd's Weekly News*, sporting papers like the *Winning Post* (1904), and crime papers like the *Illustrated Police Budget* (1893).[198]

Importantly, the initial *commercial* success of the paper was solely the result of Newnes's editorial acumen and marketing skills – he was apparently offered £30,000 for it in 1882 by a London publisher.[199] It was at first printed on a flat-bed press – he introduced the modern cost-saving American Hoe Rotary Press, which turned out 25,000 finished copies an hour, only in 1892 – and until May 1886 it carried no advertisements.[200] In effect, it prospered commercially without advertising revenue, serial fiction, or advanced technology; and by 1889, with a socially diverse weekly readership of at least two to three million, its *cultural* impact was unparalleled.[201] Whereas the mid-Victorian penny weeklies had possessed all the qualities of an unexpected archaeological find for literary commentators like Wilkie Collins in the 1850s and James Payn in early 1881, by the end of the 1880s, primarily as a consequence of *Tit-Bits's* unprecedented ascendancy, these papers had become a conspicuous, though for literary purists a no less distasteful, cultural force.[202] In December 1889, the *Scots Observer*, responding to a survey by the trade journal the *Newsagent and Advertiser's Record* (1889), saw *Tit-Bits* as the archetypal reading of the 'real general public': the 'millions' who 'weakened their brains' on this kind of 'weekly drivel'. It was, Henley's observer went on, chiefly read by men who could often be seen cramming 'such fare' in the 'railway carriage' and on the ''bus'.[203] Writing in the autumn of 1890, George Gissing echoed these views in his latest three-volume novel *New Grub Street* (1891). Whelpdale, who is, like Jasper Milvain, a champion of the new profiteering spirit which the novel suggests is degrading late-Victorian literate culture, founds an enormously successful paper called *Chit-Chat*. Composed largely of 'bits of stories, bits of description, bits of scandal, bits of jokes, bits of statistics, bits of foolery', it is, Gissing implies, perfectly suited to the intellectual competence of its intended readership – the 'quarter-educated; that is to say, the great new generation that is being turned out by the Board Schools' who 'as a rule care for no newspapers except the Sunday ones'.[204] In response to such attacks, the *Newsagent* defended both Newnes and the trade it represented by arguing that, if publications like *Tit-Bits* and *Answers* were not, 'perhaps, the highest form of literary food', they were 'useful in their place' and they had the 'one virtue, not universal among cheap publications, that they [were] fit for the young to read'.[205] Four years earlier, Edward Salmon, writing in the *Nineteenth Century*, replied to the objection that the 'reading of the scraps printed in these papers tends to develop a habit of loose reading' by claiming that 'if the working classes did not read these papers they would read hardly anything save the novelette or the weekly newspaper; and, even though gained in a disjointed fashion, it is surely better for them to acquire pieces of historical information thuswise than never to acquire them at all'.[206]

Having moved his growing enterprise to London in 1885, and with *Tit-Bits* apparently yielding an annual profit of £30,000 by 1890, Newnes was soon ready to diversify.[207] In January 1890, he launched a second venture, the *Review of Reviews*, which he co-founded with W. T. Stead, the crusading editor of the *Pall Mall Gazette*.[208] Stead had approached him in late 1889 with the idea of creating a sixpenny magazine in the form of a monthly digest of selected essays published in the reviews.[209] Using the *Tit-Bits* model, but adopting the cultural ideals of Archibald Grove's *New Review* (1889), Stead proposed to make the established mid-Victorian 2s 6d critical reviews more easily accessible, in format and price, to a wider readership. In the prospectus to the first issue, he quoted Arnold's view of culture as the best that is thought and said, and added that his own aim was 'to make the best thoughts of the best writers in our periodicals universally accessible'.[210] With Stead, this broad cultural programme had, of course, a grandiose political objective: his inexpensive digest was intended to redeem the 'untutored democracy' by reviving 'civic faith' and by fostering Carlyle's 'new clergy', the natural *aristoi* Stead believed existed at every level of society. Importantly, the need for this high-principled mission was, in his view, made all the more urgent by the manifest 'decadence of the press': 'The Mentor of the young Democracy', he complained, 'has abandoned philosophy, and stuffs the ears of its Telemachus with descriptions of Calypso's petticoats and the latest scandals of the Court'.[211] Though the new digest flourished – by May 1890 Stead put the circulation at 60,000 and anticipated it would soon reach 100,000 – the partnership between its two promoters soon foundered.[212] They had their political differences – broadly, Newnes was a progressive, but old-style, Liberal; while Stead was a notoriously combative Radical Imperialist, with Socialist and Suffragette leanings – but their brief partnership broke down primarily because of their conflicting views on the social function of journalism.[213] Their initial disagreements over management and policy eventually came to a head when Stead published a strident attack on the *Times* in the March issue, which Newnes feared would be libellous, and then announced he would publish Tolstoy's latest novel *The Kreutzer Sonata* in April as part of the condensed novel series.[214] As he explained in his preface to the story in that issue, he had visited Tolstoy for a week in 1888, during which they had discussed 'the relations between men and women, the right ordering of which is the foundation of every healthy society'. In the course of these discussions,

Tolstoy mentioned he was working on a novel that would expose 'the conventional illusion of romantic love' and the inequities of apparently 'respectable' Russian marriages. This pro-feminist perspective had an immediate appeal for Stead, and over the next two years he set about arranging an English translation for his new magazine. Despite the fact that the novel was banned by censors in Russia, that Tolstoy himself said it would not go down well in England, and that Miss Hapgood, the American translator Stead employed, was too horrified to undertake her commission, Stead remained resolute.[215] Finally, when Newnes refused to back down, Stead moved to terminate the partnership. On 3 April 1890, he bought out Newnes's interest in the venture for £10,000 and moved from the *Tit-Bits* Offices to new premises in Mowbray House.[216]

As the dispute over *The Kreutzer Sonata* revealed, Newnes's steadfast respectability made him as hostile to the combative improprieties of the literary avant-garde as he was to the indecencies of some sectors of the established popular press. According to his biographer, his first concern, as an editor of popular magazines, was to serve a public which he believed, with some justification, cared little for 'so-called problem stories' or 'decadent or materialistic fiction', but welcomed 'tales dealing in a natural way with healthy human emotions, adventures and experiences'.[217] For him a 'wholesome' story about male–female relations typically depicted a chivalric Englishman rescuing a pure English woman from some form of distress, a scenario which recurred frequently in the *Strand* of the 1890s from Grant Allen's 'A Deadly Dilemma' to Mrs L. T. Meade's series *The Adventures of a Man of Science* and, of course, the Holmes saga.[218] Added to this, Newnes had little sympathy for any New Women – the Suffragettes in fact burned his house down a few months after his death in 1910.[219] Yet the particular disagreement over the Tolstoy was also only a symptom of a deeper conflict of interests. As Newnes explained in a tactful letter to Stead, their partnership represented an uneasy alliance between two distinct positions in the field of journalism:

There is one kind of journalism which directs the affairs of nations; it makes and unmakes Cabinets; it upsets governments, builds up Navies and does many other great things. It is magnificent. This is your journalism. There is another kind of journalism which has no such great ambitions. It is content to plod on, year after year, giving wholesome and harmless entertainment to crowds of hard-working people, craving for a little fun and amusement. It is quite humble and unpretentious. That is my journalism.[220]

The letter was, of course, strategically designed to defuse tensions and to bring the partnership to an amicable conclusion. Yet the strict cultural divisions it implied – glamorous and controversial journalism for the governing classes, on the one hand; modest but wholesome entertainment for the masses, on the other – fudged the issue as far as the *Review of Reviews* was concerned. Stead's main objective, after all, had been to create a magazine that might overcome these exclusive categories by bringing serious, and, if necessary, controversial, public debate to a wider audience. Later, in an interview for the *Idler*, Newnes made his own position more explicit. When asked if he thought it would 'ever be possible' to provide 'the masses with a higher journalism, with a sort of *Saturday Review*, or *Nineteenth Century*', he replied:

I don't think, Radical as I am, and absolute believer in the sovereignty of the people, that the masses will ever take to any paper which consists of essays or leaders. They want things served up with other interesting matter, and with as much of the personal element as it is possible to give them . . . They work hard enough in everyday life, their recreation and their literature *must*, therefore, be as light as possible.

Earlier in the same interview, he argued that *Tit-Bits* provided light relief not only from hard work, but also from the 'hardness and narrowness' which he believed characterized the educational regime of the Board Schools.[221] In short, though he was willing to underwrite 'higher journalism' in other areas of the periodical market – he founded the Liberal *Westminster Gazette* in 1893 – he believed, from the start, in the existence, and validity, of a separate, ostensibly apolitical, popular sphere.[222] He was, in other words, less a politically inspired cultural democrat, in the style of Stead, Grove, and O'Connor, and more an entrepreneur with the social conscience of a late-Victorian middle-class improver. The most he expected from his entertaining but respectable publications was that they might encourage readers to 'take an interest in higher forms of literature'.[223] This broad outlook left him open to attacks both from political reformers like Stead and from literary purists like Gissing, Gosse, and Henley, but it earned him official honours in 1895. When he was nominated for a baronetcy that year, Lord Rosebery wrote to him saying he wished 'to commemorate not only [his] political services but the good work that [he had] done in the cause of healthy popular literature'.[224]

For all the heat produced by the *Kreutzer Sonata* episode, when Stead finally came to read the novel, he was as reluctant to print it as Newnes though for different reasons. 'It is not only that [the author's] expressions are often coarse and brutal', Stead argued in his preface, 'but [that] I profoundly dissent from the whole strain and tendency of his teachings'. While he appreciated Tolstoy's protest against marriages founded on lust alone, and thanked him for 'his stern rebuke of the false views which are so widely accepted as to the exception of one sex from the obligations of the moral law', he strongly objected to the strain of 'pessimistic Orientalism' which he felt dominated the work. Tolstoy's advocacy of celibacy, on the grounds that Pozdnyshev's extreme lusts led to violent jealousy and murder, was logically absurd according to Stead. It was 'as revolting and as unreal as a theory of diet which assumed that we all were cannibals and only dined because we wished to recall the toothsome delight of a human spare-rib or roast baby'. What was particularly unappealing about Tolstoy's extremism was that his beliefs would inevitably 'lead to the extinction of the race'. For an arch-Imperialist like Stead, that would entail nothing less than national suicide and the end of the Empire. In the end, despite his objections, he decided to publish the story, minus the first section in which Pozdnyshev describes his libidinous bachelor days. And, for good measure, he added to his own warnings authoritative quotations from Milton (*Paradise Lost*, Book IV, lines 750–65) and Elizabeth Barrett Browning (*Aurora Leigh*, Book IX, lines 657–9) on the importance of love *and* sensuality in the true marriage.[225]

The *Strand* emerged directly out of the *Kreutzer Sonata* affair. 'When the *Review of Reviews* went out of my field of vision', Newnes noted, 'I had made certain arrangements with people for publishing magazine work, and so on, and I wanted something to take its place'.[226] The replacement, not unexpectedly, embodied his most cherished beliefs about popular journalism. With his new literary editor Herbert Greenhough Smith, a Cambridge graduate who had been a newspaper journalist and an associate editor of *Temple Bar*, he set out to create a model popular monthly that he hoped would capture the sixpenny market as *Tit-Bits* had the penny weeklies. This time he had to compete in a market dominated by local sixpenny illustrated magazines like *Cassell's Family Magazine* (1867) and the *English Illustrated* (1883); popular religious monthlies, also illustrated and priced at sixpence, like *Leisure Hour* (1852), *Good Words* (1860), and *Sunday at Home* (1854); and, more particularly, successful illustrated American shilling imports like *Harper's* (1880), *Century* (1881), and *Scribner's* (1887).[227] Stead described the first issue of the *Strand*, which appeared in January 1891, in his *Index to the Periodical Literature of the World*:

The ideal of the *Strand* is a sixpenny *Harper* or *Scribner*, depending for its future chiefly upon translations from foreign authors, and for its circulation upon the number and quality of its illustrations. It has achieved phenomenal success. It is well printed, smartly got up, and contains besides its foreign translations, occasional articles of general interest, and portraits of celebrities at various ages.[228]

The two founding editors were jointly responsible for this format: Newnes included his 'long-cherished notion' of a magazine with an illustration on *every* page, and the celebrities series; while Smith, who always had more ambitious cultural aspirations, suggested the translations from foreign authors.[229] At this point, too, as a matter of policy they published only self-contained short stories, not serials. Some elements of this initial policy, it should be noted, were relatively short-lived. By 1896, the magazine had begun to carry serials; and though most of the short stories in the early issues were by foreign authors – including Hugo, Daudet, Maupassant, Lermontov, Pushkin, and Voltaire – by the sixth, British authors like Besant, Allen, Clark Russell, and Hornung had begun to dominate the adult fiction sections. For all this, short stories – which, after the first Holmes series, meant the connected series in particular – and illustrations remained a prominent feature throughout the magazine's sixty-year history. By the second year of publication, its general appearance, and Newnes's main editorial principles, were settled. Throughout the 1890s, the *Strand* offered its readers an illustrated miscellany typified by the issue for August 1892:

(1) 'Dick Donovan' [the pseudonym of J. E. Muddock, a regular contributor], 'The Story of the Great Cat's Eye', no. II in his series *A Romance from a Detective's Case-book*. This short-story series continued the *Strand's* tradition of the detective series, which started with Conan Doyle, while the second Holmes series was being written.

(2) Harry How, 'Illustrated Interviews: No. XIV. – Sir Frederick Leighton, P. R. A.' Commended by Raymond Blathwayt, this series of interviews, which reflected Newnes's interest in the 'personal element' and became a staple of the magazine, started in the issue for July 1891.

(3) Charles J. Mansford, 'The Jasper Vale of the Falling Star', no. II in his *Shafts from an Eastern Quiver* series which recounted the adventures of two English explorers in Arabia.

(4) Frances H. Low, 'Boy Soldiers and Sailors'. An item on how boy soldiers and sailors are trained at the Royal Military Asylum which formed part of the magazine's tradition of 'human interest' articles focusing on public services and institutions.

(5) 'Portraits of Celebrities at Different Times of their Lives'. A series of short, illustrated biographies of various social luminaries, including notable authors, politicians, performers, royalty, academics, and clergymen, which once again emphasized the 'personal element'. This month's celebrities included the painters Philip H. Calderon, RA and Edward J. Poynter, RA; Hermann Vezin, a West End actor; Miss Julia Neilson, a West End actress; Signor Foli, an Italian opera singer; and Sir William Harcourt, QC and Liberal MP.

(6) Annie L. Coghill, 'There's Many a Slip', a love story.

(7) Arthur Morrison and J. A. Shepherd, 'Zig-Zags at the Zoo', the B-part of their whimsical, alphabetically arranged series about animals in the zoo.

(8) Saint-Juirs, 'Nicette', a love story translated from the French.

(9) Harry How, 'A Day with Dr Conan Doyle', another 'Illustrated Interview'.

(10) W. Clark Russell, 'A Nightmare of the Doldrums', described by the editors as 'a Terrible Story of the Sea, only to be read by people of strong nerves'.

(11) Unsigned, 'Grandfather's Picture-Books', an illustrated article on wood-cuts which reflected the magazine's lasting interest in 'curiosities'.

(12) Unsigned, 'The Three Lemons', a short story for children translated from the Italian.

(13) J. F. Sullivan, part of his humorous series *The Queer Side of Things*, which includes a page about anthropomorphic vegetables, two pages of illustrations showing changing fashions in outdoor garments from Roman

times to the present day, 'Pal's Puzzle Page' (drawings containing hidden figures), a picture of a strange train accident, and various cartoons.

This table of contents reflected the *Strand's* standard range of interests. Each issue, which usually comprised about 50,000 words, included 45 per cent adult genre fiction, more or less evenly divided between stories intended primarily for men and those intended for women; 45 per cent general articles and features, which focused on the 'personal element', humour, 'curiosities', and 'human interest'; and 10 per cent children's fiction, which, until the advent of Edith Nesbit in 1899, was predominantly translated. Scientific articles, though not reflected in the sample, were another regular feature. As Smith noted in 1911, 'popular science and natural history articles, written by the best authors, have been more prominent in *The Strand* than in any other magazine of its kind'.[230] These covered a broad range of specific issues, from Grant Allen on botany and Sir John Lubbock on entomology to discussions of the latest technological and scientific developments, and wider debates among leading scientists about the promise of science in general.[231] Indeed, on these issues, the magazine was always well-informed, current and responsible as is indicated, for instance, by the appearance in January 1913 of an article on Freud by William Brown, then head of psychology at King's College, London, entitled 'Dreams: The Latest Views of Science'. Here the *Strand* rivalled self-consciously avant-garde magazines, like the *New Age* which began to publicize Freudian psychoanalysis only in 1912, and it kept up with the latest publications – *The Interpretation of Dreams* was first published in Britain in 1913.[232]

As Conan Doyle remarked in a letter to Greenhough Smith, the *Strand* had a 'family circulation.'[233] Indeed, it could be argued that the suburban middle-class family, which emerged as the dominant social unit in the course of the nineteenth century, found its fullest and most successful cultural expression in Newnes's sixpenny monthly.[234] The diverse needs of this family group determined its format; and, like *Tit-Bits*, its unprecedented success depended largely on the convergence between the interests and tastes of its founder and those of its intended audience. Its enormous yield of illustrated fiction – in the first ten years it published a total of 1,800 contributions by 600 authors, including 900 short stories, 7,000 illustrations, and 10,000 photographs – not only created an income and a forum for a stable of popular authors that included Kipling, Besant, Wells, W. W. Jacobs, Conan Doyle, Clark Russell, Mrs L. T. Meade, Allen, Hornung, Hall Caine, Stanley Weyman, and Anthony Hope; as well as popular illustrators from Sidney Paget and Arthur Twidle to Paul Hardy and Max Beerbohm; it tracked, influenced, and, to a great extent, led the popular literary fashions of the period.[235] At the same time, in reflecting the broader aesthetic interests of its intended audience, the magazine became a junction at the centre of respectable popular British culture. It supplied the textual resources for home entertainments in the form of piano music and songs for the parlour, illustrated puzzles and games, guidance about *tableaux vivants*, and, of course, reading for all the family; it covered the West End's respectable theatre and opera scene (though it later welcomed the advent of the 'biograph theatre', its celebrities in the 1890s were Gilbert and Sullivan; and the stars of the Lyceum, the Haymarket, and the Royal Opera House, not the Empire, the Alhambra, or Gatti's Music Hall); each Christmas it discussed the latest pantomimes; and, in numerous articles on painters and painting, it reflected, often under the authority of the Royal Academy, a steady interest in popular British artists of the nineteenth century, with a particular emphasis on the Pre-Raphaelites and Victorian narrative painters.[236] In short, while displaying some continuities with the tastes of the mid-Victorian middle class – Dickens, for instance, was a regular *Strand* topic and standard – it established a new position in the literary field for the 1890s, distinguished by its simultaneous reaction against what were perceived to be the more morally questionable elements of established working-class culture, the pious austerity of the previous generation's religious monthlies, and the radicalism of the avant-garde. The various principles of valuation underlying this emergent position were contained in the words 'healthful', 'amusing', 'bright', 'personal', 'light', and 'instructive'.

On questions of taste, for instance, many contributors shared Mrs L. T. Meade's opinion, directed against the avant-garde, that Realism, in painting and especially in literature, was the scourge of a healthy culture. In the issue for July 1895, she applauded Burne-Jones's 'mysticism and idealism' and his commitment to the values of 'chivalry and romance', adding, apropos the 'ugly realism of the modern novel', that it was a 'good sign of our own day' that 'we are beginning to turn with relief' to the 'light fancy and stirring romance of Stevenson and other writers of his school'.[237] John Holt Schooling, another regular contributor at this time, echoed her views six months later, observing that 'in these days of literary outpouring, when there is so much "realistic literature" that is not real, but which for the most part is only nauseous, it is a relief to turn back to Dickens'.[238] Speaking for many contributors (and no doubt readers) in December 1897, James Payn asked simply: 'What right has a man to pen a story like Turganieff's [sic] 'On the Eve' to make generations of his fellow-creatures miserable?'[239] Such literary values harmonized well with the *Strand's* characteristically bright, reassuring tone and outlook; and, in this sense, 'wholesome' genre fiction, or what the magazine labelled 'Romances', contributed to its two principal objectives, namely, to provide what Smith called 'innocent entertainment' and to assure its public, sometimes in the face of contradictory evidence, that all was well with England, the Empire, and the 'white race'.[240] While Conan Doyle displayed a characteristically complex regard for such ideals – he was not quite at one with the likes of Mrs L. T. Meade – a young, cosmopolitan literary intellectual like 'George Egerton' viewed them with unmixed scorn. Writing from London to her father in Ireland on 15 March 1891, she condemned Newnes's venture for being 'Englishly nice and nicely English'. 'Coming from me', she added, 'you know what that means'.[241]

The *Strand's* circulation figures became one of the publishing sensations of the 1890s. Sales in Britain and the Colonies climbed steadily from 200,000 a month in February 1891, a normal figure for successful monthlies like *Cassell's* in the 1870s, to a regular 275,000 in 1892; and, by 1899, according to Newnes's own statements, they had stabilized at between 300,000 and 350,000.[242] By that time, the special New York edition, which ran from 1891 to 1916, was also selling 200,000 copies a month.[243] In effect, at the end of the first decade, it had a world readership, spanning Britain, the Colonies, and the United States, of well over three million.[244] As early as 1892 its achievements were clear even to a critical observer like Stead:

The phenomenal success of the *Strand*, which now prints regularly 275,000 copies a month, shows that the peculiar genius of Mr George Newnes is as great in putting together monthly illustrated articles as in compiling weekly *Tit-Bits*. The *Strand* is light reading from cover to cover; bright, entertaining, illustrated matter, admirable for passing the time, and quite safe against suggesting forbidden speculations; nor does it provoke its readers to too great exercise of thinking.[245]

Its primary intended audience, the British suburban classes, could obtain their monthly copy for sixpence from any newsagent or W. H. Smith railway bookstall, or by post on payment of an annual subscription of 9 shillings; and, twice a year, they could purchase, for 6 shillings, a volume of six issues, uniformly bound, like the first book edition of the Holmes stories, in light-blue cloth. Yet, like *Tit-Bits*, which published many of the same authors and always kept its own readers informed about the monthly's latest contents, the *Strand's* actual audience extended well beyond the middle classes. As Lady Bell's study once again indicates, sixpence, spread over a month, was still just within the budget of many skilled labourers.[246] Indeed, the response to a rare competition, launched by Smith in February 1910, suggests that the magazine had a regular working-class following. The contest was for the best examples of art by bona fide British artisans, and by May, when the results were published, the magazine had been overwhelmed with paintings and sketches from a wide range of workers, including house painters, compositors, weavers, detective officers, railway porters, bakers, miners, French-polishers, shoemakers, and bottle-washers, most of whom earned an average of 25s a week.[247] At the same time, as Smith eagerly announced, its readership in the 1890s had included Queen Victoria (who was also an occasional contributor), Cardinal Manning, Queen Margherita of Italy, and Swinburne who called it the 'ever-delightful *Strand*'.[248] Its capacity to attract and not offend this large, and socially diverse, constituency brought to its pages at the turn of the century as many as 250 different advertisers of everything from household goods and clothes to patent medicines and insurance.[249] Yet, like *Tit-Bits*, the clearest evidence of its enormous success was reflected in its impact on the magazine trade. As Newnes remarked in April 1899, 'most [sixpenny] magazines are now modelled upon the plan of THE STRAND'.[250] Among the more enduring imitations were the *Idler* (1892), *Pall Mall* (1893), *Windsor* (1895), *Pearson's* (1896), and the unsuccessful threepenny rivals that soon reverted to the standard price, *Harmsworth's Monthly Pictorial* (1898, later the *London Magazine*), and the *Royal* (1898). With the exception of the *Idler*, all of these, as well as the *Strand* itself and the older *English Illustrated* and *Cassell's*, dominated *Bookman's* list of the best-selling monthlies in England's wholesale book trade of the late 1890s.[251] Yet, as Bennett later noted, the 'natal day of the popular illustrated magazine' was in January 1891 when the *Strand* first appeared. On that day, he recalled, one of his fellow clerks, a 'family man' who had never read anything 'except possibly a halfpenny daily paper and *Tit-Bits*', became a devotee of 'imaginative literature' when he returned from lunch 'with a blue brochure', the 'just-out first issue of *The Strand Magazine*'. His conversion was a 'dramatic tribute to the correctness of the psychological insight of George Newnes, and to the remarkable skill of Mr. Greenhough Smith in bringing to full fruition George Newnes's idea'.[252] For Conan Doyle, the clearest indication of Newnes's success was that the *Strand* seemed to have become a national emblem for the English middle-class traveller abroad. As he remarked in one of his letters to Smith:

Foreigners used to recognize the English by their check suits. I think they will soon learn to do it by their *Strand Magazines*. Everybody on the Channel boat, except the man at the wheel, was clutching one.[253]

IV

Sherlock Holmes played a major part in the unprecedented commercial and cultural achievements of the *Strand*. According to Newnes, the two series of short stories that appeared in the early 1890s gave his new venture its first 'boom'; and, in the new century, as Chairman of George Newnes, Limited – the public company, capitalized at £1 million, which he had formed in 1897 – he lost no time in announcing the publication of any subsequent Holmes adventures to his shareholders.[254] At the fourth annual general meeting of the company on 31 July 1901, for instance, he was delighted to report with understandable hyperbole, apropos *The Hound of the Baskervilles*, that after trying 'for a number of years' the firm had finally managed to 'resuscitate their deceased friend Sherlock Holmes'.[255] As we have seen, the price was high, but the impact on sales was impressive: while the British edition had to go to an unprecedented seventh printing to meet demand, the American edition increased its circulation by 200,000 copies.[256] Sales and rates were not the only index of Holmes's importance to the *Strand*, however. Like many vigilant popular editors, Smith and Newnes readily adjusted their editorial policy to accommodate the new literary trends the success of the Holmes stories seemed to indicate. After the first Holmes series, the formula of the connected series of short stories, which had obvious utility for the monthly magazine market, became a staple of both the *Strand* and its imitators; and, more particularly, detective stories, or stories with scientist-heroes, by such regular contributors as Mrs L. T. Meade, Grant Allen, Arthur Morrison, and J. E. Muddock, became a well-established *Strand* tradition.[257] While such literary fare harmonized well with the magazine's general scientific interests, after the success of Holmes the editors also began to develop a specific interest in issues related to forensic science, actual detectives and their methods, and criminal psychology.[258] Advertisers, too, lost no time in capitalizing on Holmes. After 'The Final Problem' (*Memoirs*) appeared in the *Strand* for December 1893, the Beecham's Pills copywriters immediately launched a campaign under the heading 'The Last Letter from Sherlock Holmes' in which Holmes writes to a friend requesting a box of the 'indispensable'; and in October 1903, in the issue containing 'The Empty House' (*Return*), they asked readers:

Have you a clue? Do you miss anything? Is anything wrong? The 'SHERLOCK HOLMES' in cases of this kind is 'Beecham's Pills'; no fear of them getting on the wrong scent. They will soon discover the lost appetite, and restore the Rosebud of Health.[259]

To some extent, then, the Holmes stories not only made the magazine a success, they shaped it around them.

Yet, if Holmes left his mark on the *Strand*, the converse was equally true. To begin with, as Conan Doyle himself testified, the 'Holmes phenomenon' was only partly his responsibility. 'If my little creation of Sherlock Holmes has survived longer perhaps than it deserved', he argued in September 1921, 'I consider that it is very largely due to those gentlemen, who have, apart from myself, associated themselves with him'. He then specifically singled out Sidney Paget, the *Strand's* first, and his favourite, Holmes's illustrator who established the popular image of the detective-hero for British readers in the 1890s; William Gillette, the American actor who portrayed Holmes on the stage in New York and at the Lyceum Theatre in London for the first time in 1899; and Smith, the editor who first brought Holmes to a mass readership.[260] Of course, in so far as the *Strand* was not merely an immediate market for the stories, but an agent in their production, it has a uniquely privileged place in their history. Many of the stories would probably never have been written if its editors had not commissioned them and had the resources to meet Conan Doyle's increasingly high rates. Given Conan Doyle's strong bargaining position, however, their *direct* control over the publication process of the entire illustrated text should not be exaggerated. While the editorial staff, especially W. H. J. Boot, the art editor, had most say in the selection of illustrators, and artists, like Paget, decided on the style and content of their accompanying illustrations – Paget generally provided between five and ten for each short story – Conan Doyle still had some influence over who was selected and over the placing of the illustrations.[261] In addition, he generally determined which narrative form he would employ on any occasion – serial, connected series, or occasional short story – and he selected such features as the setting, character types, and crimes for each episode. As censors, the editors restricted themselves to ensuring that minor elements of the content did not offend the religious sensitivities of their family readership. Potentially blasphemous expletives were their chief concern, so the manly Captain Croker's 'Damn the beast' and 'as God is my judge' in the manuscript of 'The Abbey Grange' (*Return*) became, respectively, 'Curse the beast' and 'as Heaven is my judge' in the *Strand* text and in later printings.[262] For the rest, the *Strand's* influence over the text was mainly effected through Smith's courteous but firm editorship, which, as Conan Doyle mentioned on a number of occasions, amounted at times to unofficial collaboration, and through the simple fact that the magazine itself became a regular item on Conan Doyle's own monthly reading list. While the 'Curiosities' page occasionally provided him with minor details for a crime – the description of ancient counterfeit horseshoes in the issue for May 1903, for instance, gave him the idea for the deception in 'The Priory School' (*Return*) – other articles sometimes served as the basis of a story's entire setting and theme.[263] 'The Man with the Twisted Lip' (*Adventures*), for example, which Conan Doyle completed in August 1891, was probably inspired by an article entitled 'A Night in an Opium Den', published in the *Strand* for June that year.[264] While the accord between the stories and their magazine context can partly be ascribed to influences of this kind, it was also achieved less self-consciously. It was also an effect of the structural equivalence between Conan Doyle's socio-cultural position and that of the *Strand* and its editors. Yet, from Conan Doyle's point of view, this 'elective affinity', which had obvious advantages for both parties, was at best only partial. Despite his populism and the obvious strength of his ties to the magazine, he was never content just to be the *Strand's* detective writer. He was also an ambitious player in the larger literary field of the 1890s, and an historical novelist with lofty aspirations. This dual commitment created tensions of its own which were manifest not only in his negotiations with the *Strand's* editors, but in the textual form of the Sherlock Holmes stories themselves.

The 1890s were not a good time for an author with serious literary ambitions to write popular detective stories. For one thing one had to contend with the literary purists' anti-populist disdain. More worrying, however, was the bad press the genre received in the established reviews on account of its 'sensationalism'. A. Innes Shand, writing in the eminently respectable *Blackwoods* in August 1890, took an apparently moderate, cultural line.

Criminal fiction does little direct harm, in the sense of shortening inconvenient lives or tampering with important deeds. But it steadily demoralises the palate for anything milder and more delicately flavoured.

Yet his rhetoric hinted at more profound moral anxieties. Conjuring up the world of the temperance campaigner, he compared the regular reader of such 'sensational' fiction to the 'habitual dram-drinker' who 'will have his stimulants stronger and stronger'.[265] This analogy was more in keeping with the commentators' generally alarmist tone. In the *Westminster Review* for April 1897, 'A. C.' maintained 'it has been carefully estimated that fully 80 per cent. of the yearly output of works that may be classified as purely fictional are exclusively stories of crime and criminals'. Turning Max Nordau's attack on the avant-garde against popular authors, he then went on to claim that the success of the genre was 'the most notorious instance of collective mattoidism in our day and generation'.[266] This debate in the reviews was a more elevated version of the late-Victorian moral panic about the 'penny dreadful' which the editors of the trade journal the *Newsagent* had voiced in characteristic terms in December 1889. In a leading article on 'Cheap Pernicious Literature', they argued that these 'unwholesome' stories, which 'turn the juvenile robber into a hero and lead the youthful idea to spurn all the trammels of home and scholastic discipline', were the 'means of producing many of those sensational dramas' featured in newspaper crime columns.[267]

Conan Doyle was well aware of these anxieties. In his preface to the Author's Edition of the *Adventures*, written in 1901, he claimed that 'one strong objection to the detective story has always been that it must deal with crime, and that the idea of crime is not a wholesome one for the young'.[268] Shortly before, in an interview for *Tit-Bits*, he had remarked, more generally, that 'all work dealing with criminal matters is a cheap way of rousing the interest of the reader'.[269] His response to such concerns was to adopt a set of self-imposed rules that were intended primarily to pre-empt criticism of this kind and to protect his own literary reputation. First, unlike his brother-in-law and literary imitator, E. W. Hornung, he remained committed from the outset to the maxim that one 'must not make the criminal a hero', and, for that reason, he considered Hornung's Raffles stories, the first of which was *The Amateur Cracksman* (1899), as 'rather dangerous in their suggestion'.[270] His second rule, which followed only later, was to reduce, as far as possible, the number of legally punishable crimes represented in the saga as a whole and then to draw attention to this fact in interviews, prefaces, and in the stories themselves. As he put in the *Tit-Bits* interview, 'in dealing with criminal subjects one's natural endeavour is to keep crime in the background'.[271] This obviously put him in a delicate position as a creditable writer of *detective* stories. 'If no crime was ever committed', he acknowledged, 'the reader might feel that he was the victim of a practical joke'. His solution was to create as far as fairness could allow only an atmosphere of crime in some stories or, as he put it, to produce the required effect 'by the anticipation of what might have been, not of what is'.[272] In devising this elaborate 'bluff' he usually drew upon the social prejudices and fears of his respectable audience and traded on the fictional stereotypes of the 'shilling dreadful'.[273] In 'The Man with the Twisted Lip' (*Adventures*), for example, much is made of the degenerate and murderous aspect of the East End opium den and its denizens, especially the 'Lascar scoundrel' who runs it; of the seemingly 'abominable' and bloody murder of Neville St Clair; and of the 'hideous' accused, the 'disfigured' beggar Hugh Boone, who has all the typical qualities of a 'mutilated villain'; but, in the end, all this turns out to involve nothing more than a case of double identity and a pardonable offence of impersonating a beggar. As Holmes stresses, 'no crime, but a very great error has been committed'.[274] In effect, Conan Doyle's strategy was to play an elaborate literary game, exploiting, but at the same time repudiating, the conventions of the 'shilling dreadful' from which the Holmes saga had originally been derived, in an effort to distance himself from what he considered the more disreputable aspects of the genre. Of course, as he felt he could get away with this only about half the time, sometimes he had to give the reader a real crime, and, he added, 'occasionally I had to make it a downright bad one'.[275] But it should be remembered that, in the *Strand* stories, Holmes and Watson never directly confront grimacing corpses as they had in the more sensational scenes of *A Study* and *The Sign*.[276]

Importantly, Conan Doyle began to use this oblique device only when his career as a historical novelist was reasonably well-established and once he had decided to market Holmes in a format suited to popular family magazines; and it was only once the *Strand* commissioned the second six stories in the *Adventures* series that he began to make explicit references to it. Though three of the first six *Adventures* do not involve a serious crime – besides 'The Man with the Twisted Lip', there is 'A Scandal in Bohemia' and 'A Case of Identity' – it is only in 'The Blue Carbuncle', the first story in the next batch of six, that Watson alludes retrospectively to the fact that these three had 'been entirely free of any legal crime.'[277] Holmes, who becomes Conan Doyle's metafictional purist conscience, reinforces the point in the final story in the series, 'The Copper Beeches'. As usual, he criticizes Watson's 'literary shortcomings' but, besides adding 'The Noble Bachelor' to what he had earlier called the 'innocent category', he also defends him against the 'charge of sensationalism' on the grounds that four of the previous eleven stories had dealt with 'matters which are outside the pale of the law'.[278] Such self-reflexive debate was not a new feature of the saga, but, in these stories, its rhetorical purpose shifted explicitly to the problem of sensationalism. In *The Sign*, written in September 1889, Holmes had already commented critically on Watson's literary methods. About *A Study* he remarks disdainfully:

I cannot congratulate you upon it. Detection is, or ought to be, an exact science, and should be treated in the same cold and unemotional manner. You have attempted to tinge it with romanticism, which produces much the same effect as if you worked a love-story or an elopement into the fifth proposition of Euclid.[279]

Holmes, the scientific intellectual, is in this passage chiefly the spokesman for

Conan Doyle's revisionist intentions and manly ideals. In April 1891, while writing the first six *Adventures*, Conan Doyle took up the literary debate once again but in a slightly altered form. In 'A Case of Identity' Holmes takes his argument further, claiming that 'all fiction with its conventionalities and foreseen conclusions' is 'most stale and unprofitable'.[280] His point, which, as Green suggests, may also be Conan Doyle's retort to Wilde's remarks in 'The Decay of Lying' on the primacy of art over life, is that 'life is infinitely stranger than anything which the mind of man could invent'.[281] Watson challenges this realist assumption, arguing that newspaper 'police reports', which display 'realism pushed to its extreme limits', are 'neither fascinating nor artistic'. He then points to a case in the morning paper of 'A husband's cruelty to his wife', the 'crude' and 'vulgar' details of which he can predict without needing to read the report. Though Holmes accepts his criticism of the literary defects of police reports, admitting that a 'certain selection and discretion must be used in producing a realistic effect', he goes on to prove that the particular case Watson refers to contains incidents well beyond the 'imagination of the average story-teller'.[282] Like the discussion in *The Sign*, this literary talk serves Conan Doyle's internal dramatic purposes – namely, to bring out Holmes's qualities as a rigorously scientific intellectual and to underscore his difference from Watson who is a writer and reader of popular fiction – but, unlike the earlier remarks, it also furthers his external sociocultural ends. If Holmes's criticisms of the conventionality of all fiction reinforce Conan Doyle's revisionism, Watson's attitude to the police reports indirectly reflects his author's desire to distance his own writing from such unsavoury matter. Versions of these self-reflexive comments recur strategically throughout the saga, but after 'The Blue Carbuncle' sensationalism becomes the dominant theme. After remarking on the difficulties of selecting which cases he should 'lay before the public', Watson observes in 'The Solitary Cyclist' (*Return*): 'I shall, however, preserve my former rule, and give preference to those cases which derive their interest not so much from the brutality of the crime as from the ingenuity and dramatic quality of the solution.'[283] Later in 'The Abbey Grange' (*Return*), Holmes reiterates the point about judicious selection, but then launches the following remorseless attack, combining all the elements of his literary critique:

I must admit, Watson, that you have some power of selection which atones for much which I deplore in your narratives. Your fatal habit of looking at everything from the point of view of a story instead of as a scientific exercise has ruined what might have been an instructive and even classical series of demonstrations. You slur over work of the utmost finesse and delicacy in order to dwell upon sensational details which may excite but cannot possibly instruct the reader.[284]

This partly serious self-referential game is finally played out in 'The Blanched Soldier' (*Case-Book*), the fifth last story in the saga, which appeared in the *Strand* for November 1926. Holmes, who has agreed, under pressure from Watson, to write the narrative himself concedes that, though he has frequently accused his 'old friend and biographer' of 'pandering to popular taste', he is now beginning 'to realize that the matter must be presented in such a way as may interest the reader'.[285] Late in his career, Holmes, Conan Doyle's purist critic, becomes his populist defender.

Importantly, Conan Doyle's editors did not share his positional anxieties. Their standards of literary decorum were lower than his. While Smith and Newnes considered 'The Cardboard Box' (*Memoirs*), with its double murder, illicit love affair, and lurid dismemberment, acceptable for serial publication – it appeared in the issue for January 1893 – Conan Doyle successfully requested they suppress it from the subsequent book edition on the grounds that it was 'rather more sensational than I care for'.[286] No doubt, on reflection, Watson's apologetic 'short preface' proved too weak a defence in this case. Indeed, from the author's point of view, Watson's argument that it is 'impossible to entirely separate the sensational from the criminal' and that as a 'chronicler' he 'must use matter which chance, not choice, has provided', is merely an elaborate evasion.[287] On another occasion, in a letter of 14 May 1903, Conan Doyle defended 'The Norwood Builder' (*Return*) against Smith's criticisms, saying 'any feeling of disappointment at the end is due to the fact that no crime has been done & so the reader feels bluffed, but it is well for other reasons to have some of the stories crimeless'. None the less, in response to Smith's complaints about both this story and 'The Solitary Cyclist' (*Return*), he assured him that he had 'a strong bloody story' in 'The Dancing Men' that could 'separate the two crimeless stories', give 'a stronger start to the series', and he hoped 'make a good story for your Xmas number'.[288] Yet, if the editors were understandably eager for real crimes, when it came to other, especially non-fictional, topics covered by their magazine, they were as anxious as Conan Doyle to demonstrate their disdain for sensationalism. This was made particularly apparent in their concern to pre-empt accusations of jingoism during the Boer War. Though patriotic articles celebrating national war heroes were a *Strand* tradition – it began in March 1891 with the series 'Stories of the Victoria Cross Told by Those who have Won it' – Alfred T. Storey felt obliged to conclude his article 'Deeds of Daring and Devotion in the War' (August 1900) with the following defensive rationalization:

Many do and will continue to regret the war; but everyone must be pleased to think, not only how the nation rose to the emergency, but that it was the means of bringing to the front not only so many fine talents, but so many fine qualities to boot. It shows how secure so far the national feeling and the national tradition lie at the basis of the common life.[289]

Later, when George Newnes Ltd. published Storey's *Golden Deeds of the War*, an advertisement in the *Strand* once again revealed the company's anxiety about such subjects:

This book is not intended to be in any way a glorification of the South African War, or of any war . . . It is rather a selection, to show what our sturdy British soldiers are at their best, and to be a pattern and stimulus for those who will have to fight England's battles in other years.[290]

To this extent, though Conan Doyle, the ambitious literary author, always remained more ethically mindful than his editors, his disquiet about the propriety of the detective genre was not out of keeping with the magazine's general ethos; on the contrary, his intricately inflected narratives advanced Newnes's cultural cause. If his attempt to domesticate the 'shilling dreadful' entailed a tacit rejection of the more sensationalist traditions of late-Victorian middle-class fiction, it necessarily served to distinguish his own crime stories from those that appeared in such popular working-class publications as the 'penny dreadfuls' and the *Illustrated Police News*. In effect, his quest for distinction underscored one of Newnes's primary goals which was to supplant some elements of established working-class literate culture with wholesome entertainment for the 1890s.

Yet, as we have seen, Newnes's influential cultural position was not only defined against what he considered the baser elements of working-class culture. It was also strongly opposed to the broadly 'Realist' tendencies of the literary avant-garde. Though Conan Doyle was more tolerant of these tendencies than the *Strand's* editors and most of their contributors – again because of his own more complex literary aspirations – his choice of genres and his position as a 'manly Romantic' with populist convictions made him and his detective-hero effective allies on this second cultural front as well. In Conan Doyle's view, the Holmes adventures belonged generically in the 'fairy kingdom of romance', but they could be described more accurately as modernized chivalric fairy tales playfully masquerading as documentary history.[291] The references to precise dates (however careless on Conan Doyle's part) and places; the 'local colour' of 1890s London; the broad cast of 'realistic' character types which included hotel porters, tradesmen, clerks, typists, servants, and governesses, but emphasized those whom the *Strand* would have classed 'celebrities'; and Watson's role as a chronicler whose justifications for the gaps in publication masked Conan Doyle's real relations with the magazine market – all these devices helped to invest the stories with a beguiling aura of historical authenticity. Yet, from the outset, Conan Doyle had at the same time firmly located the saga in the tradition of the medieval romance, or, rather, a popular late-Victorian version of that tradition. In *The Sign*, Mrs Forrester exclaims after hearing Watson's carefully censored version of the story's main events:

'It is a romance!' cried Mrs Forrester. 'An injured lady, half a million in treasure, a black cannibal, and a wooden-legged ruffian. They take the place of the conventional dragon or wicked earl.'

To this Mary Morstan adds, with 'a bright glance' at Watson: 'And two knight-errants to the rescue'.[292] Other occasional references, repeated throughout the saga, reaffirmed this idea of its generic ancestry. Charles Augustus Milverton, the 'king of all blackmailers', has a safe which is likened to a 'green and golden monster, the dragon which held in its maw the reputations of many fair ladies'; and the 'queenly' Isadora Klein, who inhabits an 'Arabian nights drawing-room', is described as 'the *belle dame sans merci*' of fiction'.[293] As self-consciously literary allusions, these comparisons established a direct line of generic descent; but at the same time, as value-laden judgements, they pointed to an underlying system of ideals which, despite the saga's modernizing tendencies, was also derived from a popular romance tradition.

At the centre of this inherited system was the chivalric code of honour which, in the medieval romance, encompassed both the elaborate rules of combat followed by knightly opponents and the conventions of courtship observed by courtly lovers. In Conan Doyle's manly detective romances, both central characters, as 'gentlemen' rather than 'knights', observe every article of this code, though Holmes, the just opponent of criminals and the intellectual rival of the official police, is the principal exemplar of the rules pertaining to combat, and Watson, especially in *The Sign*, is the model gallant lover. By extension, male villains are typically identified by their disregard for either set of rules, or simply by their failure to reflect the ideals of manliness these rules enshrined. Unlike the villains, John Clay and Mortimer Tregennis, who bring suspicion on themselves by displaying signs of effeminacy, Baron Von Herling, the German diplomat and spy master, who practices '*realpolitik*' and believes 'we live in a utilitarian age', damns himself as a chivalrous opponent by dismissing honour as an out-moded 'medieval conception' and denying that it has any real influence in England.[294] Those who disdain the courtesies of courtly relations, which often means, more generally, those who abuse or mistreat women, are similarly beyond the pale. Beginning with Drebber and Stangerson, the vengeful Mormons of *A Study*, the saga traces the villainy of a large cast of rapacious men, ranging from oppressive step-fathers and abusive husbands to blackmailers and con-men. Baron Gruner, the Austrian serial womanizer in 'The Illustrious Client' (*Case-Book*), who treats women as if they were objects to collect like his butterflies or pieces of rare china; and Charles Augustus Milverton, whom Holmes calls the 'worst man in London', are the archetypes.[295] Conversely, despite Conan Doyle's fastidiousness about legal crimes and the conduct of his heroes, manly defenders of the code are granted special licence because of their noble mission. When Holmes and Watson trespass illegally onto Milverton's property in order to save the reputation of Lady Eva Brackwell, Watson notes:

I thrilled now with a keener zest than I had ever enjoyed when we were defenders of the law instead of its defiers. The high object of our mission, the consciousness that it was unselfish and chivalrous, the villainous character of our opponent, all added to the sporting interest of the adventure.[296]

Indeed, even murder, when seen to involve chivalrous motives and manly figures, is deemed pardonable, as in the cases of Captain Jack Croker in 'The Abbey Grange' (*Return*) and Dr Leon Sterndale in 'The Devil's Foot' (*Case-Book*).

If a popular version of the tradition of the medieval romance gave Conan Doyle an ideal of manliness and a code of male conduct, it also influenced the way he represented women, and especially English women. Following the chivalric model of the knight's 'fair lady', English women are figured in the saga as chaste and virtuous, idealized and idolized types. Often tall, golden-haired, blue-eyed, graceful, and queenly, they seldom do wrong, and they certainly outshine their foreign counterparts.[297] A census of the women who fulfil three invariant roles in the fifty-six short stories reveals that, of the 26 English women represented, 10 (39 per cent) are clients, 14 (54 per cent) are victims, and only 2 (7 per cent) are catalysts/criminals; whereas, among the 9 foreign women in similar roles, none are clients, 1 (11 per cent) is a victim, and 8 (89 per cent) are catalysts. The only English woman, who strictly speaking, serves as a lone catalyst – Lady Trelawney Hope in 'The Second Stain' (*Return*) – is compromised by a foreign spy, and Holmes successfully safeguards her honour. Any others who break the law are either seen to be justified in doing so, or they are shown to have been misled by foreign or dangerous men.[298] This does not mean that foreign women are without virtue. Both Beryl Stapleton in *The Hound of the Baskervilles*, who is Costa Rican, and Elsie, the German woman in 'The Engineer's Thumb' (*Adventures*), try to protect the victims of their depraved male consorts; and, of course, Irene Adler, the American adventuress of 'A Scandal in Bohemia' (*Adventures*), remains *the* woman. Yet, unlike their English counterparts, most habitually fail to live up to the ideals of feminine chastity. Foreign or simply non-English women have a monopoly on female desire, often figured negatively as sexual jealousy. Desire is the province of South American women, like Mrs Fergusan and Maria Gibson, who are both 'tropical by birth and tropical by nature'; or French women with Creole origins like the jealous Mme Fournaye; or, closer to home, non-English, lower class women like Rachel Howells who has a 'passionate Celtic woman's soul' and an 'excitable Welsh temperament'.[299] The archetype of these passion-driven non-English women is Isadora Klein, the Spanish widow of a German sugar king, who is the *femme fatale* in 'The Three Gables' (*Case-Book*), and the female counterpart of Baron Gruner – in her guise as the '*belle dame sans merci*' she destroys middle-class Englishmen like Douglas Maberley.[300] Yet, for all his patriotic idealizations of the courtly romance, Conan Doyle was capable at times of giving some women strong opinions and a life of their own. In 'The Abbey Grange' (*Return*) he made Lady Brackenstall, an Australian by birth, his first fictional pro-divorce propagandist. As a victim of a drunken and violent English husband, she supports the cause by arguing forcefully against the injustice of the 'monstrous laws' as they affect 'sensitive and high-spirited' women like herself.[301] This affirmation of an independent woman is echoed in the portrayal of Violet Hunter, the governess in 'The Copper Beeches' (*Adventures*). Though not Ann Veronica, she is the cycle's closest approximation to the New Woman: she is trilingual, cultured, and economically independent; she has the 'brisk manner of a woman who has had to make her own way in the world'; and she impresses Holmes by courageously unmasking Jephro Rucastle, one of the saga's many corrupt father figures.[302] Yet, if Conan Doyle endorsed women's civil and economic rights, and perhaps equality, he drew the line when it came to politics. Referring to the more militant post-1903 phase of the movement led by the Pankhursts, he represented the suffragettes in 'His Last Bow' (*Last Bow*) as 'window-breaking furies' who were, allegedly like the Irish insurgents, the tools of a German conspiracy to keep England unprepared for war.[303] On this last point, and more generally in his advocation of chivalric ideals, he had the support of the *Strand's* editors who, despite their apparently apolitical stance, strongly opposed female suffrage. Though real suffragettes, like Christabel Pankhurst, were included in the controlled forum of a debate, when their views could be opposed by defenders of the 'inborn chivalry of Englishmen', their fictional counterparts were banned, as Bennett discovered when the editors refused to publish *The Lion's Share*.[304]

Holmes is the heroic centre of this pseudo-historical fairy kingdom based largely on 1890s London and its surrounding counties; and, as a *scientific* detective, he is the focus of the saga's modernizing tendencies and of Conan Doyle's revisionist ambitions as a detective writer. Though Holmes often calls detection an 'art', and implies that he inherited his powers from a French painter in the family, he is, as Conan Doyle intended from the outset, primarily an exponent of late-Victorian scientific rationalism in the spirit suggested by Joseph Bell and T. H. Huxley in his essay 'On the Method of Zadig'.[305] That at least was the intention. In fact, as Conan Doyle himself admitted, Holmes is at best equipped with 'semi-scientific methods'; indeed, as Isaac Asimov has indicated, 'Conan Doyle was surprisingly poor in science, apparently, and Sherlock Holmes, as a scientific detective, does not really come off well for that reason.'[306] Among other things, Holmes displays astounding and unscientific confidence in the powers of the microscope. In 'Shoscombe Old Place' (*Case-Book*) he believes one can distinguish copper from zinc filings by microscopic visual evidence alone; and, more astonishingly, that amorphous 'brown blobs' can be accurately identified as glue by similar means.[307] Yet it is not simply the details of Holmes's scientific practice or knowledge that are questionable. His theoretical exposition of his scientific methods itself amounts only to an incoherent, even contradictory, store of alluring maxims. According to one model, his methods are derived from a strictly mechanistic brand of scientific empiricism. Following the maxim that 'it is a capital mistake to theorise before one has data', he approaches a problem with 'an absolutely blank mind'; then, moving onto the second stage of inquiry, variously called his 'brilliant edifices of deduction', his 'chain of inductive reasoning', or, more accurately, 'inference', he builds up his, invariably correct, explanation of events.[308] The only qualities he requires as a 'perfect reasoning and observing machine' are a capacity for what he calls 'observing' as opposed to mere 'seeing' and an ability to suppress the 'intrusions' of 'strong emotions' which would be like 'grit in a sensitive instrument' or a crack in a 'high-power lens'.[309] As he says to Watson, 'we were simply there to observe and to draw inferences from our observations'.[310] However, on another less mechanistic model, many other qualities and procedures come into play. In this case, Holmes emphasizes his artistic background, speaks of the 'value of imagination', of the need to form 'provisional theories', and claims that the 'first rule of criminal investigation' is that 'one should always look for a possible alternative and provide against it'.[311] As a God-like 'ideal reasoner', he now also possesses 'all knowledge which is likely to be useful to him in his work', and so is able 'accurately to state' every cause and consequence of a 'single fact' as 'Cuvier could correctly describe a whole animal by the contemplation of a single bone'.[312] To further complicate matters, Conan Doyle traced around these various notions of Holmes's detective methods an elaborate network of figures and analogies which made them as suggestive as they were vague. Though his skills are often associated with those demanded by experimental chemistry, they are also compared to those required for tracking and hunting, especially tiger- and fox-hunting, palaeontology, medical diagnosis, cryptography, and linguistic or manuscript research.

Yet, by subjecting the stories to such close critical scrutiny, one is in danger of assuming, like the many readers who fell into Conan Doyle's trap and thought the stories were histories, that Holmes is the embodiment of a substantial point of view, rather than an exercise in mythopoeic image-making designed to appeal to a particular readership. In a letter of 4 May 1892 to Holmes's role model Joseph Bell, Conan Doyle expressed doubts about Bell's 'fine' idea of a story with a 'bacteriological criminal' on the grounds that 'the only fear is lest you get beyond the average man, whose interest must be held from the first and who won't be interested unless he thoroughly understands'.[313] Rooted as it was in his populist outlook, this broad sense of his intended audience not only influenced his selection of viable material, it shaped his conception of his hero. Initially conceived as an eccentric man of science with an expert knowledge of 'sensational literature', by the time Holmes appeared in the *Strand* he had become the popular archetype of the 1890s intellectual purist.[314] Unlike Watson, who reads Clark Russell's 'fine sea stories' and 'yellowbacks', Holmes has a taste for Meredith, Flaubert, Petrarch, ancient Persian poets, Horace, Wagner, and arcane historical scholarship.[315] As a writer he habitually disdains Watson's populism, and prefers to publish learned monographs on various aspects of his art. He speaks in the epigrammatic style of a Wildean Aesthete, rejects domesticity for bohemia, and yet has the manly bearing and chivalric values of a Doylean gentleman. The object of his investigative quests, or connected series of mini-quests, is not the favour of a fair lady (much to Watson's dismay), nor is it principally justice and the defence of what he sardonically calls 'England, home and beauty': it is rather the pleasure of practising his 'art for its own sake'.[316] 'Like all great artists,' says Watson, the 'unworldly' Holmes 'lived for his art's sake'.[317] The purpose of these various signs of purist prestige is principally to lend credibility and glamour to Holmes in his primary role as the consoling rationalist who takes on and defeats the vampires, devils, and spectral hounds of ancient super-stition. As a detective, his function is not simply to solve crimes: it is to demonstrate that 'the world is big enough for us' and that master interpreters, using 'natural explanations' alone, can solve most of its encoded mysteries.[318] This intellectually confident and reassuring ethos is implicit in the popular detective genre itself, with its characters who have clear and unmixed motives, and its satisfying narrative resolutions, but in Conan Doyle's saga it is repeatedly enacted and reinforced in the Bell-like conjuring tricks which usually begin each story. By a convincing sleight of hand, Holmes, now the interpretative magician, decodes an ordinary hat, a pair of pince-nez, a pipe, a watch, or his latest client, illustrating in each case the general principle, as outlined in his article 'The Book of Life', that 'all life is a great chain, the nature of which is known whenever we are shown a single link of it'.[319] Indeed, as he confidently asserts in an uncharacteristic aside in 'The Naval Treaty' (*Memoirs*), which serves no purpose in the plot, his methods of 'deduction' do not transform only *this* world into a readable book, since even religion 'can be built up as an exact science by the reasoner'. Defying ordinary logic, Darwin, and basic botany, he argues that 'our highest assurance of the goodness of Providence seems to me to rest in the flowers'.

All other things, our powers, our desires, our food, are really necessary for our existence. But this rose is an extra. Its smell and its colour are an embellishment of life, not a condition of it. It is only goodness which gives extras, and so I say again that we have much to hope from the flowers.[320]

With such displays of Holmesian sophistry, he reveals himself not so much as the modern scientific detective he purports to be, but as the mythical figure he is: a beneficent wizard from the world of the medieval romance disguised as a charismatic late-Victorian genius bearing a reassuring message. With this hero at its centre, the saga represented an appealing literary rejoinder to what was seen to be the morbid pessimism of the avant-garde Realists, and, indeed, to the corrosive scepticism of emergent modernists, like Conrad, who figured the world as an 'unreadable sea'.[321]

After October 1891, when the *Strand's* editors first commissioned a Holmes series, author, magazine, and character began to live a complex symbiotic life. Partly by design and partly by an unplanned and partial convergence of positions, Conan Doyle produced a fictional series, the genre and form of which suited the magazine's sociocultural interests, and significantly influenced its own form as well as its cultural and commercial success. At the same time, the magazine and its editors, who added illustrations to Conan Doyle's text and to a limited degree influenced its contents, gave the series a popular, inexpensive forum with a massive British, Colonial, and American readership; and, in association with others, its editors offered Conan Doyle significant financial incentives to continue writing what they, their shareholders, and readers wanted. For his part, Conan Doyle was a shrewd and generally amenable participant and beneficiary in this successful alliance; yet, as we have seen, it did entail some serious professional dangers. In the short term, there was simply the immediate problem of Holmes, with the backing of a publication like the *Strand*, hijacking his literary career; or, as he put it in a letter to his mother of 11 November 1891, of his increasingly popular and lucrative hero taking his 'mind from better things'.[322] He solved this drastically at first by killing Holmes off after the second series, then, after the *Return* series, by staggering his composition of the subsequent occasional stories over twenty-three years and limiting his contractual obligations. In the preface to the *Case-Book* series, written in 1927, he modestly pointed to the success of this strategy: 'I have not in actual practice found that these lighter sketches have prevented me from exploring and finding my limitations in such varied branches of literature as history, poetry, historical novels, psychic research, and the drama.'[323]

The second problem, which was related to the first but was both short- and long-term, was less easily managed. As he remarked in his autobiography, with the success of Holmes he was not only in danger of having his 'hand forced', but 'of being entirely identified with what I regarded as a lower stratum of literary achievement'.[324] He attempted to remedy this with the publication of the multi-volume 'Author's Edition' of his works in 1903, a joint venture by the well-established firm of Smith, Elder, who had published some of his historical novels, and D. Appleton of America. Like most authors, he used the occasion to correct some errors and clean up various minor textual details. As he remarked, he wanted to put 'these books into their final form'. But his 'Author's Edition' was not simply revised. It was revisionist. He used it to attempt to reclaim what he considered to be his rightful position in the literary field. First, he reconstructed his *œuvre* through a process of studious suppression. He dropped his juvenilia, that is, all the short stories he had written during his decade-long literary apprenticeship as an anonymous magazine author in the 1880s. He also excluded some of his weaker novels, either because they were immature works like the early mystery novels *The Mystery of Cloomber* (1888) and *The Firm of Girdlestone* (1890), or because they were occasional pieces written principally for money, like *Beyond the City* (1893) and *The Doings of Raffles Haw* (1892). The 'Author's Edition', he noted, 'gave me an opportunity of finally casting off what my more mature judgement told me to be unworthy and of retaining what my conscience approved'. The trouble was his conscience did not approve of all the remaining key works to quite the same extent, and this is where his second revisionist strategy came in. Taking his literary reputation into his own hands, he added prefaces, both to each volume and to the collection as a whole, the purpose of which was clear: 'A preface had always seemed to me an unnecessary impertinence, until I found by experience how easily one may be misunderstood.' And so, in the general preface, he set out to correct any misconceptions about his position by ranking the selected works for 'the help of any critic'. In the 'first place' he put the 'historical romances', including *Micah Clarke*, *The White Company*, *The Great Shadow*, and *The Refugees*; then, 'on a different and humbler plane', he put the 'police romances'; and, in a third category, he included the 'medical stories' *Round the Red Lamp* and *The Stark Munro Letters*.[325] This exercise in critical self-assertion failed, however. (It was not helped by the fact that only 1,000 copies of the dignified 'Author's Edition' were printed in Britain, of which Smith, Elder bound only 510 sets.)[326] Towards the end of his career in 1924, and again in 1927, he regretfully acknowledged that he was never to be known as the Walter Scott of his generation, but as the author of the more famous Sherlock Holmes. 'If I had never touched Holmes, who has tended to obscure my higher work', he noted, 'my position in literature would at the present be a more commanding one'.[327] In fact, it could be argued that Holmes, in conjunction with George Newnes, Ltd. and their American partners, did much more than decide Conan Doyle's *literary* fate. By bringing his name to a receptive mass audience, they redefined his *social* standing as well. Jointly, they created 'Conan Doyle', the celebrity and opinion leader, who ranked himself in 1899 second only to Kipling in terms of the influence he had 'over young men, especially young athletic sporting men', and whose fame went on to make him a useful ally for numerous extraliterary groups and lobbies, including the Congo Reform Association, the Divorce Law Reform Union, and, in the aftermath of the Boer War, the British Foreign Office.[328] As E. D. Morel, one of the founders of the Congo Reform Association, put it in a note about Conan Doyle's pamphlet *The Crime of the Congo* (1909).

It was not his book – excellent as it was, nor his manly eloquence on the platform, nor the influence he wielded in rallying influential men to our cause, which helped most. It was just the fact that he was – Conan Doyle; and that he was with us.[329]

As an aspiring historical novelist, with literary and political ambitions, Conan Doyle had predicted in October 1894 that 'no statesman and no ecclesiastic will have more influence on public opinion than the novelist of the future will have'.[330] What he did not anticipate was that, in the sharply polarized literary field of the 1890s, those novelists might not be in a position to influence the public's opinion of their own literary identity; and, moreover, that that limitation might be the basis of their particular power in the world at large.

POSTSCRIPT

THE THEORY OF THE FIELD, as Bourdieu defines it and as this book has attempted to demonstrate, offers a satisfyingly inclusive methodological framework which embraces, and even transcends, many traditional divisions within cultural and literary studies. By insisting upon literature as a social practice, while avoiding the pitfalls of a naive reductionism, it enables us to move beyond the classical impasse between purely 'internalist' modes of reading, which focus on textuality *per se*, and 'externalist' modes, which threaten to dissolve the text into its non-discursive context. As Bourdieu puts it, the theory leads

both to a rejection of the direct relating of individual biography to the work of literature (or the relating of the 'social class' of origin to the work) and also to a rejection of the internal analysis of an individual work or even of intertextual analysis. This is because what we have to do is all these things at the same time.[1]

On this analysis, as we have seen, Conrad's *The Nigger of the 'Narcissus'* can be read as a manifestation of the literary field in the 1890s. Its impressionistic style and reactionary political allegory, its intertextual liaisons with the journalism and criticism of the Henley circle, its anxiously self-legitimizing preface, its material and symbolic embodiment as a *New Review* serial or a limited first book edition by Heinemann, its reception by contemporary reviewers and readers, and its place in Conrad's literary career – all this 'internal' and 'external' evidence conjointly marks it out as an 1890s-style purist text. Moreover, the unusually complete convergence between its form, style, and themes, and the literary and political outlook of the Henley circle, testifies to Conrad's eagerness as a purist newcomer to make his mark. Reading the *Nigger* – or, indeed, Bennett's serials and novels or the Sherlock Holmes stories – in this context, then, demands the combined acumen of literary critics, sociologists, economists, biographers, bibliographers, and book historians, all of whom have an independently insufficient but collectively necessary part to play in any history of the intricately structured field of the 1890s.

At the same time, by articulating the structures implicit in sociocultural relations, Bourdieu transcends not only the narrowly interactive models of literary production popular among book historians, but also the division between 'traditional' and 'populist' styles of cultural history. Even revisionist historians, like Karl Beckson, assume, for instance, that the literary culture of the 1890s is synonymous with its avant-garde. In a recent study, Beckson notes that 'for many decades, the 1890s have been casually disposed of as the Yellow Nineties, suggestive of decay, principally because of the famous periodical, the *Yellow Book* (1894-1897), and because of a relatively small but articulate band of writers, Wilde included, who proclaimed "art for art's sake" '. Against this all-too-prevalent idea, he rightly points out that the 'fin de siècle embraced such a wide variety of literary and artistic modes of expression, including Impressionism, Aestheticism, Decadence, Naturalism, and Symbolism, that reducing the late nineteenth century to one of them and branding it "decadent" merely because it was anti-Establishment is to inflict simplicity on complexity'.[2] Beckson, in effect, replaces a crudely essentialist historiography with a more sophisticated version which none the less still centres exclusively on the avant-garde. Inevitably, this methodological assumption blinds one in advance to the possibility of a significant relationship between avant-garde and 'mass culture', the purists and the profiteers, or, as we saw in chapter 2, Bennett as novelist and serialist. Part of the argument of this book has been that a more dialectical historical method has the advantage of leaving one open to the possibility of alternative contextual sources and readings. It presupposes a framework of investigation that encompasses both the purists and the profiteers (as well as those, like Conan Doyle, who occupy a more precarious position between such extremes), both canonical novels and ephemeral serials, both books and periodicals. This does not, of course, require the existence of a cultural utopia in which all symbolic forms are equal. The dialectical history, which any analysis of the field demands, is, as a matter of methodological principle, neither 'elitist' nor 'populist'. If it claims that each literary generation establishes itself against the previous one, it also insists that avant-garde and 'popular' culture are reciprocally defined in and through an ongoing cultural contest. Its object is neither avant-garde nor 'popular' literature: it is the reciprocal antagonisms that exist between them and the hierarchically structured networks that make each possible.

For Bourdieu, this style of cultural analysis is 'resolutely historicist', a view this book has clearly endorsed.[3] Any cultural or literary study which takes the field as its object sets out, I have implied, on a particularly comprehensive mission to reconstruct the context in which texts are originally written, published, printed, distributed, reviewed, and read. The object of this historical investigation, viewed from the perspective of today's reader, is to overcome the inevitable process of 'derealization' which cultural survival entails. 'Stripped of everything which attached them to the most concrete debates of their time', Bourdieu notes, texts 'are impoverished and transformed in the direction of intellectualism or an empty humanism'.[4] This studiously anti-Platonic outlook is a salutary remedy against the false idealism implicit in much literary history, but it also provides more questions than it does answers. Does such a negative conclusion, we might ask, necessarily follow from the fact that texts, for all their historical determinations, have the capacity to survive the contexts in which they are initially produced and read? Is cultural survival only an unhappy story of inevitable loss as Bourdieu implies? Michel Foucault, so often figured as his intellectual antagonist, offers, I would argue, an alternative vision of survivability in *The Archaeology of Knowledge* (1969) which points towards a less narrowly historicist response to the problem. With a characteristically Nietzschean flourish, he concludes a discussion of what he calls the 'statement', the category of discourse he considers logically prior to the 'sentence', 'proposition' or 'speech act', by focusing on the question of survival:

Instead of being something said once and for all – and lost in the past like the result of a battle, a geological catastrophe, or the death of a king – the statement, as it emerges in its materiality, appears with a status, enters various networks and various fields of use, is subjected to transferences or modifications, is integrated into operations and strategies in which its identity is maintained or effaced. Thus the statement circulates, is used, disappears, allows or prevents the realization of a desire, serves or resists various interests, participates in challenge and struggle, and becomes a theme of appropriation or rivalry.

A literary text can be seen as a composite 'statement' on this definition and, as such, it is entangled in the same process of modification and survival. This is, as Foucault suggests, 'paradoxical'. 'Too repeatable to be entirely identifiable with the spatio-temporal co-ordinates of its birth . . . too bound up with what surrounds it and supports it to be as free as a pure form', the text is, in its 'repeatable materiality', 'endowed' with what he calls 'a certain modifiable heaviness, a weight relative to the field in which it is placed, a constancy that allows various uses, a temporal permanence that does not have the inertia of a mere trace or mark, and which does not sleep on its own past'.[5] Despite his general emphasis on the field of discourse, these remarks about materiality, status, and networks of use suggest that Foucault's more favourable, and indeed more realistic, account of survivability need not be incompatible with a social theory of the field. Indeed, he appears to want to claim that texts are both conditioned by the discursive and non-discursive fields in which they are originally produced, as Bourdieu would argue, *and* that they continue to live a complex after-life in other times, places, and fields. They are edited and republished in new material formats; translated into new media like radio, film, or television; forgotten or championed or vilified by new generations of readers and writers; subjected to new styles of reading and critical scrutiny; and they become the focus of contests and debates remote from those that constituted the conditions of their production. Indeed, a few canonical texts become an established part of another semi-autonomous field, with its own history, structure, and disputes, namely, literary and cultural studies. Any further account of the field in the 1890s would have to consider this subsequent history and recognize that survival entails not only derealization but an always incomplete process of re-realization, misrealization, and even non-realization. It would have to concern itself with the initial field of writing and reading, as this book has done, and with the ongoing history of such fields, tracing the text's various material and social predicaments, and the history of its uses and meanings.

NOTES

INTRODUCTION: THE LITERARY FIELD IN THE 1890s

1 [Henry Harland], 'Books: A Letter to the Editor and an Offer of a Prize', *YB* October 1895: 128. Beckson attributes all the 'letters' signed 'The Yellow Dwarf' to Henry Harland, the literary editor of the *Yellow Book*. See Karl Beckson, *London in the 1890s: A Cultural History* (New York: W. W. Norton, 1992), 243.

2 Edmund Gosse, 'The Influence of Democracy on Literature', *Contemporary Review* April 1891: 523–36. Gosse is EG hereafter.

3 EG, 'Tennyson', *NR* November 1892: 513.

4 'Funeral of Lord Tennyson', *Reynolds's Newspaper* 16 October 1892: 5e.

5 'Tennyson's Funeral', *Times* 13 October 1892: 4a.

6 'Funeral at the Abbey', *Daily Telegraph* 13 October 1892: 7e.

7 Robert Martin, *Tennyson: The Unquiet Heart* (Oxford: Clarendon Press, 1980), 582–83.

8 'Notes', *NO* 15 October 1892: 545.

9 'Tennyson', *Star* 12 October 1892: 3c.

10 June Hagan, *Tennyson and his Publishers* (London: Macmillan, 1979), 175.

11 In their contemporary survey, Charles Booth's reporters claimed that the average West End 'tailoress' could expect between 15s and 18s a week; while the 1906 census put the average wage for a 'seamstress' as 15s 10d. See Charles Booth, ed., *Life and Labour of the People in London* vol. 4 (London: Macmillan, 1893), 152; H. L. Smith, ed., *The New Survey of London Life and Labour* vol. 1 (London: P. S. King, 1931), 332.

12 EG, 'Tennyson', *NR*: 515 and 520.

13 For the details of Gosse's career, see Ann Thwaite, *Edmund Gosse* (London: Secker and Warburg, 1984), 241–378.

14 R. J. Lister, *A Catalogue of a Portion of the Library of Edmund Gosse, Hon. M. A. of Trinity College, Cambridge* (London: The Ballantyne Press, 1893), xv. This volume, with its introduction by Gosse, was privately printed for subscribers. For a more detailed catalogue see E. H. M. Cox, *The Library of Edmund Gosse* (London: Dulau and Company, 1924).

15 EG, 'Tennyson', *NR*: 515 and *passim*.

16 [Wilkie Collins], 'The Unknown Public', *Household Words* 21 August 1858: 217–22.

17 EG, 'Tennyson', *NR*: 515 and 518.

18 EG, 'The Tyranny of the Novel', *National Review* April 1892: 167–8.

19 Evan Charteris, *The Life and Letters of Sir Edmund Gosse* (London: Heinemann, 1931), 226.

20 'The Cheapening of Poetry', *NO* 5 November 1892: 624.

21 Donald Read, *England, 1868–1914* (London: Longman, 1979), 103.

22 EG, 'Tennyson', *NR*: 515.

23 Raymond Blathwayt, 'Mr Hall Caine at Home', *Interviews* (London: A. W. Hall, Great Thoughts Office, 1893), 145.

24 Hall Caine, 'The Burials of Two Poets Laureate. – A Contrast', *Times* 17 October 1892: 11b.

25 EG, 'Tennyson', *NR*: 516 and 523.

26 Henry James, *The Notebooks of Henry James*, eds. F. O. Matthiessen and Kenneth B. Murdock (New York: Oxford University Press, 1947), 180.

27 Henry James, *The Figure in the Carpet and Other Stories*, ed. Frank Kermode (Harmondsworth: Penguin, 1986), 284.

28 For a useful account of Yates and the interview, see Weiner's essay 'Edmund Yates: The Gossip as Editor' in *Innovators and Preachers: The Role of the Editor in Victorian England*, ed. Joel H. Weiner (Westport: Greenwood Press, 1985), 259–74.

29 Blathwayt, 'The Art of Interviewing', *Interviews*, 347–53.

30 EG, 'Tennyson', *NR*: 523.

31 'Personal Tit-Bits', *TB* 22 October 1892: 575.

32 EG, 'Tennyson', *NR*: 523; 'The Small Change of Literature', *SO* 20 July 1889: 238.

33 'Small Change', *SO*, 238–9. For Salmon's early defence of *Tit-Bits*, see his essay 'What the Working Classes Read', *Nineteenth Century* July 1886: 113–14.

34 EG, 'Tennyson', *NR*: 523.

35 'Cheapening', *NO*: 625.

36 Karl Marx and Frederick Engels, *Marx and Engels on Literature and Art*, eds. Lee Baxandall and Stefan Morawski (New York: International General, 1974), 136.

37 Pierre Bourdieu, *The Field of Cultural Production* ed. Randal Johnson (Cambridge: Polity Press, 1993), 181–2.

38 Robert Darnton, *The Kiss of Lamourette* (London: Faber and Faber, 1990), 110–11. This frequently reprinted essay, entitled 'What is the History of Books?', originally appeared in *Daedalus* 3.3 (Summer 1982).

39 Leopold Wagner, *How to Publish* (London: George Redway, 1898), 56–7.

40 Bourdieu, *Field*, 37.

41 *Ibid.*, 78.

42 *Ibid.*, 179.

43 Michel Foucault, *The Archaeology of Knowledge*, trans. A. M. Sheridan Smith (1969; London: Tavistock Publications, 1972), 36–7.

44 Bourdieu, *Field*, 53 and 115–31.

45 Oscar Wilde, *The Picture of Dorian Gray* (Harmondsworth: Penguin, 1985), 3.

46 'The Society of Authors', *Times* 10 March 1887: 8d. This report on the second conference of the Society includes a verbatim account of Gosse's speech on 'The Profession of Author'. For an indispensable account of the formation of the Society, see Peter Keating, *The Haunted Study* (London: Secker and Warburg, 1989), 27–71.

47 EG, 'The Society of Authors and Mr Gosse', *Times* 10 May 1895: 11e. See the Society's official reply on 13 May 1895: 11c.

48 Rayburn S. Moore, ed., *Selected Letters of Henry James to Edmund Gosse, 1882–1915: A Literary Friendship* (Baton Rouge: Louisiana State University Press, 1988), 128. The letter is dated 10 May 1895.

49 Bourdieu, *Field*, 53.
50 W. B. Yeats, 'The Grey Rock', *Collected Poems* (1933; London: Macmillan, 1982), 115–17.
51 W. B. Yeats, ed., *The Oxford Book of Modern Verse* (Oxford: Clarendon Press, 1936), ix.
52 *Ibid.*
53 EG, *Father and Son* (Harmondsworth: Penguin, 1986), 251.
54 Roland Barthes, *Image Music Text* (London: Fontana, 1977), 146.
55 *Ibid.*, 147.
56 'The Decay of Fiction', *NO* 27 May 1893: 37.
57 EG, 'Influence', *Contemporary*, 529.
58 For a more detailed discussion of the circulating libraries, see Keating, *Study*, 22–7, and 420–5.
59 For Gosse's puzzlement over his unhappy relations with Henley, see Charteris, *Life and Letters*, 234–5.
60 Bourdieu, *Field*, 46.

I MEN OF LETTERS AND CHILDREN OF THE SEA: JOSEPH CONRAD
AND THE HENLEY CIRCLE

1 Joseph Conrad, *CL2*, 109. Joseph Conrad is JC hereafter.
2 JC, *CL1*, 390. The letter was originally written in French. For the purposes of this discussion, however, I have used the English translation provided by Karl and Davies.
3 *Ibid.*, 393, 333, and 422.
4 *CL2*, 137.
5 *CL1*, 185.
6 *CL2*, 418.
7 *Ibid.*, 137, and see also *CL1*, 296.
8 *Ibid.*, 137.
9 *Ibid.*, 138.
10 JC and Ford Madox Hueffer, *The Inheritors* (London: J. M. Dent, 1923), 24–7 and *passim*. The novel also contained an unflattering portrait of Alfred Harmsworth as Fox.
11 JC, *CL1*, 16. As Najder has argued, it is impossible to tell just how far Conrad actually committed himself to these strongly reactionary posturings at this time. Yet, as I shall argue later in this chapter, subsequent evidence points to a marked and persistent disposition towards political conservatism. See Zdzislaw Najder, *Joseph Conrad: A Chronicle* (Cambridge University Press, 1983), 87–9.
12 *CL2*, 137.
13 JC, *The Nigger of the 'Narcissus'*, ed. Jacques Berthoud (Oxford University Press, 1984), xxxix, italics mine.
14 JC, *CL1*, 333, italics mine. As it turned out, Garnett could not find a publisher for these sketches.
15 *CL2*, 418.
16 *Ibid.*, 417. It should be remembered, however, that J. B. Pinker had become Conrad's literary agent two years before he made this disparaging remark.

17 *CL1*, 266.
18 JC to A. T. Quiller-Couch, 23 December 1897, *ibid.*, 430.
19 *Ibid.*, 405.
20 *Ibid.*, 180.
21 *Ibid.*, 434.
22 Edward Garnett, 'Letters from Joseph Conrad', *The Nigger of the 'Narcissus'*, ed. Robert Kimbrough (New York: Norton, 1979), 173.
23 Najder, *Conrad*, 181. Meyers calculates that the 15,000 roubles Conrad inherited in February 1895 was worth £4,000 or $20,000 at current rates. See Jeffrey Meyers, *Joseph Conrad: A Biography* (London: John Murray, 1991), 117.
24 JC, *CL1*, 292; and see also Najder, *Conrad*, 201.
25 Without knowing it or desiring it at the time, he ended his sea career in January 1894. But he was still looking for a suitable post as late as 1898. As Najder has argued, his lack of experience on steamships, his ill-health, and his foreign origins counted against him. See Najder, *Conrad*, 181; and JC, *CL2*, 79.
26 JC, *CL1*, 306–8. If we make the generous assumption that he worked a fifty-hour week, this meant he was hoping to make an annual income of around £108. Given his circumstances, this was certainly not 'magnificent': in 1892 he was making £96 a year as first mate on the *Torrens*. See Najder, *Conrad*, 153.
27 JC, *CL1*, 266.
28 Najder, *Conrad*, 187–8.
29 JC, *The Rescue* (London: J. M. Dent, 1923), ix.
30 JC, *CL1*, 240. The story was, in fact, never placed serially.
31 *Ibid.*, 299, 330, and 372. He objected to 'An Outpost of Progress' being cut in two for *Cosmopolis* and to the instalment plan for the *Nigger* in the *New Review*.
32 *Ibid.*, 296, 301, 338, 354, 337.
33 *Ibid.*, 176, 240, and 350.
34 Based on the evidence in the letters, Conrad's earnings from magazines for his first short stories are as follows: from the *Savoy* (October 1896) about £37 16s for 'The Idiots' (10,000 words), or 1s for 13 words; from *Cornhill* (January 1897) £10 for 'The Lagoon' (5,300), or 1s for 27 words; from *Cosmopolis* (June–July 1897) £40 10s for 'An Outpost of Progress' (9,500), or 1s for 12 words; and from *Blackwood's* (November 1897) £36 for 'Karain' (16,000), or 1s for 22 words. In all these calculations, Unwin's 10 per cent commission on the magazine rights has been deducted. See JC, *CL1*, 285, 293, 350–1, 356, 367, and 408.
35 This figure includes only the following: £20 for *Almayer*, the £50 advance on *An Outcast*, and £88 6s for the magazine rights to 'The Idiots', 'An Outpost of Progress', and 'The Lagoon'. It is also worth noting that Conrad was used to earning £8 a month as a bachelor. This was his wage as first mate on the *Torrens* in 1892. See Najder, *Conrad*, 153.
36 According to the family budgets described in *Cornhill* in 1901, a working-man who earned 30s a week was 'in receipt of good weekly wages'. See Arthur Morrison, 'Family Budgets: I. A Workman's Budget', *Cornhill* April 1901: 446.
37 JC, *CL2*, 7.
38 *CL3*, 112–13, and 142.

39 *Ibid.*, 184. The story was called 'Benavides' (later incorporated into 'Gaspar Ruiz'). The *Strand* turned it down. See *CL3*, 170–1 and 181.

40 *Ibid.*, 112.

41 See Najder, *Conrad*, 199, and F. R. Karl, *Joseph Conrad: The Three Lives* (London: Faber and Faber, 1979), 381.

42 JC, *Rescue* , ix.

43 Kimbrough, ed., *Nigger*, 174.

44 *CL1*, 308 and 312.

45 *Ibid.*, 330; and Kimbrough, ed., *Nigger*, 175.

46 JC to various correspondents, June–August 1896, *CL1*, 285–6, 290–4, and 298.

47 *Ibid.*, 308–10.

48 *CL3*, 115.

49 *CL1*, 315.

50 Kimbrough, ed., *Nigger*, 174–5.

51 *CL1*, 317–19.

52 Kimbrough, ed., *Nigger*, 168.

53 *CL1*, 323 and 329.

54 *CL2*, 109.

55 *CL3*, 115.

56 JC, *Last Essays* (London: J. M. Dent, 1923), 95–6.

57 Todd G. Willy, 'The Conquest of the Commodore: Conrad's Rigging of "The Nigger" for the Henley Regatta', *Conradiana* 17.3 (1985): 167.

58 *CL1*, 211.

59 Unsigned review, *NO* 14 September 1895: 513. See also Norman Sherry, ed., *Conrad: The Critical Heritage* (London: Routledge and Kegan Paul, 1973), 69.

60 Unsigned review, *NO* 18 April 1896: 680. See also Sherry, *Heritage*, 69–70.

61 JC to T. Fisher Unwin, 22 April 1896, *CL1*, 276.

62 Willy, *Conradiana*, 166. By September 1895 Henley was nine months into his editorship of the *New Review*. In other words, Willy is right about the personal score with Henley, but wrong about the evidence for this.

63 Sherry, *Heritage*, 51–2 and 73–6.

64 Willy, *Conradiana*, 167.

65 Bourdieu, *Field*, 116.

66 Joseph Conrad, *Under Western Eyes* (London: J. M. Dent, 1923), 10–14.

67 Linda Marie Fritschner, 'Publishers' Readers, Publishers, and their Authors', *Publishing History* 7 (1980): 48. Fritschner's is a useful social study of the difference between purist readers, like Garnett, and profiteering readers, like Geraldine Jewsbury who worked for Bentley between 1860 and 1875.

68 His more complex relationship with Marguerite Poradowska marked an earlier stage in the process of co-optation.

69 Bourdieu, *Field*, 77.

70 JC to Garnett, 14 August and 16 September 1896, *CL1*, 300 and 307.

71 For instance, Garnett wrote the first general appreciation of Conrad. It appeared in the *Academy*, 15 October 1898, 82–3. See also Sherry, *Heritage*, 104–8.

72 Meredith to The Earl of Plymouth, *c.* 5 July 1907, *The Collected Letters of George Meredith*, ed. C. L. Cline, vol. 3 (Oxford: Clarendon Press, 1970), 1600.

73 *Ibid.*

74 Rudyard Kipling, *Something of Myself* (London: Macmillan, 1937), 82; W. B. Yeats, *Autobiographies* (London: Macmillan, 1955), 124.

75 JC to various correspondents, May 1896–January 1897, *CLi*, 281, 320, and 329.

76 'Subsidising Literature', *NO* 10 December 1892: 77.

77 'Literature and Democracy', *NO* 11 April 1891: 528.

78 'The Prospects of Literature', *NO* 29 April 1893: 591. By contrast, in early 1889 the *Scots Observer* called the Society an 'excellent body', and added that it was 'a matter of the utmost importance that something like a trade's union should exist among literary men'. See 'The Protection of Authors', *SO* 27 April 1889: 628–9.

79 'The Literary Agent', *NO* 16 July 1892: 216–17. Though Besant was a key figure behind the formation of the Society of Authors, both the Society and its founder were, as Keating has shown, in fact against literary agents in principle. See *Haunted Study*, 65.

80 *Ibid.* See also 'The Sorrows of *The Author*', *NO* 13 June 1891: 85–6.

81 'An Academy of Letters', *SO* 1 November 1890: 601.

82 'Author's Rights', *NO* 5 December 1891: 57.

83 'Literature and Democracy', *NO* 11 April 1891: 528.

84 'The Cheapening of Poetry', *NO* 5 November 1892: 624. Toynbee Hall, named after the radical Oxford economic historian Alfred Toynbee, was the first permanent 'settlement' in the East End for university graduates. Opened in 1884, it was part of a largely Christian Socialist project of social improvement. See Read, *England*, 103 and 298.

85 'The Prospects of Literature', *NO* 29 April 1893: 591.

86 Charles Whibley, 'The True Degenerate', *NR* April 1895: 425–32.

87 'Modern Men: Mr. H. Rider Haggard', *SO* 27 April 1889: 631.

88 For Lang's views on Romance see John Gross, *The Rise and Fall of the Man of Letters* (1969; Harmondsworth: Penguin, 1991), 146–53.

89 'Modern Men: Mr. R. L. Stevenson', *SO* 26 January 1889: 264.

90 'Modern Men: Walter Pater', *NO* 2 May 1891: 608–9.

91 Henley to Charles Whibley, 19 January 1897, Connell, *Henley*, 316. An abridged version of *What Maisie Knew* appeared in the *New Review* from February to September 1897.

92 [Charles Whibley], 'Modern Men: Henry James', *NO* 23 May 1891: 10–11. For the attribution, see Unpublished ALS, Henley to Whibley, 6 April 1891, The Pierpont Morgan Library, New York.

93 [Charles Whibley], 'Reviews and Magazines', *SO* 5 July 1890: 181. This provoked a lengthy debate in the *Scots Observer* between Wilde and the Henley circle which ran from July to August 1890. On 8 April 1895, after Wilde was arrested, Henley wrote self-righteously to Whibley who had, according to Connell, started the exchange: 'I think you'll be pleased with this result of an old campaign in the S. O.' Lord Arthur Somerset and some Post Office workers, who frequented a male brothel in Cleveland Street, were compromised by the scandal. See Connell, *Henley*, 298.

94 W. E. Henley, 'The Tory Press and the Tory Party', *National Review* May 1893: 371.

95 For an account of Henley's tenure at the *Magazine of Art*, see Simon Nowell-Smith, *The House of Cassell, 1848–1958* (London: Cassell & Co., 1958), 138–47.

96 'The Decay of Fiction', *NO* 27 May 1893: 37.
97 'Candid Fiction', *SO* 18 January 1890: 229.
98 Evelyn March Phillips, 'The New Journalism', *NR* August 1895: 182–6.
99 *Ibid.*, 184. The name 'Kodak', as Carey remarks, was specially coined by George Eastman so that it would not be misspelled by the semi-literate. The camera was introduced in 1888. See Carey, *Intellectuals*, 31.
100 '*Drivel*: Weekly 1d.', *SO* 28 December 1889: 157.
101 *Ibid. Ally Sloper's Half-Holiday*, an illustrated comic weekly, gave Charles Ross the first major forum for the eponymous cartoon character he invented in 1865. It ran from 3 May 1884 to 9 September 1916, and then again from 5 November 1922 to 29 September 1923. For detailed discussion of the magazine, see Peter Bailey, '*Ally Sloper's Half-Holiday*: Comic Art in the 1880s', *History Workshop* 16 (1983): 4–31.
102 [Charles Whibley], 'Modern Men: George R. Sims', *SO* 23 November 1889: 11–12. For the ascription see Connell, *Henley*, 167.
103 *Ibid.*, 11.
104 [Henry Harland], 'Dogs, Cats, Books, and the Average Man', *Yellow Book* July 1896: 12–22. Max Beerbohm, who coined the phrase the 'Henley Regatta', expressed similar views about the Henley circle earlier in the *Yellow Book's* run. See Max Beerbohm, 'A Letter to the Editor', *Yellow Book* July 1894: 283.
105 'Log-roller', 'Books and Bookmen: 'Log-roller's' Literary Notes of the Week', *Star* 30 July 1891: 2e, emphasis added. Le Gallienne was referring to Henley's *Views and Reviews* (London: Nutt, 1890).
106 Vernon Blackburn, 'A Poet's Corner', *NR* May 1895: 526.
107 'The Fogey Speaks', *NO* 10 February 1894: 313.
108 'ΘΑΥΜΑ ΘΕΑΣΘΑΙ', *NO* 21 April 1894: 588–9. Though the weekly announced Henley's resignation in the issue of 7 April, his stamp and some of his contributors were still very much in evidence at this point.
109 See *CLi*, 386, 394, 405.
110 'The Bugbear of Realism', *NO* 23 July 1892: 235.
111 'Modern Men: Emile Zola', *SO* 25 January 1890: 262.
112 O. Winter, 'The Cinematograph', *NR* May 1896: 512.
113 See 'Cinematograph', *NR*: 510; 'Bugbear of Realism', *NO*: 235; and George Wyndham, 'A Remarkable Book', *NR* January 1896: 33.
114 Henley, according to Yeats, was affected by the Pre-Raphaelites 'as some people are affected by a cat in the room'; while Ford Madox Ford claimed that Henley and the literature he encouraged pointed the way out of the 'stifling atmosphere of Pre-Raphaelism'. See Yeats, *Autobiographies*, 125; and Ford, *Ancient Lights*, 228.
115 Winter, 'Cinematograph', *NR*: 509–10.
116 Arthur Morrison, 'What is a Realist?', *NR* March 1897: 327–8. Kiddo Cook and Pigeony Poll are characters from the East End who feature in *A Child of the Jago*.
117 [Whibley], 'Sims', *SO*: 11.
118 'X', 'A Sane Critic', *NR* January 1896: 90–1. This is a review of R. A. M. Stevenson's *The Art of Velasquez* (1895).
119 Henley, *Views and Reviews*, 49.

120 'The Bugbear of Realism', *NO*: 235. The article is a response to William Barry's criticisms in his essay 'Mr. Rudyard Kipling's Tales', *Quarterly Review* July 1892: 132–61.

121 'Mr. Whistler's Etchings', *NO* 28 January 1893: 261.

122 *Ibid.*, and R. A. M. Stevenson, 'Corot', *NR* April 1896: 409.

123 Stevenson, 'Corot', *NR*: 408–11.

124 See Edward H. Cohen, 'Henley's *In Hospital*, Literary Realism, and the Late-Victorian Periodical Press', *Victorian Periodicals Review* 28.1 (Spring 1995): 4–5. As Cohen points out, Wilde made his remark in a review for *Woman's World* (1889), while the Symons quote comes from an article in *Harper's New Monthly Magazine* (1893). Cosmo Monkhouse and Alice Meynell echoed their views.

125 'Studies in the New Poetry', *Punch* 4 June 1892: 268.

126 [Charles Whibley], 'Modern Men: Guy de Maupassant', *SO* 25 October 1890: 583. For the ascription, see Unpublished ALS, Henley to Whibley, 3 October 1890, The Pierpont Morgan Library, New York.

127 Wyndham had been on the 'inner council' of the *National Observer* since October 1892, and became the driving figure behind the *New Review*. Whibley called him Henley's 'pupil in letters'. George Wyndham, *Essays in Romantic Literature*, ed. Charles Whibley (London: Macmillan, 1919), x–xi; Wyndham, 'Remarkable Book', *NR*: 33.

128 Winter, 'Cinematograph', *NR*: 510.

129 Unpublished ALS, W. E. Henley to Lord Windsor, 18 October 1895, The Pierpont Morgan Library, New York. MA 1617 (3). The dates for the Stevenson stories refer to the year in which they began to appear in *Young Folks*.

130 [Whibley], 'Maupassant', *SO*: 583.

131 [J. H. Millar], 'Reviews: Crumbs of Criticism', *SO* 12 July 1890: 202. Millar was reviewing Henley's *Views and Reviews* (1890). For the ascription, see Connell, *Henley*, 190.

132 Charles Whibley, 'Slang', *NO* 30 December 1893: 164. Whibley was reviewing volume 3 of Henley and Farmer's *Slang and its Analogues*.

133 'Mr. Vizetelly's Recollections', *NO* 18 November 1893: 18–19.

134 'Penny Dreadfuls', *SO* 2 August 1890: 268.

135 'The Worst of Fiction', *SO* 7 September 1889: 425; and 'Candid Fiction', *SO*: 229. This second article was a response to a symposium on the topic published in Archibald Grove's *NR*. See Walter Besant, Mrs Lynn Linton, and Thomas Hardy, 'Candour in English Fiction', *NR* January 1890: 6–21.

136 G. W. Steevens, 'The New Ibsen', *NR* January 1895: 39.

137 *Ibid.*; and 'Modern Men: Henrik Ibsen', *SO* 11 May 1889: 687.

138 [Charles Whibley], 'The New Journalese', *SO* 26 April 1890: 627–28. For the ascription, see Unpublished ALS, Henley to Whibley, 25 April 1890, Pierpont Morgan Library, New York.

139 G. W. Steevens, 'The New Ibsen', *NR* January 1895: 39–44.

140 '*Drivel*: Weekly 1d.', *SO* 28 December 1889: 157.

141 'The Small Change of Literature', *SO* 20 July 1889: 239; '*Drivel*: Weekly 1d.', 28 December 1889: 157

142 'Art and the Mob', *SO* 15 August 1890: 315.

143 James Bertrand de Vincheles Payen-Payne, ed., *Some Letters of William Ernest Henley* (London: Privately Printed, 1933), 49–50.

144 Yeats, ed., *Modern Verse*, vi.

145 'Outis', 'The Great Democratic Joke', *NR* February 1895: 161–2.

146 W. S. Lilly, 'The New Divine Right', *NR* May 1895: 508–9.

147 'Z', 'Two Demagogues: A Parallel and a Moral', *NR* April 1895: 364–70.

148 James Annand, 'The Decline of the Politician', *NR* November 1897: 703–4. The final two lines from 'Invictus' are: 'I am the master of my fate: / I am the captain of my soul.' See W. E. Henley, 'Echoes: IV', *Poems* (London: David Nutt, 1898), 119. The poem is dated 1875.

149 Lilly, 'Divine Right', *NR*: 509.

150 'Socialism *In Excelsis*', *SO* 23 February 1889: 376–7. See also Read, *England*, 99–100.

151 'Cheapening of Poetry', *NO*: 624. See Read, *England*, 103 and 297.

152 W. Roberts, 'The Free Library Failure', *NR* September 1895: 316. As the article claimed, all issued over 75% fiction, and nine over 80%. For a more detailed account of the problems associated with the public libraries, see Keating, *Haunted Study*, 411–20.

153 'The Triumph of Sentimentality', *SO* 29 November 1890: 33.

154 W. S. Lilly, 'The Problem of Purity', *NR* January 1895: 85.

155 'Anti-Woman', *NO* 7 May 1892: 633.

156 'After the Strike', *SO* 29 June 1889: 146; Lilly, 'Problem of Purity', *NR*, 84. Lilly was particularly critical of the attacks on marriage in Pearson's *The Ethic of Free Thought* and Morris and Bax's *Manifesto of the Socialistic League*, claiming that as Socialism would 'abolish pauperism by making all men paupers, so it would abolish prostitution by making all women prostitutes'.

157 'Sentimentality', *SO*: 33.

158 See the following unsigned articles in the *National/Scots Observer*: 'Why Women May Not Vote', 30 April 1892: 607; 'Pampering the Unemployed', 19 November 1892: 5–6; 'Philanthropy on Trial', 31 January 1891: 269–70; 'The Submerged Tenth', 6 December 1890: 64–5; 'The New Nigger Question', 17 January 1891: 214–15.

159 James Annand, 'The Demoralisation of Liberalism', *NR* September 1895: 248–56; 'The Liveliness of Radical Socialism', *SO* 20 July 1889: 229.

160 'Sentimentality', *SO*: 33.

161 'Anti-Woman', *NO* 7 May 1892: 633.

162 'The Submerged Tenth', *SO* 6 December 1890: 65. In his study of poverty in England and Wales *In Darkest England* (1890), Booth estimated that the 'Submerged Tenth', the most abject and impoverished residuum of late-Victorian society, numbered about 3 million or roughly one-tenth of the population. The book was co-authored by W. T. Stead. See Read, *England*, 34–5.

163 'Pampering the Unemployed', *NO* 19 November 1892: 5–6.

164 Paul Cushing, 'For England's Sake', *NO* 16 April 1892: 561.

165 C. De Thierry, 'Imperialism', *NR* September 1897: 317; and 'Colonial Empires', August 1897: 152. Henley wrote an approving introduction to her collection of essays *Imperialism* (London: Duckworth, 1898).

166 'The Nigger of Fact', *SO* 10 October 1890: 526.

167 'The New Nigger Question', *NO* 17 January 1891: 214. See also 'Our Black Question', *NO* 9 May 1891: 630. Here they argue for a strong policy towards the West Indies specifically.

168 *Ibid.*, 215.

169 W. E. Henley, *The Song of the Sword* (London: David Nutt, 1892), 10.

170 'Modern Men: Thomas Hardy', *NO* 7 February 1891: 301.

171 W. E. Henley, 'The Early Life of Jean-François Millet,' *Cornhill* March 1882: 299.

172 'Hardy', *NO*: 301.

173 Morrison, 'Realist?', *NR*: 328, and 330–1.

174 Morrison, *A Child*, 53–4.

175 In the echo chamber of the magazine this quotation was consciously taken up by an essayist to vilify another group of 'false prophets': in this case the Liberal Free Traders who argued against Ernest E. Williams's pro-protectionist series 'Made in Germany' published in the *NR* in 1896. See Ernest E. Williams, 'My Critics', *NR* November 1896: 609.

176 Morrison, 'Realist?', *NR*: 329.

177 See Lionel Deck, 'The Murder in Africa', *NR* December 1895: 585–98; and H. R. Fox-Bourne, 'The Congo Failure', March 1897: 342–52. The Congo Reform Association was formed only in 1904. Both these articles reveal that it was not difficult to be strongly in favour of British Imperialism, as Henley was, and severely critical of other European empire-builders at the same time. The criticisms served only to demonstrate the superiority of the British Imperial order. Such views persuade one that some of Conrad's political attitudes, particularly those implied by *Heart of Darkness,* are not as radical as one might at first think.

178 'The Small Change of Literature', *SO* 20 July 1889: 239.

179 'Some New Journals of the Year', *Newsagent* 30 May 1891: 14.

180 Advertisement, *Saturday Review* 25 May 1889: after 652. See also Walter E. Houghton and Elizabeth Evans, '*The New Review*', *The Wellesley Index to Victorian Periodicals: 1824–1900*, vol. 3 (London: Routledge and Kegan Paul, 1979), 303. The other major essay on the *New Review* is Anne Murtagh's '*The New Review*: A Glimpse of the Nineties', *Victorian Periodicals Review* (Spring 1981): 11–20.

181 Houghton, *Index*, vol. 3, 303.

182 Archibald Grove, 'Special Announcement' *NR* January 1894: 127.

183 'Less than Halfpenny a Line!', *NO* 11 March 1893: 406.

184 Grove, 'Announcement', *NR*: 127. Houghton and Evans misleadingly suggest that Grove was responding to competition from periodicals such as the *Illustrated London News* (1842). Clearly, by 1894, the pressure came from illustrated monthlies like the *Strand*. See Houghton, *Index*, vol. 3, 304–5.

185 *Ibid.*

186 *Ibid.*, 128.

187 *Ibid.*

188 *Advertisement, NR June 1894: viii.*

189 Houghton, *Index*, vol. 3, 305.

190 George Wyndham, *Letters of George Wyndham*, ed., Guy Wyndham, vol. 1 (Edinburgh: T. and A. Constable, 1915), 346.

191 Keating, *Haunted Study*, 35.

192 Advertisement, *Modern Men from The Scots Observer* (London: Edward Arnold, 1890), 128; Wyndham, *Letters*, 346.

193 Connell, *Henley*, 231; Advertisement in *The Newsagent and Bookseller's Review* 30 May 1891: 17.

194 All these advertisements, which were typical throughout Henley's editorship, appear in the issue of April 1896.

195 Connell, *Henley*, 148; and Herbert Stephen, 'W. E. Henley: As a Contemporary and an Editor', *The London Mercury* February 1926: 399.

196 Insert, *NR*, July 1897.

197 [Millar], 'Crumbs of Criticism', *SO*: 202.

198 Stephen, 'W. E. Henley', *Mercury*: 398.

199 Blaikie and Bruce put in £3,000 each over the same period. In 1891, newsagents could purchase one quire (or 26 copies) of the *Observer* at the wholesale price of 9s (or just over 4d per copy). This meant the average weekly sales revenue of just over £31 barely covered the production costs of £30. Without any significant advertising revenue, the promoters were left with the bill for all the editorial costs, including Henley's salary of not more than £400. See *Newsagent* 30 May 1891: 17; Connell, *Henley*, 140 and 148.

200 [Arnold Bennett], 'D'You Know?', *Woman* 11 April 1894: 6. Though Bennett was only one of a number of writers who produced 'Marjorie's' weekly gossip column, his later accusations of plagiarism suggest that he had a personal investment in the paragraph. On 16 May, in his 'Book Chat' column, he gently criticized the *Student*, a magazine produced for University Extension students, for understandably stealing it from *Woman* for their editorial. See 'Barbara', 'Book Chat', *Woman* 16 May 1894: 8.

201 Wyndham, *Letters*, 346.

202 Letter to Whibley 19 April 1895, see Connell, *Henley*, 300.

203 Stephen, 'W. E. Henley', *Mercury*: 399.

204 Wyndham, *Essays*, xi.

205 Wyndham, *Letters*, 346.

206 *Ibid.*, 348. Wyndham considered Jameson to be 'a man after my own heart' and admired him enormously. See *Letters*, 349 and 352. Harris's article, 'The Fate of South Africa', appeared in the *New Review* for March 1896.

207 'The Monthly Report of the Wholesale Book Trade', *Bookman* April 1896: 8. See also reports for May and September 1896.

208 'Editorial Note', *NR* September 1896: on the unnumbered inside content's page.

209 'News Notes', *Bookman* July 1896: 101.

210 Advertisement, *NR* September 1896: i.

211 Anthony West, *H. G. Wells: Aspects of a Life* (London: Hutchinson, 1984), 216.

212 Stephen, 'W. E. Henley', *Mercury*: 399.

213 Edwin Pugh, 'The Mother of John', *NR* May 1896: 559–71. Houghton and Evans oddly speculate that the story was Elizabeth Robins's 'A Lucky Sixpence' which appeared in Grove's issue of January 1894. See Houghton, *Index*, vol. 3, 306. For a discussion of the problems surrounding this attribution, see Sue Thomas, 'Eliza-

beth Robins and the *New Review*', *Victorian Periodicals Review* 28:1 (Spring 1995): 63–6.

214 Stephen, 'W. E. Henley', *Mercury*: 399.

215 Wyndham, *Essays*, xi.

216 Insert, *NR* December 1897. In a letter Wyndham called it a 'raft' built 'out of the wreckage of the "New Review" '. See Wyndham, *Letters*, 387.

217 *CL2*, 32.

218 *CL1*, 321.

219 'The Monthly Report', *Bookman* December 1897: 60.

220 *CL2*, 8 and 273; and *CL4*, 324. In the letter of 19 May 1900 Conrad remarked that the *Nigger* had brought him nearly £200 at a 17.5% royalty. Taking this to be approximately 1s per copy, the total sales to that date must have been about 4,000.

221 *CL2*, 18 and 3.

222 *Ibid.*, 273.

223 *Ibid.*, 8–9.

224 Sherry, *Heritage*, 11. See also Edward Garnett, ed., *Letters from Joseph Conrad, 1895–1924* (New York: Charter Books, 1962), 16.

225 *Ibid.*, 93.

226 JC, *Nigger*, ed. Berthoud, 150.

227 Sherry, *Heritage*, 83.

228 *Ibid.*, 95. See also I. Zangwill, review, *Academy* 1 January 1898: 1–2.

229 Letter of 7 January 1898, *CL2*, 5–6.

230 Unsigned review, *Literature* 26 March 1898: 354.

231 Sherry, *Heritage*, 11–12 and 88–9.

232 JC, *Nigger*, ed. Berthoud, 22, 108, and 149.

233 Sherry, *Heritage*, 83, 92–6.

234 JC to A. T. Quiller-Couch, 23 December 1897, *CL1*, 430.

235 'Candid Fiction', *SO* 18 January 1890: 229.

236 JC, *Nigger*, ed. Berthoud, 4–7.

237 JC to A. T. Quiller-Couch, 23 December 1897, *CL1*, 430–1.

238 Sherry, *Heritage*, 85–8.

239 JC to Garnett, *CL1*, 395.

240 *Ibid.*, 432 and *CL2*, 28. See also *CL1*, 354–5.

241 *CL2*, 138.

242 JC, *Nigger*, ed. Berthoud, vii–x.

243 Wyndham, 'Remarkable Book', *NR*: 32–40.

244 JC, *Last Essays*, 120.

245 For examples of the various uses of the unrestricted third-person narrator, see *Nigger*, 93, 99, 109, and 113.

246 Sherry, *Heritage*, 96.

247 Unsigned review, 'Novel Notes', *Bookman* January 1898: 131.

248 Sherry, *Heritage*, 86.

249 Letter of 24 December 1897, *CL1*, 432–3.

250 JC to ?[a reviewer of the *Nigger*], *CL1*, 421.

251 JC, *Nigger*, ed. Berthoud, 29, 54, and 162–3.

252 *Ibid.*, 90.

253 JC, *Last Essays*, 95.
254 JC, *Nigger*, ed. Berthoud, 7, 26, and 130.
255 *Ibid.*, 25.
256 *Ibid.*, 6, 24–5, 89, and 137.
257 *Ibid.*, 25, 90, 134.
258 *Ibid.*, 10–14, 41, 45, 101–10, 123, 167, and 169 (my italics).
259 *Ibid.*, 9, 11, 17, 41, 45, 84.
260 *Ibid.*, 115–16 and 150.
261 *Ibid.*, 25, 138–40, 152, and 160.
262 *Ibid.*, 42, 99, 120, 127, and 129.
263 *Ibid.*, x–xi.
264 Najder, *Conrad*, 167 and 171.
265 Bourdieu, *Field*, 95

2 PLAYING THE FIELD: ARNOLD BENNETT AS NOVELIST, SERIALIST, AND JOURNALIST

1 Arnold Bennett and Eden Phillpotts, *The Sinews of War* (London: T. Werner Laurie, 1906), 343. Arnold Bennett is AB hereafter.
2 AB, *LAB2*, 11.
3 AB, *The Truth About an Author* (1903; London: Methuen, 1914), 2 and 71.
4 *Ibid.*, 29; and AB, *Sketches for Autobiography*, ed. James Hepburn (London: George Allen and Unwin, 1979), 5.
5 AB, *Truth*, 37–40.
6 AB, *Truth*, 45, 52, and 139. See also Cash-Book for 1894, holograph, Henry W. and Albert A. Berg Collection, The New York Public Library, Astor, Lenox and Tilden Foundations, New York, n. p.
7 *Ibid.*, 52. See also, Cash-Books for 1894 and 1895, Berg, n. p.
8 AB, Cash-Books for 1894 and 1895, Berg, n. p.
9 AB, *Truth*, 49, and *LAB2*, 9.
10 *LAB2*, 12, and 19–20.
11 AB, *Truth*, 61–2,
12 *LAB2*, 15, and 22–3.
13 James, *Notebooks*, 180.
14 AB, *Truth*, 61.
15 *LAB2*, 11–12 and 35.
16 AB, *Truth*, 79.
17 *Ibid.*, 62; and *LAB2*, 29.
18 AB, *Truth*, 80.
19 AB, *A Man from the North* (Stroud: Alan Sutton, 1994), 4.
20 James Hepburn, ed. *Arnold Bennett: The Critical Heritage* (London: Routledge and Kegan Paul, 1981), 139–47.
21 AB, *The Journals of Arnold Bennett, 1896–1910*, ed. Newman Flower (London: Cassell and Company, 1932), 11 and 68; *Truth*, 64.
22 AB, *Truth*, 64. Harris has a useful discussion of this formal characteristic of the

'Keynotes Series'. See Wendell V. Harris, 'John Lane's Keynotes Series and the Fiction of the 1890s', *PMLA* 83: 5 (October 1968), 1407–13.

23 Hepburn, *Critical Heritage*, 140. The review originally appeared in *Hearth and Home* for 3 March 1898 under Bennett's pseudonym 'Sarah Volatile'. The weekly later published Bennett's first 'sensational serial' *Love and Life*. As Mrs C. S. Peel's 'Household Management' column indicates, the predominantly female readership ranged from those who lived on £160 a year, rented two-roomed flats, and employed an occasional servant, to those with an annual income of £650, a house that cost £120 a year, and two permanent domestic servants who together cost £39 a year. See *Hearth and Home* 26 July 1900: 499 and 2 August 1900: 530.

24 *LAB2*, 26.

25 *Ibid.*, 26 and 38; *Truth*, 62 and 66.

26 AB, *Truth*, 63.

27 *LAB2*, 55; and *A Man*, 53.

28 AB, *Truth*, 66; and *A Man*, 113.

29 *LAB2*, 27.

30 AB, *Truth*, 70–1.

31 *LAB2*, 27.

32 Wagner, *How to Publish*, 52.

33 'Barbara', 'Book Chat', *Woman* 5 February 1896: 7. 'Barbara' was Bennett's pseudonym for his book review column.

34 AB, *Truth*, 61; and *LAB2*, 27.

35 AB, *Journals, 1896–1910*, 19; *Truth*, 72.

36 Holbrook Jackson, *The Eighteen Nineties* (1913; London: Century Hutchinson, 1988), 53.

37 J. Lewis May, *John Lane and the Nineties* (London: The Bodley Head, 1936), 217.

38 Stetz quotes this advertisement from the first issue of the *Yellow Book* (April 1894). See Margaret Diane Stetz, 'Sex, Lies, And Printed Cloth: Bookselling at the Bodley Head in the Eighteen-Nineties', *Victorian Studies*, 35:1 (Autumn 1991), 76.

39 For the best account of Lane's early years, see James G. Nelson, *The Early Nineties: A View from the Bodley Head* (Cambridge, Mass.: Harvard University Press, 1971).

40 Richard Le Gallienne, *The Romantic '90s* (New York: Doubleday, Page & Co., 1925), 163.

41 Ella D'Arcy, Some *Letters to John Lane*, ed. Alan Anderson (Edinburgh: The Tragara Press, 1990), 17–18.

42 [Margaret Oliphant], 'The Looker-on', *Blackwood's*, January 1895: 164.

43 Leon Edel, ed., *Henry James Letters*, vol. 3 (London: Macmillan, 1980), 482. The letter is dated 28 May 1894.

44 Richard Le Gallienne, *Prose Fancies* (London: Elkin Mathews and John Lane, 1894), 121.

45 Susan Otis Thompson, *American Book Design and William Morris* (New York: R. R. Bowker Co., 1977), 11 and 15.

46 For Lane's exploitation of the copyright act, see P. H. Muir, 'Ignoring the Flag', *New Paths in Book Collecting*, ed. John Carter (London: Constable, 1934), 89.

47 William Dana Orcutt, *In Quest of the Perfect Book* (Boston: Little, Brown & Co., 1926), 56.

48 Unsigned and undated note, John Lane Archives, British Library, London. These details about the production of Bennett's first novel reinforce Brown's account of Lane's business practices in the early 1890s. See R. D. Brown, 'The Bodley Head Press: Some Bibliographical Extrapolations', *The Papers of the Bibliographical Society of America*, 61 (1967): 39–50.

49 Stetz, 'Sex, Lies', 75, 79, and 84.

50 May, *Lane*, 206–7.

51 Karl Beckson, *Henry Harland: His Life and Work* (London: The Eighteen Nineties Society, 1978), 79–80.

52 *Ibid.*, and AB, Cash-Book for 1895, Berg, n. p. Bennett was paid £3 3s for the 2,700-word story 'A Letter Home', and Harland expected to have to pay James £75 for 'The Next Time' which was 19,000 words.

53 Beckson, *Harland*, 67.

54 'George Egerton', *A Leaf from The Yellow Book*, ed. Terence De Vere White (London: The Richards Press, 1958), 42.

55 J. W. Lambert and Michael Ratcliffe, *The Bodley Head, 1887–1897* (London: The Bodley Head, 1987), 105–18. In a letter of 10 November 1896 'George Egerton' complained about Lane pressurizing her to 'bowdlerize' *Symphonies*. See 'Egerton', *A Leaf*, 42.

56 Bourdieu, *Field*, 78.

57 John Buchan, *Memory Hold-the-Door* (1940; London: J. M. Dent, 1984), 41, and 49–50.

58 John Buchan, *Scholar Gypsies* (London: John Lane, The Bodley Head, 1896), 12; and Lambert and Ratcliffe, *Bodley Head*, 117.

59 Lambert and Ratcliffe, *Bodley Head*, 116.

60 AB, *Journals, 1896–1910*, 10–11.

61 Lambert and Ratcliffe, *Bodley Head*, 117.

62 AB, *Truth*, 74–5. This printed version of the conversation has Bennett saying that the notorious novel was by 'Mrs. – '. Though Lane had had another controversial success in the interim – Grant Allen's *The Woman Who Did* (1895) – 'Egerton's' was his most successfully controversial novel by a woman. 'Egerton's' maiden name was Mary Chavelita Dunne, but she was known at this point by her married name Mrs Clairmonte. For the details about the publication of her first novel, see Nelson, *Early Nineties*, 287.

63 Unpublished ALS, E. A. Bennett to John Lane, 6 October 1896, ms Ogden 96/1, University College Library, London.

64 AB, *Journals, 1896–1910*, 69.

65 Unpublished TLS (Contract form letter), John Lane to E. A. Bennett, 15 December 1897, John Lane Archives, Reading Library, Reading.

66 AB, *Truth*, 79.

67 *LAB2*, 12.

68 AB, *Truth*, 76.

69 AB, *Journals, 1896–1910*, 79–80.

70 See Eden Phillpotts, *Eden Phillpotts (1862–1960): Selected Letters*, ed. James Y. Dayananda (Lanham: University Press of America, 1984), 1–18 and 127.

71 *LAB2*, 115.

72 AB, *Journals 1896–1910*, 101.

73 *Ibid.*, 26.

74 *Ibid.*, 80.

75 *LAB2*, 115.

76 *Ibid.*, 118.

77 AB, Cash-Books for 1894 and 1895, Berg, n. p.

78 Margaret Drabble, *Arnold Bennett: A Biography* (1974; Boston: G. K. Hall, 1986), 86–7; and AB, *The Savoir-Vivre Papers*, *TPW*: 'Running Away from Life', 17 August 1906, 210; 'What is the Simple Life?', 24 August, 242; 'Those Petty Artificialities', 7 September, 306; 'The Simple Life Controversy', 21 September, 370. As Drabble points out, however, he experimented for a while by going part-shares in a weekend-cottage in Witley, Surrey from the autumn of 1898.

79 AB, *Truth*, 149.

80 AB, *Journals 1896–1910*, 90–91.

81 AB, *Truth*, 102. For a detailed account of the history and business practices of the Tillotson firm, see Frank Singleton, *Tillotsons, 1850–1950* (Bolton and London: Tillotson and Son, 1950), especially 41–48; Michael Turner, 'Reading for the Masses: Aspects of the Syndication of Fiction in Great Britain', *Book Selling and Book Buying: Aspects of the Nineteenth-Century British and North American Book Trade*, ed. Richard G. Landon (Chicago: American Library Association, 1978), 52–72; and Keating, *Haunted Study*, 43–45.

82 *Ibid.*, 104.

83 Reginald Pound, *Arnold Bennett: A Biography* (London: Heinemann, 1952), 114. Pound quotes from an unpublished journal entry of 13 January 1898.

84 AB, *Truth*, 102–4. Though Bennett's description is broadly accurate, Turner's more thorough account indicates that the rights Tillotson, in particular, bought and sold were more complex. See Turner, 'Reading for the Masses', 63–4.

85 AB, Holograph Journal, vol. 3: 7 December 1897–27 May 1901, Henry W. and Albert A. Berg Collection, The New York Public Library, Astor, Lenox and Tilden Foundations, New York, 17–19. This entry is for Thursday, 13 January 1898.

86 *Ibid.*; and AB, *How to Become an Author: A Practical Guide* (London: C. Arthur Pearson, 1903), 120. Bennett claimed Phillpotts was earning 5 guineas per thousand in January 1898.

87 In a letter to George Sturt of 5 January 1899, Bennett claimed he wrote five trial stories at this time. The first was a 'damn silly story' entitled 'The Marriage of Jane Hendra', which appeared in *Woman* on 26 October 1898; he considered the one described in the text, 'The Dragons of the Night', as his best, and it appeared in *Hearth and Home* on 1 December. In addition, he sent two stories to his agent, who was at this time William Morris Colles, only one of which is known, namely 'Mr. Penfound's Two Burglars'. And finally he published a children's story in *Woman*, entitled 'The Great Fire at Santa Claus's House', on 7 December 1898. See *LAB2*, 115–17.

88 *LAB2*, 112 and 116.

89 AB, *Journals, 1896–1910*, 87.

90 AB, Holograph Journal, vol. 3: Berg, 93. This entry is for Wednesday, 18 January 1899.

91 AB, *Journals, 1896–1910*, 90-1.

92 Bennett gave two different versions of his pseudonym. See AB, *Truth*, 109; and AB, *Journals 1896–1910*, 91.

93 *LAB2*, 116.

94 AB, Holograph Journal, vol. 3: Berg, 165–6. This entry is for Tuesday, 10 April 1900.

95 AB, *Truth*, 110–13. Not much is known of the process of production in this case. Yet, in a letter to H. G. Wells of 2 August 1900, Bennett claims to be working on the serial, and adds that, as progress is being impeded by an abscess, Tillotsons have generously given him a six-week extension on the deadline. See *LAB2*, 135. Turner notes that Philip Gibbs, later Sir Philip Gibbs, was the 'Bureau's' editor from 1899 to 1902. See Turner, 'Reading for the Masses', 59.

96 James Hepburn, ed., *Arnold Bennett: The Critical Heritage* (London: Routledge & Kegan Paul, 1981), 18. Given this payment, Bennett's popular fiction was only slightly more remunerative than his serious fiction at this point in his career. In the Cash-Book for 1902 he recorded two payments (£90 in March and £10 in August) from Chatto and Windus, presumably as advances on royalties for the 80,000-word *Anna of the Five Towns* which was published in September. If, as Hepburn suggests, Tillotsons bought the entire rights to *The Grand Babylon Hotel*, also published by Chatto and Windus in 1902, then he would have earned nothing from book rights, and these payments can only be attributed to *Anna*. Of course, if one takes into consideration the time involved in producing the popular fiction, then it was still very much more lucrative than the serious work. See AB, Cash Book for 1902, Berg, n. p.

97 AB, *Truth*, 113.

98 Advertisement, *Golden Penny* 26 January 1901: 73.

99 AB, *Journals 1896–1910*, 109.

100 *LAB2*, 147; AB, *Truth*, 113–14.

101 Hepburn, ed., *Heritage*, 19 and 149–52; AB, *Truth*, 114.

102 Drabble, *Bennett*, 84.

103 AB, *Truth*, 114.

104 Philip Gibbs, *The Pageant of the Years: An Autobiography* (London: Heinemann, 1946), 32.

105 AB, Holograph Journal, vol. 3: Berg, 109–10. This entry is for Wednesday, 22 February 1899. His career as a dramatist began informally in February 1899, and in 1900 he went on to collaborate with Arthur Hooley and Eden Phillpotts.

106 AB, *Truth*, 127–8.

107 *LAB2*, 145; and AB, *Truth*, 128–9. The two plays written in collaboration with Arthur Hooley in 1900 were *The Chancellor* and *A Wayward Duchess*.

108 For his views on reading for Pearsons, see *Truth*, 132–7. In his Cash-Books for 1901 and 1902, he records that he received £43 19s 6d and £64 9s, respectively, from Pearsons. See Berg, n. p.

109 AB, Cash-Book for 1901, Berg, n. p.; AB, *Journals 1896–1910*, 107.

110 AB, Cash-Book for 1902, Berg, n. p.

111 G. Colmore, 'Family Budgets: III. Eight Hundred a Year', *Cornhill* June 1901: 790–800; AB, *Truth*, 65. According to the survey, £800 a year would have been

considered normal for a young married couple where the husband was at the beginning of a professional or Civil Service career. Bennett's recorded expenses for the year came to only £422 13s 8d. See AB, Cash-Book for 1902, Berg, n. p.

112 *LAB2*, 147. Julia Neilson was an actress, producer, and theatre manager.

113 AB, *Truth*, 114.

114 *Cupid and Commonsense*, a dramatization of *Anna of the Five Towns*, was produced in January 1908.

115 Until 1907, Chatto and Windus, who published most of his early serials in book form, including *The Grand Babylon Hotel* (1902), *The Gates of Wrath* (1903), *Teresa of Watling Street* (1904), *Hugo* (1906), *The Ghost* (1907), and *The City of Pleasure* (1907), were standardly paying a £75 advance on royalties, and at this time he usually expected at least £30 for translation rights. In March that year he claimed never to have earned more than £90 in royalties from them. In November 1904 he estimated that *Hugo* was worth altogether about £300, and as late as June 1907 he considered £300 to be a minimum for the English serial and book rights to *Helen with the High Hand*. See *LAB1*, 54, 72, 83, 91, and 110.

116 As he claimed in a letter of 28 November 1903, negotiations with *T. P.'s Weekly* had broken down at the end of 1902 when he refused to accept less than 15 guineas per instalment (standardly 5,000 words). Though, as Wilfred Whitten, the executive editor, told him privately, they would probably have agreed to the relatively decent rate of twelve guineas per instalment (1s for 20 words or just over £150 for a standard serial). In July 1904 he maintained he would be happy if Tillotsons agreed to pay 3 guineas per thousand for *The City of Pleasure*, his sixth serial, though he stressed that this did not include translation rights for which he expected a further £30. See *LAB1*, 42 and 54.

117 *LAB1*, 42 and 61.

118 *Ibid.*, 64.

119 *Ibid.*, 38, 71, 75, and 83.

120 *Ibid.*, 65. Bennett argued that £450 for 100,000 words brought them down to the 'decidedly insufficient' rate of £4 10s a thousand; that a serial of over 80,000 words would bore the reader; and, finally, that *T. P.'s Weekly* would get the same serial anyway whether it was 80,000 or 100,000 words.

121 *Ibid.*, 57. Though Bennett accepted O'Connor's judgement, he was not convinced that the offending scene was all that lay behind the refusal. As he remarked to Pinker, 'I regard T. P.'s explanation that they refused the story on account of that chapter as grotesque.' As an earlier letter suggests, he thought O'Connor was also prejudiced against him because Whitten, the managing editor, had 'always rammed me down his throat' and that he was trying to cut costs. See *LAB1*, 54–5.

122 Eden Phillpotts, A L S to J. B. Pinker, 13 January 1906, Berg Collection, New York Public Library, New York.

123 AB, *Journals 1896–1910*, 225.

124 *LAB1*, 66.

125 *Ibid.*, 68 and 72. As Bennett added that his was a minimum figure which did not take account of any good luck as far as sales were concerned, it presumably comprised his share of the British serial rights and the advances on British and American book rights. *The Sinews of War* was published in America under the title

Doubloons at the same time as the British publication in November 1906. It was Bennett's first American publication since *The Grand Babylon Hotel* which was published in New York as *T. Racksole and Daughter* by the New Amsterdam Book Company in 1902. See *LAB1*, 67.

126 Phillpotts noted in a letter to William Morris Colles of 9 March 1906 that they had £1,500 for serial rights and advances as well as £50 for the Tauchnitz edition. See Phillpotts, *Selected Letters*, 158.

127 *LAB1*, 70.

128 AB, *Journals 1896–1910*, 225–6 and 230–1. He began writing on 26 January 1906.

129 Eden Phillpotts, A L S to AB, 23 February 1906, Berg Collection, New York Public Library, New York.

130 Advertisement, *TPW* 23 February 1906: 233.

131 *LAB1*, 70.

132 Unsigned Review, *Spectator* 8 December 1906: 938; Unsigned Review, *Bookman*, December 1906: 154.

133 Advertisement, *TPW* 9 November 1906: 604.

134 Unsigned Review, *Athenaeum* 1 December 1906: 687.

135 Unsigned Review, *Academy* 17 November 1906: 503.

136 *LAB1*, 90. The fate of *The City of Pleasure* was similar. According to Chatto and Windus, 2,500 copies were printed in August 1907, of which 1750 were bound that year and sold at 6s. In 1910 they reduced the price to 3s 6d, but it took until 1919 to sell the remaining copies. See *LAB1*, 111.

137 AB, Cash-Book for 1906, Berg, n. p. His expenses, which included the costs of his failed engagement to Eleanor Green, came to £1,046 15s 10d. Under 'Special Expenses' he listed £191 12s 6d as 'Private', but at another point he attributed this figure to 'Women'. He was, for the most part, receiving at this stage a regular payment of £50 a month from Pinker.

138 Drabble, *Bennett*, 157–8. As Drabble notes, the book rights for *The Statue* were sold to Cassell's in August 1907 for £600. It was published in March 1908. In addition to the two serials, Bennett also collaborated with Phillpotts on four plays, none of which was ever produced.

139 *LAB1*, 91, 93, 110, 156, and 167.

140 Drabble, *Bennett*, 191–2. The breakdown of his income for 1913 gives an indication of the commercial importance of his dramatic career at this stage: of the total £15,449 17s 1d, £6,924 18s 1d came from books, and £8,524 19s from plays. See AB, *Journals, 1911–1921*, 76.

141 AB, *Journals 1896–1910*, 26.

142 Alvin Sullivan, ed., *British Literary Magazines: The Victorian and Edwardian Age, 1837–1913* (Westport, Connecticut: Greenwood Press, 1984), 4.

143 H. G. Wells, *Tono-Bungay* (London: Macmillan, 1909), 285–7.

144 Keating, *Haunted Study*, 75. As my discussion suggests, the *Academy* was not as irretrievable as Keating claims.

145 Sullivan, ed., *Literary Magazines, 1837–1913*, 5.

146 AB, *The Savour of Life: Essays in Gusto* (London: Cassell and Company, 1928), 146.

147 'Barbara', 'Book Chat', *Woman* 5 February 1896: 7; 10 April 1895: 7; and 1 January

1896: 6. The serial, by G. A. Greene and Arthur Hillier, appeared in the magazine from 16 May to 8 August 1894.

148 C. Lewis Hind, *Authors and I* (London: John Lane, 1921), 50 and 53.

149 AB, *Truth*, vi-viii. According to Bennett, Andrew Chatto was the first to guess who it was, and from then on everyone knew.

150 E. A. B., 'Mr. Silas Hocking's Popularity: An Enquiry', *Academy* 1 July 1899: 17-18. See also AB, *Fame and Fiction: An Enquiry into Certain Popularities* (London: Grant Richards, 1901), 146-53. In the following week's issue, Hocking, who was on the whole very appreciative of Bennett's remarks about his work, objected strongly to this last claim. Bennett was, in his view, guilty of precisely those kinds of prejudice he had allegedly been trying to dismantle, since he appeared to 'accept the traditional idea that [the Nonconformists] are "Philistine" to the core'. Bennett defended himself in the next issue by claiming his right to speak with authority on these matters, seeing as he knew the class 'from the inside', and by pointing out that he been careful not to include all Nonconformists in his criticism, but only those who belonged to the specific class and region he mentioned. See the 'Correspondence' column in the *Academy* for 8 July 1899: 44; and 15 July 1899: 69.

151 Unsigned, 'The Novel of the Moment: An Enquiry', *Academy* 18 November 1899: 575-6. See also *Fame and Fiction*, 111-16.

152 E. A. B, 'The Revolution in Journalism: An Enquiry', *Academy* 10 March 1900: 207. See also *Fame and Fiction*, 123-32.

153 E. A. B, 'The Fiction of Popular Magazines: An Inquiry [sic]', *Academy* 24 February 1900: 167. See also *Fame and Fiction*, 133.

154 E. A. B, 'Revolution in Journalism', *Academy*: 207.

155 AB, *Truth*, 18-19 and 106-7.

156 As Keating points out in his discussion of late-Victorian ideas of the artist, both du Maurier and Puccini drew extensively on Henry Murger's *Scenès de la vie de bohéme* (1847) which Watson is shown to be reading in *A Study in Scarlet*. *La Bohème* was first performed in England in 1897. See Keating, *Haunted Study*, 80-1; and Arthur Conan Doyle, *A Study in Scarlet*, ed. Owen Dudley Edwards, (Oxford University Press, 1993), 46.

157 For his comments about the attitudes of the reading public, see *Arnold Bennett: The Evening Standard Years, 'Books and Persons' 1926-1931*, ed. Andrew Mylett (London: Chatto & Windus, 1974), 298. The article, entitled 'This "Bosh" About Art For Art's Sake', originally appeared on 22 August 1929.

158 AB, *The Author's Craft* (London: Hodder and Stoughton, 1914), 125.

159 AB, *Books and Persons: Being Comments on a Past Epoch, 1908-1911* (London: Chatto and Windus, 1917), 243.

160 *Ibid.*, 244.

161 AB, *Evening Standard Years*, 84.

162 *LAB1*, 135; *Craft*, 130.

163 AB, *Books and Persons*, 88-92 and 100-2.

164 AB, *Craft*, 113-14.

165 See AB, *Books and Persons*, 143 and 186; and Drabble, *Bennett*, 287.

166 AB, *Craft*, 113 and 115. His private interest in sexuality is readily apparent in the many parts of his journal censored by Newman Flower in the 1930s. As the MS of

the journal, which forms part of the Berg Collection in New York, reveals, he had an ongoing and lively fascination with issues ranging from lesbianism to the horrors of childbirth, and female hysteria to his own erotic dreams.

167 See John Carey, *The Intellectuals and Masses* (London: Faber and Faber, 1992), 153; and Drabble, *Bennett*, 289–94.

168 AB, *Truth*, x. For Wells's favourable remark, see *LAB2*, 180.

169 Unsigned Review, *Athenaeum* 22 August 1903: 253.

170 [Charles Whibley], 'Musings Without Method', *Blackwood's* October 1903: 535–8.

171 St. John Lucas, 'Two Kinds of Author', *The Author* 1 October 1903: 23–4. Bennett's tract was not universally accepted in the pages of *The Author*, however. 'Artifex', in the next month's issue, whose literary career had been one of 'unceasing struggle', claimed it described the exception rather than the rule. He was so desperate that he was even thinking of taking a research job with a German manufacturer, though he 'detest[ed] Germans' and 'abhor[red] trade'. See 'Artifex', 'The Truth about an Author', *The Author* 1 November 1903: 51–2.

172 Carey, *Intellectuals*, 152.

173 *LAB1*, 17 and 34. As he noted in his diary and cash-book for 1902, *T. P.'s Weekly* offered 15s a column (about 700 words) for general articles, 31s 6d for reviews (generally 1,500 words), and 5 guineas for 1,500-word short stories. The rates for the reviews and general articles were not substantially different to those he had been getting from the *Academy*. See AB, Cash-Book for 1902, Berg, n. p.

174 E. A. B, 'Revolution in Journalism' *Academy*, 207.

175 T. P. O'Connor, 'Confession of Faith', *The Star* 17 January 1888: 1.

176 T. P. O'Connor, 'The Gospel According to "The Sun"', *Sun* 27 June 1893: 2.

177 T. P. O'Connor, 'The Sun's First Anniversary', *Sun* 27 June 1894: 2.

178 T. P. O'Connor, 'Our Anniversary', *TPW* 6 November 1903: 729; and 'Literature the Consoler', 14 November 1902: 17.

179 T. P. O'Connor, 'Consoler', *TPW* 14 November 1902: 17.

180 T. P. O'Connor, 'Anniversary', *TPW* 6 November 1903: 729.

181 O'Connor noted on 22 January 1909: 'Self-culture, unguided or misguided, is almost as futile as the absence of the attempt to gain a taste for culture at all. This is the want which, on the appeal of my readers, I am now trying to supply.' The College began officially on 5 February 1909. The response, especially to the course on reasoning (called 'Mental Training'), was overwhelming. The editor noted that 'hundreds' of readers were signing up for it, and, according to the course examiner, entrants of various ages came from all over the country, with Scotland being particularly well-represented: most were young men and women, but there were some older men from the 'learned professions' and one lady of sixty-three. See T. P. O'Connor, 'A Word in Advance', *TPW* 22 January 1909: 99; 'Special Supplement', *TPW* 29 January 1909; [Editorial Note], 11 February 1909: 241; and 'An Interesting Report of the Examiner-in-Chief', 5 March 1909: 312.

182 Keating, *Haunted Study*, 77.

183 An advertisement in *Bookman* reported that over 200,000 copies of the first issue were sold within a few hours of publication, but, by 1904, Bennett reported that it had 'a solid regular public of 150,000 a week', while the paper itself published a more modest average weekly sale for the year of 117,487 copies. In the Christmas

number for 1904, O'Connor was pleased to report a 'steady growth' in the number of subscriptions – though he added that many readers still bought directly from newsagents – as well as a continued widening of the 'geographical sphere' of his audience: by then copies were being sent to Syria, Australia, South Africa, India, Canada, Bolivia, and Borneo. All of this, he added, was a clear sign of the paper's 'acceptance and prosperity'. By 1905 he noted that, given the 'substantial advance' on the previous year's sales, new printing machinery had been set up to meet the demand. Unreliable though these various figures and comments might be, taken as a whole, it would seem safe to assume that at its best the average weekly circulation was between 120,000 and 175,000 copies; and, on the conservative assumption that four people read parts of each issue, that it had a weekly readership of at least half a million. See Advertisement, *Bookman* December 1902: xxviii; *LAB1*, 46; Unsigned, 'Special Notice', *TPW* 24 March 1905: 369; T. P. O'Connor, 'A Word of Greeting', *TPW* Special Christmas Number for 1904: 1; and T. P. O'Connor, 'Our Anniversary', *TPW* 6 November 1903: 729.

184 AB, *Become an Author*, 67 and 105.

185 T. P. O'Connor, 'Anniversary', *TPW* 6 November 1903: 729.

186 Representative articles covering the eight topics mentioned are in order: 'Savoir-Faire Papers: Alone in London', a seven-part mini-series which ran from 11 September to 23 October 1903; 'The Savoir-Faire Papers: The City Lunch', 28 November 1902: 83; 'The Savoir-Faire Papers: The Modern Woman', 2 January 1903: 243; 'The Savoir-Vivre Papers: Running Away from Life', 17 August 1906: 210; 'The Rising Storm of Life', 5 July 1907: 14; 'The Savoir-Vivre Papers: The Duty of Marriage', 26 January 1906: 114; 'The Adventure of Marriage', 2 February 1906: 146; 'The Two Ways of Marriage', 9 February 1906: 178; the six-part series *The Revolt of Youth* , 22 October–26 November 1909; and 'The Savoir-Faire Papers: The Importance of Going to Belgium', 14 November 1902: 19.

187 Both were subsequently published as volumes of pocket philosophy: see *The Human Machine* (London: The New Age Press, 1908), and *Literary Taste: How to Form it* (London: The New Age Press, 1909).

188 Advertisement, *TPW*, 6 November 1903: 739; and [AB], 'The Savoir-Vivre Papers: Wanted: A Mental Sandow', 18 May 1906: 652.

189 AB, *The Human Machine* (New York: George H. Doran and Co., 1911), 20–1.

190 [AB], 'The Savoir-Faire Papers: Time to Read', *TPW*, 14 August 1903: 338.

191 AB, *Human Machine*, 113.

192 [AB], 'Savoir-Faire Papers: Reading', *TPW* 30 January 1903: 365. See also AB, *Literary Taste: How to Form it* (London: New Age Press, 1909), 114.

193 AB, *Literary Taste* , 9.

194 See 'Savoir-Faire Papers: Some Cosmopolitan Literature', *TPW* 27 February 1903: 499; and 'My Literary Heresies: III Concerning the Living', 23 September 1904: 392.

195 AB, *Literary Taste* , 14, 22 and 61.

196 [AB], 'The Savoir-Faire Papers: Alone in London, VI', *TPW* 16 October 1903: 626.

197 Though generally happy about the new publishing initiative, which the editors of *T. P.'s Weekly* eagerly supported, Bennett had some misgivings about the fact that

the 'series' format made reader's dependent on publisher's choices and that the selections tended to be too limited. As his suggestions for the library indicate, he always advocated a broad and catholic attitude to book-buying in order to overcome these problems. [AB], 'The Savoir-Vivre Papers: The Physical Side of Books', *TPW* 16 February 1906: 210; AB, *Literary Taste*, 89–112; and, for the editor's remarks, see Wilfred Whitten, 'A River of Reading: Mr. Dent's Great Series: Everyman's Library', *TPW* 23 February 1906: 233.

198 AB, *Literary Taste*, 7–8, 11–13, 28, 35–6, 43–51, and 117.

199 'C. T. of Oldam', T. P.'s Letter-Box', *TPW* 14 July 1905: 60; and 'Dernier Cri', 'Literature and Isolation', 15 September 1905: 329.

200 'T. P.'s Letter-Box', 3 March 1905: 284.

201 'T. P.'s Letter-Box', *TPW* 5 December 1902: 124.

202 [AB], 'Time to Read', *TPW* 14 August 1903: 338.

203 'By its Owner', 'A Working Woman's Library', *TPW* 1 September 1905: 262; and 'T. P.'s Letter-Box', 31 January 1908: 152.

204 J. J. D., 'T. P.'s Letter-Box: The Worker's Mental Life', *TPW* 13 October 1905: 476.

205 'By Its Owner', 'A Working Man's Library', *TPW* 19 August 1904: 231.

206 E. H., 'T. P.'s Letter-Box', *TPW* 1 September 1905: 284.

207 'H. R. J. (of Birmingham), 'T. P.'s Letter-Box', *TPW* 26 March 1909: 414.

208 'T. P.'s Letter-Box', *TPW* 9 April 1909: 480.

209 Carey, *Intellectuals*, 154, 172, and 174.

210 AB, *Truth*, 63.

211 AB, *A Man*, 113.

212 Woolf worked out her case against Bennett in three famous essays – 'Modern Novels' (1919), 'Mr Bennett and Mrs Brown' (1923) and 'Character in Fiction' (1924) – all of which appear in Virginia Woolf, *The Essays of Virginia Woolf, 1919-1924*, ed. Andrew McNeillie, vol. 3 (London: The Hogarth Press, 1988).

213 AB, *The Old Wives' Tale*, ed. John Wain, (1908; Harmondsworth: Penguin, 1988), 82.

214 *Ibid.*, 37–40.

215 AB, *Man*, 46.

216 AB, *Wives'*, 37–44.

217 Ibid., 42–7 and 65–7.

218 AB, *The Grim Smile of the Five Towns* (Harmondsworth: Penguin, 1946), 130.

219 AB, *Craft*, 17–18. For his views on the way the novels set out to subvert conventional language, and on the way names designating social functions, like 'policeman', could reduce the individual to an 'algebraic symbol', see *Craft*, 30–2.

220 Ibid., 9.

221 AB, *Truth*, 85.

222 AB, *Fame*, 9, 11, and 15–19.

223 [AB], 'The Sensational Serial: An Enquiry', *Academy* 2 May 1901: 387–8.

224 AB and Phillpotts, *Sinews*, 244.

225 AB, *Fame*, 14.

226 AB, *The Gates of Wrath, Myra's Journal: The Leader of Fashion* (November 1899), 29; *Hugo* (New York: G. H. Doran, 1907), 67 and 166.

227 AB, *Riceyman Steps* (London: Cassell, 1945), 177.

228 AB, 'Sensational Serial', *Academy*: 387.

229 AB, *Journals, 1896–1910*, 274 and 299.

230 AB and Phillpotts, *Sinews*, 14, 20, 75, 128–29, 211, and 216.

231 AB, *Love and Life, Hearth and Home* (21 June 1900): 283.

232 *Ibid.*, (17 May 1900), 88–9.

233 AB, *Hugo*, 2–3, 7, 34, 63, and 95.

234 AB, *The City of Pleasure* (New York: G. H. Doran, 1907), 1–10, 13, and 35.

235 AB, Evening Standard *Years*, 81.

236 AB, *Journals, 1896–1910*, 31.

237 AB, *Sinews*, 141; *Teresa of Watling Street* (London: Ward, Lock, 1931), 13 and 19.

238 AB, *The Grand Babylon Hotel* (1902; London: Eveleigh Nash and Grayson, 1923), 168.

239 AB, *Savour of Life*, 142.

240 AB, *Wives'*, 46.

241 AB, *Teresa*, 227; *Hugo*, 35–6.

242 AB, *Wives'*, 32–3.

243 AB, *Hugo*, 323.

244 *LAB1*, 54–7.

245 Drabble, *Bennett*, 212.

246 AB, *Journals, 1896–1910*, 190 and 311.

247 *LAB1*, 49, 52, and 162.

248 *LAB2*, 232–5.

3 LIGHT READING AND THE DIGNITY OF LETTERS: GEORGE NEWNES LTD. AND THE MAKING OF ARTHUR CONAN DOYLE

1 Quoted in Pierre Nordon, *Conan Doyle* (London: John Murray, 1966), 46. Mary Doyle, who sympathized with the Boer cause, was attempting, without success, to dissuade her forty-year-old son from volunteering to go to South Africa to assist in the Anglo-Boer War.

2 [Harland], 'Dogs, Cats', *YB* July 1896: 15.

3 'The Real Sherlock Holmes: An Interview by our Special Commissioner', *NO* 29 October 1892: 606–7.

4 'Novel-Reader', 'Warning to Novelists?', *NR* September 1897: 309, and 313–14. The crisis centred on the boundary disputes between Venezuela and British Guiana. Feeling that its paramountcy in the Western Hemisphere was at risk, the United States stepped in demanding the right to arbitrate in the dispute and threatening war if that was denied.

5 Raymond Blathwayt, 'A Talk with Dr. Conan Doyle', *Bookman* May 1892: 51.

6 J. M. Gibson and R. L. Green, eds., *The Unknown Conan Doyle: Letters to the Press* (London: Secker and Warburg, 1986), 47–9. The letter appeared on 7 January 1896.

7 As his own professional career and the career trajectories of his siblings suggest, despite the near-poverty of his early life, he came from the educated middle classes of mid-Victorian Edinburgh: he trained as a medical doctor at Edinburgh University (MB, CM 1881; MD 1885), many of his sisters went on to become

governesses, and his brother became a Brigadier-General. For Doyle as a cultural philistine, see Ronald Pearsall, *Conan Doyle: A Biographical Solution* (1977; Glasgow: Richard Drew Publishing, 1989), 123. For a more complimentary, and usefully concise, overview of Doyle's background, outlook, and personal history see Owen Dudley Edwards, *The Quest for Sherlock Holmes* (Edinburgh: Mainstream Publishing, 1983), 11-20.

8 Christopher Roden, 'In Conversation with . . . Air Cmdt Dame Jean Conan Doyle', *A. C. D.: The Journal of the Arthur Conan Doyle Society* March 1990: 117-18.

9 Nordon, *Doyle*, 338. As the family archives, of which the journal forms a part, have been closed to researchers following a lawsuit, Nordon remains one of the primary sources for this material. For Bennett's views on the Post-Impressionist exhibition organized by Clive Bell, Roger Fry, and Desmond Macarthy, see Drabble, *Bennett*, 180. Bennett stated his controversial views on the controversial exhibition in a letter to the *Nation* of 10 December 1910.

10 Arthur Conan Doyle, *The Poems of Arthur Conan Doyle* (London: John Murray, 1922), 99–101. Conan Doyle is ACD hereafter.

11 Nordon, *Doyle*, 338.

12 ACD, *Memories and Adventures* (London: Hodder and Stoughton, 1924), 256. See also ACD, *Through the Magic Door* (London: Smith Elder and Company, 1907), 213-14.

13 According to Carey, the *New Age*, under A. R. Orage, featured 'some eighty items relating to Nietzsche between 1907 and 1913'. See Carey, *Intellectuals and Masses*, 4. For a discussion of the *Savoy's* articles on Nietzsche, see Beckson, *London*, 251-2.

14 Havelock Ellis, 'Friedrich Nietzsche: I', *Savoy* April 1896: 79; and Nordon, *Doyle*, 338. Ellis contributed a three-part article on Nietzsche which appeared in April, July, and August 1896.

15 ACD, *To Arms!* (London: Hodder and Stoughton, 1914), 28-9.

16 Nordon, *Doyle*, 338.

17 'A Dinner to Dr. Doyle', *Critic* 1 August 1896: 79.

18 Blathwayt, 'Doyle', *Bookman*: 51. 'Lucas Malet' was the pseudonym used by Mary Kingsley, daughter of Charles Kingsley.

19 ACD, 'Mr. Stevenson's Methods in Fiction', *National Review* February 1890: 650.

20 Gibson and Green, eds., *Letters to the Press*, 43–4. The letter first appeared in the *Daily Chronicle* for 1 May 1894. Though common among the intelligentsia of the 1890s, this attack on the booksellers was not entirely fair. As Wilson has shown, Smith's boycotts were invariably the result of a complex interplay of factors encompassing company policy, editorial tastes, lobbies from prominent public figures, contractual obligations to the railway companies, and other legal considerations. See Charles Wilson, *First with the News: The History of W. H. Smith, 1792–1972* (London: Jonathan Cape, 1985), 365–75.

21 ACD, *Memories*, 79. As I shall argue in the next section, Wilde made a lasting and influential impression on Doyle.

22 ACD, *Magic Door*, 11.

23 ACD, *Memories*, 153, 160, 347 and 365.

24 ACD, 'Stevenson's Methods', *National*: 650–2.

25 ACD, *Magic Door*, 16.

26 *Ibid.*, 25 and ACD, 'Stevenson's Methods', *National*: 654.

27 ACD, 'Stevenson's Methods', *National*: 656.

28 ACD, *Memories*, 260–1. He claimed his was not 'equal to the task'.

29 ACD, 'Stevenson's Methods', *National*: 646–7.

30 ACD, *The White Company* (London: Smith, Elder and Co., 1903), vi–vii.

31 'Doyle', *Critic*: 79.

32 Blathwayt, 'Doyle', *Bookman*: 50.

33 'Doyle', *Critic*: 79.

34 ACD, *White Company*, viii–ix.

35 'Doyle', *Critic*: 78–9. Given the general sentiments and much of the wording of the speech, it is clear Doyle referred back to it when writing his preface for the 1903 edition. The draft of the speech was also published in *The Queen* 4 July 1896: 18–19.

36 *Ibid.*

37 J. M. Gibson and R. L. Green, *A Bibliography of Arthur Conan Doyle* (Oxford: Clarendon Press, 1983), 404–5.

38 ACD, *Memories*, 72–3.

39 *Ibid.*, 70; and ACD, 'My First Book', *McClure's Magazine* August 1894: 227. This article first appeared in the *Idler* January 1893: 632–40.

40 J. M. Gibson and R. L. Green, eds., *The Unknown Conan Doyle: Uncollected Stories* (London: Secker and Warburg, 1982), x.

41 ACD, *The Memoirs of Sherlock Holmes*, ed. Christopher Roden (Oxford University Press, 1993), 273. The article originally appeared in H. Greenhough Smith, ed., *What I Think – a Symposium on Books and Other Things by Famous Writers of To-day* (London: George Newnes, 1927).

42 ACD, *Memories*, 97.

43 *Ibid.*, 102.

44 Gibson and Green, eds., *Letters to the Press*, 52–3. The letter originally appeared in the *Daily Chronicle* on 7 August 1897.

45 ACD, *The Adventures of Sherlock Holmes*, ed. Richard Lancelyn Green (Oxford University Press, 1993), xxviii–xxix.

46 John Dickson Carr, *The Life of Sir Arthur Conan Doyle* (London: John Murray, 1949), 196.

47 ACD, 'The Three Garridebs', *The Case-Book of Sherlock Holmes*, ed. W. W. Robson (Oxford University Press, 1993), 89.

48 Gibson and Green, eds., *Letters to the Press*, 54. Doyle wrote three letters on this issue which originally appeared in the *Daily Chronicle* on 16 and 18 May 1899. He was himself a victim of W. Robertson-Nicoll's multiple-reviews of *A Duet with an Occasional Chorus* (1899). See Gibson and Green, *Bibliography*, 423.

49 In his 'Musings without Method', Whibley attacked 'syndicates, agents, and multiple-reviewers' for having degraded the high profession of literature. See [Charles Whibley], 'Musings without Method', *Blackwood's* October 1903: 537.

50 Bennett, *Truth*, 101.

51 See Gibson and Green, *Bibliography*, 415–16.

52 ACD, 'First Book', *McClure's*: 226.

53 Gibson and Green, eds., *Uncollected Stories*, xii.

54 Doyle, *Memories*, 73. The story eventually appeared in the issue for January 1884.

55 For a more detailed discussion of Payn's position, see Keating, *Haunted Study*, 35, 83, and 402–4.

56 Sullivan, ed., *Literary Magazines 1837–1914*, 83.

57 ACD, 'First Book', *McClure's*: 227. In his autobiography he claimed he realized this 'about a year' after his marriage, that is, sometime in 1886. See ACD, *Memories*, 74.

58 The compositional history of Doyle's first attempts at writing a full-length novel has recently been clarified. According to Gibson and Green, he began his ill-fated first novel *The Narrative of John Smith*, subsequently lost in the post, 'at the end of 1882, or thereabouts'; according to Edwards, this was followed by *The Mystery of Cloomber*, begun in 1883 but published by Ward & Downey only in 1888; and, according to Carr, *The Firm of Girdlestone*, which he thought came second, was begun in early 1884 but published by Chatto & Windus only in 1890. See Gibson and Green, eds., *Uncollected Stories*, xiii; Owen Dudley Edwards, 'The Mystery of *The Mystery of Cloomber*', *ACD* Autumn 1991: 101–33; and Carr, *Life*, 60.

59 Carr, *Life*, 62.

60 Nordon, *Doyle*, facing 212. Nordon reproduces the draft from the closed family papers.

61 ACD, *Memories*, 74–5.

62 'Detective Fiction', *The Saturday Review* 4 December 1886: 749. Vizetelly published Gaboriau's novels, which originally appeared as serials and then books in France in the 1860s, in red paper covers at one shilling per volume and distributed them through all booksellers and railway bookstalls. By 1885 he had brought out fifteen titles, including *The Lerouge Case* (1881), *Lecoq, the Detective* (1881), and *The Gilded Clique* (1884). In 1885 he added Fortune du Boisgobey, Gaboriau's successor, to his list, publishing in that year his *The Old Age of Lecoq, the Detective*. The American Anna Katherine Green is usually considered to be the first women detective fiction writer.

63 Carr, *Life*, 60. Though Carr quotes Doyle's own letter which lists the English titles of the novels, in an interview for *Tit-Bits* (15 December 1900) Doyle claimed he had been reading 'half-a-dozen or so detective stories, both in French and English' at about that time. See Richard Lancelyn Green, ed., *The Uncollected Sherlock Holmes* (Harmondsworth: Penguin, 1983), 346.

64 Nordon, *Doyle*, facing 212.

65 Though many literary models lay behind Holmes, including Poe's Dupin, Gaboriau's Tabaret (from *L' Affaire Lerouge*), and Wilkie Collins's Sergeant Cuff, Doyle from the start made much of Bell's influence. See Harry How, 'Illustrated Interviews: A Day with Dr. Conan Doyle', *Strand* August 1892: 186–8. As Green points out, Doyle's second short story, 'The Recollections of Captain Wilkie', probably written in 1879, contained a tribute to Bell. See Green, ed., *Uncollected Sherlock*, 16.

66 ACD, *Memories*, 74.

67 Green, ed., *Uncollected Sherlock*, 346.

68 For a more detailed discussion of the many borrowed threads that made up the fabric of the story, see ACD, *Study*, xiii–xxxviii.

69 In his essay on Stevenson, Doyle singled out the 'Mormon story' in the *More Arabian Nights: The Dynamiter* (1885) series for special approval. Though the series was mostly the result of a collaboration between Stevenson and his wife, Fanny Osborne, she

was entirely responsible for 'The Destroying Angel'. See ACD, 'Stevenson's Methods', *National*: 648.

70 ACD, *Study*, 18–19.

71 In the final text, Holmes is as critical of Lecoq, but more disdainful towards Dupin, than he had been originally. His denunciations are, however, now modified by Watson's amiable presence. He is 'indignant at having two characters whom I had admired treated in this cavalier style'. He is left thinking Holmes 'very conceited'. See ACD, *Study*, 21.

72 *Ibid.*, 15–17, 25, 37, 42, and 44. At one point, Holmes alludes to Darwin's view, outlined in *The Descent of Man* (1871), that the human capacity to produce and appreciate music predated language in human development.

73 Green, ed., *Uncollected Sherlock*, 41–2.

74 'Hugh Conway' was the pseudonym of Frederick John Fargus and *Called Back* was published by Arrowsmith in book form in 1884.

75 Carr, *Life*, 68.

76 ACD, *Memories*, 75.

77 See ACD, *Study*, 128–9; and Green, ed., *Uncollected Sherlock*, 43.

78 ACD, *Memories*, 75.

79 *Ibid.*

80 The two plays were R. Andre's 'Food for Powder', described by reviewers as a 'vaudeville', and J. Hamilton's 'The Four-Leaved Shamrock', a 'drawing-room comedietta in three acts'. For the review, which originally appeared in the *Glasgow Herald* on 17 December 1887, see Richard Lancelyn Green, ed., *The Sherlock Holmes Letters* (Iowa City: University of Iowa Press, 1986), 63.

81 ACD, *Study*, 132–4. A second impression appeared only in March 1889.

82 Green, ed., *Holmes Letters*, 58–9. This extended, informed, and sometimes critical review originally appeared as a leader on 2 December 1887. *The Hampshire Post* was at that time one of Doyle's local papers.

83 ACD, *Study*, 133.

84 'Detective Fiction', *Saturday*: 749.

85 Andrew Lang, 'At the Sign of the Ship', *Longman's* January 1889: 335–6. Lang accepted *Micah Clarke* on 29 October 1888, and the novel was published on 25 February 1889. See Green, 'Pocket Diary', *ACD*: 23.

86 Edwards has a more detailed discussion of the pantomime elements in the story in his introduction; see ACD, *Study*, xxiii–xxvii.

87 See ACD, *Study*, 48–9.

88 Green, ed., *Uncollected Sherlock*, 350.

89 ACD, *Micah Clarke* (London: Smith Elder, 1903), vi.

90 ACD, *Case-Book*, 4.

91 ACD, *Memories*, 80.

92 Carr, *Life*, 88.

93 Blathwayt, 'Doyle', *Bookman*: 50.

94 Carr, *Life*, 90.

95 'A Chat with Conan Doyle', *Idler* October 1894: 348.

96 ACD, 'First Book', *McClure's*: 228.

97 Green, 'Pocket Diary', *ACD*: 23; *Bibliography*, 16.

98 ACD, *Memories*, 76.

99 Green, 'Pocket Diary', *ACD*: 23.

100 ACD, *Memories*, 81.

101 ACD, *The Sign of the Four*, ed. Christopher Roden (Oxford University Press, 1993), xii–xiii.

102 This new version of the events surrounding the commissioning of *Sign* was first convincingly made by Roden in his 1993 introduction. See ACD, *Sign*, xiii–xvi.

103 ACD, *Memories*, 78.

104 Green, 'Pocket Diary', *ACD*: 25.

105 ACD, *Sign*, xvi.

106 Green, ed., *Uncollected Sherlock*, 49 and 347.

107 ACD, 'A Dinner', *Critic* 1 August 1896: 79.

108 Green, 'Pocket Diary', *ACD*: 25. He was paid in full by Lippincott's on 2 November.

109 Green, ed., *Uncollected Sherlock*, 49–50.

110 *Ibid.*, xxvi.

111 Green, ed., *Uncollected Sherlock*, 130–1.

112 ACD, *Sign*, 16, 58, and 119.

113 Gibson and Green, eds., *Letters to the Press*, 19–21 and 32–3.

114 ACD, *Sign*, 22–4. For a more detailed discussion of Doyle's indebtedness to Wilde see Roden's introduction and notes, xxiv–xxvii and 126–7; and Lionel E. Fredman, 'Oscar at Pondicherry Lodge', *ACD* March 1990: 91–3.

115 As Roden indicates 'there would have been little public reaction to Holmes's use of [cocaine] as it was easily obtainable in those days'. Yet, as Holmes's motives for taking it and Watson's solicitude suggest, his addiction is figured in the story as being part of his eccentric and anti-bourgeois life style. See ACD, *Sign*, 121.

116 *Ibid.*, 4 and 79.

117 *Ibid.*, 79; and ACD, *Study*, 7.

118 ACD, *Memories*, 78.

119 ACD, *Sign*, 5; and ACD, *Adventures*, 270.

120 For a more detailed account of the publishing history of *The Sign of the Four*, see ACD, *Sign*, xvi and xxxvii; and Gibson and Green, *Bibliography*, 40–2.

121 For an account of the reviews, both of which appeared in December 1890, see ACD, *Sign*, xxxix–xli.

122 For more details on the background to this decision see ACD, *Adventures*, xi.

123 Carr, *Life*, 73–4.

124 ACD, *Adventures*, xii.

125 Gibson and Green, *Bibliography*, 50–1.

126 ACD, *Adventures*, xiii.

127 ACD, A L S to A. P. Watt, 23 September 1890, Henry W. and Albert A. Berg Collection, The New York Public Library, Astor, Lenox and Tilden Foundations, New York. This was a covering letter Doyle sent along with his short story 'A Straggler of 15'.

128 A. P. Watt, A L S to ACD, 31 March 1891, *Letter-Books: March–June 1891*, vol. xxv, ts. and ms., Berg, New York, 30.

129 *Ibid.*, 11 April 1891, 165. According to the date stamped on the MS, the *Strand* received 'A Scandal' from Watt on 6 April. See ACD, *Adventures*, xxii.

130 Harry How, 'Illustrated Interviews: A Day with Dr. Conan Doyle'. *Strand* August 1892: 187.

131 Pearson, *Doyle*, 92.

132 A. P. Watt, A L S to ACD, 13 May 1891, *Letter-Books*, 545.

133 ACD, *Adventures*, xxiv. *Beyond the City* actually appeared in *Good Cheer*, the special Christmas number of *Good Words*.

134 For the accounts given by Doyle and Smith, see ACD, *Adventures*, xxii–xxiv.

135 A. P. Watt, A L S to ACD, 22 April 1891, *Letter-Books*, 290.

136 ACD, *Memories and Adventures* (London: Hodder and Stoughton, 1924), 95–6.

137 E. A. B., 'The Fiction of Popular Magazines: An Inquiry', *Academy* 24 February 1900: 167.

138 A. P. Watt, A L S to S. S. McClure, 14 April 1891, *Letter-Books*, 186.

139 A. P. Watt, A L S to ACD, 11 April 1891, *Letter-Books*, 165.

140 ACD, *Adventures*, 5–6, and 299–300.

141 A. P. Watt, A L S to Herbert Greenhough Smith, 14 April 1891, *Letter-Books*, 182.

142 ACD, *Adventures*, 6.

143 ACD, A L S to A. P. Watt, 23 September 1890, Berg, New York.

144 A. P. Watt, Autograph account for Dr. Doyle, 28 April 1891, *Letter-Books*, 335.

145 A. P. Watt, Autograph account for Dr. Doyle, 23 May 1891, *Letter-Books*, 335.

146 A. P. Watt, T L S to Miss Doyle, 20 May 1891, *Letter-Books*, 623.

147 According to Watt's letters, Mrs Oliphant was receiving £4 per thousand words, and Mrs Lynn Linton £5. See A. P. Watt, T L S to Herbert Greenhough Smith, 3 April 1891, *Letter-Books*, 62.

148 A. P. Watt, T L S to S. S. McClure, 14 April 1891, *Letter-Books*, 186.

149 A. P. Watt, T L S to ACD, 22 April 1891, *Letter-Books*, 290.

150 ACD, *Memories*, 97.

151 ACD, *Adventures*, xiii–xiv.

152 Gibson and Green, *Bibliography*, 47; Pearson, *Doyle*, 106–7. He earned £150 for the British serial rights to *Haw*, another £150 for *Beyond the City*, and £184 for the first six Holmes stories from the *Strand*. Both *Haw* and *City* were written on commission. See also Gibson and Green, *Bibliography*, 51 and 70.

153 'Joint Stock Publishing Companies: (9) George Newnes, Limited', *The Newsagent and Bookseller's Review* 28 November 1891: 435. According to the list of prominent share holders, Doyle had subscribed £250, Grant Allen £200, while J. C. Eno of Eno's Fruit Salts had put up £1,000.

154 Pearson, *Doyle*, 106–7.

155 Carr, *Life*, 86.

156 ACD, A L S to Mary Doyle, 11 November 1892, MS facsimile in Carr, *Life*, facing 64.

157 ACD, *Adventures*, xxv.

158 Carr, *Life*, 91.

159 In August 1892 *Bookman* put the *Strand's* circulation at 'about 300,000 copies a month'. Based on the conservative assumption that at least four people read each issue – or at least the latest Holmes story – this puts the readership at 1.2 million.

This is a doubly conservative estimate for 1893 however, since, again according to *Bookman*, the circulation was at times increasing in 1892 at the rate of 15,000 copies a month. See 'News Notes', *Bookman* March 1892: 199; and August 1892: 133.

160 ACD, letter to Mary Doyle, 6 April 1893, cited in Green, ed., *Uncollected Sherlock*, 60; see also 61–6.

161 In 1894 he continued to contribute to the *Idler*, and from then until 1911 he occasionally sent stories to other popular illustrated monthlies, including *Windsor*, *Pearson's*, and *London*. Yet from 1895 most of his fictional output appeared in the *Strand*, and from 1912 till his death in 1930 they took all but three stories. See Gibson and Green, *Bibliography*, 404–14.

162 Cameron Hollyer, 'Author to Editor: Arthur Conan Doyle's Correspondence with H. Greenhough Smith', *A.C.D.* 3 (1992): 28.

163 *Ibid.*, 30. The letter is dated 14 September 1904.

164 For the details surrounding the publication of the story, see ACD, *The Return of Sherlock Holmes*, ed. Richard Lancelyn Green (Oxford University Press, 1993), xxv–xxvii. Colliers of New York paid $4,000 (£800) per story for Doyle to resurrect Holmes in this series.

165 Green, ed., *Uncollected Sherlock*, 96.

166 Cameron Hollyer, ' "My Dear Smith": Some Letters of Arthur Conan Doyle to his Strand Editor', *Baker Street Miscellanea* 44, Winter 1985: 17.

167 *Ibid.*, 20.

168 All the dates refer to the *Strand* publication. For the *Return* payments, see ACD, *Return*, xvii. As Green points out, Colliers commissioned at least six and ideally twelve of the stories, and, under pressure, Doyle satisfied them by producing the full dozen. The thirteenth, 'The Second Stain', was written for S. S. McClure, but at the suggestion of the junior editor of the New York *Bookman*, Arthur Bartlett Maurice, one of the founding 'Sherlockians'.

169 Hollyer, *Baker Street*: 7.

170 *Ibid.*, 14.

171 Cited in Hollyer, 'Author to Editor', *A.C.D.*: 19.

172 Herbert Greenhough Smith, 'Some Letters of Conan Doyle', *Strand* October 1930: 393. Smith is HGS hereafter.

173 Hollyer, 'Author to Editor', *A.C.D.*: 21.

174 See Green's notes and introduction to ACD, *Adventures*, passim; and *Return*, passim; and Green, ed., *Uncollected Sherlock*, 53–4.

175 Hollyer, *Baker Street*: 24.

176 The biographical details relating to Newnes's early life are taken from Hulda Friederichs's often unreliable *The Life of Sir George Newnes, Bart.* (London: Hodder and Stoughton, 1911), 3–48; and from Albert Dawson, 'An Interview with Sir George Newnes, Bart.', *Bookman* May 1899: 38–40.

177 Dawson, 'Newnes', *Bookman*: 39.

178 Keating, *Haunted Study*, 36.

179 In a short editorial note on the first page of the issue for 15 April 1882, Newnes announced that there were now eleven imitations on the market.

180 The future Lord Northcliffe began as a contributor to *Tit-Bits* in the mid-1880s, and then went on to found *Answers* which was based on the Newnes model in 1888.

Pearson won his position on the *Tit-Bits* editorial staff in a competition in 1884. See Richard Bourne, *Lords of Fleet Street: The Harmsworth Dynasty* (London: Unwin-Hyman, 1990), 11–12; and Friederichs, *Newnes*, 104.

181 An article in the *Strand* for July 1897 put total sales of the first number of *Tit-Bits* at 12,000, while Newnes mentioned in his interview for *Bookman* that 'in Manchester alone newsboys sold in two hours some 5,000 copies'. See 'Ourselves in Figure and Diagram', *Strand* July 1897: 37; and Dawson, 'An Interview', *Bookman*: 39.

182 Collins based his disparaging arguments about the 'average intelligence of the Unknown Public' on the 'Answers to Correspondents' columns found in the five 'penny journals' he examined. In these columns, editors offered advice on, among other things, practical matters, questions of social etiquette, and legal issues. See Collins, 'Unknown Public', *Household Words*, 217 and 219–20.

183 *Ibid.*, 221; and Raymond Blathwayt, 'Lions in their Dens: George Newnes at Putney', *Idler* March 1893: 172.

184 Ellegård claims that the *Family Herald*, which had a circulation of 200,000 in from 1850 to the 1870s, had a readership among 'lower to middle class, chiefly women, with a large proportion of domestic servants'. See Ellegård, 'The Readership of the Periodical Press' *Victorian Periodicals*, September 1971: 20–1.

185 Reginald Pound, *The Strand Magazine, 1891–1950* (London: Heinemann, 1966), 24–5.

186 Advertisement, *Strand* January 1891: vii.

187 For a useful discussion of the reaction against the 'penny dreadful', see John Springhall, ' "Pernicious Reading"? "The Penny Dreadful" as Scapegoat for Late-Victorian Juvenile Crime', *Victorian Periodicals Review* 27.4 (Winter 1994): 326–49; and for a general account of the middle-class reaction against working-class culture, see Gareth Stedman Jones, 'Working-Class Culture and Working-Class Politics in London, 1870-1900: Notes on the Remaking of a Working Class', *Journal of Social History* (Summer 1974): 460–508.

188 'Tribute to Sir G. Newnes', *Times* 9 September 1902: 2f. The report contains a verbatim account of Conan Doyle's speech on the occasion of a bust being unveiled in the village of Lynton in recognition of Newnes's philanthropic services to the local community.

189 Friederichs, *Newnes*, 56 and 62.

190 On the first page of the issue for 29 October 1881, Newnes announced that 'great expense is being incurred in advertising *Tit-Bits* in London and the provinces', and on 3 December he claimed to have made arrangements with W. H. Smith and all newsagents.

191 Friederichs, *Newnes*, 75 and 80.

192 According to an article in *Tit-Bits*, 353 hopefuls sent in *Matthew* chapter two. See Gibson and Green, eds., *Uncollected Stories*, xiv; and Charles Stevens, 'The Best Description of *Tit-Bits*', *TB* 8 September 1894: 399. This article, which gives a useful outline of the history of *Tit-Bits*, was itself the result of a prize competition. Stevens, who came from Finsbury Park in London, won £10 for it.

193 Dawson, 'Newnes', *Bookman*: 39.

194 Moreover, in 1899, Dawson made the following claim: 'The circulation of *Tit-Bits* has long exceeded half a million, and that being the most profitable output, Sir

George is not anxious to increase it.' It probably never went much above the 671,000 figure in other words. See Dawson, 'Newnes', *Bookman*: 40. Friederichs makes the claim for 1883; Stevens's article in *Tit-Bits* gives the 1889 figure; and the *Strand* mentions the 1897 figure. As Stevens points out, for the promotional drive in 1889 Newnes offered to donate £10,000 to various hospitals if the circulation reached 500,000 by the end of the year. Since it reached only 430,318, he ended up giving out only £2,235 11s 4d. See Friederichs, *Newnes*, 86; Stevens, 'Best Description', *TB*: 399; and 'Figure and Diagram', *Strand*: 37.

195 A survey, the results of which were published in the trade journal the *Newsagent* in December 1889, asked which twelve weeklies newsagents considered the most saleable. The response was as follows: 1,926 voted in *Tit-Bits*; *Ally Sloper's Half-Holiday* got 1,362; *Weekly Budget* 1,275; *Family Herald* 727; *Christian Herald* 574; *Reynolds's Newspaper* 529; *Scraps* 503; *Cassell's Saturday Journal* 467; *Lloyd's Weekly News* 418; *Family Reader* 396; *Answers* 391; and *Princess Novelette* 359. This result should, however, be compared to the circulation figures listed in the same journal in October that year which gave *Lloyd's Weekly News* a circulation of 612,000 while *Tit-Bits* was put at 500,000. Though the editors were admittedly sceptical about the accuracy of these figures, Ellegård's findings support the *Lloyd's* figure. See 'Survey', *Newsagent* October 1889: 55; December 1889: 50; and Ellegård, 'Readership of the Periodical Press', *Victorian Periodicals* September 1971: 6.

196 *TB* 19 November 1881: 1; and 26 November 1881: 1.

197 J. C. Breach, 'Hints to Unmarried Ladies', *TB* 10 December 1881: 9. See also the 'Where to Go' column which ran from 3 June to 29 July 1882.

198 Lady Bell, *At the Works: A Study of a Manufacturing Town* (1907. London: Virago Press, 1985), 145–55.

199 Friederichs, *Newnes*, 60.

200 *Bookman* in August 1892 carried a short note about the 'new machinery for printing *Tit-Bits*' and added that 'nothing at all like it has before been seen in England'. This was the Hoe Rotary Press which printed, folded, cut, and bound the paper in one connected process. According to the *Strand's* description of the entire process of producing the paper, composition was always done by hand – though the linotype machine had been available in Britain since about 1890 – and then the made-up pages were stereotyped. Pound gives the details about the early printing process. See Unsigned note, *Bookman* August 1892: 137; 'A Description of the Offices of the *Strand Magazine*', *Strand* December 1892: 601–6; and Pound, *Strand*, 20.

201 If we take Newnes's projected family of four, then in 1889 each issue was read, at least in part, by a minimum of 2 million readers. By 1897 this had risen to just under three million.

202 In an article on 'Penny Fiction' published in January 1881, Payn responded to Collins's earlier essay about the class of penny papers observing that the 'luxuriance of its growth has since become tropical' but that the 'Unknown Public remains practically as unknown as ever'. Thomas Wright, who described himself as a 'Journeyman Engineer' and, as a former member of the 'Unknown Public', took issue with both Collins and Payn in February 1883 in a convincing counter-assessment of the place of penny papers. See James Payn, 'Penny Fiction', *Nineteenth*

Century January 1881: 145–6; and Thomas Wright, 'Concerning the Unknown Public', *Nineteenth Century* February 1883: 279–96.

203 *'Drivel*: Weekly, 1d.', *SO* 28 December 1889: 157–8.

204 George Gissing, *New Grub Street*, ed. Bernard Bergonzi (Harmondsworth: Penguin, 1985), 496. The novel was written in the autumn of 1890, published by Smith, Elder in 1891, and set in the years 1882–6.

205 'The Latest and Biggest on Record', *Newsagent* January 1890: 26. This remark was made in a direct response to the *Scots Observer's* attack which the journal had reprinted in part.

206 Edward G. Salmon, 'What the Working Classes Read', *Nineteenth Century* July 1886: 113.

207 Newnes and his business moved from Manchester to London in 1885 and, in June 1886, he moved into new premises in Burleigh Street (later Southampton Street) on the Strand. See Pound, *Strand*, 23 and 25.

208 Stead was the editor, Newnes was the major partner (he put up £10,000), and C. A. Pearson was business manager. See Friederichs, *Newnes*, 114; and Pound, *Strand*, 28–9.

209 The new monthly first appeared in January 1890, and, according to Newnes, it took only a month to set up. It is probable, then, that Stead first approached him with the idea sometime in late 1889. See Blathwayt, 'Newnes', *Idler*: 168.

210 [W. T. Stead], 'Programme', *Review of Reviews* January 1890: 14.

211 [W. T. Stead], 'To All English-Speaking Folk', *Review of Reviews* January 1890: 18–19.

212 [W. T. Stead], 'To My Readers', *Review of Reviews* May 1890: 363.

213 Newnes was a Liberal and a Home Ruler. Though never a very effective parliamentarian, he held the seat first for Newmarket from 1885 to 1895, and then for Swansea Town from 1900 to his death in 1910. He was not sympathetic to the Socialist or Suffragette movements. When the Liberal *Pall Mall Gazette* was taken over by Conservatives, he founded and then consistently underwrote the *Westminster Gazette* (1893). Stead, by contrast, committed himself to numerous radical programmes, including an Anglo-American Alliance (like Doyle), the Suffragettes, Socialist reform, and Home Rule. See Friederichs, *Newnes*, 149; Pound, *Strand*, 51. Stead himself gives the clearest exposition of his own views at this time in the *Review of Reviews*: [Stead], 'English-Speaking Folk', *Review of Reviews* January 1890: 15–20.

214 [W. T. Stead], 'Character Sketch: *The Times*', *Review of Reviews* March 1890: 186–9; and Sullivan, ed., *Literary Magazines, 1837–1913*, 353. As Joseph O. Baylen points out in his essay on the *Review*, the more commercially minded Newnes 'would not tolerate Stead's haste to establish overseas affiliates of the *Review*, or his use of the *Review* to propagate his own ideas, or his penchant for controversy.' In the first three months the condensed series featured a religious novel, *Ellen Middleton: A Tale of a Tortured Soul* by Lady Georgina Fullarton (January), Mark Twain's satirical attack on English institutions *A Yankee at the Court of King Arthur* (February), and Ismar Thiusen's utopian *The Diothas; or, a Far Look Ahead* which speculated about the coming Electrical Age (March). The Tolstoy was planned for April.

215 [W. T. Stead], 'Count Tolstoi's [sic] New Tale', *Review of Reviews* April 1890: 330–2.

216 Sullivan, ed., *Literary Magazines, 1837–1913*, 353.

217 Friederichs, *Newnes*, 118.

218 Grant Allen's 'A Deadly Dilemma' appeared in the first issue of the *Strand* in January 1891; and Mrs L. T. Meade's series, which she co-wrote with Clifford Halifax, ran from July 1896 to February 1897. In the first story in Mrs L. T. Meade's series an intrepid scientist-hero solves a crime and protects an aristocratic English lady's honour by means of the newly discovered Röntgen rays. See Mrs L. T. Meade and Clifford Halifax, *The Adventures of a Man of Science*: No. 1 – 'The Snake's Eye', *Strand* July 1896: 57–8.

219 Pound, *Strand*, 113.

220 George Newnes, letter to W. T. Stead, quoted in Friederichs, *Newnes*, 116–17.

221 Blathwayt, 'Newnes', *Idler*. 172–3.

222 When the *Pall Mall Gazette* was taken over by Conservatives, Newnes founded the *Westminster Gazette* to maintain a Liberal voice in the market for middle-class evening papers. It remained a private venture and, according to Pound, he lost £180,000 in the first five years of his proprietorship. It apparently had a circulation of only 25,000. The paper would go down in literary history for its call to have the *Yellow Book* suppressed (18 April 1894). Newnes sold it in 1908. See Pound, *Strand*, 51; and Beckson, *London*, 245.

223 Pound, *Strand*, 24–5.

224 *Ibid.*, 50.

225 [Stead], 'Count Tolstoi', *Review of Reviews* April 1890: 333–4.

226 Blathwayt, 'Newnes', *Idler*. 169.

227 In April 1899 Newnes noted: 'At the time when *The Strand Magazine* first appeared, I have no hesitation in saying that British magazines were at a low ebb. American magazines were coming here, and, because they were smarter and livelier, more interesting, bright and cheerful, they were supplanting those of native birth. *The Strand Magazine* checked that, and established a new record of sales in this country.' See Sir George Newnes, 'The One Hundredth Number of *The Strand Magazine*', *Strand* April 1899: 364.

228 Stead, ed., *Index*, 29–30.

229 Dawson, 'Newnes', *Bookman* May 1899: 40. Newnes made Smith's contribution clear in an interview for the *Caxton Magazine* in 1901, see 'Men of Mark: V. Sir George Newnes, Bart., MP', *The Caxton Magazine: A Magazine for the Printing, Paper, Stationery, and Allied Trades* September 1901: 269. Until 1898, most of the illustrations were woodcuts, and from then on 'process engraving' predominated.

230 [HGS], 'The Twenty-First Birthday of "The Strand Magazine"', *Strand* December 1911: 618.

231 For a detailed list of the *Strand's* scientific contributions in the 1890s, see Peter McDonald, 'Three Authors and the Magazine Market', D.Phil thesis, Oxford University (1994), 177.

232 See Keating, *Haunted Study*, 121.

233 Hollyer, *Baker Street*, 17.

234 For a useful discussion on the rise of the middle-class family, see Catherine Hall's

essay 'The Sweet Delights of Home', which appears in *The History of Private Life*, ed. Michelle Perrot, vol. 4 (Cambridge, Mass.: Belknap Press, 1990), 47–93.

235 The figures come from the *Strand* itself, see George Newnes, 'To Friends of 'The Strand', Old and New, Near and Far, – Greeting', *Strand* December 1900: 603–4. In the same article the editors claimed to receive an average of 4,000 MSS a year.

236 For a more detailed list of the range of materials provided by the *Strand* in the 1890s, see McDonald, 'Three Authors', 178.

237 Mrs L. T. Meade, 'Sir Edward Burne-Jones, Bart.', *Strand* July 1895: 16.

238 John Holt Schooling, 'Charles Dickens's Manuscripts', *Strand* January 1896: 29.

239 James Payn, 'The Compleat Novelist', *Strand* December 1897: 636.

240 [HGS], 'Twenty-First Birthday', *Strand*: 622. For examples of the magazine's confidently superior outlook, see 'Dusky Dandies', May 1897; Symposium, 'The Mind of the Savage: A Symposium of Missionaries', May 1909; Anon., 'Where John Bull Leads', March 1911; Symposium, 'Which is the Finest Race?', February 1912; Symposium, 'Is England on the Downgrade?', October 1912.

241 'George Egerton', *A Leaf from The Yellow Book*, ed. Terence de Vere White (London: The Richards Press, 1958), 10.

242 According to advertisements in *Tit-Bits*, the first issue sold 350,000 copies, but in February these went down to 200,000. Stead reported that the *Strand* had a regular sale of 275,000 in 1892, and Newnes himself gave the figures for 1899. This last set of figures compares with the *Strand's* own estimate of its average sales between 1891 and 1897, namely, just 330,000 a month. Though first printed by Unwin Brothers, by 1892, after Newnes formed a private limited company, he took over the entire process of production. It was produced on 2 Hoe Rotary Webb Presses, 2 Hoe Art Presses, 1 Hoe Stop Cylinder Press, and 2 Hoe Perfecting Presses with after processes being done with a Lovell-Bredenberg covering machine and Dexter folders. Most of this machinery was American. Like *Tit-Bits*, composition was always done by hand; but, unlike *Tit-Bits*, the plates were produced by electro-typing, rather than stereotyping. For the circulation figures, see Advertisement, *TB* 17 January 1891: 229, and 7 February 1891: 275; W. T. Stead, Preface to *The Annual Index of The Review of Reviews* (London: *Review of Reviews* Offices, 1892), v; Dawson, 'Newnes', *Bookman*: 40; and 'Figure and Diagram', *Strand*: 40. For details about the process of production, see 'Newnes', *Caxton* September 1901: 270–1; and 'A Description of the Offices', *Strand*: 600–3.

243 Dawson, 'Newnes', *Bookman*: 40. The New York edition of the *Strand* was edited by James Walter Smith and distributed by The International News Company.

244 This is again based on the conservative assumption that at least four members of a family read parts of each issue. To cater to its Colonial readership, the editors introduced an 'Overseas Empire Supplement', which ran from 1909 to 1911 and included articles on India, Australia, South Africa, and Canada.

245 Stead, ed., 'Preface', *Index*, v.

246 Bell, *At the Works*, 145.

247 'The Art of the British Working Man', *Strand* May 1910: 559–65. The idea for the competition was inspired by an article on an exhibition of art by German workers in Berlin which appeared in the February issue. See G. Valentine Williams, 'The Soul of the Workman', *Strand* February 1910: 205–8.

248 [HGS], 'Twenty-First Birthday', *Strand*: 615.

249 Pound, *Strand*, 79–80.

250 Newnes, 'One Hundredth Number', *Strand*: 363.

251 See *Bookman's* 'Monthly Reports of the Wholesale Bookselling Trade' from 1897 to 1900.

252 Bennett, Evening Standard *Years*, 83.

253 HGS, 'Letters of Conan Doyle', *Strand* October 1930: 395.

254 'Newnes', *Caxton*: 269; and Green, ed., *Holmes Letters*, 91 and 118. Reports of the annual general meetings, which Green reproduces, were regularly published in *Tit-Bits*.

255 Green, ed., *Holmes Letters*, 91. The report originally appeared in *Tit-Bits* on 10 August 1891.

256 Green, ed., *Uncollected Sherlock*, 95–6; and Gibson and Green, *Bibliography*, 130.

257 See, for instance, Mrs L. T. Meade's three series *Stories from the Diary of a Doctor* (July 1893–December 1895), *The Adventures of a Man of Science*, co-written with Clifford Halifax (July 1896–February 1897), and *The Brotherhood of the Seven Kings*, co-written with Robert Eustace (January-October 1898); Grant Allen's series, which featured female detective-heroines, *Miss Cayley's Adventures* (March 1898-February 1899), and *Hilda Wade* (March 1899–February 1900); Arthur Morrison's *Martin Hewitt, Investigator* (March–September 1894); and J. E. Muddock's *A Romance from a Detective's Case-book* (July–November 1892).

258 For a detailed list of detective-style articles in the *Strand*, see McDonald, *Three Authors*, 182.

259 Green, ed., *Holmes Letters*, 80; and Advertisement, *Strand*, October 1903: inside front cover.

260 Green, ed., *Uncollected Sherlock*, 299–302. This was the speech Doyle gave on 28 September 1921 at the Stoll Convention dinner which Smith attended.

261 Doyle always lobbied for his favourite illustrators, Paget and later Arthur Twidle; and on a number of occasions he complained to Smith that some ill-placed illustrations undermined his carefully concealed mysteries, and he requested that the artists find ways of avoiding this at all costs. He also insisted that Holmes's dignity be preserved in all illustrations. Paget, who died in September 1908, illustrated the *Adventures, Memoirs, Hound*, and *Return*. For a detailed discussion of his correspondence with Smith about the issue of illustrations, see Hollyer, 'Author to Editor', ACD 26–8.

262 Many examples of these slight alterations have been identified by the Oxford University Press editors, but these are typical cases. See ACD, *Return*, 286, 288, and 402.

263 See Green's notes to ACD, *Return*, 357.

264 The article describes a visit to an Opium den, run by a Chinaman, in London's East End. Like the story, it contains allusions to De Quincey, and, in addition to some similar descriptive detail, it is strongly critical of the addicts and of the moral and social atmosphere of the place. In his notes, Green also points out that Doyle probably borrowed some ideas for the double identity elements of the story from *Tit-Bits*. See 'The author of 'A Dead Man's Diary'', 'A Night in an Opium Den', *Strand* June 1891: 625; and ACD, *Adventures*, 344.

265 [A. Innes Shand], 'Crime in Fiction', *Blackwood's*, August 1890: 173.

266 A. C., 'Crime in Current Literature', *Westminster Review* April 1897: 430 and 435. For a more hysterical contribution to the debate, see Arnold Smith, 'The Ethics of Sensational Fiction', *Westminster Review* August 1904: 188–94.

267 Unsigned editorial, 'Cheap Pernicious Literature', *Newsagent* December 1889: 32.

268 ACD, *The Adventures of Sherlock Holmes* (London: Smith, Elder and Co., 1903), viii.

269 Green, ed., *Uncollected Sherlock*, 350. The interview originally appeared in *Tit-Bits* on 15 December 1900.

270 Green, ed., *Uncollected Sherlock*, 77.

271 *Ibid.*, 350.

272 ACD, *Adventures* (1903), viii.

273 Green, ed., *Uncollected Sherlock*, 350.

274 ACD, *Adventures*, 131–3 and 144.

275 Green, ed., *Uncollected Sherlock*, 350–1.

276 Another clear example of Doyle's rewriting of the 'shilling dreadful', and, indeed, of *The Sign of the Four*, is 'The Crooked Man' (*Memoirs*).

277 ACD, *Adventures*, 150.

278 *Ibid.*, 150 and 271. 'The Copper Beeches' itself is a non-criminal case, making the total for the *Adventures* five out of twelve.

279 ACD, *Sign*, 5.

280 ACD, *Adventures*, 30.

281 *Ibid.* 30 and 308. 'The Decay of Lying' first appeared in the *Nineteenth Century* in January 1889.

282 ACD, *Adventures*, 30–1.

283 ACD, *Return*, 52.

284 *Ibid.*, 266–7.

285 ACD, *Case-Book*, 151.

286 Green, ed., *Uncollected Sherlock*, 61. Green quotes from a letter Doyle wrote to Smith on 28 August 1893. The story was not included in the first English edition of the *Memoirs* (Newnes, 1893), but it did appear in the first American edition (Harper, 1894). Its first appearance in a British book was as part of *His Last Bow* (Murray, 1917). Edwards speculates that Doyle may have been influenced to withdraw the story 'by sensitivity within his family over the question of violence brought about by alcoholism' – Doyle's father was an alcoholic. This biographical argument seems unnecessary, however. In the first place, he had already established the connection between drunkenness and violence in 'The Five Orange Pips' (*Adventures*) and he would return regularly to the theme throughout the saga, most explicitly in 'The Abbey Grange' (*Return*). Moreover, on the question of alcoholism, the implied ethics of the story, which could be read as a temperance tract, are above suspicion. The suppression is, however, sufficiently explicable when seen in the light of the contents of the story and Doyle's concern about his reputation. See ACD, *Memoirs*, xxi.

287 ACD, *Memoirs*, 30.

288 Hollyer, *Baker Street*, 7 and 9.

289 Alfred T. Storey, 'Deeds of Daring and Devotion in the War', *Strand* August 1900: 160.

290 Advertisement, *Strand* October 1900: xxxvi.

291 ACD, *Case-Book*, 4.

292 ACD, *Sign*, 70–1.

293 ACD, *Return*, 158 and 168; *Case-Book*, 146–7.

294 ACD, 'His Last Bow', *His Last Bow*, ed. Owen Dudley Edwards (Oxford University Press, 1993), 158. John Clay appears in 'The Red-Headed League' (*Adventures*) and Mortimer Tregennis, who is contrasted throughout with the robust and manly explorer Dr Leon Sterndale, is the villain of 'The Devil's Foot' (*Last Bow*).

295 ACD, 'Charles Augustus Milverton', *Return*, 158.

296 *Ibid.*, 168.

297 Women who fit this stereotype either wholly or in part are particularly prevalent in the *Return* series, see Violet Smith in 'The Solitary Cyclist', Mrs Staunton in 'The Missing Three-Quarter', and Lady Trelawney Hope in 'The Second Stain'. Though Lady Brackenstall in 'The Abbey Grange' is Australian by birth, she also conforms to this general type.

298 See, for instance, Eugenia Ronder (the only other English woman who fills the function of a catalyst) in 'The Veiled Lodger' (*Case-Book*), the unnamed English lady who shoots Milverton (*Return*), Mary Holder in 'The Beryl Coronet' (*Adventures*), and Miss Fraser in 'The Disappearance of Lady Frances Carfax' (*Last Bow*).

299 See, respectively, ACD, 'The Sussex Vampire', *Case-Book*, 79, and 'The Problem of Thor Bridge', *Case-Book*, 28; 'The Second Stain', *Return*, 305; and 'The Musgrave Ritual', *Memoirs*, 118 and 131. Countess Morcar in 'The Blue Carbuncle' (*Adventures*) is the only foreign woman who fills the function of victim. But, since the plumber John Horner is the principal victim (he is falsely accused of stealing her diamond), she is only the secondary victim as far as the narrative is concerned.

300 ACD, 'The Three Gables', *Case-Book*, 146. This repeated stereotype puts in doubt Edwards's claim that the various responses to the death of old enemies evinced by the restrained Miss Burnett, the English governess of 'Wisteria Lodge', and the exuberant Italian, Emilia Lucca of 'The Red Circle', is simply a matter of their difference in age. See ACD, *Last Bow*, xxv–xxvi.

301 ACD, 'The Abbey Grange', *Return*, 269. Doyle returned to this issue in 'The Devil's Foot' (*Last Bow*), which was published in the *Strand* for December 1910. There Dr Leon Sterndale, the manly big game hunter who has been abandoned by his wife, puts the case from the man's point of view. Doyle served as president of the Divorce Law Reform Union from 1909 to 1919.

302 ACD, 'The Copper Beeches', *Adventures*, 272.

303 ACD, 'His Last Bow', *Last Bow*, 158.

304 The Hon. Mrs Fitzroy Stewart and Christabel Pankhurst, 'Women's Rights – and Men's', *Strand* May 1911: 525. The editor introduced this debate with this remark: 'We hear a great deal in these days about the privileges which Law and Custom afford to men but deny to women. There is, however, no doubt another side of the question – namely, the case of privileges which women enjoy but from which men are barred.' The heroine of Bennett's serial was a vacillating supporter of the cause, and few of the other suffragettes portrayed were treated sympathetically. For a discussion of the circumstances surrounding the banning of this story, see Drabble, *Bennett*, 213–16. For other anti-feminist material in the *Strand*, see

'Facsimile of the Notes of a Speech by John Bright', February 1891 [this was a copy of his speech of 26 April 1876 opposing female suffrage]; 'The Foundling Hospital', September 1891; 'Muzzles for Ladies', November 1894; E. A. B. Hodgetts, 'Girton and Newnham Colleges', November 1894; Symposium, 'Should Women Serve as Soldiers?', July 1910.

305 ACD, 'The Greek Interpreter', *Memoirs*, 193; T. H. Huxley, 'On the Method of Zadig', *Science and Culture and Other Essays* (London: Macmillan, 1882), 128–48. Huxley's essay, which first appeared in the *Nineteenth Century* in 1880, compares the methods of Voltaire's Zadig to those of Georges Cuvier (1769–1832), the French naturalist and palaeontologist. This may be a further source, in addition to the Gaboriau and Oliver Wendell Holmes references pointed out by Green, for Doyle's comparison between Holmes and Cuvier in 'The Five Orange Pips'. See ACD, 'The Five Orange Pips', *Adventures*, 114 and 341.

306 ACD, 'Some Personalia about Mr Sherlock Holmes', *Strand* December 1917: 534; and Isaac Asimov, 'Sherlock Holmes as Chemist', *The Roving Mind* (Buffalo: Prometheus Books, 1983), 127. Asimov's essay originally appeared in *Science Digest* for August 1980.

307 ACD, 'Shoscombe Old Place', *Case-Book*, 220; and Asimov, *Roving Mind*, 128–9. Asimov points out many more of Holmes's scientific blunders, including his faulty knowledge of the chemical composition of carbuncles ('Blue Carbuncle'), his implausible test for a reagent to precipitate blood (*Study*), and his belief that dissolving hydrocarbons is a major scientific problem (*Sign*).

308 ACD, 'A Scandal in Bohemia', *Adventures*, 8; 'The Cardboard Box', *Memoirs*, 42; 'The Abbey Grange', *Return*, 279; 'The Six Napoleons', *Return*, 196; 'The Musgrave Ritual', *Memoirs*, 116.

309 ACD, 'A Scandal in Bohemia', *Adventures*, 5.

310 ACD, 'The Cardboard Box', *Memoirs*, 43.

311 ACD, 'Silver Blaze', *Memoirs*, 18; 'The Sussex Vampire', *Case-Book*, 79; 'Black Peter', *Return*, 149.

312 ACD, 'The Five Orange Pips', *Adventures*, 114–15.

313 Green, ed., *Uncollected Sherlock*, 19.

314 ACD, *Study*, 16.

315 ACD, 'A Case of Identity', *Adventures*, 48; 'The Red-Headed League', *Adventures*, 74; 'The Boscombe Valley Mystery', *Adventures*, 83, 87, and 89; 'The Five Orange Pips', *Adventures*, 103; 'The Red-Circle', *Case-Book*, 115.

316 ACD, 'The Bruce-Partington Plans', *Last Bow*, 62; 'The Copper Beeches', *Adventures*, 270. As Edwards indicates in his notes on *His Last Bow*, Holmes was quoting from Samuel Jones Arnold's rhapsodic elegy 'The Death of Nelson'.

317 ACD, 'Black Peter', *Return*, 134.

318 ACD, 'The Sussex Vampire', *Case-Book*, 73; 'The Devil's Foot', *Last Bow*, 73.

319 ACD, *Study*, 18–19.

320 ACD, 'The Naval Treaty', *Memoirs*, 227.

321 This phrase is taken from Conrad's only *Strand* publication 'The Tale' which appeared in the issue for October 1917. Like many of Conrad's unresolved stories about doubt and irresolution, especially *Heart of Darkness* and *The Secret Agent*, it can be read as a literary attack on the assumptions underlying the detective genre in

general, and the Sherlock Holmes stories in particular. See Joseph Conrad, 'The Tale', *Tales of Hearsay* (London: Dent, 1928), 80.

322 ACD to Mary Doyle, MS facsimile in Carr, *Life*, facing 64.

323 ACD, *Case-Book*, 4.

324 ACD, *Memories*, 99.

325 ACD, *White Company*, v–vi.

326 Gibson and Green, *Bibliography*, 229.

327 ACD, *Memories*, 81. He made the same argument in his preface to the *Case-Book* series in 1927. See ACD, *Case-Book*, 4.

328 Nordon, *Doyle*, 46. Doyle's patriotic pamphlet *The War in South Africa: Its Cause and Conduct* (1902) was partly funded by the Foreign Office. As a systematic defence of Britain's role and conduct in the Boer War, it was consciously designed to rebut critical allegations made by the likes of Stead in Britain but, more especially, by German and other foreign supporters of the Boer cause. See ACD, *Memories*, 191 and 193.

329 Nordon, *Conan Doyle*, 77. The original letter to A. St John Adcock appeared in *Bookman*, November 1912: 97.

330 'Doyle', *Idler*: 348.

POSTSCRIPT

1 Pierre Bourdieu, *In Other Words: Essays Towards a Reflexive Sociology*, trans. Matthew Adamson (Cambridge: Polity Press, 1990), 147.

2 Beckson, *London*, xvii.

3 Bourdieu, *Field*, 190.

4 *Ibid.*, 32.

5 Foucault, *Archaeology*, 104–5.

BIBLIOGRAPHY

MANUSCRIPTS

Bennett, Arnold. Cash-Books for 1894–7, 1901–2, 1905–8, mss. Berg Collection, New York Public Library, New York.

Conan Doyle, Arthur. Letter to A.P. Watt, 23 September 1890, ms. Berg Collection, New York Public Library, New York.

Henley, W. E. Letter to Lord Windsor, 18 October 1895, ms. The Pierpont Morgan Library, New York.

Phillpotts, Eden. Letter to J.B. Pinker, 13 January 1906, ms. Berg Collection, New York Public Library, New York.

Letter to Arnold Bennett, 23 February 1906, ms. Berg Collection, New York Public Library, New York.

Watt, Alexander Pollock. *Letter-Books: March–June 1891*, vol. 25, ts. and ms. Berg Collection, New York Public Library, New York.

BOOKS

Primary

Arnold, Matthew. *The Last Word*, ed. R. H. Super. Ann Arbor: University of Michigan Press, 1977.

Bell, Lady. *At the Works: A Study of a Manufacturing Town*. 1907. London: Virago Press, 1985.

Bennett, Arnold. *Arnold Bennett: The* Evening Standard *Years, 'Books and Persons' 1926–1931*, ed. Andrew Mylett. London: Chatto and Windus, 1974.

The Author's Craft. London: Hodder and Stoughton, 1914.

Books and Persons: Being Comments on a Past Epoch, 1908–1911. London: Chatto and Windus, 1917.

Buried Alive. London: Chapman and Hall, 1908.

The Card. London: Methuen, 1911.

The City of Pleasure. New York: G. H. Doran, 1907.

Clayhanger, ed. Andrew Lincoln. Harmondsworth: Penguin, 1989.

Fame and Fiction: An Enquiry into Certain Popularities. London: Grant Richards, 1901.

The Grand Babylon Hotel. London: Eveleigh Nash and Grayson, 1923.

A Great Man. London: Chatto and Windus, 1904.

The Grim Smile of the Five Towns. Harmondsworth: Penguin, 1946.

How to Become an Author: A Practical Guide. London: C. Arthur Pearson, 1903.

How to Live on 24 Hours a Day. London: The New Age Press, 1908.

Hugo. New York: G. H. Doran, 1907.

The Human Machine. New York: G. H. Doran, 1911.

Journalism for Women: A Practical Guide. London: John Lane, The Bodley Head, 1898.

The Journals of Arnold Bennett, ed. Newman Flower. 3 vols. London: Cassell, 1932–3.

The Letters of Arnold Bennett, ed. James Hepburn. 3 vols. London: Oxford University Press, 1966–70.

The Lion's Share. New York: G. H. Doran, 1916.

Literary Taste: How to Form it. London: New Age Press, 1909.

The Loot of the Cities. London: Alston Rivers, 1905.

A Man from the North. London: John Lane, 1898.

The Old Wives' Tale, ed. John Wain. Harmondsworth: Penguin, 1988.

Riceyman Steps. London: Cassell, 1945.

The Savour of Life: Essays in Gusto. London: Cassell, 1928.

Sketches for Autobiography, ed. James Hepburn. London: George Allen and Unwin, 1979.

Teresa of Watling Street. London: Ward, Lock, 1931.

The Truth About an Author. 2nd edn. London: Methuen, 1914.

What the Public Wants. London: Duckworth, 1909.

Bennett, Arnold, and Eden Phillpotts. *The Sinews of War*. London: T. Werner Laurie, 1906.

The Statue. London: Cassell, 1908.

Besant, Walter. *The Pen and the Book*. London: Thomas Burleigh, 1899.

Blathwayt, Raymond. *Interviews*. London: A. W. Hall, Great Thoughts Office, 1893.

Booth, Charles, ed. *Life and Labour of the People in London*, vol. 4. London: Macmillan, 1893.

Buchan, John. *Memory Hold-the-Door*. 1940; London: J. M. Dent, 1984.

Scholar Gypsies. London: John Lane, The Bodley Head, 1896.

Conan Doyle, Arthur. *The Adventures of Sherlock Holmes*. London: Smith, Elder, 1903.

The Captain of the Polestar and Other Tales. London: Longmans, Green, 1890.

Memories and Adventures. London: Hodder and Stoughton, 1924.

Micah Clarke. London: Smith, Elder, 1903.

The Oxford Sherlock Holmes, eds. Owen Dudley Edwards, et al. 9 vols. Oxford University Press, 1993.

The Poems of Arthur Conan Doyle. London: John Murray, 1922.

Through the Magic Door. London: Smith, Elder, 1907.

To Arms! London: Hodder and Stoughton, 1914.

The White Company. London: Smith, Elder, 1903.

Conrad, Joseph. *The Collected Letters of Joseph Conrad*, eds. F. R. Karl and L. Davies. 4 vols. Cambridge University Press, 1983–90.

The Collected Works of Joseph Conrad. London: J. M. Dent, 1923.

Letters from Joseph Conrad, 1895–1924, ed. Edward Garnett. New York: Charter Books, 1962.

The Nigger of the 'Narcissus', ed. Jacques Berthoud. Oxford University Press, 1984.

The Nigger of the 'Narcissus', ed. Robert Kimbrough. New York: Norton, 1979.

Cox, E. H. M. *The Library of Edmund Gosse*. London: Dulau and Company, 1924.

Crane, Stephen. *The Correspondence of Stephen Crane*, eds. Stanley Wertheim and Paul Sorrentino. 2 vols. New York: Columbia University Press, 1988.

D'Arcy, Ella. Some *Letters to John Lane*, ed. Alan Anderson. Edinburgh: The Tragara Press, 1990.

Edel, Leon, ed. *Henry James Letters*, vol. 3, London: Macmillan, 1980.

'Egerton, George'. *A Leaf from The Yellow Book*, ed. Terence De Vere White. London: The Richards Press, 1958.

Ford, Ford Madox. *Ancient Lights and Certain New Reflections*. London: Chapman and Hall, 1911.

Memories and Impressions. London: The Bodley Head, 1971.

Forster, E. M. *Howards End*, ed. Oliver Stallybrass. Harmondsworth: Penguin, 1989.

Gettmann, Royal A., ed. *George Gissing and H.G. Wells: Their Friendship and Correspondence*. London: Rupert Hart-Davis, 1961.

Gibbs, Philip. *The Pageant of the Years: An Autobiography*. London: Heinemann, 1946.

Gissing, George. *New Grub Street*, ed. Bernard Bergonzi. Harmondsworth: Penguin, 1985.

Gosse, Edmund. *Father and Son*. Harmondsworth: Penguin, 1986.

Henley, W. E. *Poems*. London: David Nutt, 1898.

Some Letters of William Ernest Henley, ed. James Bertrand de Vincheles Payen-Payne. London: Privately Printed, 1933.

The Song of the Sword. London: David Nutt, 1892.

The Works of W. E. Henley. London: Macmillan, 1921.

Henley, W. E. and J. S. Farmer. *Slang and its Analogues, Past and Present, a dictionary, historical and comparative, of the heterodox speech of all classes of Society for more than three hundred years, with synonyms in English, French, German, Italian, etc.* 7 vols. London: D. Nutt, 1890–1904.

Hind, C. Lewis. *Authors and I*. London: John Lane, 1921.

Huxley, T. H. *Science and Culture and Other Essays*. London: Macmillan, 1882.

Jackson, Holbrook. *The Eighteen Nineties*. 1913; London: Century Hutchinson, 1988.

James, Henry. *The Figure in the Carpet and Other Stories*, ed. Frank Kermode. Harmondsworth: Penguin, 1986.

The Notebooks of Henry James, eds. F. O. Matthiessen and Kenneth B. Murdock. New York: Oxford University Press, 1947.

Kipling, Rudyard. *Something of Myself*. London: Macmillan, 1937.

Le Gallienne, Richard. *The Romantic '90s*. New York: Doubleday, Page and Co., 1925.

Prose Fancies. London: Elkin Mathews and John Lane, 1894.

Lister, R. J. *A Catalogue of a Portion of the Library of Edmund Gosse, Hon. M. A. of Trinity College, Cambridge*. London: The Ballantyne Press, 1893.

May, J. Lewis. *John Lane and the Nineties*. London: The Bodley Head, 1936.

Meredith, George. *The Collected Letters of George Meredith*, ed. C. L. Cline. 3 vols. Oxford: Clarendon Press, 1970.

Moore, Rayburn S., ed. *Selected Letters of Henry James to Edmund Gosse, 1882–1915: A Literary Friendship*. Baton Rouge: Louisiana State University Press, 1988.

Morrison, Arthur. *A Child of the Jago*, ed. Peter Keating. London: MacGibbon and Kee, 1969.

Nordau, Max. *Degeneration*, ed. George L. Mosse. Lincoln: University of Nebraska Press, 1968.

Orcutt, William Dana. *In Quest of the Perfect Book*. Boston: Little, Brown and Co., 1926.

Phillpotts, Eden. *Eden Phillpotts (1862–1960): Selected Letters*, ed. James Y. Dayananda. Lanham: University Press of America, 1984.

Smith, Herbert Greenhough. *Odd Moments: Essays in Little*. London: George Newnes, 1925.

Smith, H. L., ed. *The New Survey of London Life and Labour*, vol. 1. London: P. S. King, 1931.

Sprigge, S. Squire. *The Methods of Publishing.* 2nd edn. London: Henry Glaisher, 1891.

Stevenson, Robert Louis. *The Works of Robert Louis Stevenson.* London: Waverley Book Co., 1924.

Wagner, Leopold. *How to Publish.* London: George Redway, 1898.

Wells, H. G. *The First Men in the Moon.* London: George Newnes, 1901.

The Time Machine. London: Heinemann, 1895.

Tono-Bungay. London: Macmillan, 1909.

Whitten, Wilfred. *The Joy of London and Other Essays,* ed. Frank Witaker. London: George Newnes, 1943.

Wilde, Oscar. *The Letters of Oscar Wilde,* ed. Rupert Hart-Davis. London: Rupert Hart-Davis, 1962.

The Picture of Dorian Gray. Harmondsworth: Penguin, 1985.

Willing's Press Guide. London: James Willing, 1890–1914.

Woolf, Virginia. *Mr. Bennett and Mrs. Brown.* London: The Hogarth Press, 1924.

Wyndham, George. *The Letters of George Wyndham,* ed. Guy Wyndham. 2 vols. Edinburgh: T. and A. Constable, 1915.

Yeats, W. B. *Autobiographies.* London: Macmillan, 1955.

Collected Poems. 1933; London: Macmillan, 1982.

The Oxford Book of Modern Verse. Oxford: Clarendon Press, 1936.

'£600 a year from it.' *How to Write for the Magazines.* London: Grant Richards, 1900.

Secondary

Adorno, Theodor W. *The Culture Industry: Selected Essays on Mass Culture,* ed. M. Bernstein. London: Routledge, 1991.

Altick, Richard. *The English Common Reader.* Chicago: University of Chicago Press, 1957.

Writers, Readers, and Occasions. Columbus: Ohio State University Press, 1989.

Asimov, Isaac. *The Roving Mind.* Buffalo: Prometheus Books, 1983.

Bailey, Peter, ed. *Music Hall: The Business of Pleasure.* Milton Keynes: Open University Press, 1986.

Barthes, Roland. *Image Music Text.* London: Fontana, 1977.

Beare, Geraldine. *Index to the* Strand Magazine, *1891–1950.* Westport, Connecticut: Greenwood Press, 1982.

Beckson, Karl. *Henry Harland: His Life and Work.* London: The Eighteen Nineties Society, 1978.

London in the 1890s: A Cultural History. New York: W. W. Norton, 1992.

Benjamin, Walter. *Illuminations,* ed. Hannah Arendt. Trans. Harry Zohn. London: Jonathan Cape, 1970.

Bourdieu, Pierre. *The Field of Cultural Production,* ed. Randal Johnson. Cambridge: Polity Press, 1993.

In Other Words: Essays Towards a Reflexive Sociology. Trans. Matthew Adamson. Cambridge: Polity Press, 1990.

Bourne, Richard. *Lords of Fleet Street: The Harmsworth Dynasty.* London: Unwin-Hyman, 1990.

Buckley, Jerome. *W. E. Henley: A Study in the 'Counter-Decadence' of the Nineties.* Princeton: Princeton University Press, 1945.

Carey, John. *The Intellectuals and the Masses: Pride and Prejudice among the Literary Intelligentsia, 1880–1939.* London: Faber and Faber, 1992.

Carr, John Dickson. *The Life of Sir Arthur Conan Doyle.* London: John Murray, 1949.

Carter, John, ed. *New Paths in Book Collecting*. London: Constable, 1934.

Charteris, Evan. *The Life and Letters of Sir Edmund Gosse* London: Heinemann, 1931.

Connell, John. *W. E. Henley*. London: Constable, 1949.

Coyle, Martin, et al., eds. *Encyclopaedia of Literature and Criticism*. London: Routledge, 1990.

Cross, Nigel. *The Common Writer: Life in Nineteenth-Century Grub Street*. Cambridge University Press, 1985.

Crossick, Geoffrey, ed. *The Lower Middle Class in Britain, 1870–1914*. London: Croom Helm, 1977.

Daiches, David. *Some Late Victorian Attitudes*. London: André Deutsche, 1969.

Darnton, Robert. *The Kiss of Lamourette*. London: Faber and Faber, 1990.

Dooley, Allan C. *Author and Printer in Victorian England*. Charlottesville: University Press of Virginia, 1992.

Drabble, Margaret. *Arnold Bennett: A Biography*. 1974; Boston: G. K. Hall, 1986.

Dudek, Louis. *Literature and the Press: A History of Printing, Printed Media, and their Relation to Literature*. Toronto: Contact Press, 1960.

Edwards, Owen Dudley. *The Quest for Sherlock Holmes*, Edinburgh: Mainstream Publishing, 1983.

Ellmann, Richard. *Oscar Wilde*. London: Hamish Hamilton, 1987.

Eliot, Simon. *Some Patterns and Trends in British Publishing, 1800–1919*. London: The Bibliographical Society, 1994.

Feather, John. *A History of British Publishing*. London: Routledge, 1988.

Feltes, Norman. *Modes of Production of Victorian Novels*. University of Chicago Press, 1986.

    Literary Capital and the Late Victorian Novel. Madison: University of Wisconsin Press, 1993.

Flora, Joseph M. *William Ernest Henley*. New York: Twayne Publishers, 1970.

Friederichs, Hulda. *The Life of Sir George Newnes, Bart*. London: Hodder and Stoughton, 1911.

Foucault, Michel. *The Archaeology of Knowledge*. Trans. A. M. Sheridan Smith. 1969; London: Tavistock Publications, 1972.

Fyfe, Hamilton. *T. P. O'Connor*. London: George Allen and Unwin, 1934.

Gatrell, Simon. *Hardy the Creator: A Textual Biography*. Oxford: Clarendon Press, 1988.

Gibson, J. M., and R. L. Green, eds. *A Bibliography of Arthur Conan Doyle*. Oxford: Clarendon Press, 1983.

    The Unknown Conan Doyle: Letters to the Press. London: Secker and Warburg, 1986.

    The Unknown Conan Doyle: Uncollected Stories. London: Secker and Warburg, 1982.

Green, Richard Lancelyn, ed. *The Sherlock Holmes Letters*. Iowa City: University of Iowa Press, 1986.

    The Uncollected Sherlock Holmes. Harmondsworth: Penguin, 1983.

Gross, John. *The Rise and Fall of the Man of Letters*. 1969; Harmondsworth: Penguin, 1991.

Guillaume, André. *William Henley et Son Groupe: Néo-Romantisme et Impérialisme à la fin du XIXe siècle*. Paris: C. Klincksieck, 1973.

Hagan, June. *Tennyson and his Publishers*. London: Macmillan, 1979.

Harris, Jose. *Private Lives and Public Spirit: Britain, 1870–1914*. Harmondsworth: Penguin, 1994.

Hepburn, James, ed. *Arnold Bennett: The Critical Heritage*. London: Routledge and Kegan Paul, 1981.

Houghton, Walter E., ed. *The Wellesley Index to Victorian Periodicals: 1824–1900*. 4 vols. London: Routledge and Kegan Paul, 1966–87.

Hughes, Linda K. and Michael Lund. *The Victorian Serial*. Charlottesville: University Press of Virginia, 1991.

Karl, F. R. *Joseph Conrad: The Three Lives*. London: Faber and Faber, 1979.

Keating, Peter. *The Haunted Study: A Social History of the English Novel, 1875–1914*. London: Secker and Warburg, 1989.

Kunzle, David. *The History of the Comic Strip: The Nineteenth Century*. Berkeley: University of California Press, 1990.

Lambert, J. W., and Michael Ratcliffe. *The Bodley Head, 1887–1897*. London: The Bodley Head, 1987.

Landon, Richard G., ed. *Book Selling and Book Buying: Aspects of the Nineteenth-Century British and North American Book Trade*. Chicago: American Library Association, 1978.

Leavis, Q. D. *Fiction and the Reading Public*. London: Chatto and Windus, 1932.

Lee, Alan. *The Origins of the Popular Press in England, 1855–1914*. London: Croom Helm, 1976.

Le Mahieu, D. L. *A Culture for Democracy: Mass Communication and the Cultivated Mind in Britain between the Wars*. Oxford: Clarendon Press, 1988.

Lester, John. *Journey Through Despair, 1880–1914: Transformations in British Literary Culture*. Princeton University Press, 1968.

Martin, Robert. *Tennyson: The Unquiet Heart*. Oxford: Clarendon Press, 1980.

Marx, Karl, and Frederick Engels. *Marx and Engels on Literature and Art*, eds. Lee Baxandall and Stefan Morawski. New York: International General, 1974.

McAleer, Joseph. *Popular Reading and Publishing in Britain, 1914–1950*. Oxford: Clarendon Press, 1992.

McDonald, Peter. 'Three Authors and the Magazine Market'. D.Phil. thesis, Oxford University, 1994.

McKenzie, D. F. *Bibliography and the Sociology of Texts*. London: The British Library, 1986.

Meyers, Jeffrey. *Joseph Conrad: A Biography*. London: John Murray, 1991.

Miller, Anita. *Arnold Bennett: An Annotated Bibliography, 1887–1932*. London: Garland Publishing, 1977.

Najder, Zdzislaw. *Joseph Conrad: A Chronicle*. Cambridge University Press, 1983.

Nelson, James G. *The Early Nineties: A View from the Bodley Head*. Cambridge, Mass.: Harvard University Press, 1971.

Nordon, Pierre. *Conan Doyle*. London: John Murray, 1966.

Nowell-Smith, Simon. *The House of Cassell, 1848–1958*. London: Cassell and Company, 1958.

Pearsall, Ronald. *Conan Doyle: A Biographical Solution*. 1977. Glasgow: Richard Drew Publishing, 1989.

Pearson, Hesketh. *Conan Doyle*. 1943. London: Unwin Paperbacks, 1987.

Perrot, Michelle, ed. *The History of Private Life: From the Fires of Revolution to the Great War*, vol. 4. Cambridge, Mass.: Belknap Press, 1990.

Pound, Reginald. *Arnold Bennett: A Biography*. London: Heinemann, 1952.

The Strand Magazine, 1891–1950. London: Heinemann, 1966.

Read, Donald. *England: 1868–1914*. London: Longman, 1979.

Rose, Jonathan and Patricia J. Anderson, eds. *Dictionary of Literary Biography: British Literary Publishing Houses, 1881–1965*, vol. 112. Detroit: Gale Research, 1991.

Said, Edward W. *The World, the Text, and the Critic*. Cambridge, Mass.: Harvard University Press, 1983.

Shattock, Joanne and Michael Wolff, eds. *The Victorian Periodical Press: Samplings and Soundings*. Leicester: Leicester University Press, 1982.

Sherry, Norman, ed. *Conrad: The Critical Heritage*. London: Routledge and Kegan Paul, 1973.

Singleton, Frank. *Tillotsons, 1850–1950*. Bolton and London: Tillotson and Son, 1950.

St John, John. *William Heinemann: A Century of Publishing, 1890–1990*. London: Heinemann, 1990.

Stetz, Margaret D. and Mark Samuels Lasner. The Yellow Book: *A Centenary Exhibition*. Cambridge, Mass.: The Houghton Library, 1994.

Stokes, John. *In the Nineties*. London: Harvester Wheatsheaf, 1989.

Sullivan, Alvin, ed. *British Literary Magazines: The Victorian and Edwardian Age, 1837–1913*, vol. 3 of 4. Westport, Connecticut: Greenwood Press, 1984.

Sutherland, John A. *Victorian Novelists and Publishers*. London: Athlone Press, 1976.

Thompson, John B. *Ideology and Modern Culture: Critical Social Theory in the Era of Mass Communications*. Cambridge: Polity Press, 1990.

Thompson, Susan Otis. *American Book Design and William Morris*. New York: R. R. Bowker Co., 1977.

Thwaite, Ann. *Edmund Gosse*. London: Secker and Warburg, 1984.

Watts, Cedric. *Joseph Conrad: A Literary Life*. Basingstoke: Macmillan, 1989.

West, Anthony. *H. G. Wells: Aspects of a Life*. London: Hutchinson, 1984.

Wiener, Joel H., ed. *Papers for the Millions: The New Journalism in Britain, 1850s to 1914*. Westport, Connecticut: Greenwood Press, 1988.

Innovators and Preachers: The Role of the Editor in Victorian England. Westport: Greenwood Press, 1985.

Williams, Raymond. *Culture*. London: Fontana, 1981.

The Long Revolution. Harmondsworth: Penguin, 1965.

Wilson, Charles. *First with the News: The History of W. H. Smith, 1792–1972*. London: Jonathan Cape, 1985.

Wolff, Michael, et al., eds. *The Waterloo Directory of Victorian Periodicals, 1824–1900*. Waterloo, Ont.: Wilfred Laurier University Press, 1976.

PERIODICALS

Contemporary

A. C. 'Crime in Current Literature'. *Westminster Review* April 1897: 430.

Annand, James. 'The Decline of the Politician'. *New Review* November 1897: 699–709.

'The Demoralisation of Liberalism'. *New Review* September 1895: 248–56.

'Artifex'. 'The Truth About an Author'. *The Author* 1 November 1903: 51–2.

'The Author of 'A Dead Man's Diary.'' 'A Night in an Opium Den'. *Strand* June 1891: 624–7.

Beerbohm, Max. 'A Letter to the Editor'. *Yellow Book* July 1894: 281–4.

[Bennett, Arnold]. 'Book Chat'. *Woman* 5 February 1896: 7.

'D'You Know?' *Woman* 11 April 1894: 6.

'Faust and Marguerite'. *Humanitarian* March 1894: 217–20.

The Gates of Wrath. *Myra's Journal: The Leader of Fashion* October 1899: 28–31; November 1899: 28–31; December 1899: 28–32; January 1900: 28–31.

'A Letter Home'. *Yellow Book* July 1895: 93–102.

Love and Life. *Hearth & Home* 17 May 1900: 88–90; 24 May: 128–30; 31 May: 178–80;

7 June: 212–14; 14 June: 248–50; 21 June: 284–6; 28 June: 320–2; 5 July: 370–2; 12 July: 411–12; 19 July: 442–4; 26 July: 474–6; 2 August: 506–7.

'The Sensational Serial: An Enquiry'. *Academy* 2 May 1901: 387–8.

'Why I am a Socialist'. *New Age* 30 November 1907, 90.

Blathwayt, Raymond. 'A Talk with Dr. Conan Doyle'. *Bookman* May 1892: 50–1.

'Lions in their Dens: George Newnes at Putney'. *Idler* March 1893: 161–73.

Burgess, Gelett. 'Impressions of Literary London'. *Bookman* September 1898: 155.

Caine, Hall. 'The Burials of Two Poets Laureate. – A Contrast'. *Times* 17 October 1892: 11b.

[Campbell, Mrs J. (Weston)]. 'Imperialism (Part I)'. *New Review* September 1897: 316–33.

'Colonial Empires'. *New Review* August 1897: 151–62.

Collins, Wilkie. 'The Unknown Public'. *Household Words* 21 August 1858: 217–20.

Colmore, G. 'Family Budgets: III. Eight Hundred a Year'. *Cornhill* June 1901: 790–800.

Dalgleish, John. 'The Bounder in Literature'. *New Review* October 1897: 409–17.

Dawson, Albert. 'An Interview with Sir George Newnes, Bart.'. *Bookman* May 1899: 38–40.

'The Pearson People and their Publications'. *Bookman* December 1898: 72–5.

Doyle, Arthur Conan. 'My First Book'. *McClure's Magazine* August 1894: 225–8.

'Some Personalia about Mr. Sherlock Holmes'. *Strand* December 1917: 531–5.

'Mr. Stevenson's Methods in Fiction'. *National Review* February 1890: 646–57.

Ellis, Havelock. 'Friedrich Nietzsche: I'. *Savoy* April 1896: 79–94.

Gosse, Edmund. 'Tennyson'. *New Review* November 1892: 513–23.

'The Influence of Democracy on Literature'. *Contemporary Review* April 1891: 523–36.

'The Society of Authors and Mr Gosse'. *Times* 10 May 1895: 11e.

'The Tyranny of the Novel'. *National Review* April 1892: 167–8.

[Harland, Henry]. 'Books: A Letter to the Editor and an Offer of a Prize'. *Yellow Book* October 1895: 125–43.

'Dogs, Cats, Books, and the Average Man'. *Yellow Book* July 1896: 11–23.

Henley, W. E. 'The Early Life of Jean-François Millet'. *Cornhill* March 1882: 289–302.

'The Tory Press and the Tory Party'. *National Review* May 1893: 357–74.

How, Harry. 'Illustrated Interviews: A Day with Dr. Conan Doyle'. *Strand* August 1892: 182–88.

Lang, Andrew. 'At the Sign of the Ship'. Rev. of *A Study in Scarlet*. *Longman's* January 1889: 335–6.

Lilly, W. S. 'The New Divine Right'. *New Review* May 1895: 505–13.

'The Problem of Purity'. *New Review* January 1895: 78–88.

Lucas, St. John. 'Two Kinds of Author'. *The Author* 1 October 1903: 23–4.

Meade, Mrs L. T. 'Sir Edward Burne-Jones, Bart.' *Strand* July 1895: 16–26.

Morrison, Arthur. 'Family Budgets: I. A Workman's Budget'. *Cornhill* April 1901: 446–56.

'What is a Realist?' *New Review* March 1897: 326–36.

Newnes, George. 'To Friends of "The Strand", Old and New, Near and Far, – Greeting'. *Strand* December 1900: 603–4.

'The One Hundredth Number of *The Strand Magazine*.' *Strand* April 1899: 363–4.

'A Novel-Reader'. 'A Warning to Novelists?' *New Review* September 1897: 306–15.

O'Connor, T.P. 'The Book of the Week: The Song of the Clogs'. *T. P.'s Weekly* 9 June 1905: 705–6.

'Confession of Faith'. *The Star* 17 January 1888: 1.

'A Forward and Some Reminiscences'. *T. P.'s Magazine* October 1910: 3–7.

'The Gospel According to "The Sun"'. *Sun* 27 June 1893: 2.

'Literature the Consoler'. *T. P.'s Weekly* 14 November 1902: 17.

'The New Journalism'. *New Review* October 1889: 423–34.

'Our Anniversary'. *T. P.'s Weekly* 6 November 1903: 729.

'The Sun's First Anniversary'. *Sun* 27 June 1894: 2.

'A Word in Advance'. *T. P.'s Weekly* 22 January 1909: 99.

'A Word of Greeting'. *T. P.'s Weekly* Special Christmas Number for 1904: 1.

[Oliphant, Margaret]. 'The Looker-on'. *Blackwood's* January 1895: 164.

'Outis'. 'The Great Democratic Joke'. *New Review* February 1895: 161–70.

Payn, James. 'Penny Fiction'. *Nineteenth Century* January 1881: 145–54.

'The Compleat Novelist'. *Strand* December 1897: 633–40.

Phillips, Evelyn March. 'The New Journalism'. *New Review* August 1895: 182–9.

Pugh, Edwin. 'The Mother of John'. *New Review* May 1896: 559–71.

Roberts, W. 'The Free Library Failure'. *New Review* September 1895: 316–24.

Salmon, Edward G. 'What the Working Classes Read'. *Nineteenth Century* July 1886: 108–17.

Schooling, John Holt. 'Charles Dickens's Manuscripts'. *Strand* January 1896: 29–40.

[Shand, A. Innes], 'Crime in Fiction'. *Blackwood's* August 1890: 173.

Smith, Arnold. 'The Ethics of Sensational Fiction'. *Westminster Review* August 1904: 188–94.

Smith, Herbert Greenhough. 'The Passing of Conan Doyle'. *Strand* September 1930: 227–30.

'Some Letters of Conan Doyle'. *Strand* October 1930: 390–5.

'The Twenty-First Birthday of "The Strand Magazine"'. *Strand* December 1911: 615–22.

Smith, Johnston. 'Magazines of the "Nineties"'. *Chambers's Journal* January 1945: 8–10.

Stead, W. T., ed. *The Index to the Periodical Literature of the World (covering the year 1891)*. London: The Office of *The Review of Reviews*, 1892.

'Character Sketch: *The Times*'. *Review of Reviews* March 1890: 185–91.

'Count Tolstoi's [sic] New Tale'. *Review of Reviews* April 1890: 330–4.

'Programme'. *Review of Reviews* January 1890: 14.

'To All English-Speaking Folk'. *Review of Reviews* January 1890: 15–20.

'To My Readers'. *Review of Reviews* May 1890: 363.

Stephen, Herbert. 'W. E. Henley: As a Contemporary and an Editor'. *The London Mercury*. February 1926: 387–400.

Stevens, Charles. 'The Best Description of *Tit-Bits*'. *Tit-Bits* 8 September 1894: 399.

Stevenson, R. A. M. 'Corot'. *New Review* April 1896: 408–16.

Stewart, The Hon. Mrs Fitzroy, and Christabel Pankhurst. 'Women's Rights – and Men's'. *Strand* May 1911: 525–30.

Storey, Alfred T. 'Deeds of Daring and Devotion in the War'. *Strand* August 1900: 153–60.

Tainton, Clifton F. 'Civil War in South Africa'. *New Review* March 1897: 294–317.

Unsigned. 'Our Awards for 1898'. *Academy* 14 January 1899: 65.

Rev. of *The Sinews of War*. *Academy* 17 November 1906: 503.

Rev. of *The Sinews of War*. *Athenaeum* 1 December 1906: 687.

Rev. of *The Truth About an Author*. *Athenaeum* 22 August 1903: 253.

'The Monthly Report of the Wholesale Book Trade'. *Bookman* April 1896: 8; September 1896: 160; December 1897: 60.

'The Harmsworths and their Publications'. *Bookman* December 1897: 67–8 and 97–8.

'News Notes'. *Bookman* March 1892: 199; and August 1892: 133.

'Novel Notes'. Rev. of *The Nigger of the 'Narcissus'*. *Bookman* January 1898: 131.

'Novel Notes'. Rev. of *The Sinews of War*. *Bookman* December 1906: 154.

'Men of Mark: V. Sir George Newnes, Bart., MP'. *The Caxton Magazine: A Magazine for the Printing, Paper, Stationary, and Allied Trades* September 1901: 266–73.

'A Dinner to Dr. Doyle'. *Critic* 1 August 1896: 78–9.

'Funeral at the Abbey', *Daily Telegraph* 13 October 1892: 7e.

'An Interview with the Author'. *The Golden Penny* 26 January 1901: 66.

'A Chat with Conan Doyle'. *Idler* October 1894: 340–9.

Rev. of *The Nigger of the 'Narcissus'*. *Literature* 26 March 1898: 354.

'The Bugbear of Realism'. *National Observer* 23 July 1892: 235–6.

'The Cheapening of Poetry'. *National Observer* 5 November 1892: 624–5.

'*Exit* Mrs. Grundy'. *National Observer* 1 March 1891: 400–1.

'The Literary Agent'. *National Observer* 16 July 1892: 216–17.

'Literature and Democracy'. *National Observer* 11 April 1891: 528–9.

'Modern Men: Henry James'. *National Observer* 23 May 1891: 10–11.

'Modern Men: Thomas Hardy'. *National Observer* 7 February 1891: 301–2.

'Modern Men: Walter Pater'. *National Observer* 2 May 1891: 608–9.

'The New Nigger Question'. *National Observer* 17 January 1891: 214–15.

'Notes'. *National Observer* 15 October 1892: 545.

'Our Black Question'. *National Observer* 9 May 1891: 630.

'Pampering the Unemployed'. *National Observer* 19 November 1892: 5–6.

'The Real Sherlock Holmes: An Interview by our Special Commissioner'. *National Observer* 29 October 1892: 606–7.

'Mr. Whistler's Etchings'. *National Observer* 28 January 1893: 261.

'Cheap Pernicious Literature'. *The Newsagent and Advertisers' Record: The Trade Journal for Newspaper Distributors, Stationers, Printers, and Advertisers* December 1889: 32–3.

'Interview'. *The Newsagent and Advertiser's Record: The Trade Journal for Newspaper Distributors, Stationers, Printers and Advertisers* July 1889: 7–8.

'Joint Stock Publishing Companies: (9) George Newnes, Limited'. *The Newsagent and Bookseller's Review* 28 November 1891: 435–6.

'The Latest and Biggest on Record'. *The Newsagent and Advertisers' Record: The Trade Journal for Newspaper Distributors, Stationers, Printers, and Advertisers* January 1890: 26.

'Some New Journals of the Year'. *The Newsagent and Bookseller's Review* 30 May 1891: 14.

'Survey'. *The Newsagent and Advertisers' Record: The Trade Journal for Newspaper Distributors, Stationers, Printers, and Advertisers* October 1889: 55; and December 1889: 50.

'Funeral of Lord Tennyson'. *Reynolds's Newspaper* 16 October 1892: 5e.

'Detective Fiction'. *The Saturday Review* 4 December 1886: 749.

'After the Strike'. *Scots Observer* 29 June 1889: 145–6.

'Candid Fiction'. *Scots Observer* 18 January 1890: 229.

'*Drivel*: Weekly 1d'. *Scots Observer* 28 December 1889: 156–8.

'The Liveliness of Radical Socialism'. *Scots Observer* 20 July 1889: 228–30.

'Modern Men: Emile Zola'. *Scots Observer* 25 January 1890: 262–3.

'Socialism *In Excelsis*.' *Scots Observer* 23 February 1889: 376–7.

'The Submerged Tenth'. *Scots Observer* 6 December 1890: 64–5.

'The Triumph of Sentimentality'. *Scots Observer* 29 November 1890: 33.

Rev. of *The Sinews of War*. *Spectator* 8 December 1906: 938.

'Tennyson'. *Star* 12 October 1892: 3c.

'A Description of the Offices of the *Strand Magazine*.' *Strand* December 1892: 594–606.

'The Art of the British Working Man'. *Strand* May 1910: 559–65.

'Ourselves in Figure and Diagram'. *Strand* July 1897: 37–42.

'Tennyson's Funeral'. *Times* 13 October 1892: 4a.

'Special Notice'. *T. P.'s Weekly* 24 March 1905: 369.

[Whibley, Charles]. 'Musings Without Method'. *Blackwood's* October 1903: 528–38.

'The True Degenerate'. *New Review* April 1895: 425–32.

'The Real Pepys'. *New Review* April 1896: 367–75.

Winter, O. 'The Cinematograph'. *New Review* May 1896: 507–13.

Wright, Thomas. 'Concerning the Unknown Public'. *Nineteenth Century* February 1883: 279–96.

Wyndham, George. 'A Remarkable Book'. Rev. of *The Red Badge of Courage*. *New Review* January 1896: 30–40.

'Z'. 'Two Demagogues: A Parallel and a Moral'. *New Review* April 1895: 363–72.

Later Studies

Bailey, Peter. '*Ally Sloper's Half-Holiday*: Comic Art in the 1880s'. *History Workshop* 16 (1983): 4–31.

Brown, R. D. 'The Bodley Head Press: Some Bibliographical Extrapolations'. *The Papers of the Bibliographical Society of America* 61 (1967): 39–50.

Davis, Kenneth W., and Donald W. Rude. 'The Transmission of *The Nigger of the "Narcissus"*'. *Conradiana*. 5.2 (1973): 20–45.

Ellegård, Alvar. 'The Readership of the Periodical Press in Mid-Victorian Britain: II. Directory'. *The Victorian Periodicals Newsletter* 13 (September 1971): 3–22.

Fritschner, Linda Marie. 'Publishers' Readers, Publishers, and their Authors'. *Publishing History* 7 (1980): 48.

Green, Richard Lancelyn. 'Conan Doyle's Pocket Diary for 1889'. *A.C.D.: The Journal of the Arthur Conan Doyle Society* 1.1 (September 1989): 21–9.

Hollyer, Cameron. 'Author to Editor: Arthur Conan Doyle's Correspondence with H. Greenhough Smith'. *A.C.D.: The Journal of the Arthur Conan Doyle Society* 3 (1992): 11–34.

'"My Dear Smith": Some Letters of Arthur Conan Doyle to his *Strand* Editor'. *Baker Street Miscellanea* 44 (Winter 1985): 1–24.

Jones, Gareth Stedman. 'Working-Class Culture and Working-Class Politics in London, 1870–1900: Notes on the Remaking of a Working Class'. *Journal of Social History* (Summer 1974): 460–508.

Murtagh, Anne. '*The New Review*: A Glimpse of the Nineties'. *Victorian Periodicals Review* 14.1 (Spring 1981): 11–20.

Roden, Christopher. 'In Conversation with . . . Air Cmdt Dame Jean Conan Doyle'. *A.C.D.: The Journal of the Arthur Conan Doyle Society* 1.2 (March 1990): 117–18.

'Conan Doyle and *The Strand Magazine*'. *A.C.D.: The Journal of the Arthur Conan Doyle Society* 2.2 (Autumn 1991): 135–40.

Stetz, Margaret Diane. 'Sex, Lies, And Printed Cloth: Bookselling at the Bodley Head in the Eighteen-Nineties'. *Victorian Studies* 35:1 (Autumn 1991): 76.

Vicinus, Martha. 'The Study of Victorian Popular Culture'. *Victorian Studies* (June 1975): 473–83.

Willy, Todd G. 'The Conquest of the Commodore: Conrad's Rigging of "The Nigger" for the Henley Regatta'. *Conradiana* 17.3 (1985): 163–82.

INDEX